GERARD KEEGAN

HIGHER PSYCHOLOGY

Approaches and Methods

Hodder & Stoughton

A MEMBER OF THE HODDER HEADLINE GROUP

DEDICATION

This is written in loving memory of my dad Arthur Keegan, who gingerly gave me my first psychology book in 1974. A Lev Vygotsky to many of Glasgow's schoolchildren, you were absolutely right about Mark Twain, Coco the Clown, and the nature–nurture debate. The Jock Stein, Bill Shankley and Matt Busby of teaching, you are with me every day.

If you can talk with crowds and keep your virtue,
Or walk with kings - nor lose the common touch;
If neither foes nor loving friends can hurt you;
If all men count with you, but none too much;
If you can fill the unforgiving minute
With sixty seconds' worth of distance run -
Yours is the Earth and everything that's in it,
And - which is more - you'll be a Man my son!

From 'If' by Rudyard Kipling

Orders: please contact Bookpoint Ltd, 130 Milton Park, Abingdon, Oxon OX14 4SB. Telephone: (44) 01235 827720. Fax: (44) 01235 400454. Lines are open from 9.00 - 6.00, Monday to Saturday, with a 24 hour message answering service. You can also order through our website: www.hodderheadline.co.uk

British Library Cataloguing in Publication Data

A catalogue record for this title is available from the British Library

ISBN 0 340 85028 0

First Published 2002

Impression number 10 9 8 7 6 5 4 3 2 1

Year 2008 2007 2006 2005 2004 2003 2002

Typeset by GreenGate Publishing Services, Tonbridge, Kent.

Printed in Great Britain for Hodder & Stoughton Educational, a division of Hodder Headline Plc, 338 Euston Road, London NW1 3BH by Martins the Printers Ltd., Berwick-upon-Tweed.

Contents

Preface

My students, colleagues, friends, and family will tell you that I don't just like psychology; I love it. I am a 'real gone kid' when it comes to the science of mind and behaviour and I just don't care! One reason for this is that psychology saved my life. You see, from my teenage years onwards I had a wee problem, which became a big problem. Drink. Initially brilliant for the companionship, laughs and adventures it brought, alcohol became my personal demon. Over too many years I became what psychology calls *dysfunctional*. I denied the fact that my behaviours were becoming increasingly 'abnormal'. I was mentally unwell.

One day I noticed the new subject of 'psychology' in a SCOTVEC catalogue and went to my boss to ask if I could teach it. She said: 'There is really no call for psychology in Ayrshire, Gerry.' I, however, just knew that there was. I asked her whether, if I could prove demand, she would consider introducing a day class the next year. She said, 'yes'. I walked the streets of Kilmarnock putting up handmade posters in community centres to raise enough interest for a viable night class to go ahead. I even tried to persuade my drinking compadres to come along! Some did, as did others. I had that all-important night class, and the next year my first day class had seventy students.

I realised that I was on to something. Psychology, a previously inaccessible university subject, littered with enormously long words and difficult concepts, was attracting the ordinary people of Scotland in their droves. It was down to me to keep them coming into class on wet winter nights and sunny summer afternoons. I turned to the Soviet psychologist Lev Vygotsky for help. Lev is someone you may recognise later. He was to become a major asset to my teaching. I was taking a bit of a chance being as 'edgy' as this, but needn't have worried. My students responded magnificently and began to turn in psychology assessments of outstanding quality and obvious potential. This was amazing, if only because most had left school with no qualifications. Many wanted 'more psychology' and came back year after year, module after module, morning, noon and night. All memorable, one particular night class had a manic depressive, an anorexic, a victim of obsessive–compulsive disorder and a lady with eight multiple personalities sit side by side with a police officer, a nurse, a social worker and someone who had just been released from jail. The patter was brilliant, the mutual respect and love given to everyone for what they brought in the way of personal experience was awesome.

In psychology there are all sorts of theories and therapies. In the cognitive approach there is cognitive–rational and cognitive–emotional therapy. The gist of these are that if you can change the way a person thinks, you can change the way a person feels and behaves. Psychology was doing this for ordinary people right before my very eyes. It was changing the way they thought, felt and behaved, and at more than just an academic level.

It was also changing me. Teaching psychology is like mental colonic irrigation! The more of it I did, the more I realised my thoughts and feelings didn't square with my bad behaviours. I was being hypocritical and inconsistent, in that I had been theorising and analysing everyone else's thoughts, feelings and behaviours, but not my own! This is something to which even the greats of psychology are prone and seldom recognise. One Saturday morning I woke up, realised the chaos of my personal life, and broke down. I embraced the fact of my addiction there and then, stopped drinking, and have never looked back. I applied my subject to myself and discovered its inherent power. What you can get from psychology is more than just the sum of its parts. What it gives, over and above its alluring content, differs in degree and application between people. Thus psychology, its story, and how it might personally apply, I now leave for you to uncover. To tell you any more would be like telling you the end of *The Lord of the Rings*!

I would like this book to be a developing and dynamic resource. If you have any suggestions, queries, or comments I'd love to hear from you. I would also be delighted to hear from anyone, anywhere who has picked up this book and would like to pursue Higher Psychology by distance learning. Go for it, and write to me.

Gerry Keegan
Hurlford
August 2002

gerrykeegan@kilmarnock98.freeserve.co.uk

Picture credits

Alex Machin: p22; p38; p49; p70; p88; p90; p54; p198; p224; p267.
American Statistical Association: p175.
AP Photos: p4.
Cambridge University Press: p202.
Camelot: p52.
Corbis: p3; p6; p11; p30; p 37; p45; p87; p143; p144; p149.
Fortean Photo Library: p177.
Illustrated London News: p122.
The Image Man: p147.
Mary Evans Picture Library: p24.
PA Photos: p85; p178.
Professor Allen Gardner: p276.
Professor Albert Bandura: p226.
Rex Features: p273; p274.
Robert Hunt Library: p32.
Science Photo Library: p40; p121.
Topham Picturepoint: p89; p108; p140.

Acknowledgements

A couple of years ago I was so busy with the implementation of psychology in Scotland that I didn't send Christmas cards to anyone. Forgetting people is a cardinal sin in my family; so if I've inadvertently missed anyone out, oops!

Thanks first to Tim Gregson-Williams, Deputy Managing Director, for your friendship, support, and encouragement over the last three years. You have given me an opportunity I will never forget. Thank you also to everyone at Hodder involved in the production of this book, especially Emma Woolf, my editor, John Mitchell, my Sales and Marketing Director and Anna Carroll and all at GreenGate. You are just the business.

Thank you to my readers, Jason Bryce, Dawn Burns, Fiona Gibson, Michael Gilius, Joe Lappin, Marie Morrison, Karen Officer and Sandy Robertson. A singularly huge hug to Phyllis Copeland, psychology lecturer at Cardonald College. For a lot of reasons you are a star who has been in my firmament ever since we met. A big clap also for your students, and mine, of Kilmarnock College, Kilmarnock Academy, and Queen Margaret Academy, Ayr, who helped pilot the emerging chapters, materials and ideas over the last year.

I would like to thank my mum, Anna Keegan, for her incredible faith. My dear partner Caroline McKenzie for being herself, and daughters Sarah and Toni for my stories. You have been a constant source of inspiration in the teaching of psychology in the classroom! Not forgetting Nana, Catherine, Elaine, Sally, Ian and Christopher Angus. Thanks also for their love and anecdotal contribution to Scottish psychology to my brothers Lawrence, Bryan and Desmond, their partners and their families, and the Redemptorist community. The late Jim Ward, and my much loved Aunt Helen. Anne, Catherine, Frances, Helena and Patricia Ward, their partners and families. My much missed cousin Anne; Tommy Bradshaw and girls; Henry, Marie and Jackie Keegan, Pat Chisholm and families, and also Len and Lise Keating and family in Cape Town.

To my lecturers and friends 1974–9 at Glasgow Caledonian University – pure dead brilliant it was. Thank you colleagues, past and present, at Kilmarnock College, a great place to work; and now you have hard evidence to detain me under the Mental Health (Scotland) Act! Of my senior management particular thanks to John McMaster, a constant encouragement, and Dougie McColl, a superb example of the power of the human spirit. You have yet to see the irony in our friendship! The Yellow Workroom, most especially Gianna, Iris, Liz, Una, Avril, Sandy, Theresa, Gette and Kath for giving me the space of late, and their love, support and concern over many years. Thanks to God's gift to sociology, Charlie Coyle, and our other fellow believer, my mentor and comrade, Peter Kerr. It is indeed better to die on your feet, than live on your knees.

Finally thank you to my students. You have been my inspiration. Of these, two deserve special mention. Richard Wilson of Shortlees, Kilmarnock, who encouraged my dream of establishing psychology as a subject in Scotland for the ordinary person; and Monica Fuller of Melbourne, Australia – because, astonishingly, that is just how far away that dream has now stretched. Across a wheen of miles and twenty years, you both encapsulate the reason behind why I do what I do. You all make a wee Glaswegian teacher of psychology very happy.

Let's now get some work done!

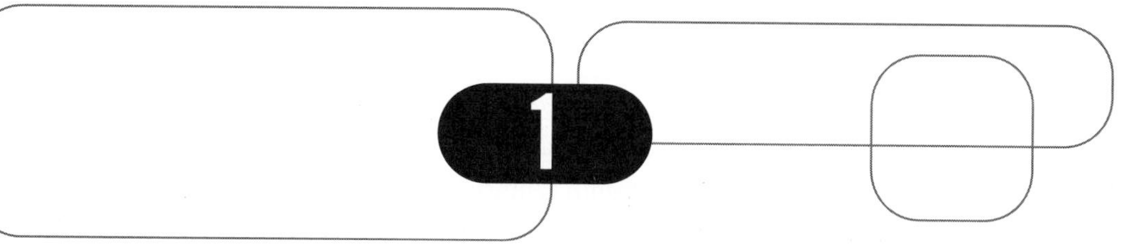

What *is* psychology, then?

- What is the book all about?
- What is psychology?
- Psychology's five approaches
- What is, and how do you become, a psychologist?

What is the book all about?

Higher Psychology: Approaches and Methods is intended to support students studying the compulsory Approaches and Methods unit of the Higher Psychology course awarded by the Scottish Qualifications Authority. It is also appropriate for mature Intermediate students, those doing an HNC Psychology A unit, and anyone new to the subject at university level.

The aim of the book is to develop an understanding of the approaches, methods and applications underpinning **psychology**. This is to encourage an ability to interpret, analyse, and evaluate critically psychological approaches, their associated theory, and research methodology. The book examines each psychological approach with its distinct, but complementary, explanations of human behaviour and mental processes. It further endeavours to establish an eclectic, holistic and integrated view of psychology, our research methods and related areas of application.

The rationale of the book is largely dictated by the knowledge, skills and understanding required by the Higher Psychology: Approaches and Methods internal assessment and external examination. By the end of the book you should be able to explain:

- the theoretical approaches found in psychology
- applications of these theoretical approaches
- the limitations of the theoretical approaches
- research designs in psychology
- related research methods
- the advantages and disadvantages of these research methods, and
- the relationship between research methods and psychological approaches.

What is psychology?

The word psychology comes from the Greek words, *psyche* (mind) and *logos* (study). When the subject of psychology began in the late nineteenth century, it was interested solely in the study of the mind. However, this early study of our mind and its mental processes such as perception, attention, language, memory and thinking was heavily criticised. The reason for this is that our mind and its elements are hypothetical constructs. A hypothetical construct is something that does not exist in reality. Something that does not exist in reality is very difficult to support scientifically. The methods used to study the mind in the early days did not give rise to the production of such scientific evidence. This was problematic because a science, or any subject claiming to be a science, needs objective (factual) data to support what it discovers. An ability to generate this **empirical data** was seen as vital to the new subject of psychology, which dearly wished to be a *science* like physics and chemistry. Empirical data is data about our experiences obtained by us through our senses.

Psychology, as exclusively the study of the mind, thus declined in popularity for a while.

From the 1910s to the 1960s, psychology instead emphasised the study of *observable behaviour*. This was because behaviour exists. As behaviour is real, behaviour can be controlled, observed, and measured. This is important because the control, observation, and measurement of phenomena, the hallmarks of a *science*, allow for the generation of essential empirical data. Observed behaviours were studied extensively by psychology in the first half of the twentieth century, especially in the USA. The study of the mind did, however, make a comeback in the 1960s when the methodological difficulty in producing objective, factual, empirical data about our mental processes was overcome.

Psychology: the scientific study of behaviour and mental processes

It is then generally agreed nowadays that psychology is the scientific study of *both* behaviour and mental processes. According to *Higher Psychology Arrangements* (5th edition, July 2001) published by the Scottish Qualifications Authority, psychology can also be further defined as 'the scientific study of behaviour and mental processes in humans and animals'. This reflects the importance psychology gives to the *scientific* study of mind and behaviour in order to generate scientific support, or otherwise, for the many rich and diverse theories regarding why we think, feel and behave as we do.

Why study psychology?

> *'I really enjoy psychology because it helps me understand why I am as I am.'*
>
> *Salva Sgarlata (2000)*
>
> *Queen Margaret Academy, Ayr*

Salva's reason for liking psychology is mirrored in the author's belief that an understanding of psychology will influence in a positive way those exposed to its message. Its study allows us to understand why we are as we are, and how and why we become what we become. It helps explain why other people are as they are, and how and why they become what they become. Psychology's attraction lies in the insight it gives us into how and why we all think, feel and behave as we do.

A brief history of psychology

Psychology emerged from philosophy

As far back as Plato (427–347 BC) and Aristotle (384–322 BC), the earliest psychologists were often philosophers. Philosophers spent, and spend, a great deal of time analysing their own feelings and mental experiences in order to develop ideas about what it means to be human. This pure self-analysis of feelings and mental experience is called **introspection** or looking within. Introspection, as a method of enquiry has been around for tens of thousands of years. Philosophy, the parent of psychology, has used introspection ever since it began asking questions like: Who am I? What am I? Where have I come from? What will I become?

Descartes

It was the French mathematician and philosopher René Descartes (1596–1650) who first questioned the belief that we were *unexplainable* creatures of God's will. He tried to be analytical and set about exploring answers to the questions posed above, and developed the notion of *ex machina* – that humankind can be studied and understood like a machine. Humans, understood as machines, are made up of two parts, mind (our knowledge, awareness, consciousness and free will) and body (our physiology: arms, legs, heart, lungs and so on). In his theory of interactive dualism, Descartes suggested that mind and body interact in the pineal gland in the brain. As we will read in the chapter on the biological approach, this still mysterious structure is thought to have something to do with sleep and hormonal activity controlling the body's internal environment and our motivation to eat, drink and reproduce.

Figure 1.1 René Descartes

Empiricists and *tabula rasa*

Britain also played its part in the early formation of psychology. In the seventeenth century philosophers John Locke (1632–1704) and Thomas Hobbes (1588–1679) founded the **empiricist** movement. Empiricism tries to understand the human mind in a systematic, factual and objective way. As already stated, data collected in a systematic, factual and objective way is known as empirical data. The empiricists thought the content of the human mind came about as a result of our interaction in, and thus sensory experience of, our world. This is reflected in Locke's idea that when we are born our mind is *tabula rasa*, which means *blank slate*. For empiricists, our human awareness or consciousness is made up of all the sensory experiences we get of objects, ideas, events and people as we journey through life.

Nativists and innate abilities

The empiricist position of *tabula rasa*, or born with a mind like a blank slate, is in sharp contrast to that of Descartes who thought *some* human abilities were present at birth. Any ability we possess when born is called an innate ability. Innate abilities are abilities *universal* to a species. An example of a universal innate ability in a species would be sparrows' ability to fly. Any innate ability particular to any species usually has a high survival value for it. In our example a sparrow with an innate ability to fly can avoid danger better and escape to warmer climates when the weather gets colder. An innate ability like flight is a huge asset to a species in its individual, and general, struggle for survival.

Those who follow in the tradition of Descartes and believe that we naturally possess innate abilities at birth are called **nativists**. Those, like Locke and Hobbes, who believe we become what we become as a result of experiences in our environment, are, as we now know, called empiricists. The degree to which nature (innate abilities) or nurture (experiences in our environment) explain why we think, feel and behave as we do is known in psychology as the nature–nurture debate. Also known as the heredity–environment, or **nativist–empiricist** debate, the influence of heredity, environment, and their interface are studied in many areas of psychology. These include the study of intelligence, personality, and atypical, or abnormal, behaviour.

The Advent of Scientific Psychology

In the early part of the nineteenth century German physiologists Weber, Helmholtz and Fechner made further contributions to the emerging subject of psychology.

A physiologist is a scientist interested in the study of bodily processes and functions.

Weber offered to early psychology his theory of touch and tactile perception. He discovered, for instance, that we have the ability, by using touch alone, to perceive differences in weight between two similar objects. Helmholtz provided us with his theories on nerves, nerve fibres, nerve impulses, colour vision, hearing and resonance. Fechner gave to early psychology information on our senses and perception, and emphasised the use of the experimental method in psychological investigation. The **experimental method**, as we will read later, emphasises the observation and measurement of phenomena under controlled conditions.

Wilhelm Wundt 1879

Germany is presently credited with founding psychology as a scientific discipline. In 1879 Wilhelm Wundt (1832–1920) opened up the first psychology laboratory at the University of Leipzig. An introspectionist, he began in controlled laboratory conditions to measure and record people's reactions to a stimulus. A **stimulus** (plural: stimuli) is an object, event or person that makes or motivates us to think, feel and behave as we do. It was Wilhelm Wundt's emphasis on the observation, measurement and control of experiences that began to set psychology apart from philosophy. Indeed, the controlled observation and measurement of our behaviours and mental processes is the hallmark of modern day scientific psychology.

Figure 1.2 Wilhelm Wundt

Nineteenth-century schools of psychology

Structuralism

Wundt established a particular school of thought, in nineteenth-century psychology, called structuralism. Structuralists tried to discover the processes and elements that make up human sensory experience. Searching for the elements of our conscious experience, structuralism investigated its component parts, such as sight, sound, taste, smell and touch. Wundt would ask his subjects to self-report those elements they thought made particular visual experiences for them. One such experience is *apparent movement*. An example of apparent movement is the experience you might have had of sitting on a train in Central Station, Glasgow, when the train alongside pulls out. For a few seconds you think it is *your* train that is moving. Wundt would ask his participants to try to isolate the mental processes of that movement. He would ask them to identify the sensations and feelings that accompanied such visual experience.

Structuralists analysed other human experiences, such as taste perception; thinking that taste perception was based purely on those structures responsible for our ability to sense information from our outside world. An example of this is their work investigating the bitter- and sweet-detecting regions on the tongue. Structuralists ultimately saw human consciousness and its elements, such as our ability to be aware of such things as taste, as comprising many independent sensations, feelings and images drawn together in our mind.

Remarkably, Wundt taught three other major figures in the history of psychology: Edward Titchener (1867–1927), the British-born founder of the first psychology laboratory in the USA in 1892; James McKeen Cattell (1860–1944) who had a leading role as founder of the American Psychological Association, and Charles Spearman, born in 1904, and still very influential in the areas of intelligence, intelligence testing and statistics.

Structuralists did however experience difficulties in finding agreement on the common elements of those mental experiences that we share. Confirmation of results was exacerbated by their use of the non-scientific method of introspection. Introspection is subjective, and so can be accused of personal bias, which is of no use in a scientific enquiry.

Science, and subjects like psychology, which claim a scientific identity, need more than mere opinion upon which to base their theories. Structuralism eventually declined because of its introspection, its inability to confirm its findings, and the advent of more attractive schools like functionalism, psychoanalysis, and behaviourism. It is now fair to say that structuralism is only of historical importance to psychology today.

Functionalism

Functionalism, another early school in psychology, was also established by the late nineteenth century. Functionalism was heavily influenced by biology, and became concerned with the function, or purpose, of human mental activity. Functionalism investigated what the mind does and why. Its historical influence can be seen in present-day psychology, because nowadays we look to the *purpose* behind why we think, feel and behave as we do.

William James

Figure 1.3 William James

Influential functionalists include William James (1842–1910) and Charles Darwin (1809–82), about whom you will read more when we look at the biological approach. Suffice to say here that James was a brilliant American who believed that the function of consciousness was to enable us to survive. His book *Principles of Psychology* (1890) is perhaps the most influential text in the history of psychology. James had been impressed with Charles Darwin's book *On The Origin of Species By Means of Natural Selection* published in 1859, and agreed with Darwin that any evolutionary characteristic a species has must serve some purpose or function for it. James thought consciousness had an important function for humans. Essentially, he believed that our *consciousness*, and aspects of it such as our emotions, had evolved over time. The purpose of human consciousness was, and is, to give us a better chance of survival in our environment.

James's work prompted others such as James McKeen Cattell and John Dewey (1859–1952) to begin to explore other avenues of psychological interest such as intelligence testing and child psychology. Intelligence and intelligence testing are today studied in the psychology of individual differences. Child psychology has become developmental psychology. Developmental psychology examines physical, cognitive (mental), social and emotional change and development within and across the human lifespan.

Psychology's competing early influences of structuralism and functionalism were to contribute towards an unsettled definition of the subject for a hundred years. In the study of our various approaches we shall see that some psychologists, like Freud, investigated the mind. Others, like Pavlov and Skinner, investigated observable behaviour in response to an environmental stimulus. And yet others, like Tolman and Piaget, looked at the interaction, and relationship between mind and environment. All heavily influence our idea of what psychology is today: the scientific study of behaviour and mental processes.

Psychology today has five approaches

What do we mean by an approach in psychology?

An approach is a perspective or school of thought. In psychology an approach is one particular view as to the origin and development of behaviours and mental processes. Psychology has developed five approaches, and each has a different outlook on why we think, feel and behave as we do. Each offers different solutions as to how to help people. This is because each approach favours a particular course of treatment, or **psychotherapy**, based on what is believed to be the root cause of a particular behavioural or mental difficulty. Each approach thus puts forward its own psychotherapeutic techniques determined by what each believes to be the cause of a psychological problem or dysfunction.

The five approaches in psychology are:

- the psychoanalytic approach
- the behaviourist approach
- the cognitive approach
- the biological approach, and
- the humanistic approach.

Overview of the five approaches

The **psychoanalytic approach** states that thoughts, feelings and behaviours are the result of unconscious mental processes formed by early childhood experiences.

The **behaviourist approach** states that thoughts, feelings and behaviours are the result of learning in our environment.

The **cognitive approach** states that thoughts, feelings and behaviours are the result of thinking or problem solving. Thinking and problem solving are also referred to as information processing.

The **biological approach** states that thoughts, feelings and behaviours are the result of genetics and physiology.

The **humanistic approach** states that thoughts, feelings and behaviours are the result of a psychologically healthy or unhealthy self, or self-image.

Is any one approach *better* than another?

> *'Most psychologists are not adherents to schools but are theoretical eclectics who use different concepts for different phenomena'.*
>
> *Brown & Herrnstein (1975)*

In psychology no single approach is necessarily viewed as better than another. Psychology is a *holistic* subject. Holistic means having a place for *all* approaches, which allows for a more comprehensive and rounded psychological understanding of phenomena.

In the case of a *person* who seeks treatment, one particular approach may be more appropriate than another. This is because an application of an approach, in the form of a treatment, should be driven by what is best for the individual. When you apply the most appropriate approach in psychology to a person, object, event, or situation, you are taking an *eclectic* view.

It should also be noted that our approaches should be seen as *complementary* to one another. This is reflected in the world of clinical application where often a *variety* of psychotherapies from *different* approaches are used together to help an individual.

What is, and how do you become, a psychologist?

In order to decide whether you want to become a psychologist, here is an idea of what they do:

- Psychologists conduct research.
- Psychologists work in the community.
- Psychologists help people learn.
- Psychologists promote good mental and physical health.
- Psychologists study, and contribute to, the world of work.

To become a psychologist you would first have to go to university and get an *accredited* degree in psychology. An accredited psychology degree is one that allows Graduate Basis for Registration (GBR) with the British Psychological Society (BPS).

The British Psychological Society

Founded in 1901, the BPS, with over 34,000 members in the UK, is the representative body for psychologists and psychology in Britain. Its Royal Charter gives it responsibility to guide psychology for the public good and to be concerned with ethical issues.

The BPS has divisions for particular specialist areas. On the basis of your GBR you *could* pursue a career in psychology such as:

- **Clinical psychologist:** A clinical psychologist helps people with mental health problems.
- **Educational psychologist:** An educational psychologist provides learning support for children, parents and teachers within the school system.
- **Counselling psychologist:** A counselling psychologist helps people with personal and relationship problems.
- **Health psychologist:** A health psychologist promotes mental health, and helps people to adjust to, or recover from, physical illness. Health psychologists also foster an understanding of the relationship between mind, body and environment.
- **Forensic psychologist:** A forensic psychologist helps to understand and change criminal behaviour and often works alongside the police.
- **Research psychologist:** A research psychologist conducts research in academic, industrial or other settings.
- **Consumer psychologist:** A consumer psychologist works with businesses and other organisations to understand customer behaviours.
- **Sports psychologist:** A sports psychologist helps enhance individual performance and works with organisations, teams, and sports clubs. Sports psychologists work alongside coaches, and also teach.
- **Occupational psychologist:** An occupational psychologist helps to enhance training and work-related performance of people in employment.

It should also be said that psychology graduates are employed in many other areas, such as health, social work, industrial, commercial, and retail management, teaching psychology in schools and further education colleges, finance, information technology, marketing, public relations, advertising, journalism and the media.

If you intend studying psychology at university it is imperative that you check precisely what qualifications your intended university requires. If in doubt – ask. All should be happy to hear from you. Application should be made to UCAS (University and Colleges Admissions Service). Details of UCAS procedures can be obtained from your school, college, or local careers office and from UCAS itself at http://www.ucas.ac.uk/

Entry to HE courses from 2002 is based on a points system. All pre-university qualifications have point weightings. Called the UCAS Tariff system, an A in a Higher is worth 72 points, a B 60, and a C 48. An A at Intermediate 2 is worth 42 points. Total points needed to study psychology will vary from institution to institution. In Scotland in the 2002 entry year there were seventeen single-subject psychology courses on offer, and another 164 courses where psychology was a major element. To embark *somewhere* on a Scottish University Bachelor of Science (BSc), Bachelor of Arts (BA) or Master of Arts (MA) undergraduate degree course with psychology, in whole or in part, you should investigate what entry requirements are needed. A number of psychology departments in Scotland emphasise that progression into second and subsequent years of psychology depends entirely on your performance in university examinations.

To help you decide where to study psychology you might like to browse *http://www.psych.bangor.ac.uk/Links/BIPsychDepts/index.html*

This site details all psychology departments in Britain and Ireland.

The Learning and Teaching Support Network (LTSN) for psychology is also worth consulting. LTSN is a UK network of 24 UK university psychology departments, whose aim is to promote high quality teaching and learning of psychology in our universities. LTSN can be found at *http://www.psychology.ltsn.ac.uk/students.html*

INTERACTIVE

1. Imagine you are a journalist. Using http://www.utm.edu/research/iep/d/descarte.htm write a short obituary of René Descartes, possibly including graphics, artwork and photographs.
2. Starting off @ http://www.indiana.edu/~intell/wundt.html and http://www.ship.edu/~cgboeree/wundtjames.html report in no more than 50 words what you understand by 'apperception'.
3. Using http://www.emory.edu/EDUCATION/mfp/james.html find out how William James defined psychology. What did he see (hint, hint...) as the goal of psychology?
4. Go to the British Psychological Society @ http://www.bps.org.uk/careers/careers2.cfm#essential and read about the work of six types of psychologist.

Glossary

Empirical data: objective, factual data obtained by sensory experiences

Empiricist: someone who believes we are born *tabula rasa*, and become what we become as a result of experiences in our environment

Experimental method: the scientific method of enquiry, which emphasises the control, observation and measurement of phenomena in strict (e.g. laboratory) conditions

Introspection: self-reporting on experiences

Nativist: someone who believes we are born with certain innate abilities

Nativist–empiricist debate: a debate concerning the influence of nature and/or nurture on development

Psychology: the scientific study of behaviour and mental processes

Psychotherapy: the application of an approach as a treatment

Stimulus: plural stimuli. Any object, event or person that prompts us to think, feel and behave as we do

Tabula rasa: literally ‘a blank slate’

2

The psychoanalytic approach

BY THE END OF THIS CHAPTER YOU SHOULD BE ABLE TO:

- **define and explain the psychoanalytic approach with reference to its key features**
- **explain applications of the psychoanalytic approach**
- **explain the limitations of the psychoanalytic approach.**

Overview of the psychoanalytic approach

The psychoanalytic approach was founded by Sigmund Freud around 1900. The aim of the psychoanalytic approach is to understand thoughts, feelings and behaviours by analysing unconscious mental processes formed by early childhood experiences. Diagnosis and treatment of any dysfunction we might acquire is carried out in psychoanalytic psychotherapy. Here the psychoanalytic psychotherapist helps the patient understand him- or herself by exploring their unconscious. Psychoanalytic treatment involves the patient being made aware of the unconscious drives that make him or her think, feel and behave the way he or she does.

In this chapter we will explore the main features of the psychoanalytic approach. We will examine the structure and the function of the unconscious as proposed by Freud. We will also look at his psychodynamic theory of personality, and theory of adult personality development. The psychoanalytic approach as a psychotherapy will be discussed and developed using applications from mental health and childcare. The case study research method will be used to evaluate the strengths and weaknesses of the approach.

We will look finally at the emergence of the broader, and more modern, psychodynamic approach, which came about because of criticisms of the sexual emphasis of psychoanalysis.

Figure 2.1 Sigmund Freud

Alternatively, this approach suggests that it is our social world, of which sexual experience is only a part, that is of greater significance in the development of personality.

SIGMUND FREUD

Sigmund Freud was born into a Jewish family at 6.30pm on the sixth of May 1856, at 117 Schlossergasse, Freiberg, Moravia, now part of the Czech Republic. He died from cancer of the mouth on the 23 September 1939, at 20 Maresfield Gardens, London, at the age of 83. During his lifetime he developed psychoanalytic theory and its related psychoanalytic psychotherapy as a means of helping people in psychological distress. He is probably the best-known psychologist in history, and his ideas have had a huge impact on Western culture, with reflections of his work to be found even in situation comedies and dramas to illustrate what can happen when people with different personalities are thrown together.

WHAT IS THE PSYCHOANALYTIC APPROACH?

The psychoanalytic approach is both a theory and a therapy, the two being closely linked.

Central to psychoanalytic theory is the need to understand that our thoughts, feelings, and behaviours are influenced by unconscious mental processes formed by early childhood experiences. As stated in the Overview, the application of a theory in everyday clinical practice in psychology is called psychotherapy. Those who seek the help of a psychoanalyst (someone trained in Freud's psychoanalytic theory and techniques) would then be undergoing psychoanalytic psychotherapy, which is the application of psychoanalytic theory in everyday clinical practice.

NEUROSIS AND THE UNCONSCIOUS

The psychoanalytic approach believes that the cause of thoughts, feelings and behaviours is a result of unconscious mental processes formed by early childhood experience.

Freud thought that the causes of all mental and behavioural difficulties lie deep within the unconscious, and that personality is influenced from birth by the contents of the unconscious. Any mental and behavioural difficulties that arise, he termed neuroses. A **neurosis** is a mental condition with no known medical (physical/biological) cause. A neurosis is distressing to the individual and influences their life in a negative way. Examples of neuroses that originate in our unconscious include phobias, compulsions, anxieties, panic disorders and **hysterias**.

We are unaware of our unconscious and what it contains. The purpose of psychoanalytic psychotherapy is thus to access – in order to bring to the patient's *conscious awareness* – the *unconscious causes* of their neurosis. This will hopefully help the patient, as the client is termed in psychoanalysis, to understand the causes and symptoms of their distress. The psychoanalytic approach aims to restore the patient's personality to health. Knowing the cause of a neurosis is immensely helpful in coming to terms with its mental, emotional and social effects. You can deal with yourself better and you become psychologically healthier.

Neurosis

Neurosis is a general term used to denote a wide range of disorders and is characterised by the following:

- Unrealistic anxiety is accompanied by associated problems such as phobias or compulsions.
- The neurotic individual retains complete contact with reality (in contrast with **psychosis**).
- The disorder tends not to transgress wider social norms, although it is recognised as unacceptable to the neurotic individual.

Source: Mike Cardwell (2000) *The Complete A–Z Psychology Handbook.* 2nd edition. Hodder & Stoughton.

Key features of the psychoanalytic approach

The structure and function of the unconscious

Psychoanalytic theory is concerned with the unconscious mind. Using what is called *the iceberg analogy*, the mind can be likened to an iceberg. Only the tip of an iceberg can be seen above the surface of the ocean, while the great remainder is hidden under the water line. The part of us of which we *are* aware is our conscious mind. Freud believed that people are only consciously aware of this small part of themselves. The greater parts of the mind – our deepest thoughts, instincts, traumas, fears and passions – are hidden from us in our unconscious. Our hidden unconscious is full of these forces that have much more influence over our behaviour than we might at first think.

The iceberg analogy

Our conscious/consciousness is our awareness. Consciousness is the rational decision-making part of our mind. Our preconscious is our dream state. Often we waken up aware of what we have just dreamt about. By remembering dream content we have brought some of our preconscious to our conscious awareness. R.M. Ryckman, in his *Theories of Personality* (2000), says that our preconscious is also that part of our mind that contains information we *could* bring to conscious awareness with little effort. This includes recent experiences, an example being remembering what you had for breakfast yesterday. We are not normally aware of our unconscious at all, probably because it is too scary! It contains our instincts (sex and aggression), traumas, fears and passions. As we age the *sea of life* gets choppier and choppier. This sees the iceberg of our mind thrown

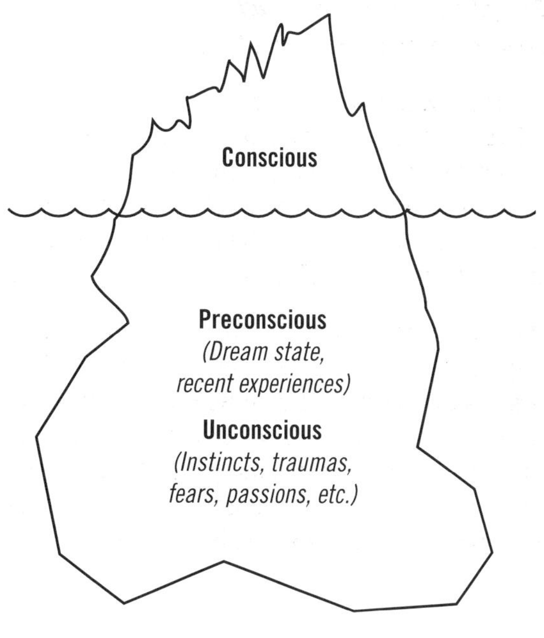

Figure 2.2 The iceberg analogy

about. Parts of the iceberg – previously hidden under the water line – can then break off and float to the surface. In psychoanalytic terms, as life progresses parts of our unconscious can fragment and *manifest* themselves in our conscious awareness as phobias, compulsions, anxieties, panic disorders and hysterias.

Instincts

Freud identified two instincts in our unconscious that influence our personality: *Eros* and *Thanatos*. Eros and Thanatos are innate and biological in origin. Thanatos, or death wish, shows itself in people who show highly aggressive or self-destructive behaviours. Eros, originally described as an instinctual drive for sexual pleasure, is nowadays seen as more of a pleasure-seeking instinct within us. This sees us from the early months of life seeking pleasure and gratification in a number of ways. The satisfaction of libido, via the instinctual drive of Eros, can be seen with a baby sucking its thumb. It derives great pleasure from this and other oral activities such as breast-feeding. The satisfaction of our instincts influences the development of our personality.

Parapraxes

Freud called faulty acts *parapraxes*. Parapraxes are of two kinds and show how our unconscious can influence our thoughts, feelings and behaviours. The first type of parapraxis is *forgetting* to do something. This is because it is painful for you somehow. Examples would be forgetting to do an essay or forgetting to keep a dental appointment. The other type of parapraxis is a slip of the tongue or a *Freudian slip*. This is where we accidentally reveal what we unconsciously mean, like 'I'm glad to see you go' as opposed to 'I'm sad to see you go'. Often parapraxes are sexual in content. This was important for Freud with regard to his view of the influence of sex on the development of personality. In 1980 a student union officer at Glasgow Caledonian University Students Association brought the house down when, at a meeting concerning an incident in the Student Union bar, he said 'I had no alternative but to send in the bouncers to ejaculate the troublemakers from the premises'!

The psychodynamic structure of personality: id, ego and superego

According to Freud, our personality is the pattern of thoughts, emotions and intellectual skills that makes us unique. He also believed personality to be largely unconscious.

Personality

Although personality is what prompts each of us to act in the ways we do, we cannot study it directly. This is because personality is internal to us. Since it does not exist as a tangible reality, personality is another hypothetical construct. Freud thought he could investigate the influence of the unconscious on personality indirectly, by listening to people's free associations (thought associations), and reports of their dreams. From notes made of these sessions with his patients, Freud put together various theories where experiences in childhood are seen as central to the development of personality.

For example, Freud came up with a theory concerning the structure of personality. For him personality is made up of three parts: the *id*, the *ego* and the *superego*. *Id* means 'it' in Latin, and *ego* means 'I'. *Id, ego* and *superego* comprise the psychodynamic structure of personality.

Id

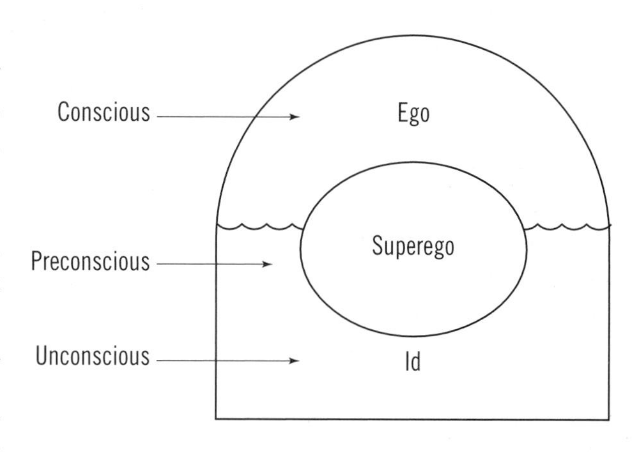

Figure 2.3 The psychodynamic structure of personality

The *id* is the most primitive part of our personality. Present from birth, the *id* is the centre of an instinctive psychic energy Freud called *libido. Libido* constantly demands to be satisfied. The *id*, which is found in the unconscious, in order to satisfy libido, operates on what is called the pleasure principle. The pleasure principle drives us to seek pleasure and avoid pain. This can be seen in babies who demand that their needs are satisfied immediately. If they are hungry, need changing or are uncomfortable, they cry, and we respond immediately to satisfy their id desires. A baby's personality consists principally of id. The id continues to function throughout life, and its job is the immediate satisfaction of instinctive needs. Selfishness, sex and aggression are three manifestations of the demands of the id. They can be seen in our behaviours.

Ego

From about two or three years of age the second more conscious part of our personality, the ego, starts to emerge. Our ego is influenced by our real-world experiences. At this stage personality structure is beginning to change. The ego part of our personality deals with those activities needed to get the demands of our id satisfied. The ego thus operates according to the reality principle. Obeying the reality principle means that the ego tries to find a realistic and socially acceptable solution to the demands of the id. A child discovers that the whining id demand of 'Muuuum! I want sweets!' accompanied by a tantrum doesn't work after a while. Their ego manages this id demand by coming up with a more 'acceptable' solution to what it wants, such as the child using the strategy of 'Mum, if I behave will you buy me sweets?' The id gets what it wants, but in an acceptable manner, based on the ego's experience of how other people get things.

> *'The ego seeks to bring the influence of the external world to bear upon the id and its tendencies. For the ego, perception plays the part, which in the id falls to instinct. The ego represents reason and common sense, in contrast to the id, which contains the passions.'*
>
> *(Freud,* The Ego and the Id*, 1923)*

Superego

The third part of our personality to emerge at around four to six years is the superego. Like a watchdog, or internalised parent, over our entire personality the superego is our conscience. It holds a model of what we think, largely unconsciously, we ought to be like. It punishes us with feelings of guilt if we do not come up to these expectations. The superego is formed as a result of our upbringing. The superego is not dominated by the need to satisfy instinctive drives. However it is not as rational as the ego, and can keep us in tight moral check by producing such feelings of guilt that result in anxiety and irrational behaviour. The superego operates on what is called the morality principle.

Id, ego, and superego: a psychodynamic relationship

A maturing, and mature, personality is the result of continuing clashes and compromises between these three parts of our personality. The id, ego and superego are therefore in a changing, psychodynamic, relationship with one another. Sometimes the id will make demands of the ego that the ego cannot satisfy in an acceptable way. There is no 'safe' realistic solution to these id demands. We then may act in ways we know are 'bad'. This could include underage drinking, truanting from school, taking drugs, or having an affair. If we engage in these activities, the superego produces feelings of guilt as a consequence of our id-driven quest for pleasure.

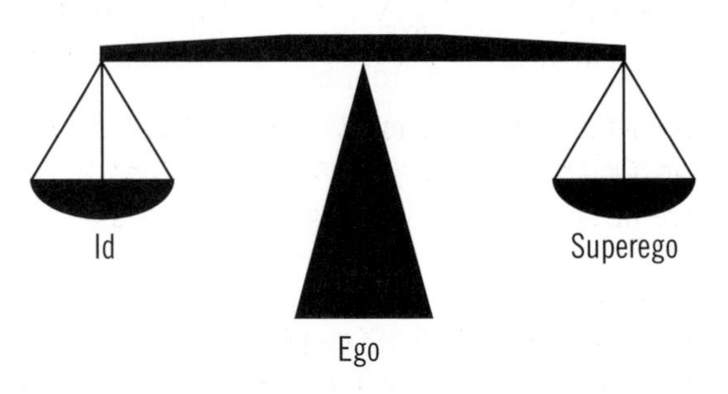

Figure 2.4 The psychoanalytic view of a healthy adult personality is that that person will be a delicate balance between their id and their superego. Their ego tries to balance each antagonistic demand in a realistic manner

A *healthy* adult personality is never entirely id or entirely superego. The diplomatic ego is continually working out solutions to square the conflicting pulls of id and superego. The all-id or all-superego personality is seen as psychologically unhealthy. The id personality is permanently self-centered and overly pleasure-seeking. They hurt others, and perhaps ultimately themselves, to get what they want. Popular music and show business are littered with celebrities who have recognised that they have been or are id-driven personalities. Pleasure seeking excess in the form of sex, drugs and alcohol was, and is, their undoing. Sir Elton John, Billy Connelly and George Best courageously themselves confirmed this when interviewed on Parkinson on BBC in 2001.

Superego personalities also abound. These are highly moralistic individuals fraught with guilt about their own, and others' thoughts, feelings and behaviours. They are often the first to condemn, and there are many examples to be seen in popular culture, such as Mrs Mack in STV's 'Take The High Road' and Dot Cotton in the BBC's 'Eastenders'.

One interpretation of the long-running BBC comedy 'Last of The Summer Wine' is that the three main characters represent the three parts of personality. Foggy, the ex-officer type, is 'superego'. Clegg, the realist, is 'ego'. Compo is 'id'. Its success turns on the changing psychodynamic relationship between the personalities of the three central characters as they enjoy their later years. Id, ego and superego can also be recognised in the central characters of *The Brothers Karamazov* written by the famous Russian author Fyodor Dostoyevsky in 1880.

INTERACTIVE: APPLIED FORENSIC PSYCHOLOGY

- ☐ When did Dostoyevsky write *The Brothers Karamazov*?
- ☐ When was Freud's work first published?
- ☐ What idea could Freud have got from *The Brothers Karamazov*?
- ☐ Is this possible?
- ☐ Does it matter?
- ☐ Try reading *The Brothers Karamazov* for more clues.

The component parts of personality, id, ego, and superego are in a psychodynamic relationship with each other. This is because the ego has to try to keep an even balance between the demands of the id and, at the same time, the demands of the superego.

Sometimes we need to have fun and let our id have a wee adventure. An example might be going on a night out after your Approaches and Methods internal assessment. However, at other times we need to listen to our superego and stick to life's rules more strictly. Like not dodging classes!

Freud thought a child had to learn how to manage the developing conflict between the demands of their id, ego, and superego. Achieving a healthy balance between id, ego and superego is not easy. It takes time. Freud also said we must go through various stages in personality development that further influence the personality we become.

The psychodynamic struggle of id, ego and superego

Imagine that you go out one night and have a marvellous time. So brilliant, in fact, that you forget you are in a relationship with someone else! As a result, you get romantically involved with another person at a level you might not normally – if you were not so carried away. This is your *id* driven by the pleasure principle. In the morning when you wake up you are consumed with remorse and guilt. You don't want to go outside. You don't want to meet up with your friends whom you think will look at you with disgust or glee! Most of all you dread the consequences of your actions if your unsuspecting partner ever finds out. This is your *superego* driven by the morality principle. As the day wears on, you begin to rationalise about the situation. Why did it happen? You might blame alcohol, drugs or the heat of the moment. By the time you go to bed, you have convinced yourself that something else was to blame, that it was a 'one-off' incident and that it will never, ever happen again. This is your *ego* as driven by the reality principle playing its part.

While not recommended, and moral issues aside, Freud would say this psychodynamic tussle between id, ego, and superego, and the way it is resolved, is the sign of a healthy adult personality.

Freud's psychosexual theory of adult personality development

The oral stage (birth–twelve months)

In the first year of life, a baby's mouth is the centre of its universe. Look at any baby's oral behaviour to confirm this. They are constantly putting things in their mouths, and getting much satisfaction as a result. Freud thought this was because, when born, a psychic energy known as libido is centred on our mouth. Libido fuels the id, which is of course the part of our personality present from birth. As libido is initially centred on the mouth we see id-driven oral behaviours in babies such as sucking, biting and breast-feeding. The satisfaction got by such oral activities is evidence of oral gratification demanded by libido.

Fixations

If a child becomes stuck in the oral stage, because of too much or too little oral stimulation, Freud said the child could grow up orally fixated. **Oral fixations** can be seen in people who like to put things into their mouths, e.g. the smoker, nail-biter, finger-chewer, lip-sucker. Freud thought that oral fixations came about because of too much/too little breast-feeding when an infant, and would be very interested in the current fashion among young people for tongue piercing! He would say that this, and other oral behaviours, displayed an oral personality. Oral fixations often surface when we are under stress. The nail-biters have no fingernails left when they leave an exam hall, while the student smoker reaches for a cigarette.

As the child's personality develops, libido shifts to another erogenous zone in the body. An erogenous zone is a part of the body from which we derive sexual pleasure.

THE ANAL STAGE (TWELVE MONTHS–TWO YEARS)

The anal stage of personality development comes at toilet-training time. At about 12 months a toddler begins to learn to control his or her bowels and bladder. During this time libido moves to the anus. The ability to control our bowels and bladder becomes of prime importance to us during the anal stage. As toddlers we get a feeling of delight and satisfaction at managing bowel control. It sees us becoming independent. Alternatively, if made to feel a failure when an 'accident' occurs, as toddlers we can become anxious and afraid. If 'accidents' are not commented upon, this can make us unsure, and this may result in our developing an **anal fixation**.

INTERACTIVE: BE A PSYCHOANALYTIC PSYCHOTHERAPIST

There is a family of four boys in Glasgow. All are now in their forties. L.H. is the second eldest of the four. For as far back as the family can remember, when they all meet with cousins, aunts and uncles at Christmas, L.H. is always reminded of his toilet training experiences! His mum taught her children to control their bowels in the same way her mother taught her. At certain times of the day each child was placed on the potty and advised by mum to *perform*. His eldest and younger brothers did not seem to have a problem with this. L.H. did. When put on the potty he would just not cooperate. Even when he needed to go, aided by doses of child laxative, he would fight to control his faeces. Sitting on the potty, his wee fat face puffed up like a balloon. He would then go various shades of pink, red and scarlet. Finally, gravity took over! He'd lost the battle. As a teenager, he had to share a room with his eldest brother. LH's side of the room was always neat and tidy. His clothes were always hung up, spick and span. He lent nothing to his scruffy eldest brother whose half of the room was a bombsite in comparison. Many a fight was had about this. As an adult he seems obsessed with 'looking good', buys clothes he can ill-afford, is extremely tidy, and a bit tight with his cash.

In around 250 words analyse L.H.'s personality from the viewpoint of the psychoanalytic approach.

Freud thought there were two types of anal fixation, resulting in either an anal retentive or anal expulsive personality in adulthood. Anal-retentive personalities are overly possessive, stubborn and very clean and tidy, while anal expulsive are personalities who give things away. Symbolically they are sharing their faeces.

THE PHALLIC STAGE (THREE YEARS–FIVE YEARS)

The third psychosexual phase of personality development is the one for which Freud is most renowned. During the phallic stage libido moves to the genitals. The pleasure-seeking nature of libido is seen in childhood genital stimulation.

Freud said that from the age of about three, a small boy falls in love with his mother. This state of affairs, and how it is resolved, is known as the Oedipus complex. Because he now sees his father as a rival for his mother's love, the little boy suffers strong feelings of jealousy and resentment towards his father. These uncomfortable feelings make the small boy anxious, coming to believe his father will punish him by cutting off his penis. The small boy of three or four then adopts an interesting strategy to avoid this castration anxiety.

The resolution of the Oedipus complex

In order to get into his dad's good books, he begins to imitate his dad's behaviour. This process is called *identification*. Through identification with his father the little boy comes to realise his gender identity is masculine. Identification is the successful resolution of the Oedipus complex. In successfully resolving his conflict with his dad in this way the small boy subsequently learns his gender role. The $64,000 dollar question here is 'What might transpire if a little boy cannot resolve his Oedipus complex?' Any ideas?

It is worth noting that Freud himself never addressed the female equivalent of the Oedipus complex. Known as the Electra complex, this was left to later neo-Freudians like daughter Anna Freud to explain. A neo-Freudian is a follower of Freud. Freud's reluctance to talk about female sexuality lies in a possible answer to the question posed above – and the times he was writing in (1900). The failure to resolve the Oedipus complex has been cited as a *possible* explanation of male homosexuality.

The latent stage (five years–twelve years)

Freud believed that between the ages of five and twelve years children's psychosexual development went into a latent or dormant phase. Libido is expressed outwards in social and academic development. It is called the latent stage because nothing psychosexual seems to occur. Boys are boys and girls are girls mostly 'doing their own boy or girl thing'. Toni, the ten-year-old Brownie pictured opposite, reports that at her primary school discos only one primary 7 boy and girl have ever been seen dancing together. Little girls dance with each other while the boys apparently just run around playing.

Figure 2.5 Toni

The genital stage (eleven/twelve years–adulthood)

The final stage of sexual development begins at adolescence and continues throughout adult life. This is when the young person enters puberty and progresses towards adult sexual relationships. The genital stage is characterised by sexual experimentation. It is resolved in our twenties or so when we settle down in a one-to-one, hopefully permanent, loving relationship with another person. This is, according to Freud, the successful resolution of the genital stage of psychosexual adult personality development.

What is a case study?

- A case study is a investigation into an individual, or group of individuals, who are unique in some way.
- A case study nowadays involves intensive study of evidence from a variety of sources. These includes family, doctors, work colleagues and psychologists. A history of the individual is constructed from all of the information gathered.
- A case study proper can see various methods being used to gather information. Common methods are interviews, surveys and observations.
- Case studies can be retrospective. This means you investigate the person's past.
- Case studies can also be longitudinal. A longitudinal case study is carried out over an extended period of time into the future. This is to monitor development, progress and changes in the individual or group.

Little Hans

Freud carried out a case study of a child in the phallic stage of personality development. Little Hans was four years old and had a phobia about horses. He lived opposite a large coaching inn where horses, horse-drawn carriages and horse-drawn trams came and went all the time. He had once seen a horse collapse in the street and die. Little Hans was frightened to go outside preferring instead to stay indoors with his mother. Hans's dad was interested in Freud's new therapy called psychoanalysis and his mother had been a patient of Freud's. Hans's father wrote to Freud reporting Hans's symptoms. Freud replied by return, listing questions to ask Hans. Freud interpreted the written answers sent to him by Hans's father according to the principles of his psychoanalytic theory. One letter said that Hans often dreamed that his mother would leave him. Freud interpreted this as a fear aroused by guilt at his incestuous desire of his mother. Freud suggested that Hans's fear was based on the child being in the phallic stage of development. He was showing an awakening of sexual feelings. Hans desired his mother but was consequently frightened of castration. Freud felt that Hans had made a connection between his father's facial characteristics and those of a horse (moustache – hairy face, glasses – blinkers). Whatever their cause, Hans's phobic behaviours got him lots of attention from his mother. Maybe not coincidently, she had recently given birth to Hans's sister Hanna. The father was told by Freud to give Hans continual reassurance. Hans's father spent more time with him and after a while the phobia disappeared. Freud thought this was due to his analysis of the problem and the use of the talking cure of reassurance given to Hans by his dad. Hans had resolved his Oedipus complex. Freud met Hans only once.

1. What criticisms can be made of the way Freud conducted his study of Little Hans? There are at least three.
2. What alternative reasons might be given for Hans's phobia? There are at least two.
3. In your opinion why did Hans's phobia of horses disappear?

Ego-defence mechanisms

The ego has a number of defence mechanisms that it uses to protect itself (us) from unpleasant feelings of anxiety or guilt. These feelings can arise because we feel threatened by a real danger, or because our id or superego becomes too demanding of us. We use ego defence mechanisms to reduce these anxieties.

It is important to understand that the use of defence mechanisms is not under our conscious control. Defence mechanisms are then non-voluntaristic. In conjunction with the ego, the unconscious will use one or more ego-defence mechanisms to protect us when we come up against a stressful situation in life: Here are some examples of ego-defence mechanisms.

- **Repression:** this happens when you experience something so painful and traumatic that you push it out of your conscious awareness. You permanently forget that it ever happened. The 'affect' (or emotion) attached to the memory cannot be repressed, however, and is still evident in your behaviour, perhaps as neurotic symptoms. Freud used dream analysis, slips-of-the-tongue (parapraxes) and free association to uncover patients' repressed information on the origin of their problems. This repressed information gave him a clue as to the cause of their psychological distress. Repression is the unconscious act of forgetting a deeply disturbing trauma or event. Someone who has suffered the trauma of child sexual abuse may understandably use repression as an ego-defence mechanism. It is just too horrific for them to contemplate.
- **Displacement:** this involves the transfer of ideas and impulses from one object or person to another. For example, you may feel hostile and aggressive towards your boss as a result of getting the blame for something you did not do. You feel like lashing out, verbally, physically or both. This is not realistic. You could lose your job. You thus use displacement and snap at and criticise a colleague instead. Another example of displacement might be where you may be getting a telling-off from your mum. You want to lash out. Instead you hit your wee brother or try to kick the cat.
- **Regression:** this occurs when a person behaves in a manner more suitable to an earlier stage of life, e.g. adults who resort to childish behaviours like stamping, kicking, and/or shouting in an effort to get their own way. Regressive behaviours such as thumb sucking can be seen when individuals are in a stressful situation like examination time, a first date or a job interview.
- **Denial:** this is when someone refuses to believe difficult events are happening or have happened. Denial convinces us that there is no problem to worry about. For example, a child may refuse to admit that a parent is dead and insist that he or she is coming home soon. An alcoholic may refuse to admit that he or she is dependent on alcohol. They read the concerns of other people as over-exaggerated. It is other people who have a problem, not them! This is not of course true; the alcoholic is in denial.
- **Rationalisation:** this is where we explain away any uncomfortable thoughts, feelings, and behaviours as positive and logical. Rationalisation helps us feel better about the things we do, in that we rationalise out irrational (!) excuses for what we do. An example is the full-time student at college who wastes his time in the pub, when he should be at classes, or doing homework. He fails his exams. This is extremely painful. He avoids the pain by rationalising that it must have been his 'crap' teachers' fault.
- **Projection:** this is where our ego projects undesirable characteristics, desires or feelings we may have onto another person. A person who is aggressive may not like to think this is a problem. They may, as part of their personality, project their aggression onto another person. This allows them to feel that it is the *other* person who is being aggressive towards them and not the other way round. Many in Scotland have experienced

Figure 2.6 Ego-defence mechanisms

projection when innocently walking along the street and confronted with the phrase 'What's your problem, pal?!' In his case, projection.

- **Suppression:** this is when we suppress our at-first conscious feelings of sexual desire for friends or suppress anger towards objects, events and people that have disturbed us in the past. The ego-defence of suppression uniquely originates in our *preconscious*. We use suppression when we are confronted with the stimuli about which we have sexual/aggressive feelings. This might be when you see a friend you have secret sexual feelings towards. You keep these to yourself. Another example might be the teacher who finds a student, with whom they have recently had a row, in their class. They may still be angry and the sight of the student makes them realise this! The stimulus of the student brings their preconscious feelings towards them to their conscious awareness. They then use the ego-defence mechanism of suppression and keep their thoughts to themselves.

Ego-defence mechanisms were for Freud natural and normal. When they get out of proportion, neuroses develop, such as anxiety states, phobias, obsessions or hysteria. These disorders affect emotional and intellectual functioning, relationships, health, well-being and quality of life.

As we will read, further features of the psychoanalytic approach can be found in the application of theory to clinical practice. In psychoanalytic psychotherapy the interpretation of dreams and free association are used to bring to the patients' conscious awareness the root cause of their problem. Cause lies in the unconscious. Dream interpretation and free association are therefore used to bring the cause of the patient's *neurosis* to light. But what actually is the interpretation of dreams?

Die Traumdeutung

In 1896, Freud's father Jacob died. His death had a powerful effect on Freud. At the time Freud was developing a theory that neurosis was caused by sexual seduction in childhood. Freud began to think that his father had sexually abused both himself and his brothers and sisters in childhood. This was because most of his brothers and sisters had neurotic symptoms similar to those of his own patients, and his neurotic patients had indicated childhood sexual abuse in their visits to Freud's surgery. Freud considered this and began to look to a cause behind his *own* neurotic symptoms. He surmised that he was neurotic because he *himself* had been abused when younger. Freud was uncomfortable with thoughts that his own father could be to blame, and then said he was neurotic as a result of childhood abuse – by his nanny. His abuse in childhood, and his later symptoms of adult neuroses, like soreness of the arm and heart problems, were consistent with what his patients told him about similar experiences they had had when young.

The interpretation of dreams

Freud's allegation of abuse against his nanny came as a result of a dream which he interpreted as *symbolising* the origins of his own neuroses. For Freud, dreams were somehow connected with neuroses, and he began to think and write about his patients' *dream content*. His subsequent book, *The Interpretation of Dreams* (1900), was initially a flop, selling only 129 copies in its first six weeks. Freud's publisher, Franz Deuticke began to worry, rather prematurely as it happened. By the time of Freud's death in 1939 the book was a worldwide bestseller and remains so today. *Die Traumdeutung – The Interpretation of Dreams* – has had a great impact on psychology, psychoanalysis, sexual issues, language and twentieth-century culture – as we shall now see.

Dream analysis

> *'Dreams, are invariably the product of a conflict ... [they help sleep] releasing tensions that come from unattainable wishes.'*
>
> *Freud (1900)*

In Freud's *The Interpretation of Dreams* (1900) dreams are the royal road to a knowledge of the activities of the unconscious mind. What *the royal road to the unconscious* means is that our dreams bring to our preconscious, aspects of our unconscious. We can sometimes be aware of what it is we are, or were, dreaming about. Most dreams, Freud said, are wish fulfilment – we dream about those things we want in reality. Freud also argued that we all dream in commonly shared symbols, many of which he said were sexual in nature. If we were to have a dream in which a sword appeared, Freud said this symbolised the male penis. If we had a dream in which a door opened and closed, this symbolised sexual intercourse (see Table 2.1). According to Freud, we bury our feelings during the day, and they later reappear in our dreams as a means of wish fulfilment, as do any suppressed sexual feelings we might have for others. A hundred years after the publication of *The Interpretation of Dreams* there is little scientific evidence to support Freud's claims about commonly shared dream symbols. If you have a dream that figures a large white stallion, it is perhaps as likely to be reminding you to put money on the large white dead cert in the 3.30 at Kempton the next day, rather than being connected with sexual wish fulfilment. (But only go into a bookie's if you are over eighteen of course!)

The Interpretation of Dreams gave Freud a clue to the main causes of our psychological problems. He said that neuroses and hysterias originated in the structure, the formation, and the function of our unconscious. Reflect once again on the relationship between neurosis, the unconscious, the preconscious and the conscious and you should be able to see why dream analysis is still used today in classical psychoanalytic psychotherapy.

Table 2.1 Common dream symbols and their interpretation

Symbol	Interpretation
Kings and queens	Parents
Beginning a journey	Dying
Falling	Desire to return to a state where one is satisfied and protected
Climbing stairs or ladder, driving cars, riding horses, crossing bridges	Sexual intercourse
Elongated objects, tree trunks, umbrellas, neckties, snakes, and other phallic symbols	Male genitals
Enclosed spaces: ovens, closets, caves, pockets, boxes	Female genitals

Josef Breuer and Anna O

From 1886, Freud worked in private practice in Vienna where he had some patients who suffered from hysteria. Hysteria is a physical symptom brought on by a psychological cause. Freud tried hypnosis to remove their hysterical symptoms but was unsuccessful. He then discussed his inability to help his patients with a colleague Josef Breuer, who had a patient called Anna O. Anna O, whose real name was Bertha Pappenheim, was to have a profound effect on Freud and his career.

Figure 2.7 Anna O

Anna had come to Breuer with symptoms of hysteria such as a severe nervous cough, a squint in one eye, visual disturbances and paralysis in her right arm. She had a peculiar speech problem in that she understood Breuer when he talked to her in German, but often replied to his questioning in English. She would also suffer hysterical seizures similar to epilepsy. During these seizures she would go into a trancelike state, writhe about, and shake uncontrollably. She would *talk to herself* which seemed to help her *come out* of these hysterical attacks. Later in conversation she would talk about her fears and experiences. She talked about her upbringing, childhood traumas, and important events in her life. This *talking cure*, known as catharsis or the **cathartic method**, used during and after her hysterical attacks seemed to help Anna feel better. It relieved her hysterical symptoms. It was thought that Anna's paralysis stemmed from her feelings of inadequacy to help her father who was at the time seriously ill. She talked about a dream where she saw a snake slither towards him and she felt powerless to stop it. At the level of the unconscious this was interpreted as how she felt about her inability to help her father in his illness. Once this was brought to her attention and explained, the paralysis in her right arm disappeared. Later, when her father did die, Anna experienced new hysterias. These included hydrophobia (a fear of drinking liquids). Once again, using hypnosis and the talking cure, Breuer traced the cause of her hydrophobic fear to a past experience buried in her unconscious. Breuer discovered Anna had once seen a dog drinking out of a glass normally used by humans. Using the cathartic method Breuer helped Anna recover from her traumas, and she went on to lead a most interesting life. Anna could be said to be a forerunner of the Women's Aid movement in that she became a leading social worker and feminist, and in 1907 established a home for single mothers where she dedicated the rest of her life to rescuing victims of sexual abuse. She is said to have written two separate wills just before she died – in completely different and distinct handwriting.

Hysterias

Since Freud's time hysterical paralysis, blindness and mutism have been identified. Hysterias are psychological in origin and have no physical (medical) cause. In normal circumstances visual impairment comes about due to damage, disease or accident to the eyes and visual cortex. Hysterical blindness, paralysis and mutism however can be triggered by deep personal trauma or tragedy. Hysterias have been found in some soldiers when confronted with the horror of war. Pat Barker's excellent Booker prize winning novel *Regeneration*, based on true events, reports a First World War British officer literally being struck dumb by the horrors of the Western Front. He is sent to Craiglochart in Edinburgh where he sees an army psychiatrist. The officer agrees to treatment and is strapped into a dentist's chair. His head is fixed in a device and his mouth is held open by clamps. The psychiatrist then electrocutes the officer's tongue. Within minutes the officer had recovered his speech! The psychiatrist had a 100% success rate with this treatment. The prospect of a worse trauma like another electric shock overcame the effect of the earlier trauma of the battlefield. His hysterical mutism was cured. This treatment is longer used today. For 'other ranks' suffering the psychological effects of war the treatment was more drastic. They were shot – for what today would be regarded as symptoms of post-traumatic stress disorder.

Free association

The Anna O case encouraged Freud to develop a therapeutic technique called free association. Free association comes from the German word *einfall*, meaning irruption or sudden idea. Not too dissimilar to Breuer's cathartic method, Freud's technique of free association saw him encourage patients themselves to freely recall events in their lives. Freud said these freely recalled events formed patterns of thought associations that are unique to each individual. Further, there are many common chains of thought used by everyone. Freud studied these chains of thought or free associations, and found many **universal** symbols in the form of words, pictures, or events that he said symbolised something else. Using free association the patient and the psychotherapist, then as now, work together on the associations, or connections, between the freely recalled events of the past and the patient's present psychological difficulties. Free association is a central feature of psychoanalytic psychotherapy today.

Applications of the psychoanalytic approach

Mental health

The application of a theory in everyday clinical practice in psychology is called a psychotherapy. The most obvious application of the psychoanalytic approach is psychoanalytic psychotherapy.

The aim of psychoanalytic psychotherapy is to give the patient an insight into the root cause of their neurosis. This is carried out using psychoanalysis. Psychoanalysis sees the bringing of repressed memories from the patient's unconscious to their conscious awareness. As stated earlier, dream analysis and free association are used in psychoanalytic psychotherapy, as are other psychoanalytic techniques such as the interpretation of resistance and transference and hypnosis.

Resistance

As can be seen in Table 2.1 classical psychoanalytic psychotherapists make a symbolic interpretation of any dream content reported to them by their patients. Classical psychoanalysis, as Freud himself laid down some 100 years ago, is still practised today. Sometimes called **analysands**, patients in therapy sometimes offer resistance to dream interpretations by their psychoanalyst. One goal of psychoanalytic psychotherapy is thus to highlight and break down any resistance. By doing so the therapist hopes to make more understandable the cause of the neurotic symptoms from which the individual is suffering, as symbolised in their dream.

Transference

A major feature of the psychoanalytic approach in therapy is transference. Transference is a natural and inevitable part of the therapy, of which the patient is initially unconscious. It refers to the transferring of emotions felt in childhood onto the therapist. The psychoanalytic psychotherapist reconstructs, and plays out, these personality-forming childhood experiences with their patient. The psychoanalyst then interprets the patient's verbal reactions and behaviours to this reconstruction. The reason is to get further insight into their unconscious. For it is within the unconscious, of course, that the patient's neurosis is to be found. Using transference, and the interpretation of related free associations, the cause of neurosis can more easily be brought to light and to the patient's attention. Prior to psychoanalytic psychotherapy, the patient would be unaware of the cause(s) of their neurosis, as these would be hidden, buried in their unconscious.

Hypnosis

Another technique used in the application of the theory in psychotherapy is hypnosis. Some psychoanalysts use hypnosis to regress (send back) their patient to an earlier stage in their life. This is usually a period in childhood where the trauma causing them to think, feel and behave as they do, originally occurred. Regression via hypnosis helps bring difficulties to conscious awareness.

Psychoanalytic psychotherapy is difficult to access through the National Health Service. It should also be noted that some clinical psychologists (and psychiatrists), more often in the private sector, use one of the many newer forms of psychoanalysis that are around today. Briefer than classical psychoanalysis, these sessions are more likely to be conducted face-to-face, in upright chairs, rather than in the traditional psychoanalytic manner with the therapist sitting at the head of a couch upon which their patient lies.

PLAY THERAPY

Some followers of Freud thought play was a form of purposeful behaviour which could be used to unlock the secrets of the unconscious mind. In the same way that dreams and parapraxes can be interpreted to identify the difficulties that an adult might be trying to deal with, a therapist may use play to identify the difficulties a *child* may be experiencing. This idea was strengthened by the work of Melanie Klein, a neo-Freudian, who used play therapy to analyse behavioural problems of children as young as two years old.

In play therapy, children play and the psychoanalytic psychotherapist observes what is happening in the play situation. In this way unresolved difficulties may come to light. This is because play therapy overcomes the problem of getting a child to explain verbally the thoughts, feelings and behaviours they may have. Play therapy may be appropriate in cases of abuse. This is because children repeat everyday experiences in their play. Play also shows the child's real life use of ego-defence mechanisms. They may, for example, *project* certain feelings they have about themselves, or others, onto their toys. A child may in their play suggest that a doll is frightened of going to hospital. Unconsciously they mean themselves. Children may also *displace* anger felt towards a parent onto a toy. This anger may be causing difficulties at home. Play therapy can make the child, the therapist and the parents aware of the cause of the problem.

An example: Dibs

A good example of play therapy was conducted by V.M. Axline (1971). She conducted a case study of a child called Dibs in 1964. Dibs, when he was five, went to an American Elementary School where his behaviour gave some cause for concern. He was thought to be, to use the term of the time, mentally retarded. He seemed to have learning challenges, was withdrawn, a loner, and did not seek company. He was also very reluctant to go home when school came to an end and often fought and scratched his teachers when they came to help him do things like put his jacket on. Dibs was referred to Axline, who was developing non-directive psychoanalytic play therapy at the time.

Dibs was encouraged to explore Axline's playroom. When he picked up toys and tried to get her opinion on them, Axline would only confirm what they were. She showed no approval, disapproval, surprise or preference. Dibs began to play with the dolls, dolls' house and sandbox in much the same way as any other child of five. The crucial difference was in the *content* and subsequent *analysis* and *interpretation* of his play. He gave the mummy doll long walks around the 'park'. The sister doll, he took to 'school'. The soldier doll was treated differently. It stayed inside the dolls' house and wouldn't 'go to the park'. 'It couldn't be bothered', said Dibs. Dibs took the boy doll from its room in the dolls' house and put it outside. The soldier doll was buried upside down in the sandbox. When Axline asked why he had behaved in such a fashion, Dibs broke down and told her that his father often locked him in his room when he was angry with him. This distressed him greatly. The soldier doll represented his father. Dibs was angry about his father's temper, a temper now revealed by Axline as being often directed at Dibs. The burying of the doll in the sandpit symbolised the way Dibs felt about this. Axline was able to persuade Dibs that his negative thoughts, feelings and behaviours towards his father, and others, were normal. He had a right to feel hurt about his father's temper. Now that his thoughts, feelings, and behaviours towards his father and his family were brought to Dibs's attention, and explained, Dibs and his family learned to live together better.

INTERACTIVE

From a psychoanalytic point of view what is the cause of Dibs's atypical behaviours? Give reasons for your answer.

Limitations of the psychoanalytic approach

Methodology

Freud used a number of case studies as evidence for his theories. As you will later read in Chapter 12, the case study as a method of enquiry has disadvantages. Freud said his theories were *universal* and applied to us all, yet the few case studies on which his theories are based were mainly of middle-class neurotic Viennese women. Freud's sample was not only too small, but also biased in that it was made up of these privileged women. It was not *representative* of a wider society. In the same way, his theory on child personality development was based on only a single case of a child, Little Hans (see page 20).

INTERACTIVE

Read 'Disadvantages of the case study' on page 280. What general disadvantages does the case study method of research attract?

Hypothetical constructs

Another limitation to the approach is that psychoanalytic theory is impossible to test in a scientific way. We are unable to physically identify the structures of personality – the id, ego and superego – because they are hypothetical constructs. This creates a difficulty in that we discuss them as though they are real entities instead of a *model* of something that does not actually exist. This criticism also applies to other psychoanalytic concepts, such as libido or fixation, which are not real and are difficult to ascertain.

To illustrate this point, let us consider a study by Yarrow (1973), who looked at the age at which thumb-sucking children had been weaned (when a mother stops breast-feeding). Sixty-six mothers were surveyed and asked about when their children were weaned, and if they were thumb-suckers. Yarrow found there was a correlation between thumb-sucking in childhood and early weaning. In Chapter 7 you will read that a correlation is a relationship between certain factors, called co-variates. The related factors or co-variates here are of course age of weaning and later thumb-sucking behaviour. Yarrow (1973) suggests then that there *is* a relationship between early weaning and thumb-sucking children.

However, as a correlation only shows a relationship between two things, and does not provide any evidence of cause and effect, Yarrow's (1973) study is not sufficient to *scientifically* support the existence of the oral fixation of thumb-sucking. Neither can Yarrow (1973) conclusively claim the existence, and unsuccessful resolution, of the oral stage of personality development, as possibly demonstrated by thumb-sucking children, teenagers and adults.

Time-consuming

As a therapy, psychoanalytic psychotherapy can take months or years to get to the root cause of a patient's neurosis. In private, non-National Health Service psychoanalytic psychotherapy a patient would normally visit their analyst two hours per week, twice a week for two years. This type of psychotherapy is out of the reach of ordinary people. Quite simply, it costs too much.

Over-emphasis on the sexual world

Probably most critically of all, many people were, and are, unhappy about Freud's emphasis on children's sexual experience as being *the* factor that influences personality development. There is no evidence, for example, that the phallic stage exists. Indeed some followers parted company with him on his over-insistence that the sexual world is of such personality-shaping importance. Adler, Jung and Erikson, who went on to establish the broader psychodynamic approach, while appreciating the role of the unconscious, believed our social world is of much more importance.

A study by the English anthropologist Malinowski (1929) of Trobriand Islanders investigated the Oedipus complex. In the Trobriand Islands, found off the coast of New Guinea, the father of a male child does not bring that child up. This role falls to the mother's brother – the male child's uncle. Malinowski found that male children of between four and six years did not show any aggression towards their fathers. According to Freud, aggression towards the father during this time would have been evidence of the Oedipus complex. Further, Freud would have been concerned because if the uncle brought the male children up there did not seem to be an opportunity for sex-role identification with the father for the successful resolution of the Oedipus complex. Freudian theory at the very least would suggest that the Trobriand male child would grow up confused about his sexuality. Malinowski found, however, that Trobriand male children had no problem with sexual identification. In adulthood they managed to fulfil their appropriate sex roles without appearing to have needed to resolve an Oedipus complex at the phallic stage of childhood – given such a hypothetical construct affecting personality development exists in the first place.

The effectiveness of psychoanalytic psychotherapy

The late British Professor Hans Eysenck also criticised Freud's psychoanalytic approach as applied in therapy. Eysenck (1952) evaluated reports on the recovery of two groups of neurotic patients. One group received psychoanalytic therapy and the other group did not. Of those studied, 44 per cent were cured or much improved after psychoanalytic therapy, compared with 72 per cent who were cured or much improved, with no treatment at all. No friend of psychoanalysis, Eysenck is famous for his observation, '… the more psychotherapy, the smaller the recovery rate' (Eysenck, 1952).

Important figures in the development of the broader psychodynamic approach

Carl Gustav Jung (1875–1961)

Figure 2.8 Carl Gustav Jung

Jung left Freud's inner circle in Vienna in 1913. Jung was opposed to the emphasis Freud gave to sex. He disagreed about the nature of libido, ego and the unconscious. The libido, for Jung, was a biologically driven motivating force within us – but was non-sexual in origin. Jung said that the role of the ego is to provide us with information from the past that will help us to deal with our present reality. The ego is part of our process of consciousness. The unconscious consists of two parts: the personal unconscious and the collective unconscious. Jung agreed with Freud that the personal unconscious contains our repressed memories. Some material in the personal unconscious is not however necessarily forbidden or censored. It has merely fallen into decay through lack of use by our awareness or consciousness. The personal unconscious is considered to be the 'opposite' of our conscious mind. This means for Jung that an extrovert with an outgoing passionate temperament is unconsciously an introvert with a thoughtful reserved temperament. The personal unconscious compensates for weaknesses in our personal conscious.

The collective unconscious contains information that we hold in common with others in our evolution and is genetically transmitted. Our collective unconscious contains many concepts which Jung calls universal archetypes, such as a God, demons, fear of the dark, fire, snakes and spiders. We react to the dark, fire, snakes and spiders in the same way as our ancestors did because of our connected evolutionary biology. Our collective unconscious has survival value for us. Its ability to make us wary of snakes or spiders would have been especially important in our prehistoric past when spiders were the size of plates! Avoiding them increased your life expectancy. Jung had three stages of personality development, the pre-sexual period (age 3–6), characterised by growth and nutrition, and the pre-pubertal stage which is similar to Freud's latent stage. The last phase is the stage of maturity comparable to Freud's genital stage. In psychotherapy, Jung was more concerned with a patient's future goals, than past history. He saw the cause of neuroses – thoughts, feelings and behaviours – as being rooted in the present, as opposed to the past. Jung's analytical psychology is still of great interest in the psychodynamic approach today.

Figure 2.9 Alfred Adler

Alfred Adler (1870–1937)

Alfred Adler left Freud's 'Vienna circle' in 1911. His initial interest in Freud's psychoanalytic theory of personality stemmed from a shared belief in the biological foundations of human behaviour. Both Freud and Adler thought the biological and the psychological were interlinked. Adler went on to develop his own theory known as individual psychology. Individual psychology sees us as striving for perfection in our personality. Further, we are motivated to confirm our personality – or who we think we are. We have a biological drive towards self-preservation and a 'will to power'. Will to power is a striving for superiority over others. Our drive to superiority over others is influenced by any feelings of inferiority aquired during childhood. For individual psychology our goal is to be socially significant. Adler disagreed with Freud's view of the importance of sexuality to the development of personality. Instead, Adler concentrated on how we come to terms with feelings of inferiority originating in childhood. Feelings of insecurity or inferiority in childhood can be the consequence of congenital or environmental physical deformity, our gender and perceived gender role. Gender role is learnt, in part by the internalisation of stereotypes of what is masculine and feminine in our society. Simply put, boys are encouraged to be strong and superior, girls (in his day anyway) were/are encouraged to be weak and inferior. Birth order or where you come in the family also affects feelings of inferiority. The second eldest in a large family can feel 'left out' or less loved than say the eldest (first born) and the youngest (last born or 'baby'). Further feelings of inadequacy arise due to negative learning experiences with adults such as being neglected, spoilt or unloved as a child.

All these factors can lead to feelings of inferiority or an 'inferiority complex' in adulthood. As we have an instinctive urge to be powerful, or at least to demonstrate that we have power, Adler thought that people showed their 'will to power' in ways that reflected their inferiority complex. They compensate for their unconscious feelings of inadequacy. An example is the little man who makes a great show of smoking large cigars or driving a big car. (The next time you see a Volvo, look at the size of the person driving it!) Adler explained the development of our personality as arising from whatever compensations we make for our feelings of inferiority and related low self-esteem.

For Adler, inferiority is almost natural. As individuals we deal with it in one of three ways. The particular strategy we adopt will affect our personality. The first strategy Adler calls successful compensation. This is where we compensate in a positive and constructive way for whatever handicap we have. Successful compensation is all about making the best of whatever we have as individuals. It is our successful adjustment to Adler's three challenges in life – society, work and sex. An excellent example of successful compensation is the career of the Scottish classical percussionist Evelyn Glennie who became profoundly deaf in childhood. She turned a calamity to her advantage.

Another technique is overcompensation for your feelings of inferiority, by trying too hard to achieve things in life. Often our goals are beyond us or exist only in our imagination. The person above with the Volvo or big cigar could be said by Adler to be overcompensating for a height inferiority, for example.

Finally, there is 'escape from combat'. Escape from combat is shown by someone who reduces failure to a minimum by never trying to succeed in the first place. Often they place impossibly high demands on themselves and tackle things that they are not yet ready to do. Individuals who escape from combat might feign illness as an excuse for doing poorly in an internal assessment, for instance. The use of illness or running away from things can become a way of life. It becomes a cover for personal failure. Never having tried at all is *their* way of expressing power over others. What these individuals don't understand is that they are only damaging themselves at the end of the day. Everyone else moves on. Many physicians, social workers and public in Europe and America accepted Adler's views. His popular, simpler view of the role of inferiority in the development of personality was welcomed. Adler was an impassioned advocate of the relatively new subject of psychology; he died in Aberdeen while on a lecture tour of Scotland in 1937. His influence remains today in the work of other psychodynamic psychoanalysts such as Karen Horney.

Erik Erikson (1902–94)

More recently, Erik Erikson disagreed with Freud with his over-emphasis on psychosexual stages of development during childhood, though he accepted the idea that children are sexual beings. Instead, he saw a link between our social experiences and personality development. Unlike Freud who saw the first five years of life alone as crucial to personality, Erikson saw experiences throughout the whole of our lifetime as being important influences on personality. His main contribution is called Erikson's psychosocial theory of personality development. It is an age-stage related theory of adult personality development. It shows that it is the interaction of the person and his or her social environment, which gives rise to personality characteristics. Unsuccessful resolution of key age-stages can lead to an individual experiencing a *psychosocial crisis* that can affect their mental health, and thus their personality. Erikson's theory is still used today, especially in teaching, nursing, social care and social work training. His emphasis on the social aspects of life as influences on what we become should not be underemphasised.

Figure 2.10 Erik Erikson

Conclusion

On his death in London in 1939 Sigmund Freud left psychology a rich inheritance. His bravery in identifying child sexual abuse must be applauded. That his psychoanalytic approach has had an importance in psychology is an understatement. His psychoanalytic legacy led to research and alternative theories both in psychoanalysis and in psychology in general. His method and techniques for understanding why we think, feel and behave as we do lives on today in applied psychoanalysis and related psychodynamic theory and therapies.

Summary of the psychoanalytic approach

The psychoanalytic approach, pioneered by Sigmund Freud, understands us in the light of our unconscious and early childhood experiences. The conflict between forces in our unconscious, of which we are unaware, and our conscious reality, of which we are aware, can give us a neurosis. A neurosis is an anxiety state that affects the quality of life. Freud's structure of personality suggested that our behaviour is influenced by our id, ego and superego. We are born id, and acquire ego and superego by puberty. Our personality development occurs in psychosexual stages during childhood. If we fail to resolve conflicts associated with a particular stage (oral, anal, phallic, latent and genital) of personality development, Freud believed we could develop fixations. These can show themselves in our personality-related behaviours; thus an adult thumb-sucker would be said to have an oral fixation. We all have ego-defence mechanisms that we unconsciously use to protect ourselves from the anxieties of life. An application of the approach is found in psychoanalytic psychotherapy. Features of psychoanalytic psychotherapy include free association, dream analysis, analysis of parapraxes, resistance, regression using hypnosis and transference. The main limitation of the psychoanalytic approach is evidence generated in its support. The case study is non-scientific. Further, it is hugely difficult, scientifically or otherwise, to find support for hypothetical constructs like id, ego and superego. Also, Freud used a small sample of neurotic middle-class Viennese women, and generalised his findings to apply to all of us. His emphasis on the psychosexual saw splits with Adler and Jung. Erikson also later questioned his sexual emphasis on the emerging personality. Adler, Jung and Erikson went on to develop the broader psychodynamic approach (that includes psychoanalysis). The psychodynamic approach believes that it is the social, rather than the sexual, world of childhood that more greatly influences our personality development.

INTERACTIVE

1 Go to http://www.freud.org.uk/index.html and visit the Freud Museum, London. Write a short report entitled 'What is psychoanalysis?'.

2 Watch the video *Regeneration*, or read the book by Pat Barker. What evidence is there to support Freud's view that trauma results in neuroses?

3 Go to: http://65.107.211.206/science/freud/Division_of_Mind.html and write a short resumé on Freud's structure of personality. To emphasise the psychodynamic relationship between id, ego and superego include examples of six psychic conflicts.

4 Go to Star Trek on Freud @ http://ryoung001.homestead.com/Freud.html. What evidence can you find to support the idea that Captain Kirk, Dr McCoy and Mr Spock have id, superego and ego personalities?

Structured questions with answer guidelines

1 *Explain the psychoanalytic approach in psychology.*

With reference to the preceding chapter, structure your answer around the following model:

- State that the aim of the psychoanalytic approach is to understand thoughts, feelings and behaviours as being influenced by unconscious mental processes formed by early childhood experiences. Give brief historical background. Then explain the following features of the psychoanalytic approach:
  - structure and function of the unconscious
  - psychodynamic structure of personality: id, ego and superego
  - ego-defence mechanisms
  - psychosexual stages of adult personality development.

2 *How is the psychoanalytic approach applied in practice?*

Structure your answer as follows:

- Identify the application of the approach as a treatment, i.e. psychoanalytic psychotherapy. Explain what a psychotherapy is. Then discuss and explain features of psychoanalytic psychotherapy such as:
  - interpretation of dreams
  - free association
  - hypnosis/regression
  - What purpose do the above features have in therapy? Explain cause, diagnosis, and treatment as regards the unconscious and early childhood trauma.
  - Further, make reference to play therapy. Good idea to give details of a relevant study.

3 *What criticisms may be made of the psychoanalytic approach?*

Structure your answer as follows:

- Say that Freud's methodology is the main limitation of the psychoanalytic approach. Then give details and discuss the following:
  - The problems with the small biased sample on which Freud's theories are based. Problem with generalisation of his theories to us all on this basis.
  - The use of the case study. Briefly say what a case study is. Make reference to limitations of Little Hans as evidence for Oedipus complex. Say why.
  - The difficulty falsifying Freud's hypothetical constructs. Explain what a hypothetical construct is. Give examples. Also use research examples to help you.
  - The over-emphasis on the sexual world of childhood being *the* personality-forming variable in life. Social, rather than sexual experiences are now seen as more important with the emergence of the psychodynamic approach. Mention Jung, Adler, Erikson.

Glossary

Analysand: name sometimes given to a patient in psychoanalysis. It came about because psychoanalytic psychotherapists themselves have to undergo psychotherapy, and a number complained about being labelled with a patient tag

Anal fixation: anal fixations are of two types. If parents are too lenient in enforcing rules about bowel control, a child may get pleasure and a feeling of success from their bowel movements. They may develop an 'anal expulsive personality' or fixation, which can be seen in their behaviours. The anal expulsive can be excessively untidy, disorganised, reckless and careless. On the other hand, if a child is punished or put under pressure from parents during toilet training, they may experience anxiety about bowel control. The anal retentive personality, or fixation, may result. Anal retentives are obsessively clean, orderly and tidy. They can also be very cautious, stubborn and meticulous

Cathartic method: the origins of free association, attributed to Breuer. It is the talking cure, which helps a patient relieve their distressful symptoms

Hysteria: a condition displaying physical symptoms/behaviours that have no known physical (medical/biological) cause. They are psychological in origin

Neurosis: a term covering a range of disorders that include phobias and compulsions. The neurotic person still maintains contact with reality. An example of a neurosis is claustrophobia – a fear of confined spaces

Oral fixation: linked to breast feeding, symptoms of those who might have an oral fixation include smoking, chewing and nail biting. Freud thought both insufficient or enforced breast feeding could result in such oral personalities in adulthood

Psychosis: a term covering any medical condition where sufferers lose contact with reality, reality being what is experienced as normal by most others. An example of a psychosis is schizophrenia.

Transference: a feature of psychoanalytic psychotherapy, where the therapist plays out personality-forming experiences from the patient's past

Universal: applicable to us all

3

The behaviourist approach

BY THE END OF THIS CHAPTER YOU SHOULD BE ABLE TO:

- **define and explain the behaviourist approach with reference to its key features**
- **explain applications of the behaviourist approach**
- **explain the limitations of the behaviourist approach.**

Overview of the behaviourist approach

In this chapter, readers will be introduced to the behaviourist approach as the approach in psychology that emphasises **learning**. Reference to the work of the Soviet physiologist Ivan Pavlov, and Americans E.L. Thorndike and B.F. Skinner, will illustrate how the simple stimulus–response units of learned behaviours they observed in animals came to explain human learning and behaviours. One type of learning called classical conditioning will be examined in the light of learning by association, extinction, reinforcement, **spontaneous recovery**, stimulus generalisation and stimulus discrimination. A second type of learning, **operant conditioning**, is viewed in terms of reinforcers, positive and negative reinforcement, behaviour shaping and schedules of reinforcement. The chapter will also explain areas of application associated with the behaviourist approach, such as behaviour modification and programmed learning. Finally the limitations of the behaviourist approach as being reductionist, mechanistic, and deterministic will be considered.

Key features of the behaviourist approach

Just as our unconscious is vital to a psychoanalytic explanation as to why we think, feel and behave as we do, central to the behaviourist approach is the idea that we can be explained from the point of view of learning. The behaviourist **paradigm** therefore concerns learning in environment. A paradigm is the agreed subject matter, assumptions and beliefs of a science. For behaviourists, organisms, both human and animal, are explicable as the sum total of stimulus–response units of behaviour, learned as we journey through our environment. How this happens is explained by important behaviourist concepts such as classical and operant conditioning.

Learning, or *conditioning* as it is referred to in the behaviourist approach, can be defined as any relatively permanent change in our behaviour that comes about as a result of experience.

J.B. Watson

In 1915 John Broadus Watson, Professor of Psychology at John Hopkins University in the USA, delivered a paper to the American Psychological Association entitled 'Psychology as the behaviourist views it'. This speech laid the foundations to an approach, thereafter called behaviourism, which was to dominate psychology for the best part of the twentieth century. It was to see great emphasis placed on psychology being concerned with the scientific study of observable behaviour in animals and humans.

Figure 3.1 J.B. Watson

The Behaviourist Manifesto

The Behaviourist Manifesto was an important development, in that in 1915 psychology was all about the study of the mind. Previously, notables like Wilhelm Wundt and William James had been trying to understand the structure and function of *consciousness*, a significant aspect of the mind. Freud had himself been particularly concerned with the study of the *unconscious* mind. Watson was critical of this, because for him, the mind, and what was thought to make it up, are hypothetical constructs. Hypothetical constructs do not exist in reality and are therefore immeasurably difficult to study in a meaningful way.

Further, how Wundt and Freud investigated the mind – by self-report or introspection from participants/patients – was for Watson unscientific. Watson wanted psychology to be a science like physics and chemistry. The study of the mind by introspection was not a route psychology should follow. This was because Watson saw the mind as private and personal.

The Behaviourist Manifesto said the mind was to be left alone and advised psychology to concern itself only with the study of behaviour. For Watson psychology was then to be:

> *'... that division of Natural Science which takes human behaviour, the doings and sayings, both learned and unlearned as its subject matter'.*
>
> *Watson (1919)*

Table 3.1 Key points of the Behaviourist Manifesto, '*Psychology as the behaviourist views it*' Watson (1915)

All behaviour is learned. When born our mind is *tabula rasa*.
We learn how to behave in response to our environment, by forming stimulus–response (S–R) units of behaviour.
Behaviours can be 'unlearned' by breaking these previously formed, stimulus–response (S–R) connections.
What behaviourism discovered concerning stimulus–response learning in animals is equally applicable to human beings.
The mind is private and personal and consists of concepts difficult to study in a scientific way. An organism's observable outcomes – their behaviour – should therefore be the focus of study in psychology.
For psychology to be thought a true science, its theories need to be supported by empirical data obtained through the careful and controlled observation and measurement of behaviour in an experimental setting.

This was mainly because behaviour is observable. Behaviour can be seen, it is public and open to enquiry. Because behaviour can be observed, Watson said it could be also be controlled in an experimental environment to get an even better idea as to what might be its cause. This saw importance placed in the behaviourist approach on the use of the experimental method of research in the investigation of learning.

The behaviourist approach believes that the cause of our thoughts, feelings and behaviours is learning in our environment.

Behaviourism and tabula rasa

The Behaviourist Manifesto said that when born we are *tabula rasa*, which means that our mind is like a blank slate. What we come to understand as our mind, and what is in it, for the behaviourist comes about as a consequence of learning in our environment. Behaviourism believes that we consist of learning experiences, called stimulus–response units **(S–R)** that we use, then and thereafter, to navigate our way through life. Behaviourists consequently fall on the 'nurture', or empiricist, side of the nature–nurture debate, because for them it is our environment that makes us what we are. The influence of the environment on what we teach and learn led Watson (1925) to write:

> *'Give me a dozen healthy infants ... and my own specified world to bring them up in and I'll guarantee to take any one at random and train him to become any type of specialist I might select – doctor, lawyer ... and yes even beggarman and thief'.*

Our behaviour arises because we become conditioned to respond to stimuli

Figure 3.2 Conditioned response to stimulus

The Soviet scientist Ivan Pavlov had had a huge influence on Watson, who became attracted to Pavlov's earlier idea that all organisms, animal and human, learn behaviours as a result of having to respond to the stimuli (objects, events and people) they come across in their environment. Pavlov and Watson agreed that we learn to operate, or behave, in our world by forming associations between a particular stimulus and the most appropriate behavioural response to it.

Take the stimulus of a bus. We learn that the best way to get a bus to stop is to stand at a bus stop and stick our hand out when we see a bus coming. Thereafter if we want a bus to stop we use this associated stimulus–response unit of conditioned, or learned, behaviour to board buses. Watson thought all animal and human behaviours are learned in terms of conditioned associations between a stimulus and a response, and set out to find support for this. He also thought that as all behaviours are learned, they could be 'unlearned', by breaking the learned stimulus–response association.

Little Albert

Let us here consider a classic piece of research conducted by Watson and his colleague Rosalie Rayner into phobias. Before this study, phobias had been understood from the point of view of the psychoanalytic approach and our unconscious. Watson and Rayner set out an alternative *behaviourist* explanation for phobias proposing that they are a learned irrational emotional response to an object. They were interested in discovering whether they could teach Little Albert to fear an object that he previously did not fear, by associating it with an unpleasant stimulus, and so creating a learned, conditioned fear response. Once this S–R unit of behaviour had been established, they also wanted to know if Little Albert would generalise this response to other objects, how long the conditioned response would last, and whether the conditioned response could be removed using the same learning technique.

Albert B. (Little Albert), the nine-month-old son of a nurse in a children's hospital, was physically described by Watson and Rayner as 'healthy from birth' and as having a 'stolid and unemotional' personality.

STUDY

Watson, J.B. & Rayner, R. (1920) 'Conditioned Emotional Reactions', *Journal of Experimental Psychology,* 3(1), 1–14.

Aim: To investigate the proposition that phobias are learned.

Method/procedure: Experiment, case study and observation.

When he was nine months old Albert was tested for his reaction to a number of individual stimuli. These included a white rat, a rabbit, a dog, a monkey, hairy and hairless facemasks, cotton wool, burning newspapers, and a hammer striking a four-foot steel bar placed just behind his head. Albert was afraid only of the loud noise made by the hammer hitting the bar.

At about eleven months old Albert was reintroduced to a white rat, to which he previously had shown affection. However, on this occasion when Albert reached out to stroke the rat, Watson hit the hammer on the steel bar

continued

prompting Albert to jump out of his skin! The conditioning (learning) process of the same association of events, white rat → loud noise, was repeated seven times over the next seven weeks.

Results: By the end of the seven weeks the presentation of the rat alone elicited phobic fear behaviours from Albert. He had learned to fear a stimulus with which he had been previously happy. Further, when shown similar objects such as the rabbit, the dog and cotton wool, Albert became distressed. This is called stimulus generalisation. Five days after conditioning Albert's phobia continued. Thirty days later he was still fearful of the white rat. Albert's mother then moved away from the hospital with her baby, and Watson and Rayner never got an opportunity to decondition Albert regarding his phobia.

Conclusion: Phobias are learned conditioned behaviours. In this instance Albert's phobia came about as a result of classical conditioning where a learned association was produced between the stimuli of the rat/loud noise and his subsequent feared response.

Questions

1 In your everyday experience identify and describe a fear you, or someone you know, has. From the point of view of the behaviourist approach how might this have come about? Give reasons for your answer.
2 Describe the procedure used by Watson and Rayner to condition Albert to fear the white rat.
3 What ethical criticism can be made of Watson & Rayner (1920)?

Classical conditioning

As mentioned earlier, the beginnings of behaviourism are credited to the famous Russian Ivan Pavlov (1849–1936). Pavlov was an animal physiologist, who studied the reflex response of salivation in dogs. As a consequence of his research he gave to the behaviourist approach his theory of classical conditioning. Classical conditioning means learning by association. For Pavlov, an organism learns to behave towards its environment because of stimulus–response associations. This, as we read earlier, had a profound effect on J.B. Watson and the subsequent development of behaviourism on a global scale.

Figure 3.3 Ivan Pavlov

Stimulus and response

A stimulus is any person, event or object which causes us to respond to or behave towards it in some way. According to the behaviourist approach, we act or behave as we do because we have formed stimulus–response units of learned behaviours. We behave, or respond to stimuli coming to us from our environment in terms of S–R learned units of behaviour formed from the time we are born. The behaviourist approach thus attempts to understand our behaviour from the point of view of stimulus response units of learned behaviour. One way these S–R units of behaviour come about is considered in the theory of classical conditioning, which concerns learning by association.

Ivan Pavlov

Ivan Petrovich Pavlov was born in Ryazan, Russia, on 26 September 1849. His father, a priest, influenced Pavlov in his decision to himself study for the priesthood and in his teens he enrolled at a theological seminary. However, after reading Charles Darwin, Pavlov left for the University of St Petersburg to study chemistry and physiology. While at St Petersburg he wrote his doctoral thesis on *The Centrifugal Nerves of the Heart*, which laid the foundations for a lifetime devoted to science. He then became interested in the digestive system of dogs, and from 1891 to 1900 looked at the interaction between salivation and the working of the stomach. He found salivation and stomach action to be linked by reflexes in the autonomic nervous system. Pavlov set out to see if he could teach this reflex action of salivation without a stimulus of food. He set up an experiment where he rang a bell at the same time as he gave his experimental dogs their food. He then stopped the food, and only rang the bell. He discovered that the dogs salivated even though there was no food present. Pavlov published these results in 1903, in his paper '*The experimental psychology and psychopathology of animals*' where he identified his taught salivatory response of his dogs as a *conditioned reflex* response. What this means is that the conditioned salivatory response is learned, and can be distinguished from an innate reflex action like pulling one's hand back from a hot surface. The learning process of his dogs associating the sound of the bell with the food, Pavlov termed *conditioning*. He also believed that a learned association between a conditional stimulus (like a bell) and a conditional response (a reflex action like salivation) could become extinguished if the reinforcer (in this case food) is withdrawn. This became known as Pavlov's theory of classical conditioning. Pavlov was awarded the Nobel Prize in medicine and physiology in 1904 for his work on the digestive system of dogs. He died in 1936 at the age of 87, still working in his laboratory.

Pavlov's major works include *Lectures on Conditioned Reflexes: Twenty-Five Years of Objective Study of the Higher Nervous Activity Behaviour of Animals.*

Learning by association: S–R

In his laboratory Pavlov noticed two things about his dogs' behaviours. The first was that when they were given food (a stimulus) they proceeded to salivate (a response), and second, that they often salivated in *anticipation* of getting fed. They seemed to *know* when they were to be fed, in that they salivated when they saw a light flashing above the locked door of the laboratory. It flashed, of course, to alert Pavlov to the keeper's arrival with their food. Up until then salivation was thought to be a reflex response in animal and human organisms that only occurs on the eating or smelling of food, not in its anticipation. His dogs had, however, learned to associate the light with the imminent arrival of food and being fed. Salivation in this instance was not a reflex, but a learned response by his dogs. Pavlov thought his dogs salivated because they had become *conditioned* to associate the light with the onset of food. It was from these observations that Pavlov set up an experiment to investigate learning by association. This work led to Pavlov's theory of classical conditioning, which rapidly caught up, and began to overshadow his earlier work on the physiology of dogs that was to win him the Nobel Prize for medicine and physiology in 1904.

'The experimental psychology and psychopathology of animals'

In 1903, at the 14th International Medical Congress in Madrid, Pavlov read a paper on '*The experimental psychology and psychopathology of animals*'. This laid down the underlying principles behind his theory of classical conditioning, which suggests that animals and humans learn to behave in response to their environment in terms of conditioned, or learned, reflex actions. These conditioned behaviours are called S–R units. A stimulus–response unit of learned behaviour, or conditioned reflex action, is the mechanism that explains why we behave the way we do when we encounter stimuli in our environment. Pavlov said one way we react to our world is by associating a stimulus (S) with innate bodily reflexes (R). How we learn these associated stimulus–response units of learned behaviour is illustrated below.

Pavlov's theory of classical conditioning

Ivan Pavlov's theory of classical conditioning (stimulus–response learning by association) uses some strange and unusual vocabulary.

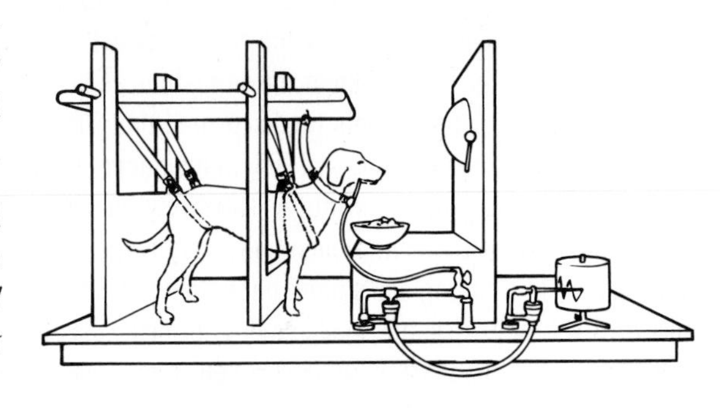

Figure 3.4 The apparatus used by Pavlov

In his classic experiment with his dogs, food is known as the *unconditional* stimulus, the US, and salivation, the *unconditional* response, or UR. Unconditional means *not learned* in that salivation is an innate reflex action found in dogs when food is presented to them. No learning is needed for this stimulus–response (S–R) link, so both stimulus and response are said to be unconditional. The tone of the bell is the *neutral* stimulus or NS. Dogs show no innate reflex reaction in response to a bell ringing.

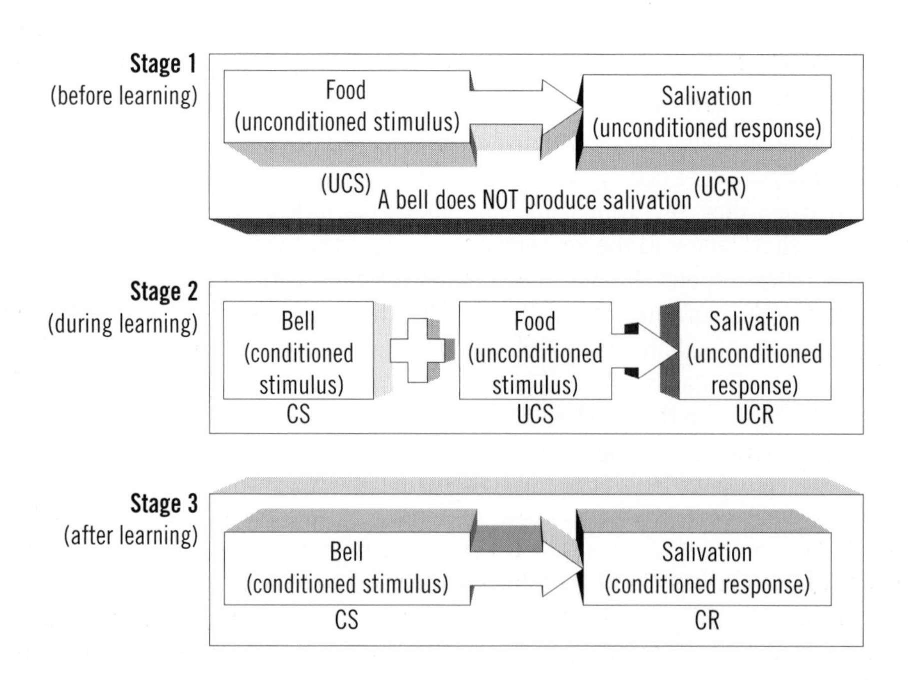

Figure 3.5 Classical conditioning

Pavlov (1927) wanted to find out if he could condition his dogs to salivate in response to a previously neutral stimulus of the tone of a bell. He set up his apparatus (see Figure 3.4) and in **Stage 1** rang the neutral stimulus of the bell. This got no response from his dogs. He then presented the unconditional stimulus of food, and his dogs salivated (the unconditional response).

In **Stage 2** he presented the bell (NS) and food (US) *contiguously*, or together in time. Known as the **law of temporal contiguity**, this simultaneous pairing of the NS of the bell with the US of the food saw the unconditional response (UR) of salivation.

In **Stage 3** he rang the bell *only*. The now conditional stimulus of the bell resulted in the conditional (learned by association) reflex response of salivation.

In behaviourist terms when a NS and US occur together they can become associated with each other, until eventually the NS causes the UR, which is here salivation. When this happens, the NS becomes known as the learned, or conditional stimulus (CS), and the reflex action, the learned or conditional response (CR).

Pavlov discovered that a conditional stimulus could produce a desired conditioned (learned) reflex response. The implications of this are immense in that Pavlov's work showed that one way we learn to respond to stimuli in our environment is by classical conditioning, or learning by S–R association. Further, classical conditioning tells us it is possible to produce S–R units of learned behaviours by associating two previously unconnected variables. In Pavlov's experiment these were the stimulus of the bell and the response of salivation. Classical conditioning is all about how a diverse range of previously neutral stimuli can come to trigger a reflex response in animal and humans.

Extinction

After a while Pavlov discovered his dogs stopped salivating in response to the bell ringing. The conditioned S–R learned behaviour of bell–salivation no longer occurred. Because they were no longer getting fed, the conditional response of salivation was *inhibited* by the non-appearance of the US of food. The dogs no longer salivated in response to the bell alone. Not responding after conditioning is called *extinction*.

Reinforcement

After extinction, to *resurrect* the conditioned S–R response of bell–salivation Pavlov had to repeat Stage 2 of the classical conditioning process. He found the *occasional* re-occurrence of bell (NS) and food (US) together, brought back the conditioned response of salivation to the bell alone (CS). In order to avoid extinction Pavlov found that *reinforcement*, the occasional re-presentation of the NS and US together, was necessary. Reinforcement makes a learned association between a stimulus and a response more permanent.

Spontaneous recovery

Pavlov discovered that if he waited up to several hours after extinguishing the conditioned S–R unit of bell–salivation (by not using reinforcement), on *later* ringing of the bell he *sometimes* saw the conditioned response of salivation re-occur. Albeit weaker than before, Pavlov called the reappearance of the conditioned response of salivation *spontaneous recovery*. What spontaneous recovery suggests is that we never entirely forget the things we learn in life. Behaviours can be modified, but never extinguished completely.

Stimulus generalisation

Two final features of classical conditioning are stimulus generalisation and stimulus discrimination. Pavlov discovered that if his dogs were conditioned to salivate to a bell of a *particular* tone, they would in Stage 3 also salivate to bells with tones slightly higher or slightly lower in pitch. This is called *stimulus generalisation*, which is an organism's associated behavioural response to stimuli it comes across in its environment that look similar to the original stimulus to which it originally was conditioned.

Stimulus discrimination

Pavlov also found that if his dogs were presented with bells whose tones were very different to the original conditional stimulus, they no longer produced the conditional response of salivation. This is called *stimulus discrimination*, which is learning to respond only to stimuli that are the same as the original conditional stimulus – in this case a specific tone of bell.

Mums with new babies sometimes experience stimulus generalisation and stimulus discrimination. Stimulus generalisation occurs when a new mum initially lactates (produces breast milk) when she hears the cries of *any* baby that might be around her. Lactation is a reflex action, and is an associated reflex response to the stimulus of a newborn's cries. Over time, mum will only lactate in response to the sound of her *own* baby crying. This is stimulus discrimination.

E.L. Thorndike

Around the end of the nineteenth century, Edward Lee Thorndike was setting the stage for an important American development regarding behaviourism. Thorndike is influential because of his law of effect. He was interested in intelligence and thinking, and in particular how cats solve problems. He used a puzzle-box into which he placed a cat. The cat could only escape when it had worked out how to open the escape hatch – by pulling on a ring-pull pulley system. Thorndike used increasingly more complex escape hatches as his experiments progressed. As an added incentive to escape, Thorndike deprived his cats of food before his experiments, and teasingly placed scraps of fish visible to them outside the box. The cats had to learn a series of interrelated steps, or S–R associated units of behaviour, in order to open the hatches to get out of the box to the food. Thorndike (1898) concluded from this that there were two laws of learning.

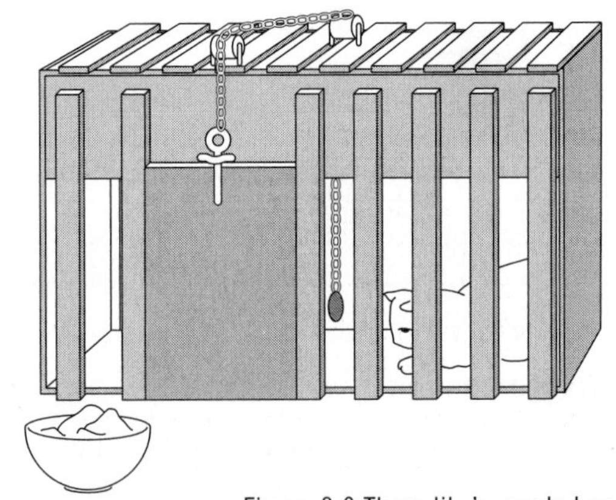

Figure 3.6 Thorndike's puzzle box

The law of exercise

The first law of learning Thorndike called the *law of exercise*. What this means is that the more times we carry out a task the better we become at it. Thorndike observed and measured the length of time it took his cats to escape from the box. He discovered that his cats escaped quicker, the more often they were put into the box. On first exposure to it they took five minutes, but by the twentieth trial they could escape in five seconds. The cats' improvement in escape performance time showed a change in behaviour as a result of experience. Learning, a relatively permanent change in behaviour as a result of experience, had taken place.

THE LAW OF EFFECT

The second law of learning is the *law of effect*. What this means is that we learn that there is a link between our behaviour and its consequences. If we get a pleasurable or positive outcome from behaving in a particular way, the law of effect says we are more likely to repeat this behaviour in the future. If, on the other hand, we behave in a way that is unpleasant in consequence, and doesn't lead to a positive outcome, Thorndike's law of effect says we are less likely to repeat this behaviour in the future.

> *'Of several responses made to the same situation, those which are accompanied or closely followed by satisfaction to the animal will, all other things being equal, be more firmly connected with the situation.'*
>
> *Thorndike (1911)*

Prior to Thorndike, learning had been understood in terms of Pavlov's S–R conditioned reflex behaviours. Thorndike's laws of learning suggested behaviours could also be seen as a learned S–R non-reflex action, used by us because it got us a positive outcome in the past. An understanding of behaviours as non-reflex actions because of learned consequence was to be of some significance to B.F. Skinner and the later development of operant conditioning.

B.F. Skinner

Burrhus Frederic Skinner was born on 20 March 1904, in Susquehanna, Pennsylvania. His contribution to the behaviourist approach was the concept of operant conditioning. Conditioning, as we discovered earlier, means learning. An operant is what reinforces our behaviours as we operate in our world. Operant conditioning occurs where 'the behaviour is followed by a consequence, and the nature of the consequence modifies the organism's tendency to repeat the behaviour in the future' (Skinner, 1938). What this means is now explained.

Figure 3.7 B.F. Skinner

Reinforcers: an environmental response

Skinner's theory of operant conditioning concerns the use of *reward* and *unpleasant consequence* in the learning process. In operant conditioning a reward/unpleasant consequence is the *environmental response*, or operant, that encourages or discourages us in the learning of behaviour. The operant of reward given to encourage a desired behaviour is called a positive reinforcer, while an unpleasant consequence given to discourage an undesired behaviour is called a negative reinforcer. According to Skinner, the process of positive reinforcement can encourage the repetition of behaviours, probably because it becomes connected with a positive outcome for an organism.

Primary reinforcer: a stimulus from our environment, whose ability to reinforce our response is based on an innate biological drive, e.g. our need for food, water and warmth

Secondary reinforcer: an environmental stimulus that has become associated with a primary reinforcer. Secondary reinforcers help precipitate primary reinforcers, e.g. we use money to purchase food

Alternatively, negative reinforcement, or an unpleasant consequence, can discourage the repetition of behaviours that have a negative outcome for an organism. Skinner came across positive and negative reinforcement in his famous experiments involving rats and his 'Skinner box'. The Skinner box, or operant chamber, allowed Skinner control over his experiments, an important factor that will be further explored when we look at the experimental method in Chapter 8.

Operant conditioning

Skinner wanted to investigate whether he could encourage the operant behaviour of lever-pressing by a rat. To do so he built a small, soundproof operant chamber that provided an experimental environment within which his rats could be studied.

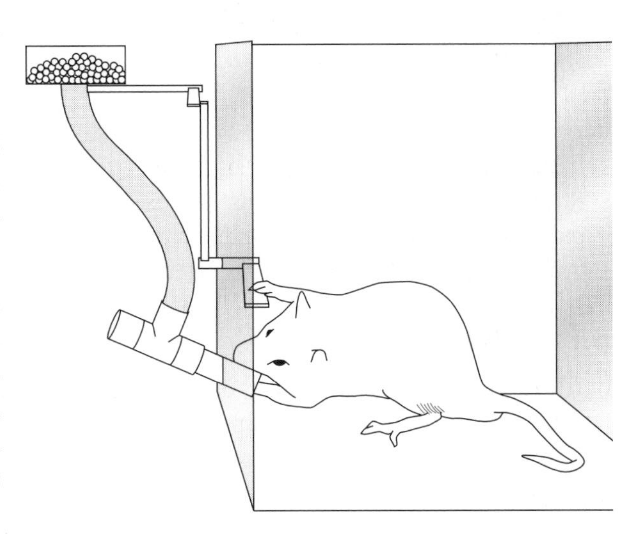

Figure 3.8 Skinner box

An operant chamber allows animals like rats to be kept apart from external influences, known in psychology as extraneous variables. The rats can then be subjected to specific experimental manipulations, called conditions. The chamber contains a bar (or lever) and there is a small tray outside the box. The tray holds the food pellets that fall into the chamber when the bar is pressed. Skinner placed his rat in the operant chamber. The rat explored the box and in doing so accidentally pressed the lever and a food pellet dropped out of the food tray. Skinner then observed increased lever-pressing behaviour by the rat, with more and more food pellets being delivered as a result. The positive outcome of a food pellet was the environmental response, or operant, that reinforced the rat's lever-pressing behaviour. In terms of operant conditioning, this shows that a behaviour followed by a reinforcing stimulus, such as the 'reward' of a food pellet, results in an increased probability of that behaviour occurring in the future. This is very much related to Thorndike' s law of effect, which said that the reason we behave the way we do, is because we have learned that to do so will have a pleasant consequence for us.

Positive reinforcement

According to Skinner, the use of positive and negative reinforcement increases the likelihood of a similar response to the stimulus in the future, while the use of punishment decreases it.

Positive reinforcement occurs where a positive reinforcer, such as a reward, is given following a desirable behaviour. We have all experienced positive reinforcement from parents, primary caregivers and teachers, to encourage us to learn particular behaviours. We also use positive reinforcement to encourage positive behaviours in others. An example of this would be where a child shows a parent or primary caregiver a piece of schoolwork they have done. If the adult shows interest and praises the child's efforts, operant conditioning tells us that this positive reinforcement of praise should encourage the continuation of schoolwork.

INTERACTIVE: COCAINE

Mestel & Concar (1994) used reinforcement in a drug rehabilitation programme with cocaine addicts. Each time a participant visited them, they gave them vouchers of increasing monetary value if their urine tested negative for cocaine use. Participants were also given counselling during their time on the programme. Their results showed that 85 per cent of participants stayed in rehabilitation for three months and 65 per cent for six months.

Please answer the following questions:

1. What was the reinforcer used by Mestel & Concar (1995)?
2. What type of reinforcement is this?
3. Explain the theory behind its use.
4. What practical consideration would have to be given to better ensure the 65 per cent who remained drug free for six months continued to do so?

Negative reinforcement

Negative reinforcement occurs where a negative reinforcer is used to end or avoid a negative behaviour, situation or consequence. Negative reinforcement avoids or discourages the continuation of this unpleasant behaviour, situation or consequence.

Negative reinforcement can be seen when young children are out shopping with an adult. The minute they see sweets or a toy, they begin to nag the adult for it. They go on, and on, and on. The adult at first usually says 'No', then 'No' again, and indeed again. Eventually the nagging becomes too much and the adult caves in and buys the child the sweets or the toy. This shows the adult's use of negative reinforcement to avoid the unpleasant situation of the annoying noise in their ears!

In using negative reinforcement, the adult unfortunately encourages the likelihood of the child using the same behavioural strategy in the future to get similar demands met. This is because the *child's* use of nagging is for *them* positive reinforcement, because they come to learn that to get something pleasurable or positive for themselves, all they need do is continue nagging.

INTERACTIVE: ABSOLUTELY SHOCKING BEHAVIOUR

A psychologist put a rat in a Skinner box. On exploring the cage, it bumped into the lever and down dropped a food pellet. This saw frantic lever pressing by the rat and its store of food pellets mounted. On the next occasion it pressed the lever it got an electric shock. The rat never pressed the lever again.

Please answer the following questions.

1. What behaviourist theory was this researcher investigating? Give reasons for your answer.
2. What is the behaviourist term given to the food pellet? Explain what is meant by this term.
3. What were the two conditions of this experiment?
4. What aspect of Skinner's work does this first condition support? Give reasons for your answer.
5. What aspect of Skinner's work does the second condition support? Give reasons for your answer.

Punishment

In a learning environment the use of punishment should reduce or eliminate the behaviour happening again. Unlike positive and negative reinforcement we do not learn anything new by the use of punishment. Behaviourism is aware that the use of punishment in the learning process is limited, and to be effective has to come immediately after the undesired behaviour has occurred. To have any effect, it also has to be consistently applied on the same occasion thereafter. If punishment is given only occasionally for the same 'offence', the undesired behaviour or response is likely to return to its pre-punishment levels.

Interestingly, in some cases the use of punishment may see an *increase* in an undesired behaviour! This is because what the punisher sees as an undesired behaviour may not be seen as such by the punished. *They* may view any unpleasant sanctions for bad behaviour as status symbols for their transgressions. The Brownie, who is photographed earlier on page 19, often asked her parents when she was seven or eight to be grounded despite the fact she had not done anything naughty. On enquiry it appeared that she wanted to be treated the same as a 'big girl' of twelve or thirteen – who reported to her when she was out playing that they were veterans of such punishment. Not so very long ago the strap was in regular use in Scottish schools. Boys of thirteen and fourteen would very often play up in some school classrooms to encourage the teacher to use the strap! League tables were often drawn up amongst the mischievous. The number of times you got the strap for bad behaviour was seen as a status symbol in your peer group, more important than the number of 'ticks' you got in your jotter for correct schoolwork!

Behaviour shaping

Behaviour shaping is the progressive use of positive reinforcement to encourage someone to behave in a complex way. Behaviour shaping is linked to the behaviourist idea that learning should be seen in terms of stimulus–response units and that complex learned behaviours are made up of a lot of related, but increasingly more complex, S–R units of learning.

Successive approximations

Behaviour shaping sees, at first, the giving of a reward for nearly getting something right; the actual behaviour being a 'successive approximation' of the desired behaviour. Thereafter the reward is given when the behaviour betters the last successive approximation of it.

Figure 3.9 Behaviour shaping

An example of behaviour shaping would be in helping people acquire a learned skill, like driving a car. On the first lesson the driving instructor will use positive reinforcement and praise the learner when they successfully manage to move the car forward safely! This is however not enough to pass the driving test. As a successive approximation reflecting the rigours of the driving test it is a long way off. As the lessons go on, the instructor will begin to positively reinforce *only* those driving behaviours that mirror the required standards. The driving instructor's progressive use of positive reinforcement helps get the learner from a distant approximation of driving-test behaviour, to a state of affairs that sees them able to pass their driving test. The instructor has successfully shaped the learner driver's behaviour and got them a positive outcome of a full driving licence.

INTERACTIVE

Write a short report on any learning experience you know of that involved Skinner's idea of behaviour shaping and successive approximations.

Schedules of reinforcement

Skinner found that *extinction* of lever-pressing behaviour occurred if the reinforcer of the food pellet was withdrawn. The futile consequence of wasting a lot of energy pressing the lever saw the rat learn not to bother! The rat is no fool. Thus, according to Skinner, a behaviour no longer followed by the reinforcing stimulus results in a decreased probability of that behaviour occurring in the future. This got him thinking about the relationship between different *degrees* of positive reinforcement and an organism's behavioural response. What developed are called schedules of reinforcement, which Skinner discovered when he tried to solve a resource problem.

He had to make his own food pellets for his operant chamber experiments. Making them was boring, so once made, he decided to make them last as long as possible. He began to restrict the number of reinforcements (food pellets) given to his rats, in that they were now not rewarded with a pellet on *every* lever press. Skinner observed nonetheless that his rats kept up their lever pressing at a similar rate to before. This led him to investigate a variety of reinforcement schedules.

Reinforcement schedules are of particular importance nowadays in education, teaching and learning. Their discovery prompted the programmed learning movement of the 1960s and 1970s. Today Skinner's work on schedules of reinforcement have led to such innovations as flexi-learning, open learning, distance learning and computer-based learning.

Types of reinforcement schedules

Continuous reinforcement schedule

A *continuous reinforcement schedule* is a reinforcement régime where every correct response by an organism leads to a reward. This is the name given to Skinner's original operant scenario where his rats got a food pellet every time they pushed the lever.

Continuous reinforcement will give rise to a low but steady rate of desired behavioural response. If the positive reinforcer is removed, fairly quick extinction of the desired behaviour occurs.

Fixed ratio schedule

The *fixed ratio schedule* was the first one Skinner discovered. In a fixed ratio schedule, the positive reinforcer of a reward is only given after a fixed number of correct responses. Using a fixed ratio schedule would have seen Skinner give a reward of a pellet after every three, five or twenty lever presses.

Fixed ratio schedules give rise to an uneven behavioural response, with the extinction of desired behaviour being fairly rapid when the positive reinforcer is removed.

Fixed interval schedule

Fixed interval schedules use a timer of some sort. With a fixed interval schedule, if the rat presses the bar at least once during a fixed interval, of say twenty seconds, it gets a food pellet. If the rat fails to press the lever within the time, it gets nothing.

Fixed interval schedules reward only once. If the rat hit the lever twenty times during the fixed interval period, it still only got one pellet. Skinner found that his rats in a fixed interval situation tended to pace themselves. They were seen to slow down their lever-pressing immediately after being positively reinforced, and speed up again when the time for reinforcement to re-occur got close.

Fixed interval schedules result in an uneven behavioural response pattern of slow, quick, slow, and quick. Under this régime, when the reinforcer of the food pellet was removed, Skinner reported the quick extinction of the conditioned lever-pressing behaviour.

Variable ratio schedule

A *variable ratio schedule* means giving a reward after a set number of correct responses around an average. Using a variable ratio schedule you could decide to positively reinforce on the first, fifth, tenth, thirteenth, seventeenth and twenty-sixth lever-press response.

A variable ratio schedule results in a high rate of desired behavioural response and is more resistant to extinction. This is because the organism comes to learn it will get a reward if it behaves in a particular way during a particular time frame. It just doesn't know *exactly* when in the time frame the reward will be forthcoming.

Variable interval schedule

A *variable interval schedule* is where you keep changing the time period – first twenty seconds, then five, then thirty-five, then ten and so on, within which time the rat has to press the lever to get a pellet. If it doesn't press the lever in the set time it gets nothing. If it presses the lever once or one hundred times within the set period, the pressing behaviour is only reinforced once in that it only gets the one food pellet.

Using a variable interval schedule desired behavioural response rate is high and steady, Extinction of learned response slowly declines when the reward is withdrawn.

Variable ratio and variable interval schedules: a clue to gambling?

Figure 3.10 Variable ratio and variable interval schedules: a clue to gambling?

Skinner got some interesting results using variable ratio and variable interval schedules. The variable ratio schedule saw his rats learn to press *just enough* to get their reward of food. They worked out the variable ratio of lever presses to reward and paced themselves accordingly. With a variable interval schedule, they no longer paced themselves because they were unable to work out a pattern between lever-pressing behaviour and reward. As a consequence, they pressed for longer periods, and at a more consistent rate. Variable ratio and variable interval schedules are very resistant to extinction, certainly in comparison with *fixed* interval and ratio schedules. Skinner saw variable ratio and variable interval schedules as the learned mechanisms behind people's gambling habits.

Variable ratio schedules might be the key to why some people, for example, play fruit machines. Players know that fruit machines will pay out, but they do not know on what occasion! They thus keep playing it for prolonged periods, possibly encouraged by the fact that they will get a positive reinforcer of a win, however small, the longer they play. Delfabbro & Winefield (1999) discovered that fruit machine players often took a rest after a win. The length of the player's post-reinforcement rest varied, and seemed dependent on both the size of the win and the player's machine-playing experience.

After a big win Delfabbro and Winefield's players may have worked out, on the basis of experience, that it was highly unlikely that the machine would pay out another big win for quite some time. Our ability to think about our learned, conditioned behaviours is a major drawback to the behaviourist approach, because behaviourism sees us as passive learners of S–R units of behaviour. This is later considered as a limitation of behaviourism, to be further explored in Chapter 4 on the cognitive approach.

The National Lottery ('Lotto')

Variable interval and variable ratio schedules may also influence our behaviours regarding the National Lottery.

Take variable ratio. The more cards you buy, the more numbers you can cover, and the more likely it is you will win something in any one week. If the Lottery hasn't paid out a jackpot, the more weeks you play further increases your chances of success. The promoters also use the psychology of the variable interval schedule as a marketing tool. If the balls haven't dropped for anyone in a few weeks, Camelot advertises the fact by reminding us that the jackpot now stands at so many million £s. This inevitably sees huge queues form for that week's draw! More tickets are sold to regulars, and to newcomers hungry to be millionaires. Probably only one will be successful, with 13,999,999 sorely disappointed, but back the next week nevertheless. Some will have begun a gambling journey they might wish to have avoided.

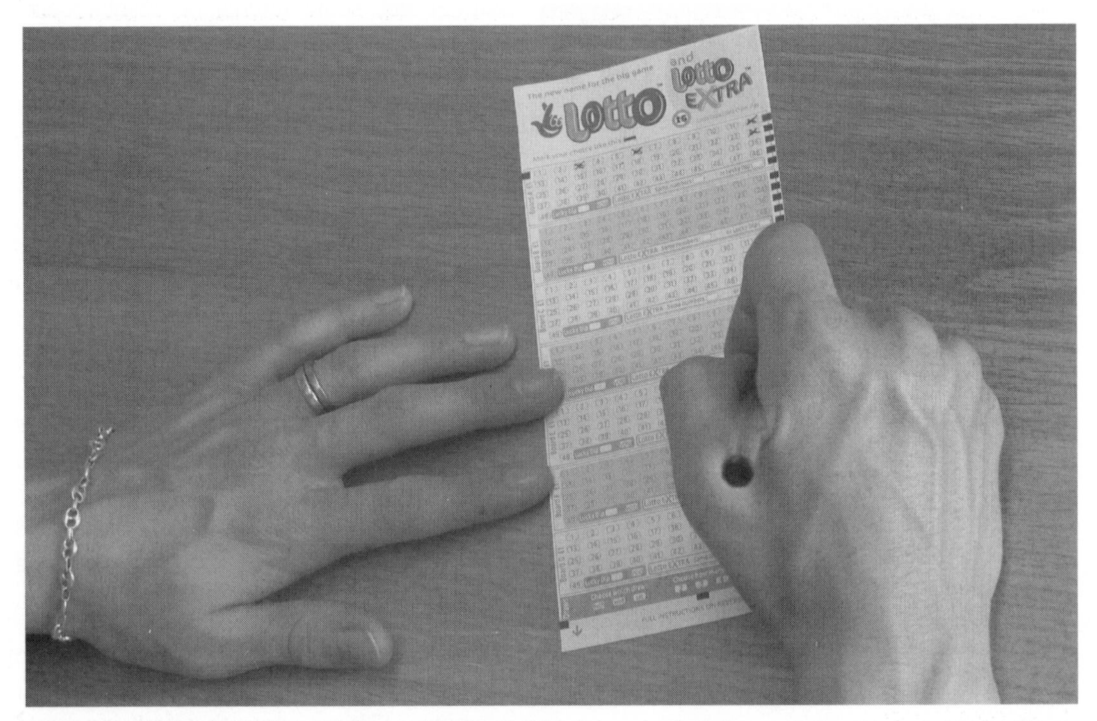

Figure 3.11 Playing the Lottery is influenced by the variable interval schedule

STUDY

Skinner, B.F. (1948) '"Superstition" in the pigeon.' *Journal of Experimental Psychology*, 38, 168–72.

Aim: To find support for the variable ratio schedule as an aid to learning.

Method/Procedure: Experimenting on eight pigeons, Skinner put each one individually into his operant chamber to try and condition them to perform certain ritual acts when they thought they might be fed. Using a fixed interval schedule of food every fifteen seconds, each pigeon was positively reinforced for behaviours such as head bobbing, or turning round, or moving towards the food tray.

Results: Skinner was able to condition six out of eight pigeons to perform a ritual act of head bobbing, turning round or moving towards the food tray in the lull between reinforcements. The pigeons learned to associate a particular behaviour, e.g. head bob/turning round/moving with the onset of food. This he likened to superstitions in humans. Athletes, for example, very often perform a superstitious act or ritual just before a big race. Footballers likewise.

Conclusion: Superstitions and rituals are learned. We learn them as a result of operant conditioning in that we associate the superstition or ritual, such as taking a lucky mascot into an exam, with a pleasant outcome of a good pass. Maybe a big sister or brother took it into their exam, and subsequently passed with flying colours. We do the same. The variable ratio nature of Lady Luck sees us take it into *all* our exams because we are never certain if we will need luck to pass, as opposed to sound prior preparation! This also shows that superstitions are very resistant to extinction. Hopefully Lady Luck will not be needed on the day of your psychology exam. But take the mascot in just in case!

Applications of the behaviourist approach

Behaviour therapy and behaviour modification

Based on Pavlov's theory of classical conditioning, *behaviour therapy* is the term given to the learning process that creates planned *associations* between a stimulus and response.

Behaviour modification, influenced by Skinner and operant conditioning, is the term used for any planned, desired change in behaviour that involves *reinforcement*.

Table 3.2 Applications of the behaviourist approach

Behaviour therapy (Pavlov)	Behaviour modification (Skinner)
Systematic desensitisation	Token economy (TE)
Implosion therapy	Programmed learning
Aversion therapy	

Behaviour therapy

Behaviour therapies are based upon Pavlov's theory of classical conditioning. As we saw earlier classical conditioning suggests that we learn behavioural units as a consequence of making an association between a stimulus and a response.

Systematic desensitisation

Systematic desensitisation is a behaviourist psychotherapy used to treat phobias by *gradually* reducing the person's fear of the phobic stimulus. In behaviourist terms, a phobia is a *learned* irrational fear of an object, event, situation, etc.

Arachnophobia: fear of spiders
Claustrophobia: fear of enclosed spaces, such as lifts and elevators
Social phobia: fear of mortification in social situations

Wolpe (1973) is credited with the development of systematic desensitisation in the behavioural treatment of phobias. Systematic desensitisation tries to get rid of a client's fear response by replacing it with a more pleasant response, such as *relaxing* when they are confronted by the stimulus that previously made them fearful and anxious. Systematic desensitisation has helped people fearful of snakes, spiders, flying and heights and has about a 70 per cent success rate (Wolpe 1973; Goldfried & Davison 1994).

INTERACTIVE

PHOBIAS AND ANXIETY STATES

A phobia produces an anxiety state where the victim may:

- suddenly feel persistent and irrational panic, dread, horror or terror in a situation that is harmless
- recognise that the fear goes beyond what would be considered normal and a real threat of danger
- feel helpless, in that their phobic reaction is automatic, uncontrollable and overwhelming. It takes over their normal thought patterns and invades the mind with imaginary threats and dangers
- suffer from the physical symptoms of extreme fear, e.g. rapid heartbeat, shortness of breath, trembling and overwhelming desire to flee the situation
- flee the feared object or situation, and thereafter go out of their way to avoid the fear-provoking stimulus. This deliberate avoidance behaviour interferes with the sufferer's quality of life. Consider, for example, how agoraphobia (fear of open spaces) could interfere with the quality of someone's life, because this phobia means that they cannot venture outside their home.

A client undergoing systematic desensitisation would be asked to list, and then prioritise, all aspects of their fear of the anxiety-provoking stimulus or situation. This produces a *hierarchy of fears*, which are mini S–R units of learned behaviour that together contribute to the total fear response. These are then dealt with one at a time.

Systematic desensitisation: a hierarchy of S–R Fears

One example is fear of the dentist. In their hierarchy of fears a sufferer might list the least fearful aspect as being the ringing of the dentist's bell before going into the surgery. The most fearful aspect might be the moment the dentist picks up their anaesthetic injection! In between might be the noise of the drill heard while sitting in the waiting room.

In systematic desensitisation the least fearful S–R association (e.g. bell-ringing and mild fear with sweaty palms) is considered first. The therapist would try to get the sufferer to picture ringing the bell, but as opposed to getting fearful, the sufferer would be encouraged to relax. Over time he or she would learn this more functional S–R unit of behaviour of dentist's bell–relax. When that has been established the therapist does the same thing with the next S–R fear response in the hierarchy. Gradually each fear response previously associated with in our example the bell, the drill, and the injection is replaced with the more pleasant emotional response association of *relax*. Systematic desensitisation allows you to become more functional in response to your environment. You have learned to deal better with going to the dentist. Depending on the complexity of your fear systematic desensitisation can however be very time-consuming and expensive.

Table 3.3 An example of a hierarchy of fears

Conditional stimulus (CS)		Conditional response (CR)
Injection	⟶	maximum fear
Noise of drill	⟶	moderate fear
Dentist's bell	⟶	mild fear

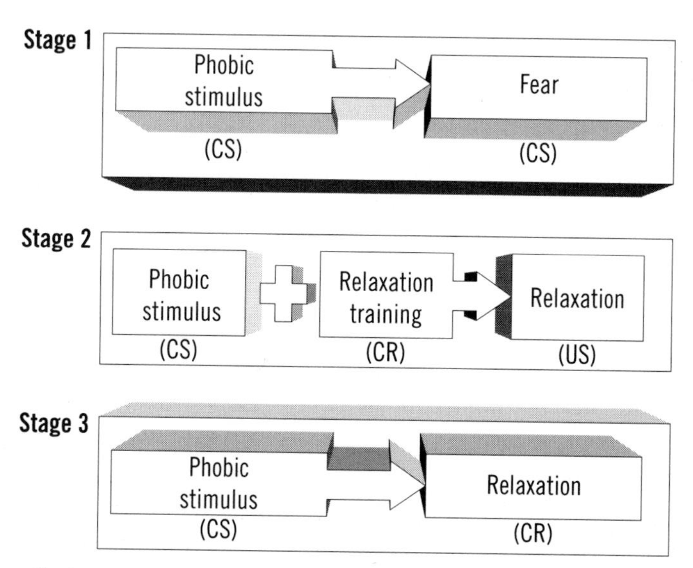

Figure 3.12 The systematic desensitisation process

Implosion therapy

Implosion therapy also relies on classical conditioning theory. Implosion therapy, or flooding, involves directly exposing the person to the feared situation or object, until their associated anxiety state is overcome. Implosion therapy is quicker than systematic desensitisation, but its suitability as a treatment will depend on the person's age, physical condition and motivation. Read carefully to understand why this is the case!

With implosion therapy clients are exposed to their phobic anxiety by being shown images of the phobic stimulus for as long as they can tolerate it, and then until they reach a point at which they no longer feel the fear. This is flooding. Implosion therapy can also be done *in vivo* (in the real situation), with clients being forced to experience anxiety through exposure to the actual phobic stimulus itself. If you were frightened of flying, *in vivo* implosion therapy could have you dealing with your phobia while the plane was in mid-air!

Virtual reality therapy

Virtual reality (VR) therapy is growing in popularity as an alternative to traditional *in vivo* implosion therapy. This is because many who are happy to try VR are wary of participating in implosion therapy in real-world environments. Confidentiality is also assured, since treatment occurs in the therapist's office. VR also offers total environmental control for the therapist in case the client cannot tolerate their fear or anxiety state and has to be removed from the situation.

According to Marks (1987), implosion therapy is even more effective than systematic desensitisation. Further, Emmelkemp & Kuipers (1979) found that of a group of agoraphobics, 75 per cent were able to cope with open spaces four years after implosion therapy. Similar results have been reported with those who suffer from obsessive–compulsive disorder, in the elimination of symptoms such as constant hand washing and an irrational fear of disease (Marks & Rachman, 1978).

Aversion therapy

Sometimes it is useful in behaviour therapy for therapists to forge an unpleasant S–R association. Aversion therapy tries to eliminate undesirable behaviours by associating them with something that causes the person to react with aversion. Examples of this would be to use classical conditioning and aversion therapy to pair the taste and smell of alcohol, or cigarettes, with nausea. To help this, an emetic drug may be prescribed. Some alcoholics have Antabuse implanted in their stomach lining. Alcohol reacts with Antabuse and causes sickness. As a result the alcoholic comes to associate the unpleasant consequences of vomiting with the stimulus of drink. To avoid the unpleasant consequences they avoid/stop drinking.

Aversion therapy has claimed a success rate of 60 per cent after twelve months with alcoholics (Weins & Menustik, 1983). Weins and Menustik did find however that over half of the 60 per cent returned to their old ways at some point after one year.

Behaviour modification

Behaviour modification is based on Skinner's work into operant conditioning, and his use of reinforcement in the learning process. The use of reinforcement encourages the repetition of behaviours that have a positive outcome for an animal or human.

Token economy (TE)

A token economy is a behaviour modification régime that uses reinforcement to encourage the learning of positive behaviours. The word *token* refers to the positive reinforcer used to do just this. It is the reward that the person gets when the appropriate behaviours being encouraged are evident. Rewards are initially given for simple responses, and thereafter for more complex behaviours.

Token economies as therapeutic learning environments can nowadays be seen in long-stay psychiatric hospitals and are also used in schools, prisons, etc.

The token economy as a behaviour modification régime came about following the work of Ayllon & Azrin (1968). The participants in their research were forty-five chronically disturbed female schizophrenic patients in a psychiatric ward. Most had been hospitalised for sixteen years or more, and exhibited atypical behaviours such as screaming for long periods, mutism, incontinence and violence. They were given plastic tokens for co-operative behaviours, which they could exchange for special privileges such as listening to music, going to the cinema, getting a private room or extra visits to the dining room.

Figure 3.13 Children respond well to a token economy, in which they are rewarded for good behaviour!

Allyon and Azrin found that a token economy could be used constructively with even the most disturbed psychiatric patients. Their research also highlighted the use of negative reinforcement of patients' negative behaviours by hospital staff. This had occurred when they had previously responded to patients' inappropriate behaviours by giving this their attention. Allyon and Azrin advised that this be stopped, and that staff only give patients positive reinforcement for their positive behaviours. Over time the use of a token economy by Ayllon & Azrin (1968) was found to help modify seriously disturbed patients' behaviours for the better.

The effectiveness of TE

Paul & Lentz (1977) compared the effectiveness of three types of treatment régimes used to normalise the behaviours of 85 hospitalised chronic schizophrenics. The eighty-five participants, for four-and-a-half years, were randomly allocated to one of three treatment conditions, a token economy, *milieu* therapy and custodial care. Custodial care was the control condition. The control condition in psychology is the condition with which you can compare the experimental condition. In this case the experimental conditions were the token economy and milieu care. Token economy and milieu care teach participants essential interpersonal and vocational skills to allow them to be able to leave hospital and live and work in the community.

Milieu therapy: is where the whole hospital becomes a therapeutic community of both staff and patients. Social interaction and pro-social behaviours are encouraged using group work. Group work and group pressure are used to establish positive attitudes, and behaviours reflecting society at large.

Custodial care: is the traditional hospital treatment of people who exhibit atypical behaviours such as schizophrenia. It sees the use of antipsychotic drugs to control the patient's condition.

Paul & Lentz (1977) report that of those who lived in the token economy, 98 per cent were eventually released back into the community. Of those exposed to milieu therapy 71 per cent went back into the community, while of those who underwent custodial care, 45 per cent were found capable of independent living. The study, which included an eighteen-month follow-up period of those going back into the community, additionally saw Paul and Lentz assess participants every six months using structured interviews and natural observation. They found overwhelmingly that the token economy was the most effective learning régime in helping to prepare patients for independent living. Milieu therapy was also found to be useful.

Thus according to Davison & Neale (1994);

> *'These regimes have demonstrated how even markedly regressed adult hospitalised patients can be significantly affected by systematic manipulation of reinforcement contingencies, that is, rewarding some behaviour to increase its frequency or ignoring other behaviour to reduce its frequency ... '.*

Programmed learning

The beginnings of programmed learning – which gave birth to flexi-learning, distance learning, open learning, computer-based learning, etc. can be attributed to Markle (1969) and Skinner (1968).

Programmed learning is based upon the following principles of operant conditioning.

- Behaviour that is positively reinforced will happen again, variable reinforcement schedules are particularly effective to the learning process.
- Information should be presented to the learner in small amounts (S–R units) so that responses can be reinforced, leading to the desired learning objective (behaviour shaping).
- Stimulus generalisation will occur in that reinforcement will encourage the generalisation of the new learned behaviour to similar stimuli.

Figure 3.14 By presenting information in small amounts and giving a fast response, distance learning aims to shape learning behaviour successively

Programmed learning, and other similar learning programmes in education, share particular features.

What is to be learned should be in the form of question (stimulus) and answer (response) teaching/learning units, which introduce the student to the subject in small steps. The learner makes a response to each S–R learning unit and should get *immediate feedback* on their performance. The level of difficulty of questions should be *fixed* so the response given by the *learner* is (hopefully) always correct, and they receive positive reinforcement. This is to encourage them to even greater learning heights. Finally programmed learning should try, where possible, to include *secondary reinforcers* to good performance such as verbal praise, prizes and the achievement of good grades.

INTERACTIVE

Think about a school or college learning experience. It could be your study of psychology. Identify aspects of operant conditioning and programmed learning such as S–R teaching/learning units, feedback, if/where fixed questions and thus positive reinforcement occur, and any use of secondary reinforcement.

Limitations of the behaviourist approach

As an approach in psychology, behaviourism is scientifically rigorous. Its use of the experiment generates sound data upon which it bases its claims. Behaviourism also gives us a good idea as to why we behave as we do in our world, as we often *do* behave in terms of stimulus–response associations, and tend to perform better at things if encouraged in a positive way. While the behaviourist approach has had a massive impact on how we learn, and the best ways to encourage learning, it does have its limitations.

Reductionist

The behaviourist approach has been accused of being reductionist. In this case, reductionist means that behaviourism explains us solely in terms of learned S–R units of behaviour. It ignores our higher-level mental processes, such as perception, attention, language and memory, and their influence on problem solving. We do appear to be able to do things with S–R units of learned behaviour, which makes us even more effective and efficient in our environment. Indeed as we shall discover in our next chapter, it was a soft behaviourist, Edward Tolman, who was to point out this major flaw in behaviourist thinking. His work contradicted the behaviourist view that we are simply passive learners of behaviours. As we shall see, Tolman indicated that we are active learners, who have a staggering capability to process and use the information that surrounds us in our environment to our advantage. Further, the behaviourist approach discounts our emotion in relation to what we learn from, and in, our environment. This we shall turn to in our chapter on the humanistic approach, particularly in relation to our personality.

Psychoanalysis would criticise behaviourism as reductionist in that it would say that behaviourism ignores the importance of relationships and the family in the learning process. Psychoanalysts would argue that the *psychodynamics* of the situation contribute to learning. For example, learning could be influenced as a consequence of whether or not a student likes a teacher or *vice versa*. Further, from a biological point of view, behaviourism discounts any effect evolution, genetics and physiology has on our behaviour – a factor, as we read in Chapter 1, that shouldn't be avoided in a complete explanation of why it is we think, feel and behave as we do. Examples abound. Seligman (1970) in his idea of *preparedness* suggests that species are biologically predisposed to learn what is important to survival. Garcia & Koelling (1966) showed that rats have a biological predisposition to learn very quickly to avoid unpleasant foods that made them sick. This biological predisposition, or adaptive advantage, to be cautious with strange foods enhances the rats' ability to live longer. Children behave very much in the same way when given foods they do not like the look of.

Many are uncomfortable with the behaviourist idea that there is little difference between animals and humans, and what it says regarding learned behaviours in rats, cats, dogs and pigeons being applicable to us as human beings. This is related to the issue of the manipulation of animals in behaviourist experiments in the investigation of learning. Extending this, the question should be asked if it is ethical for psychology in general, and the behaviourist approach in particular, to promote the notion of the control and manipulation of people in order to make them behave in some desired way.

Mechanistic

Another criticism levelled at the behaviourist approach is that it is mechanistic in its explanation of human behaviour. Mechanistic means that behaviourism sees us as merely responding to our environment and believes we have little control over it. As a result behaviourism takes the view that it is our environment that wholly decides what we learn, and thus how we behave. Behaviourism suggests that we respond to our environment in a mechanistic, or mechanical manner known as the ABC model. This is over-simplistic. Other influences play a part, as we discovered in the psychoanalytic approach, and will elaborate further when we examine the cognitive, biological and humanistic approaches.

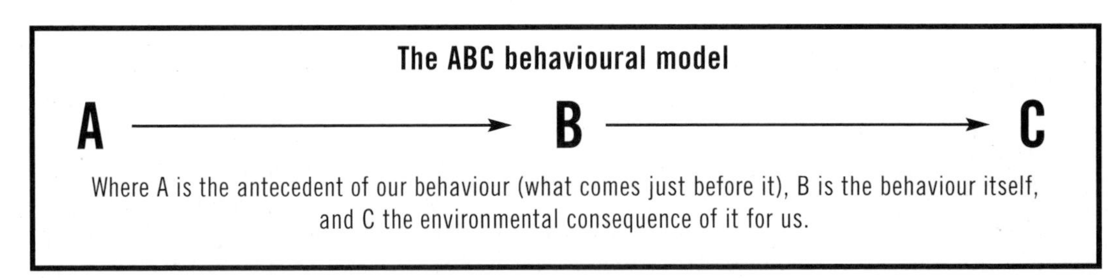

Figure 3.15 ABC behavioural model

Deterministic

Behaviourism has little place for our use of free will in learning what we learn, and thus behaving as we do. This is because behaviourism thinks we are as we are because of learning in our environment. We behave as we do because of our learned responses to our environment, through reflex associations or environmental reinforcers such as reward and unpleasant consequence. Behaviourism is therefore deterministic in that it believes it is solely our environment that shapes our behaviour. Personal choice, or free will, plays no part.

Free will, or personal agency, should not however be underestimated and is, as we shall see, a major feature of the humanistic approach to why we think, feel and behave as we do. Free will allows us to make choices, and to choose paths in life. As a result, our life is not entirely determined by our environment. We *can* take control of our environment and how it influences us psychologically.

Conclusion

As a paradigm, or body of theory and ideas, the behaviourist approach explains all organisms, animal and human, from the point of view of learned stimulus–response units of behaviour formed as we interact with our environment. It is a scientifically sound approach, and places much emphasis on the use of the experimental method in its investigation of observable events. Classical conditioning has helped psychology understand that we learn to behave in our world because of associations between a stimulus and response. Operant conditioning reminds us that reinforcement from our environment is also important to the learning of behaviours. Because of its reductionist, mechanistic and deterministic limitations the behaviourist approach is not as dominant in psychology as it once was. One reason is that the behaviourist approach, rather ironically, prompted the emergence of the cognitive approach; an approach that we shall see places importance on our higher-level mental processes in its explanation of why we think, feel and behave the way we do.

Summary

The behaviourist approach concerns the study of observed responses of humans and animals, which its proponents see as important to an understanding of human and animal behaviour. They believe that we learn to behave in response to our environment, either by stimulus–response association, or as a result of reinforcement. Important contributors to the behaviourist approach are Ivan Pavlov, with his theory of classical conditioning, and B.F. Skinner and his work into operant conditioning. Classical conditioning concerns learning by association. Operant conditioning concerns the use of environmental reinforcers in its explanation of why we learn to behave as we do. Classical conditioning emphasises conditioning, spontaneous recovery, stimulus generalisation, stimulus discrimination and reinforcement in the learning process. Operant conditioning tells us that the type of reinforcer encountered by the organism can influence this process of reinforcement. Reward, or positive reinforcement, tends to encourage the repetition of a learned behaviour. Avoidance of unpleasant consequence, or negative reinforcement, tends to discourage the repetition of a discomforting behaviour. Classical conditioning has been applied to behaviour shaping and to behaviour therapies, such as systematic desensitisation, implosion therapy and aversion therapy. Operant conditioning has been applied to behaviour modification régimes such as the token economy and the programmed learning movement. Reinforcement régimes such as fixed ratio and fixed interval schedules have been found to be of benefit in such situations when used to encourage new learning. Behaviourist ideas, especially those of B.F. Skinner, have been particularly influential on education. However, the thoughts, feelings and behaviours of higher-level species, such as human beings, are nowadays thought far more sophisticated than the behaviourist approach originally suggested. In our next chapter on the cognitive approach we will come to understand that we are more than just the sum total S–R units of learned behaviours, however formed.

INTERACTIVE

1 Go to any Internet site of your choosing and find definitions for stimulus, classical conditioning, extinction, reinforcement, stimulus discrimination, reinforcers, negative reinforcement, behaviour modification, token economy and reductionist. List any http site used in your answer.

2 Go to http://arbl.cvmbs.colostate.edu/hbooks/pathphys/digestion/misc/pavlov.html and discover how Pavlov understands the unconscious.

3 Read http://www.coe.uh.edu/courses/cuin6373/idhistory/skinner.html. What aspects of operant conditioning can you apply to Skinner's idea of a mechanical teaching machine?

4 Read http://earlybird.qeh.ox.ac.uk/rfgexp/rsp_tre/student/brief/paradigm/par_p2.htm. What do you understand by the term learned helplessness? How does the behaviourist approach explain learned helplessness in relation to the refugee experience?

Structured questions with answer guidelines

1 *Explain the behaviourist approach in psychology.*

With reference to the preceding chapter, structure your answer around the following model:

- Define the behaviourist approach as an approach that understands us from the point of view of learning. Refer to the Behaviourist Manifesto. Identify that you are going to discuss important features such as S–R, classical and operant conditioning and schedules of reinforcement.
- Explain classical conditioning with reference to:
  - S–R learning by association
  - Pavlov's theory of classical conditioning
  - extinction, reinforcement, spontaneous recovery, stimulus generalisation and discrimination.
- Explain operant conditioning with reference to:
  - Skinner's rats and operant conditioning
  - environmental reinforcers, types of reinforcers
  - schedules of reinforcement.

2 *How is the behaviourist approach applied in practice?*

Structure your answer as follows:

- Identify the application of the approach as a behaviourist psychotherapy, i.e. behaviour therapy and behaviour modification.
- Explain behaviour therapy in relation to classical conditioning with reference to
  - systematic desensitisation
  - implosion therapy
  - aversion therapy.
- Explain behaviour modification in relation to operant conditioning with reference to:
  - token economy
  - programmed learning.

3 *What criticisms may be made of the behaviourist approach?*

Identify and explain limitations, i.e.

- reductionist
- mechanistic
- deterministic.

Glossary

Law of temporal contiguity: the pairing of a neutral stimulus and unconditional stimulus at the same time, resulting in an unconditional, reflex response. Pavlov's pairing of the NS of the bell with the US of the food saw the unconditional response (UR) of salivation

Learning: a relatively permanent change in behaviour as a result of experience

Paradigm: the agreed boundaries within which a subject lies

Spontaneous recovery: the reappearance of learning thought to be extinct

Operant conditioning: Skinner's theory of learning as a non-reflex behaviour because of a learned consequence, e.g. reward

S–R: behaviourists believe our behaviour is learned. Behaviour consists of stimulus–response units of learning formed as a result of experience

Successive approximations: shaping behaviour by giving a reward for getting it nearly right. Over time the reward is only given to the learner, the more accurate the successive approximation of the desired behaviour becomes

4

The cognitive approach

BY THE END OF THIS CHAPTER YOU SHOULD BE ABLE TO:

- **define and explain the cognitive approach with reference to its key features**
- **explain applications of the cognitive approach**
- **explain the limitations of the cognitive approach.**

Overview of the cognitive approach

The cognitive approach involves the study of our information processes of perception, attention, language, memory and thinking, and how they influence our thoughts, feelings and behaviours. Also known as **mediational processes**, our information processes are the ways in which we obtain, organise and use information from our world, to help us operate successfully within it. In this chapter we will explore the active nature of information processing, with reference to the computer analogy. We will then look at three information processes, perception, memory, and thinking, to further our knowledge of how we can use this approach to understand our behaviour in our environment. While the cognitive approach is applied to information processes individually, in a psychological sense all five are very much interlinked in that we use all five simultaneously. The existence of our five information processes is *inferred* because perception and attention occur in our mind, the content, and concepts of which are hypothetical, and cannot be directly observed. Applications of the cognitive approach will see us look at advertising and marketing, and the cognitive interview technique. The limitations of the cognitive approach – its lack of agreed identity, the use of the mechanistic computer analogy, and problems concerning the ecological validity of its experimental research – will also be considered.

Key features of the cognitive approach

The cognitive approach concerns the study of how we take in information from our world, and how we actively process this information to respond to our world.

An information-processing approach

Cognitive psychologists study our higher-level cognitions of perception, attention, language, memory and thinking (or problem solving). They see our mind as consisting of these five information processes, which we individually and collectively use to operate in, upon, and through our environment. Consequently, the cognitive approach explains human behaviour and mental process from the point of view of *information processing*. Any dysfunction in our thoughts, feelings, and behaviours are due to *faulty* information processing; in other words, a problem with one or more of our five mediational processes, as identified above.

We actively process information

We are not mere passive receptors of data, according to the cognitive approach

The cognitive approach is about how we *actively* process information using our mediational processes, individually and collectively, to build up our knowledge of the world. It asks about how we make meaningful sense of stimuli in our world, and our behaviours in it as a result.

As you will discover, the cognitive approach argues that we are not passive receptors of information, as the behaviourist approach would have us believe. Our mind actively processes what information it receives, and using mediational processes changes this information into new forms. New information is combined, compared, transformed, and integrated with that which is already present. On the basis of our information processes, we build up an increasingly more complex picture of our world, and all the things in it, which affect our feelings and behaviours in our environment.

The fall and rise of the cognitive approach

From its earliest beginnings psychology has tried to understand the human *mind* in relation to feelings and behaviours. William Wundt in 1879 is remembered for his work into perception. Freud from 1901 is remembered for his work concerning the unconscious. In our previous chapter we discovered that the behaviourist approach became popular largely due to its *criticisms* of the study of such hypothetical constructs. As a consequence, the study of the mind, which was the original object of investigation in psychology, became somewhat marginalised for a good part of the twentieth century. A series of events was however to occur, aided ironically by a behaviourist, which would see the cognitive approach overcome its difficulty of generating scientific support for hypothetical constructs. This saw the rebirth of the cognitive approach from about the 1970s onwards, helped in its renaissance by developments in subjects as diverse as computer engineering and cognitive psychotherapy.

Tolman & Honzik (1930)

Behaviourism emphasises that psychology should study actual observable behaviour, and that we are to be understood in terms of stimulus–response units of learned behaviour obtained via classical and operant conditioning.

It was to be a soft behaviourist, Edward Tolman, who challenged these assumptions, when in 1930 he suggested that organisms *do* something with learned S–R units that make them even more efficient and effective in their environment. This was to stimulate the important cognitive idea that we are *active* processors of information and not passive learners as behaviourism had suggested.

In their famous experiment Tolman & Honzik (1930) built a maze environment to investigate latent learning in rats.

Latent learning

Latent learning is a kind of subliminal learning, which we don't know we possess, and don't use until there is some positive reinforcement, or environmental incentive, to do so. An example of latent learning would be where you got a lift to college from a friend every day. You may learn at a latent level the way to get to college, but as a passenger have no reason to demonstrate your learning by 'proving' that you know this. You don't even think about it. However, when you friend is sick and you have to drive yourself to college for the first time, if you drive following the same route as your friend did, then you have demonstrated latent learning.

Rats in mazes

In a variety of experiments with different kinds of mazes Tolman found that a rat when introduced to his maze initially sniffed about, and explored in an erratic fashion. If it eventually discovered food placed in a food box when it was later put back into the maze, the rat searched for the food but did not make as many errors, i.e. go down blind alleys, turn back on itself – as when first introduced to the maze.

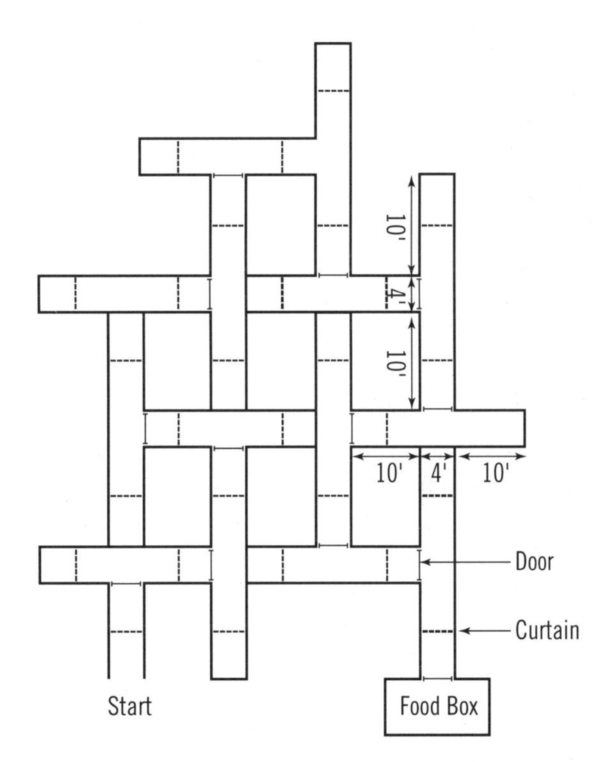

Figure 4.1 The kind of rat maze used by Tolman and Honzik

Cognitive maps

Tolman thought that what must have happened was that his rat(s) had formed a primitive *cognitive map* of the maze in their heads as a result of their first exploration of the maze. Whether they used it to their advantage, as measured by going quicker and with fewer errors to the food, depended upon this earlier exploration of the maze, and whether they had been previously rewarded, or otherwise, when coming across the food box.

Purposive behaviourism

Tolman and Honzik concluded that cognitive maps allowed the rat to understand and react better to its maze environment. The earlier behaviourists seemed to be wrong in their assumption that organisms are *passive* learners. Tolman & Honzik (1930) indicated instead that rats are active processors of information about their world. Further, organisms such as rats process what they learn about their world in a very sophisticated fashion in order to obtain some mastery over it.

This *purposive behaviourism* of non-humans, and by behaviourist definition humans, was to stimulate developments in the cognitive approach.

Behaviourism's mechanistic and deterministic view that we passively learn in response to our environment was beginning to be questioned from within behaviourism itself.

Cognitive maps

We humans form cognitive maps of our world. Saaranin (1973) got American college students to draw maps of their campus. Students tended to enlarge those buildings that were most important to them and shrink those less important. They were often found to be completely wrong when describing campus areas that were not as familiar to them. Similarly, Briggs (1971) discovered on asking people to judge how far they thought one landmark was from another, that they tended to underestimate the distance between familiar landmark objects and over-estimate the distance between unfamiliar landmarks. This research helps to explain the phenomenon of the Irish mile!

A CONUNDRUM SOLVED

Tolman and Honzik had gone some way to help solve the conundrum that had plagued cognitive research since Wundt in 1879; that is, how to investigate and generate empirical data about hypothetical constructs (which remember, don't exist in reality) in order to come to a scientific understanding of them. Tolman and Honzik *externalised* the construct of thinking in rats and studied it *indirectly* by obtaining empirical data in terms of times and errors made by the rats in the maze. Tolman & Honzik (1930) were then able to *infer* confidently on the basis of this empirical evidence that rats refine learned behaviours and thus think in a more sophisticated fashion than earlier behaviourists had believed. They had empirical data that suggested an organism actively processes learned information about its environment.

Look at the study on page 69 and then answer the questions in the Interactive box below.

INTERACTIVE

1. What do you think latent learning means? Give an example in your answer.
2. What was the relationship that behaviourism suggested existed between reinforcement and learning before Tolman & Honzik's (1930) research?
3. What are the three conditions of the independent variable in Tolman & Honzik's (1930) experiment? An independent variable is the variable the experimenter manipulates or changes in an experiment.
4. What evidence did they find that reinforcement is more related to performance of a learned behaviour, rather than the learning of the behaviour itself?

STUDY

Tolman, E.C. & Honzik, C.H. (1930) 'Introduction and removal of reward and maze-learning in rats', *University of California Publications in Psychology*, 4, 257–275

Aim: To investigate latent learning in rats and the relationship between reinforcement, learning and performance.

Method: Experiment and observation. Tolman and Honzik built a complex maze environment (see Figure 4.1). They had three groups of rats that underwent 17 trials in the maze over 17 days under three conditions. Group 1 rats were never fed in the maze, and when they reached the goal of the food box, were removed. Group 2 rats received the reinforcer of food every time they reached the food box; while on trials 1–10, Group 3 rats got no food but received reinforcement on trials 11–17.

Results: Group 1 rats always took around the same time to reach the food box and made many errors. They were observed as aimless in the maze, simply wandering around. Group 2 rats learned the intricacies of the maze quickly and over the 17 days of trials made progressively fewer and fewer errors. From day 11 Group 3 rats showed a sudden improvement in performance time to reach the food and made as few errors as Group 2 rats by the end of the experiment.

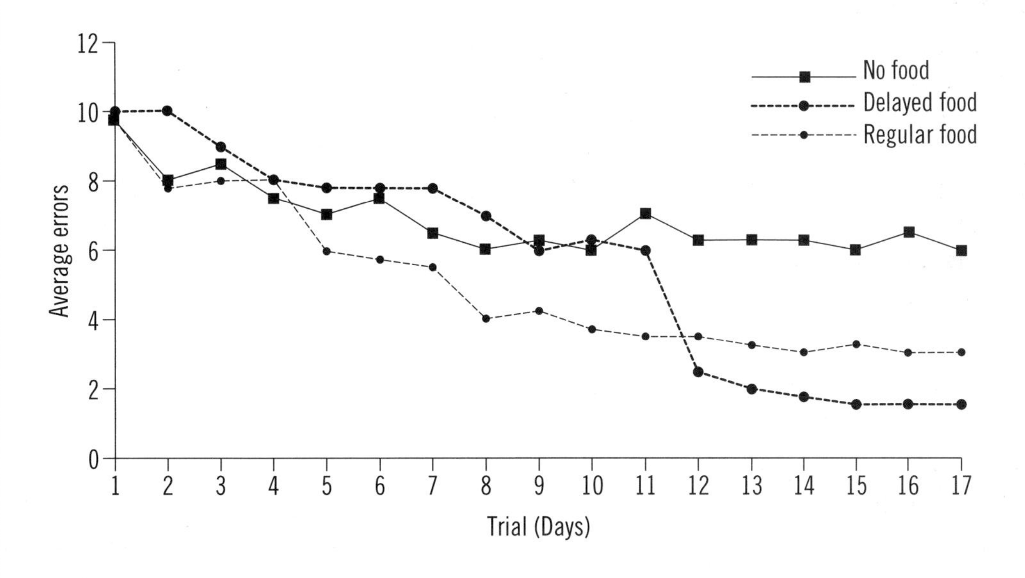

Figure 4.2 Latent learning

Conclusion: Tolman & Honzik (1930) concluded that reinforcement from the environment may not be as important to the learning process as was earlier thought. They believed reinforcement was more related to the *performance* of a learned behaviour. Further, this experiment helped Tolman infer that organisms such as rats and humans do something with learned units of behaviour to make them more efficient in their environment. Tolman (1946) was to say his rats had formed primitive cognitive maps of the maze environment in their heads. Whether they used this information depended upon a successful outcome to behaving in a particular way. We learn about things at a latent level that may see us behave in a particular way if there is some incentive from our environment to do so.

1956 – a very good year

It is entirely good fortune that the author's first birthday coincided with 1956 being the landmark year for the cognitive approach! For it would not be inappropriate to say that 1956 precipitated the growth of cognitive psychology, as it exists today. This is because in 1956 the world famous psycholinguist Noam Chomsky presented his paper on the theory of language, Jean Piaget and Bärbel Inhelder wrote about **egocentrism** in *The Child's Conception of Space*, and George Miller's work on short-term memory was published. In addition, 1956 saw Bruner, Goodnow and Austin debate concept formation, or how we develop different ways of thinking about the environment around us. 1956 was also the year of the Dartmouth Conference in the USA, which saw the beginnings of the AI (artificial intelligence) movement energised by innovations in computer technology.

Of importance here is that cognitive psychology shared with the emerging computer technologies their information-processing models about human thought and problem-solving. We share a language, in that nowadays in cognitive psychology we often come across words and concepts from information technology such as input, output, storage, retrieval, parallel processing, networking, schema and filters. The approach also uses the 'computer analogy' to help explain why it believes we think, feel and behave the way we do, which is as an active processor of information about our world.

The human mind, the cognitive approach and the computer

The cognitive approach and computer engineering share the idea that the human mind/brain can be likened to a computer. What a computer tries to do is mirror how the cognitive approach suggests that human beings solve problems.

The computer analogy assists the cognitive approach in explaining the relationship between our information processes and our behaviour in our world. Models like the computer analogy are used throughout psychology to help understand hypothetical constructs, and nowhere is their use more prevalent than in the study of perception, attention and memory. Models put forward by cognitive psychologists concerning our various cognitions have greatly influenced developments in the computing industry. The more advances that can be made in cognitive psychology, the more likely it is that the computer industry will be able to develop the ultimate in information technology – an interactive free-thinking computer that can problem-solve without direction. What the cognitive approach finds out is therefore of great interest to the likes of Bill Gates and *Microsoft*.

Figure 4.3 The human mind can be likened to a computer.

THE COMPUTER ANALOGY

In 1997, in his book called *How The Mind Works,* Steven Pinker wrote '*the behaviour of a computer comes from a complex interaction between the processor and input*'. This is very much how the cognitive approach understands our behaviour as human beings.

The computer analogy is a metaphor, or story, used by the cognitive approach to understand the relationship between our thoughts, feelings, and behaviours and our environment.

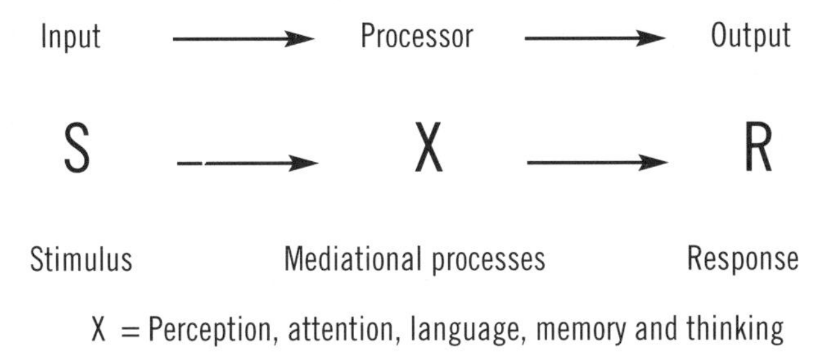

Figure 4.4 The computer analogy

Input is all the stimuli information that we encounter in our world. Input, or environmental information, about objects, people and events, comes to us via our senses in the form of light energy, sound energy, pressure – or what we see, hear and feel. All this information ultimately arrives in the brain to be interpreted, understood and acted upon. A good example of this would be the things we see in our world. What we see, or visually sense, is energy from our external environment that first strikes each eye as light waves. This information, alien to our internal biochemistry, is processed via our eyes into the only type of energy our internal body can understand: electrical energy, which ends up in our visual cortex at the back of the brain as a bundle of electrochemical impulses, or neural signals. The nature and intensity of these neural signals, we unconsciously match to what we have stored in our memory concerning the same, or a similar stimulus. Memory helps us recognise, and give meaning to, what we are visually sensing. This helps us think how best to respond, in terms of our behaviour or output, towards the stimulus object.

It is thus our information processes of perception, attention, language, memory and thinking – X – that come between the sensory inputs or stimuli (S) we receive from our world to help us understand what these sensations are, what they mean, and what might be the most appropriate way to respond (R). Mediational processes therefore intercede, or come between, external stimuli or input from our world, and our behavioural response, or output, to it. Our information processes are like the microprocessors in a computer. Microprocessors come between input in the form of keystrokes, and so on, and computer output like printouts and images.

The computer analogy helped confirm behaviourist Edward Tolman's view that we are more than just S–R units of learned behaviour. The computer analogy helps illustrate that it is our mediational processes that actively do things with the sensory information we receive, and this allows us to respond to our world in an enriched fashion.

Let us now read about three of our mediational processes, perception, memory, and thinking, aware that the cognitive approach likens our mind to a computer – the most sophisticated evolved.

Perception

As usual in psychology we try first to define the concept we are studying. The study of perception is no exception. A simple definition might be that:

Perception is an active mediational process that allows us to process, organise and interpret sensory information from our outside world.

Perception involves senses, **gestalt** abilities and past experience. Perception is an active mediational process where we take in raw sensations from our environment, which we organise and interpret using our past knowledge and understanding of the world, in order to make what we sense meaningful to us.

To put perception another way, it is '... *the process of assembling sensations into a usable mental representation of the world ...which ... creates faces, melodies, works of art, illusions etc.*' (Coon, 1983). This might seem simple enough, but be wary, as '*to perceive seems effortless. To understand perception is nevertheless a great challenge*' (Dodwell, 1995). Try the following Interactive.

INTERACTIVE

Look at Figure 4.5 opposite. What aspect of it do you perceive that does not exist in reality? To understand *reality* better, study cognitive psychology!

Figure 4.5

Our senses and perception

Central to an understanding of perception is knowing how we receive information from our environment in the first place. This is of course via our senses. We know we have five senses: sight, hearing, touch, taste, and smell, but cognitive psychology is also able to tell us we have at least one other sense called our kinaesthetic sense. This is our sense of balance. Our kinaesthetic sense is not found in one particular location in the body, unlike our nose for smelling or our tongue for tasting. Balance relies on at least three senses *sharing* information. This is a good example of cross-modal transfer: *balance* involves our *auditory* sense, our *visual* sense and our *tactile* sense, working together. Cross-modal transfer is the pooling of information from our various senses in order to obtain maximum sensory information about our world. Why might this ability be important to our personal survival?

INTERACTIVE

Complete the table below

Table 4.1

Our six senses	Function	Accessory structure
Kinaesthetic	our sense of balance	
Gustatory	our sense of taste	
Auditory	our sense of hearing	
Olfactory	our sense of smell	
Tactile	our sense of touch	
Visual	our sense of sight	Eyes

Characteristics of our senses

Each sense responds to a particular form of energy or external information, e.g. light waves, sound waves and skin pressure. Each sense has a sense organ or accessory structure, which is the first port of call for any incoming information on the road to processing and our full understanding of the perceived stimuli. Look at the list above and identify the accessory structure associated with each of our senses.

Transducers

Each accessory structure has special sense receptors called transducers. These are cells that are sensitive to particular *kinds* of energy. It is as the stimuli hit these transducers that the conversion of one type of external energy into electrical nerve impulses occurs. This electrical activity is the only kind of energy that can be processed and understood by our brains. Each sense, or sensory modality involves a different part of the brain. Visual signals go to the visual cortex, auditory signals to the auditory cortex and smell to the olfactory cortex.

Figure 4.6 It is easy to take for granted the multiple complex processes involved in perception

Absolute thresholds

In the brain we interpret these neural signals, which gives us our *sense* of awareness about an object, a person, a word, a sound or a taste. A certain minimum stimulation of a transducer is needed before we can become consciously aware of the sensory experience that is happening. These minimum requirements are called absolute thresholds, which is the level at which we can detect a stimulus 50 per cent of the time. This threshold differs between people and even within the same person, and can be affected by an individual's physical state, time of day, motivation and the manner in which the stimulus is presented. This is the area of psychophysics within psychology, which is the interface between a physical stimulus and our subjective experience of it. Psychophysics was of great importance to the development of psychology as a subject in its own right, as we saw earlier when introduced to the work of Wilhelm Wundt (1879).

Table 4.2 Where sensory information is processed, organised and interpreted

Area of the brain	Function
Prefrontal cortex	Problem solving, emotion, complex thought
Motor association cortex	Coordination of complex movement
Primary motor cortex	Initiation of voluntary movement
Primary somatosensory cortex	Receives tactile information from the body
Sensory association area	Processing of multisensory information
Visual association area	Complex processing of visual information
Visual cortex	Detection of simple visual stimuli
Wernicke's area	Language comprehension
Auditory association area	Complex processing of auditory information
Auditory cortex	Detection of sound quality (loudness, tone)
Speech centre (Broca's area)	Speech production and articulation

Visual perception

In our brief look at perception it would seem appropriate to focus on visual perception in particular. Visual perception is of immense interest to the cognitive approach.

Vision consists of two elements, sensation and visual perception. They are hard to separate out from each other but sensation is the detection and encoding of visual stimuli, whereas visual perception is our higher-level function that processes, organises, and interprets this sensory data.

Our visual system

To understand vision and visual perception a little introduction to the eye is necessary.

According to Ornstein (1975), the eye is '*the most important avenue of personal consciousness*'. We receive around 80 per cent of our information about our world via our visual system. An understanding of the structure and function of the eye is useful if only to give a clue as to how it is we receive 2-D photographic type images on our retinas, but yet interpret these two-dimensional images in three dimensions. A knowledge of our visual system is also important to how and why we can perceive colour in our world – and why it is we can see in the dark, but not as well as cats and other nocturnal animals!

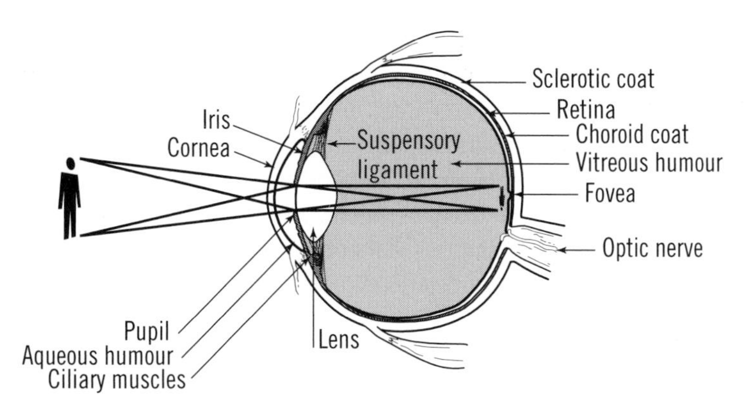

Figure 4.7 The eye

Structure and function of the eye

The pupil is an opening in the centre of the iris which looks like a small black circle at the centre of the eye. The size of the pupil is controlled by the iris and determines the amount of light that enters the eye. In dark conditions our pupils dilate to their maximum size in order to maximise the amount of light entering the eye and thus our ability to see (not too well) in the dark. A cat's ability to widen its pupils more than we humans is one of the reasons for their excellent night vision in comparison to our own.

In light conditions our pupil contracts in response to the intensity of light we experience. This protects the retina from damage. Pupil size is controlled by our autonomic nervous system (ANS), which controls our organs and glands. The ANS is linked to our central nervous system (CNS), which is our brain and spinal cord.

Vitreous humour is a clear, jelly-like substance that fills the middle of the eye. The lens of the eye is held in place by suspensory ligaments called ciliary muscles. Much like a camera, the lens focuses light on the retina as an inverted or upside down image. Ciliary muscles control the shape the lens forms as it focuses images on the retina. These muscles help our lens thicken and increase in curvature when focusing on nearby objects, and become flatter when focusing on objects far away. This changes the size of the image on the retina in relation to where it is in our visual field.

The retina at the back of each eye is where the images we see are thrown. The macula, which is a small area found on the retina, has three layers of special light-sensitive cells that help explain certain human visual abilities, and thus aid our understanding of perception. The first layer of the retina contains what are called rods and cones.

Rods and cones

Rods and cones are photosensitive transducer cells that convert light energy into electrical nerve impulses. Our 120 million rods help us see in ever-decreasing light. They account for our night vision. Rods take about twenty minutes to adjust to changing lighting conditions, and this is one reason not to put the light on when we have to go to the bathroom during the night! By switching on the bathroom light and then switching it off again you put yourself in complete darkness. Your rods are first trying to adjust to the bathroom light being switched on, and while doing so then find the light switched off again, thus completely confusing our relatively poor night vision.

Our 7 million cones allow us to experience colour or chromatic vision. Three different cone types respond to the different wavelengths of red, green and blue light as found in our world. A deficiency in red, green or blue receptor cones is the reason behind colour blindness. It is most unusual to find someone who is completely colour blind as this would mean they are deficient in all three colour-related cone receptors. Another interesting aspect to colour blindness is that it is only evident in white males (1:20) and is almost completely unknown in females.

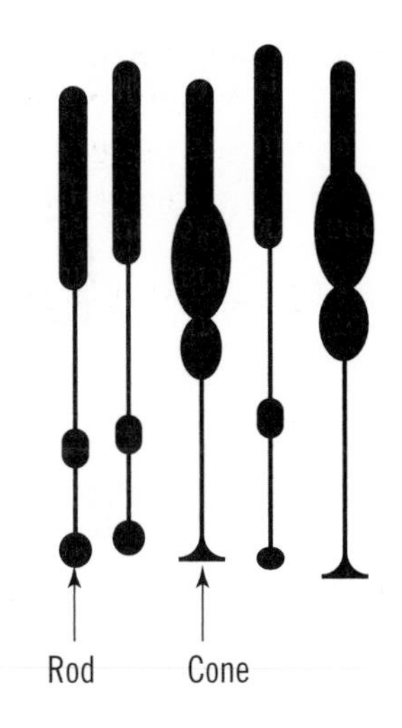

Figure 4.8 Rods and cones

Bipolar cells and ganglion cells

Bipolar cells, found at the second layer in the retina, are connected to our rods and cones, and help to relay their information to ganglion cells, which are found in the third layer of the retina.

Ganglion cells, or axons, also help form the beginnings of the optic nerve, which operates as a visual pathway to the brain. The optic nerve from each eye carries all the data that these specialised structures have detected and encoded, ultimately to the visual cortex in our brain, where according to Hubel & Wiesel (1962, 1968), three types of cell are found that respond to the features, contours and movement of objects in our visual field.

- **Simple cells** respond to the *simple features* of a stimulus, i.e. straight lines, edges, slits etc. or when something is found in a particular orientation (or way up), in our visual field.
- **Complex cells** which are direction-sensitive respond to lines of *particular orientation* wherever found in our visual field.
- **Hypercomplex cells** respond to the *length of visual stimuli,* or where a stimulus begins or ends.

Ganglion cells, or axons, also help form the beginnings of the optic nerve. The optic nerve operates as a visual pathway to the brain. The optic nerve from each eye carries all the data that these specialised structures have detected and encoded, ultimately to the visual cortex in our brain.

Each optic nerve converges and crosses over at the optic chiasma, with information from our right eye going to the left visual cortex and information from our left eye going to the right visual cortex. This is one of the reasons why we see our world in three dimensions. Because we (usually) have two eyes, each separated by our nose, the image each eye sends of the same stimulus to the left and right visual cortex is slightly different. When each is superimposed on the other at the visual cortex this slight difference gives us

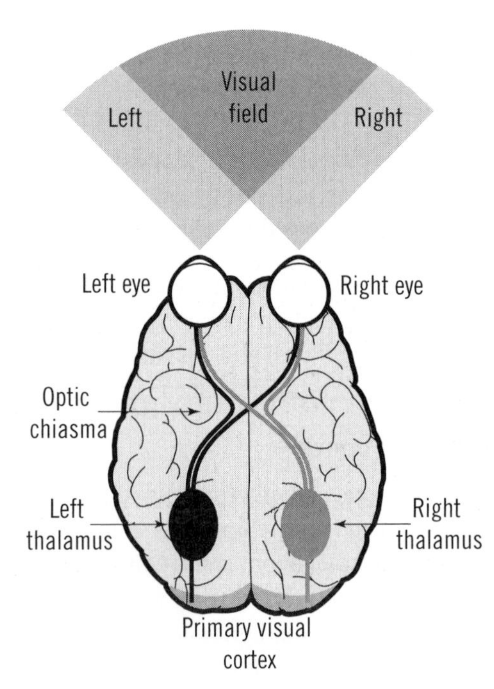

Figure 4.9 The visual system

the sensation of depth in our world. This is binocular vision, and is the biological reason behind why we experience our world in three dimensions. This does not mean to say that a person with one eye cannot experience a 3-D world however. To understand why this is so – take cognitive psychology as an option!

Where sensory data ends up

This is of course in our brain, the organ of the body concerned with consciousness. Consciousness is our *awareness*, and includes perception, attention, language, thinking and memory.

The human brain is a relatively small structure, weighing about 1.4 kg (3.1 lb) which is about two per cent of total body weight. It is housed in the skull, which acts as a protective casing. Information received about the outside world and from the rest of the body converges at the brain to be processed, understood and acted upon. We *first* begin to perceive what a particular sensation is on the basis of the sensory information that our brain receives.

What we visually sense is more then than just light focusing on the retina. Vision is an enormously complex process. What is seen must be captured by our optical system, transmitted and processed by the retina, then passed along to the brain for even more detailed processing. Areas of the brain must extract and interpret the essence of all that we see. It must recognize the colour, contour, shape, texture, movement and perspective of a stimulus and then compare all this to any memory of it we may have had. A tiny two-dimensional image that hits the retina is transformed into a meaningful three-dimensional representation in, pardon the pun, the blink of an eye!

How we reach *individual* perceptual understanding of what particular visual sensations mean for us is based on an innate ability and previous past experience.

The laws of pragnänz and visual perception

In addition to what we visually sense, visual perception involves an innate ability embodied in the **laws of pragnänz**, which are the principles of perceptual organisation put forward by early gestalt psychologists Kohler, Koffka and Wertheimer around 1910.

The laws of pragnänz account for an innate ability we humans have unconsciously to 'tidy up' the visual sensations we receive. Any innate ability has survival value for us, and with the laws of pragnänz this is to make better sense of our visual world. *Gestalt* psychology, in vogue in Germany in the early part of the twentieth century, says we have an innate disposition to perceive objects based on our inbuilt principles of grouping, or gestalten. What *gestalten* mean is our ability to construct our world in terms of organised *wholes*. It is our natural ability to organise visual sensations into a meaningful pattern. Take being in a room with a squinty picture on the wall. Gestalten allow us to perceive that the picture is not straight (what is straight anyway!?), and motivates us then to straighten the picture up, as long as nobody else is looking!

Examples of gestalten, or our innate principles of perceptual organisation include:

Proximity

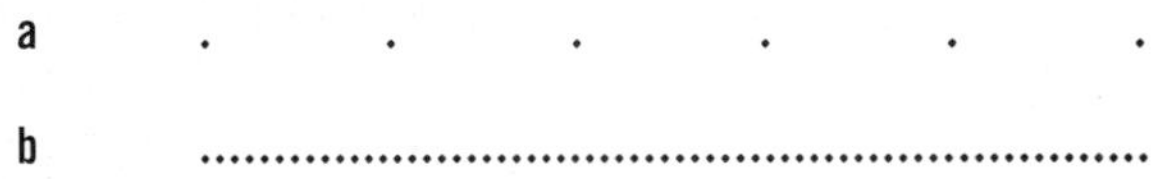

a . . . . . .

b ....

Figure 4.10 Proximity

How do you perceive **a** and **b** above? If you perceive **a** as six dots, and **b** as a line, you have applied the gestalten of proximity where we perceive objects that are close together as belonging to a *whole*, which is in the case of **b** a *line* of dots.

Similarity

We apply the gestalten of similarity when similar objects are perceived by us as belonging to the *same group*. Look again at Figure 4.5 on page 72. You may perceive and group three types of objects: squares, vertical/horizontal lines, and a third – which does not really exist! Can you see this particular example of the gestalten of similarity?

Continuity

Sensations appearing to create a continuous form are perceived by us as belonging together, e.g. a fence with slats missing is still perceived as a fence. The laws of pragnänz get us to organise sensations that appear together to form a *continuous whole.*

Do you perceive Figure 4.11 as a square made up of Xs, or 16 separate and individual Xs?

X X X X

X X X X

X X X X

X X X X

Figure 4.11 Continuity

Closure

This is probably the most influential of *gestalten* and happens when we unconsciously *fill in contours or gaps in stimuli to form a meaningful complete whole*. Closure is illustrated in Fig. 4.12. What is this shape?

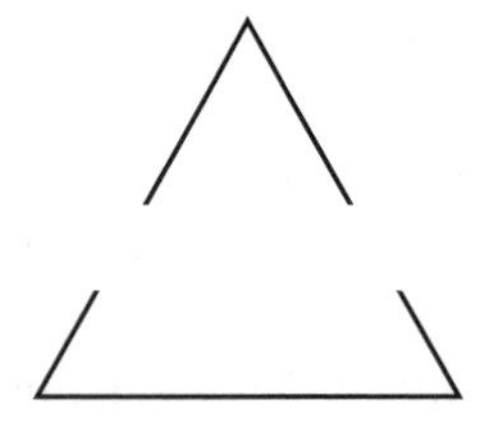

Figure 4.12 Closure

If you think that this is a triangle, it isn't! There are bits of the triangle missing. But don't worry; everyone would say this *is* a triangle. This is because of closure, an innate principle of perceptual organisation that sees us close objects in order to impose meaning on them. What you have done here is fill in the missing piece of the object in your mind's eye. Truly in this instance **the whole is greater than the sum of its parts**. The *gestalt* 'whole' is in this case a triangle. You have just demonstrated *closure*, one of the most important gestalt laws of pragnänz, which sees us 'tidy up' visual information from our outside world using these innate principles of perceptual organisation.

Texture

Another interesting gestalt is where objects of the *same texture* are perceived by us as belonging to the *same group*, e.g. grains of sand at the seaside form for us a 'beach'.

Gestalten, which are biological in origin, help further to explain perception. Perception is then a bit more than merely seeing, or sensing. Perception involves senses, plus gestalten, plus the influence of our past experience, as we will now see.

Figure 4.13 We are unlikely to perceive this scene as a collection of individual grains of sand

The influence of previous past experience

Another interesting aspect to the cognitive approach is that while we mostly all share the same mediational processes, the reason why we think, feel and behave differently, very often towards the same stimuli in our world, is because of previous past experience. Our individual experience greatly influences our perception, attention, language, memory and thinking – and ultimately our response or behaviours, towards the stimuli we encounter. Take this example.

INTERACTIVE

The Scottish Executive and Scottish Women's Aid report that one in five women in Scotland are victims of domestic abuse.

Imagine two women walking down the street. One has been the victim of domestic abuse. They both walk past a man who smiles at them.

In this example, consider the influence past experience might have on each woman's thoughts, feelings, and possible behaviours on passing the man they have just seen.

Often what you perceive is related to your expectations, culture, experience, motivation and social world. Let us look at two of these influences on the perceptual process.

Cultural variations on perception

A lot of work has been done on cultural variations in perception using visual illusions. In 1963 Segall *et al.* examined reactions from different cultures to the Müller–Lyer illusion.

Architects are Lyers, Müller

In the Müller–Lyer illusion (opposite) the two horizontal lines are actually the same length (measure them!), although the

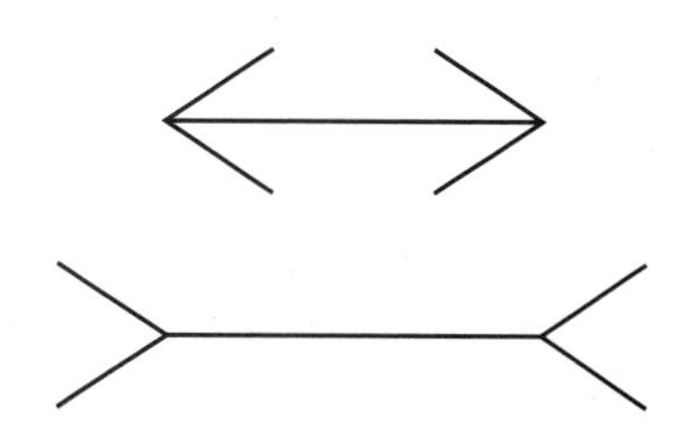

Figure 4.14 Müller–Lyer illusion

one on the bottom *looks* longer than the one at the top. In Western cultures we are surrounded by Müller–Lyer in the construction of our buildings. Look up at any top corner of a room to confirm this. Architects use Müller–Lyer to create the *impression* that rooms are bigger than they actually are.

Segall *et al.* (1963) used three groups from Africa, the Philippines and Illinois, USA. They anticipated that that those brought up in the urban West, who would have had more experience of rectangular rooms and buildings, would be more susceptible to the illusion than those brought up in a less **carpentered** environment. Segall found that the Müller–Lyer illusion was experienced more by the carpentered (Western) group than the non-carpentered Philippino and African groups.

Similarly, Pederson & Wheeler (1983) used Müller–Lyer with two groups of Navajo Indians in the USA. One group had been brought up in traditional Western housing, a carpentered environment, the other in typical rounded Navajo dwellings, a non-carpentered environment. The carpentered Navajo group had experience of angles, horizontals and verticals, the other not. Pederson and Wheeler confirmed Segall *et al.* (1963) in that the carpentered Navajo group was found to be significantly more susceptible to Müller–Lyer than the group of non-carpentered Navajo. Culture must therefore play a part in our perception of our world. Culture influences what we perceive based on our personal experience.

Our social world: prejudice and perception

Allport (1955) reports a study concerning the influence of our social world on prejudice and perception. Prejudice arises from the social world in which we find ourselves. Prejudice is learnt in environment and influences perception. Using a stereoscope (a device for presenting a separate picture simultaneously to each eye), Allport showed participants photographs of pairs of individuals from different ethnic backgrounds, one member of one race in the pair being shown to the left eye, the other to the right eye. He found people were better and more definite when picking out and categorising members of their own race – but were more unsure and cagey when categorising people of another ethnic group. White Afrikaaners however differentiated far more quickly between the different ethnic pairs presented to them. They had a very definite perception of, and raised emotional awareness towards, different racial groupings. Allport interpreted the perceptual difference, and heightened emotional reaction, as the result of strong racial prejudice held by the White Afrikaaner against others not of their colour, culture and social world.

Santa Claus

Solley & Haigh (1958) investigated whether emotion influenced perception. Children were asked to draw pictures of Santa Claus in December and again in January. Their December representations were larger and had more presents when compared to the children's January efforts. In January the drawings had shrunk and the presents were fewer! Solley & Haigh (1958) imply that emotions such as excitement and anticipation can influence perception.

Norms and values and perception

Worthington (1969) subliminally presented participants with taboo words. Taboo words, very much resembling those of the high-street retail chain FCUK, were cleverly embedded at the centre of a dot of light projected onto a screen. Dots of taboo and neutral words were presented in pairs.

Participants had to say if one dot was brighter or dimmer, or whether they were both the same. In fact the dots were all of the same luminance. Participants consistently rated dots with subliminal taboo words as being dimmer than those with neutral words. The norms and values of our social world appear to influence perception – even at a subliminal level. We seem to be able to turn down the volume of stimuli in our world we perceive as problematic – at the level of our unconscious.

INTERACTIVE

Alrite, any1 wan2 go 2 pics l8r? Gr8 mvi on. Pls!! C U L8R!!

What does the above mean to you?

Apply your knowledge of perception and explain why your granny would have difficulty understanding this! And maybe your teacher!

Senses, gestalten, experience and visual perception

In an attempt to pull all the elements of perception together, and to emphasise the use of computational models by the cognitive approach, it is useful to look at the work of David Marr, an exceptional cognitive psychologist who unfortunately died at a very young age.

Marr's four-module computational theory of vision

Visual perception begins with a retinal image of an object, from which in four stages we build a symbolic representation in our minds. At each stage the contribution and combination of our senses, gestalten and past experience can be seen.

1 The image or grey-level description

The image or grey-level stage concerns the intensity of light refracted from points on the stimulus object picked up by our retina. This helps us discover the boundaries and regions of an object.

2 Primal sketch

Here Marr says we go on to unconsciously identify surface markings, boundaries and other markings using the gestalt principles of grouping. We are still some way away from object recognition as such.

3 2½-D sketch

Here we give the object depth and orientation, or 'way up'. A picture of the percept (what we perceive) begins to emerge. The object is not yet three-dimensional. We match input against similar memories to try to account for the non-visible points of the stimulus that we cannot see. Depth and orientation are related to the biology of our eyes.

4 3-D model representation

This is where the nature of the object is confirmed or denied using such information processes as memory and thinking. The 3-D representation stage is dependent on prior knowledge got from past experience of the stimulus object. This stage creates a symbolic representation of our visual reality in our heads.

David Marr (1982) said we extract specific information about any stimulus we *see* in four stages. What we learn about specific aspects of the stimulus at each stage, we eventually put back together again in our mind to try to recognise and understand it. What we visually perceive in our mind is called a symbolic representation. A representation in psychology is a symbol, entity, or thing that refers to, or stands for, something else. Each of Marr's four stages at some point involves aspects of our visual sense, the use of gestalten and past experience. All three together give us *visual* perception.

INTERACTIVE

1 Identify where our senses, gestalten and past experience play a part in Marr's computational theory of visual perception. Give reasons for your answer.

2 What particular properties found in our eyes could account for much of Stage 1 and Stage 3 sensory input? Give reasons for your answer.

3 Is what we visually experience *real* in your view? Give reasons for your answer.

Memory

Memory is a cognitive process closely associated with perception and attention. We perceive and attend to stimuli in our world on the basis of just how meaningful it is for us. Meaning is influenced by our memories of similar stimuli in the past, as was demonstrated earlier in our domestic violence Interactive.

Memory is our active mediational process, which organises, stores, retrieves, and helps us recognise information about our world.

Where is memory?

Where memory occurs is a bit of a mystery. Research suggests that some aspects of memory are associated with particular areas of our brain. We store and retrieve memories of/for sounds in our temporal lobe. We remember what we see using our visual cortex. We recognise and remember patterns using our parietal lobe. We store and retrieve our memories of faces in our frontal lobe. Memory is a whole-brain information process. Memory of an event thus relies on widespread regions of the brain working together to create a gestalt or whole.

Our perceptions first occupy an immediate, iconic memory, and then move to short-term memory, from which some will transfer to long-term memory stores. Recall of what you are sensing depends upon past perceptual experience of it. Our perception of what it is we are sensing is often coloured by the memory we have of it. This is connected to the feelings that accompanied the event – dull events are hard to remember, life-changing ones are easy. Meaning is again central to another cognitive process; memory helps us 'make sense' of our reality based upon just how meaningful that stimulus is for us. What we remember, and just how detailed and deeply, is very personal in many ways.

How do we remember? Coding, storage and retrieval

Acoustic, visual, and semantic coding

The process we use to put information into our memory is called encoding. We store information about objects, events and people using the most appropriate code(s) relevant to the stimulus we come across. These codes come in three forms: acoustic code, visual code and semantic code.

- **Acoustic codes** represent particular events stored and remembered as a sequence of sounds. This could be the tune of a song, for example.
- **Visual codes** represent visual information stored and remembered as forms or images. This could be the words of the song as read from from a CD cover – if your eyesight is good enough!
- **Semantic codes** see us store and remember aspects of a memory on the basis of just how meaningful a stimulus is. Using our example above this could be a personal memory attached to when you heard the song in the first place. It could be that the song was the one you heard when you first met your partner.

Storage

Our ability to hold a memory in our minds is called storage. We hold memories in three main memory facilities, each with a far greater capacity compared to what came before. The cognitive approach calls these sensory register, short-term memory and long-term memory.

Sensory register

Sensory register holds information from all the senses, but only for a fraction of a second. It is more an subconscious *state of awareness* of a stimulus than a storage facility as such. An example of what is held in the sensory register would be our awareness of a sensation like a breath of wind or a raindrop hitting our cheek.

Short-term memory

According to Atkinson & Shiffrin (1968), short-term memory (STM) (or working memory) has two functions. STM helps us to form and update a picture of our world on a minute-by-minute basis, and helps us think and problem-solve. STM has a decay rate of between 15–20 seconds. If we do not use what we have stored in STM within this time, the information is lost to us. Think about trying to remember a one-off phone number that you haven't written down. If you do not use the information quickly, when you *do* go to use the phone you will have forgotten the number.

Things you maybe didn't know about STM

- **Encoding:** people from all cultures tend to use acoustic codes to encode information into STM. To remember the phone number above we often repeat, or sound, the number to ourselves until we use it. Visual codes decay faster than acoustic codes.
- **Storage capacity:** Your *immediate memory span* is the number of items you can recall perfectly after one presentation of a stimulus. In 1956 George Miller discovered our STM is between 5–9 chunks of information long.

- **The power of chunking:** breaking information up and trying to remember it in chunks can increase the capacity of our STM. The capacity of STM and the power of chunking is illustrated below.

INTERACTIVE

Without writing anything down take 30 seconds to memorise the following letter string

evarbehtdnaltocs

Please now cover up the letter string and write it down exactly as you remember it. Don't cheat! When you have done this, check how you have done. Did you remember all the letters in sequence? At what letter (fourth, fifth, etc.) did you make your first error?

The author would be very impressed if you managed to remember all 16 letters in sequence. This is because STM can only hold between 7± 2 units, or chunks, of information at any one time (Miller, 1956). You very probably tried to chunk this into short-term memory on an individual letter-by-letter basis, i.e. *e, v, a, r, b*, etc. If you got the first nine letters in sequence this is excellent. After this point, however, even those with a good STM should begin to make mistakes. Sixteen chunks are just too much.

However, if you now read the 16-letter string backwards, you may realise how this stimulus could be stored into short-term memory using only three chunks of information! By chunking information into larger bytes of information you can extend the capacity of your short-term memory, as you may now be able to see (or *perceive*, strictly speaking!).

Rehearsal and decay rate of STM

Further, if you rehearse (say over and over) the information you want to commit to STM you can extend the decay rate to more than 15–20 seconds and thus remember the information for longer. Unfortunately, as the study of attention would tell you, while doing this you would be unable to do anything much else. If you are trying to remember a phone number, and the doorbell rings, you either have to answer the door, and forget the number, or use the number and not answer the door!

Long-term memory

Long-term memory (LTM) is our third memory storage facility that allows us to remember and retain information over a long period of time. Encoding information into LTM involves a deep level of conscious processing.

Semantic encoding and LTM

Often this will involve some form of semantic coding based upon just how meaningful the event is for you. You never forget what you were doing when you hear a parent has died and events thereafter. You remember this sad time for the rest of your life in a great deal of detail. This is because most parents are very meaningful for their children.

Visual encoding and LTM

Visual codes are also used to encode information to LTM. When you study for an exam you will commit to LTM essential information in visual code form, i.e. words, phrases, etc. from your notes and reading. Visual coding is not as effective as semantic coding to LTM. While you may do well in your examination on the basis of visual coding, you would be hard pushed a week later to remember what you actually wrote. Craik & Tulving (1975) recommend we use both acoustic and visual codes to help us commit important things to memory. This is referred to as dual coding theory.

You should apply your knowledge about the different ways we encode information to LTM to improve your examination technique. Make Approaches and Methods more meaningful by attempting as many Interactives as possible. Do the online activities and structured questions. This is you using semantic and visual coding. As a consequence, you will remember more for much longer and in more detail.

The Mozart effect

Bradshaw & Anderson (1975) were interested in the influence semantics (meaning) had on LTM recall. They set up experiments where they got participants to try to remember events that occurred to famous people. In one experiment they divided participants into two groups. One group were given a lot of interesting personal observations made by the famous composer Mozart about a journey he made from Munich to Paris. The other group were only given the names of the umpteen villages and towns that Mozart's train passed through on his long journey!

The independent variable was the emphasis on semantic, personal meaning given about the journey by Mozart to the experimental group, and the absence of semantic meaning about the journey given to the control group. In the memory recall task, where participants were asked to relate details about the journey, the experimental group recalled significantly more than did the control group. This helps explain why we can remember more vividly, news items that have a visual and semantic content to them. This current generation will never forget the horrific images (visual) and personal tragedies (semantic) associated with the attack on the World Trade Centre. The very date is engrained into our LTM. Do the Interactive below.

INTERACTIVE

1. On what date did this event happen?
2. Describe what happened.
3. Now describe what happened to you two days earlier.
4. Why do you remember more about the first date than the second? Use your knowledge of memory to help you.

Figure 4.15

Unlike STM the capacity of our LTM is vast. Most theorists believe there is no limit to the amount of information that can be stored in LTM.

Types of LTM and memory retrieval

Eidetic memory

We hold different types of memory in our LTM store. The type of memory influences the amount of detail we can recall about an event. In general, memories are less clear and detailed than perceptions, but occasionally a remembered image can be recalled in every detail. This is photographic memory or **eidetic memory** (or eidetic imagery) found in 1:20 children. Children with a good eidetic memory can recall an entire page of writing in an unfamiliar language that they have seen for only a short time. They have no way of remembering it on the basis of meaning. It is gobbledegook to them. Unfortunately only the few possess eidetic memory in adulthood!

According to the Canadian psychologist Endel Tulving, we have three distinct types of LTM: episodic memory, semantic memory and procedural memory. Each stores different types of information in an organised way. Each memory store is what Tulving calls cue-dependent, meaning they store memories on the basis of one particular aspect of the stimulus.

Episodic memory

Episodic memory is our *autobiographical memory* (Tulving, 1972) and contains our personal memories of past events, people and objects. Episodic memories have a spatio-temporal significance. This means that episodic memories are those memories we remember on the basis of when and where, or the time and place, they occurred. A good example of episodic memory would be what you remember about your last birthday. In the author's case he vividly remembers he was writing this book and had to pass up a chance of going out for the evening. Indeed a lot of evenings!

Semantic memory

Semantic memory is our LTM store of general knowledge about our world including its concepts, rules and language. It is our '*mental thesaurus, organised knowledge about words and other verbal symbols, their meanings and referents*' (Tulving, 1972).

Procedural memory

Procedural memory is our 'how to' memory; it helps us remember *how to* drive a car, tie our shoelaces, play the guitar, boil an egg and so on.

Tulving's view of different and independent types of LTM store has been supported by research into different types of brain damage, and the associated difficulties patients have trying to recall different types of information – which has been encoded episodically, semantically or procedurally. Wheeler *et al.* (1997) report that brain-damaged patients could be taught to do a puzzle (procedural memory), but had problems when asked about where and when they had learned how to do the puzzle (episodic memory). Faulty retrieval of memories can be caused by damage, disease or accident to episodic, semantic or procedural memory stores.

Thinking

Our third mediational process is thinking.

Thinking as an information process is a whole-brain activity involving perception, attention, memory and language. All of which contribute towards problem solving, creativity and intellectual functioning.

Thinking permits us to manipulate words, ideas and symbols in our head to respond best to our world. It is *the* higher-level mental process, the sophistication of which distinguishes us from other higher-level primates. It is, like all other mediational processes, a hypothetical construct whose study is inferred. How we think has been of immense interest to cognitive psychology and beyond. Two of the main contributors to our knowledge of how we think are Jean Piaget and Jerome Bruner.

Jean Piaget

Figure 4.16 Jean Piaget

In order to appreciate the great contribution Piaget made to our understanding of how children think, it is necessary to consider two important Piagetian principles. These are **organisation** and **adaptation**.

Organisation

It is thought that a baby learns more in the first two years of life than in the rest of its life put together, because in their early years they must come across countless new learning experiences every day. How do they deal with this torrent of new information?

Piaget called a baby's ability to order and classify new experiences in their mind *organisation*. Organisation is an innate ability that we are born with common to all infants. Piaget said we organise these experiences into **schema**. A schema is a kind of mental file, which we open when coming across something new.

A baby when exposed to a new situation or stimulus, e.g. daddy, cows, buses, uses its innate organisational ability to form a schema *representing* this new stimulus in its mind. It creates a **mental representation** or schema of daddy, cows, buses, etc. We do this with all events, situations, people and objects. Piaget tells us organisation is the beginning of intellectual functioning for all newborns. It is not a learned ability, but biologically inherited or innate.

Adaptation

Adaptation is the infant's growing ability to *understand* its surrounding world. Adaptation cannot occur unless there is a schema already established regarding the concept, or aspect of our environment that we are trying to understand, act upon, or behave towards. A schema, as we learned above, is an internal mental representation of stimuli in our world. Adaptation of schema is a two-stage process involving assimilation and accommodation.

Assimilation: this happens when a child behaves in a way that suggests it has formed a schema about a particular stimulus. It becomes evident through their behaviours, which indicate that they have taken on board – or assimilated – the concept.

Take the example of a toddler. He is being pushed through the streets of Glasgow in his pram by his mummy and sees a bus. He points to the bus and asks what it is. His mummy says it's a bus. Thereafter anytime the infant sees a bus, he points towards it and says '*Bus, bus, bus*!' It is evident by his behaviour that he has formed a bus schema. Unfortunately he also points at caravans, lorries, and tractors also identifying them as a bus. This is assimilation – an infant's *general interpretation* of their world based upon their *existing* schema. He has not yet developed the mental ability to discriminate between stimuli, or things that look a bit like each other – but are different. For a while the infant generalises out assimilated schema to apply to similar objects.

Figure 4.17

Accommodation: this is a more advanced form of assimilation. It is where the child *restructures* existing schema in order to accommodate similar, but different, stimuli in its world. It essentially changes an existing schema so that new experiences can be added, understood and acted upon. Using our above example, accommodation would happen when the child begins consistently and correctly to identify buses, lorries, and tractors, as buses, lorries and tractors! This is accommodation – a young child's *specific interpretation* of their world based upon the *restructuring* of an existing schema. Using accommodation, the child develops the mental ability to discriminate between stimuli that seem superficially the same but are in fact different.

The development of thinking depends upon our ability to change our mental structures in order to face new challenges in life. We are able to do this from a young age. What pushes us towards having to change old schema in order to accommodate our complex world is the tussle between **equilibrium** and **disequilibrium**.

Equilibrium and disequilibrium: for a while at the assimilation stage, the child interprets buses, lorries, and tractors as buses. It is not a problem. This interpretation of his world is in equilibrium. His existing bus schema does quite well for him. As time goes on, however, and he comes across more and more buses, caravans, lorries, and tractors, and on being corrected by his mummy, he realises that a bus is different from a caravan/lorry/tractor. This puts the existing bus schema in a state of disequilibrium (imbalance) in that caravans, lorries and tractors are obviously not buses. As a consequence, accommodation, or the restructuring of his existing bus schema occurs in order to return him to a state of equilibrium (or balance) regarding the proper interpretation of his world. On seeing a bus, caravan, lorry or tractor thereafter, he identifies it correctly.

Our two innate abilities of organisation and adaptation are the building blocks of schema, essential for knowledge about our world and our ability to problem-solve in it.

INTERACTIVE

Look up The Jean Piaget Society at: http://www.piaget.org

Write a short biography of Jean Piaget.

Jerome Bruner

Figure 4.18 Jerome Bruner

Jerome Bruner, like Piaget, accepts that we are born with an innate predisposition to organise information coming to us from our world. He also says that as we age, this biological maturation allows for the development of more complex thinking and problem-solving strategies. He agreed with Piaget about the natural curiosity and inquisitiveness of children. He believed that our abstract knowledge about the world grows out of our actions and behaviours in it. Competence, or becoming good at something, comes with experience and practice.

Bruner's contribution to the cognitive approach concerns the ways children think about their world. He suggests that children have to develop progressively more sophisticated forms of knowledge in their minds to help them think and deal with life. The more complex they discover their world to be, the greater their need to use more complex ways of thinking about it. As a consequence, children use three different forms or **modes of representation** to think about their world.

- **The enactive mode,** from birth to age two, is the first mode children use to think about their world. Their world is represented (thought about/dealt with) in terms of their sensorimotor actions. This sounds complicated but all it need mean for us is that infants use a lot of gestures, facial expressions, and obvious emotions (crying, laughing), which mean something for them in their simple environment, and which others are able to interpret and act upon on their behalf.
- **The iconic mode** emerges from age two to five and concerns the growing child's use of *mental imagery* to think about, deal with, and represent their world. Showing itself just before the onset of language, the infant uses iconic mode thinking to form mental pictures to represent and remember people and objects in their environment. This is necessary because their world is becoming more complex. Gestures just will not do anymore. They begin to store *visual images* or mental pictures of their world in their mind.
- **The semantic mode** becomes evident around age seven+ when the child begins to represent or think about their world using *language*. Language is important in that it allows the young child to enquire, think about, deal with, and act upon their environment. This is

because words represent stimuli in the child's world. For Bruner, being able to use the semantic mode to think about the world is the key to intellectual growth and development.

Read more about Jerome Bruner and constructivist theory by visiting http://tip.psychology.org/bruner.html.

Applications of the cognitive approach

Here we will look at two areas of application that utilise the cognitive approach: perception and advertising, and memory and police investigations.

PERCEPTION AND ADVERTISING

Advertisers make money by attracting our attention to products they want us to buy. Very often there is very little to differentiate between similar products. One need only consider soap powder to appreciate this point. So what makes us choose between one brand and another? Whether we notice a particular product and become aware of it in the first place is the first step in the buying process. Getting our attention, and then changing our perception, is what advertising is all about. In considering advertising campaigns, it is worthwhile remembering that you cannot perceive something without attending to it, and you cannot attend to something without perceiving it.

> *'The topics of perception and attention merge into each other since both are concerned with the question of what we become aware of in our environment.'*
>
> *Greene & Hick (1984)*

INTERACTIVE

B.O.G.O.F.

Figure 4.19

Questions

1. What two posters are in each of the shop's windows?
2. Which one, if any, did you notice first?
3. What do you think the nonsense word means?
4. From the point of view of attention and perception (our senses, gestalten, and past experience), why do you think the B.O.G.O.F. campaign will be more successful than the SALE next door?

You might begin to see why psychologists are employed by the advertising, marketing, political, and public relations world? Or maybe not, it's all about ... perception!

MEMORY AND POLICE INVESTIGATIONS

The cognitive interview technique (CIT)

The globally popular CIT, developed in the 1970s and 1980s by Geiselman and Fisher in Los Angeles, is a *structured* interview where knowledge of cognitive processes is used to maximise witness recall of an event. The CIT particularly concerns perception, attention and memory. We should here note once again the integrative and active nature of our information processes.

Information is the most important element in any criminal investigation. The ability of police to get accurate and useful information from witnesses and/or victims of crimes is crucial. Often an eyewitness will tend to focus on what *they* think is important. Given the importance of *personal meaning* to our perception, attention and memory, this is understandable; however, important detail can become lost or forgotten and this can frustrate the efficiency of the police investigation.

The **cognitive interview** concerns how people remember. We store memories on the basis of particular aspects associated with them, most especially the context, or where the event happened, and just how personally meaningful the event was for us.

CIT encourages the eyewitness to (1) reconstruct the circumstances, (2) report everything, (3) recall the events in a different order, and (4) change perspectives. The method is systematic, and thus the sequence used (i.e. (1), (2), (3) and (4)) is important.

Reconstruct the circumstances

Here the officer would ask the witness to reconstruct the circumstances of the event in general. The witness essentially tells their story. This will give a general overview of the incident. The starting point might be the story of their day well before the incident itself. You ask them what they were doing, feeling or thinking.

Report everything

With an eye to the personal nature of attention and perception here the officer would encourage the witness not to withhold any detail, however trivial it might seem to be. Interestingly the interviewer here uses statements in the present tense like: 'What do you see? What is your immediate reaction?' They are trying to make the person relive the incident.

Recall the events in a different order

Here the police officer gets the witness to recount the story in different ways. This could mean from the beginning to the end, then the end to the beginning, or from a particular point from which the witness remembers a lot of detail. Other variations on this are the use of questions like: 'Of what you have told me, what stands out?' This is related to something in the study of perception called *figure and ground*. In order to make perceptual sense of our world we often unconsciously put aspects of a stimulus to the background, and other aspects of it to the foreground. Often this is done on the basis of what is important to you (foreground) and what is less important to you (background).

Recalling events in a different order is also a good lie detector! Lies are created and told in a logical order. Having a witness start at various stages confuses that order. Different order recall is most useful in catching out criminals, and naughty children too, for that matter!

Change perspective

The fourth general principle behind the CIT is where the police officer tries to get the witness to recall the incident from the perspective of where another person was standing, and involves asking questions like '*What was Richard doing while he was sitting in the Kay Park Tavern*?' or '*If you were sitting where Richard was sitting, what would you have seen?*'

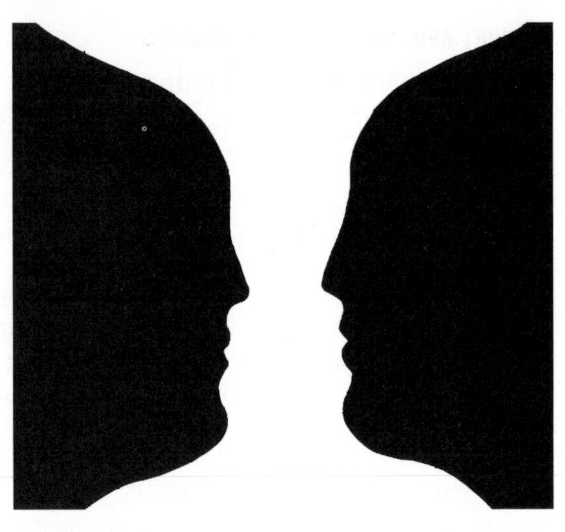

Figure 4.20 Uncannily, figure and ground work in two dimensions as well. Take this image called Rubin's Vase. What aspect of it is to the front, what aspect of it is to the back? Ask others what they see. Do you share the same figure and ground *perspective*, or point of view?

Having a witness mentally change perspectives like this enhances the quality of remembered information about the incident or event. Often a witness has a variety of perspectives on the incident, but most people will report what they remember from only one perspective, their own! Changing perspective should avoid this.

The effectiveness of CIT

Geiselman *et al.* (1986) compared the cognitive interview with the standard interview technique. Fifty-one participants saw a film of a simulated violent crime and were questioned about it two days later.

The table below shows their results, comparing the mean (average) number of items recalled using the cognitive and standard interview methods.

Table 4.3 Effectiveness of CIT

	Cognitive interview (CIT)	**Standard interview (SI)**
Items correctly recalled	42	35
Items incorrectly recalled	9	9

No difference was found in the number of errors made by participants undergoing the SI in comparison to the CIT. However witnesses questioned using SI recalled 35 correct items, whereas those questioned using the cognitive interview recalled 42 correct items.

In another set of trials based on real crime, Fisher *et al.* (1989) and Fisher & Geiselman (1988) compared the interview performance of pre- and post-CIT trained detectives. Results showed a 47 per cent gain in information got from witnesses after training. Further, in comparing information from witnesses elicited by CIT trained and untrained detectives, results showed those who used CIT got 63 per cent more information than their untrained colleagues. What CIT appears to indicate is that people often remember more than they think! The form of questioning that is used is one of the critical factors to eyewitness testimony in the reconstruction of memory.

The cognitive interview technique has come under criticism of late. Memon & Stevenage (1996) outline a number of mainly theoretical issues that concern CIT. These include the generalisability of the term itself, and the fact that in many police forces the CIT, as first proposed, has become a random and haphazard amalgam of different interview techniques.

INTERACTIVE

Investigate the University of Aberdeen Eyewitness Research Group and visit http://www.psyc.abdn.ac.uk/eyewitne.htm

Limitations of the cognitive approach

The cognitive approach assumes that our behaviour can largely be explained in terms of how the mind is felt to operate. As a result the approach likens our mind to a computer, inputting, storing and retrieving data about our external world using our information or mediational processes. As an approach it places emphasis on psychology being a science and relies heavily on laboratory experimentation upon which to base its theories. It has numerous useful applications, ranging from advice about the validity of eyewitness testimony to advertising and marketing. However, it has been criticised at a number of levels.

Lack of an agreed paradigm

Many cognitive theories exist but there is no single common overview or founding theory that holds the approach together. This is in contrast to the behaviourism with its behaviourist paradigm, as established by J.B. Watson in 1913.

Malim & Birch (1998) think that this is a consequence of no one theorist ever having dominated cognitive psychology. Many major figures are found within the approach but there is no clear link between them. Good examples of this would include Jean Piaget and his research into thinking and cognitive development in young children, R.L. Gregory (1972) and his work on visual perception and illusions, and Elizabeth Loftus (1979) with her work into memory and eyewitness testimony. Individually all these theorists have much to offer, but it is difficult to see common ground – apart from investigating one of our higher-level mental processes. It is useful to remember that while the cognitive approach studies mediational processes on an individual basis, it also tells us perception, attention, language, memory and thinking are very much integrated when seeking a comprehensive explanation regarding our behaviour.

The computer analogy: mechanistic and over-simplistic

The cognitive approach with its use of the computer analogy to explain our behaviour is limited. Likening us to a machine is mechanistic and over-simplistic. We do not think, feel and behave as computers do. Computers are infallible. They are logical and unemotional and if they produce faulty output this is always down to human error. Human beings on the other hand are very fallible! We are not logical, we make mistakes, emotions influence our behaviour or output, and so on. The computer analogy also inevitably de-emphasises the importance of our social world, and also the many internal biological factors behind what motivates us to action.

Ecological validity of cognitive research

Much research done in cognitive psychology comes from laboratory experiments. Laboratory experiments in psychology are often accused of being contrived, and therefore lacking in ecological validity. This means they are *unreal* in relation to our real-life affairs. A lot of research into memory focuses on a particular kind of memory that we came across earlier called episodic memory, or our memory for facts. There are however many different kinds of memory that we use in real life that have not been investigated too much by the cognitive approach. This may change.

There has been some interesting work done into our memory for smells, and how this might help those suffering from the very real and tragic affects of **senile dementia**. In 1969 Richman suggested a link between sensory problems and memory-related mental health difficulties in elderly people. Marcus (1983) extended this and suggested that sensory stimulation, such as the introduction of a long-forgotten smell, could be useful in bringing a *regressed* older person back in touch with their current reality. It is in all our interests that this avenue is explored further.

Conclusion

Once marginalised, the cognitive approach is nowadays at the heart of psychology. Or maybe that should be 'head'? It views us as an information processor, relying on the computer analogy to explain how we behave as we do. This is of course on the basis of how we obtain, store, use, and retrieve information about our outside world. In doing so it ignores the influence of our emotions, and how these are affected by our social experiences. The former will now be considered in the biological approach, with the relevance of social experience left until Chapter 6, and the humanistic approach.

Summary

The cognitive approach studies our information processes of perception, attention, language, memory and thinking, and how they influence our thoughts, feelings and behaviours. It considers each, and their contribution to our ability to operate successfully in our world. The cognitive approach rightfully views us as active processors of information from our outside world. We are not passive learners, as behaviourism would have us believe. This is emphasised in the mediational nature of our information processes as illustrated by the computer analogy. Individual cognitions further explore this fact. Perception for example is understood from the point of view of our senses working in tandem with an innate ability called gestalten, and our previous past experience of stimuli in our world. It is previous past experience that makes the difference between one person's perception and another's. What is meaningful to you also influences another crucial information process, memory, and as a result your ability, or otherwise, to think and problem-solve. All our information processes, while studied individually, work collectively as we operate in and through our environment. The cognitive approach has had a huge influence over the last thirty years, and continues to do so. It has been applied to the world of advertising, marketing, public relations, work, society, politics, etc. However, anything the cognitive approach discovers about our cognitions, and their influence on our behaviours has to be inferred. This is because cognitions are hypothetical constructs. This has led to criticisms, such as a lack of ecological validity, being levied at the approach. It also ignores biological and social factors as further reasons behind why we think, feel and behave as we do.

INTERACTIVE

1 Here you should find tutorials and demonstrations related to our senses. Choose a topic and have fun:
http://psych.hanover.edu/Krantz/sen_tut.html

2 Imagine you are a journalist. Using the following websites write a short biography of David Marr.
http://kybele.psych.cornell.edu/~edelman/marr/marr.html
http://www.princeton.edu/~freshman/science/marr/vision.html
http://www.richmond.edu/~pli/projects/project3/intro.html

3 Achieve good gestalt, and find out more about Koffka, Kohler and Wertheimer @
http://www.dushkin.com/connectext/psy/ch04/bio4.mhtml
http://www.unb.ca/web/courses/fields/module/textbook/ch1pt2e.html
http://www.sonoma.edu/people/Daniels/Gestalt1.html

4 Find out how good your own memory is, and learn a bit of psychology on the way, by visiting
http://www.wiu.edu/users/mfbpa/drmfirst.html

Structured questions with answer guidelines

1 *Define and explain the cognitive approach in psychology.*

With reference to the preceding chapter, structure your answer around the following model:

- Define the cognitive approach as an approach that understands us from the point of view of information processing. Possibly give brief history. Refer to perception, attention, language, memory and thinking. Identify that they help us obtain, organise and use information from our world, to help us respond to/in it. Discuss the active nature of our information processes in the light of the computer analogy (S–X–R) and mediational processes. Then explain:
  - perception: definition
  - detail of each element to perception, i.e. senses plus gestalten, plus experiences. Give examples from psychology and real life
  - memory: definition
  - detail about coding (acoustic, visual, and semantic), storage (SR, STM, LTM), and retrieval (types/storage on the basis of properties, e.g. sound, visual, semantic content). Give examples from psychology and real life
  - thinking: definition
  - detail about how we think. Piaget (organisation and schema: adaptation, assimilation and accommodation: equilibrium and disequilibrium). Bruner and modes of representation. Give examples from psychology and real life.

2 *How is the cognitive approach applied in practice?*

Structure your answer as follows:

- Identify the cognitive approach as an approach that understands us from the point of view of information processing. Explain what this means.
- Explain perception and attention with reference to:
  - advertising, marketing, etc. (this chapter has lots more than just these two practical applications of perception, e.g. the lying architect). Refer to some psychologists
  - give examples from psychology and real life
  - memory, the police and the cognitive interview technique. Refer to some psychologists, e.g. Geiselman, Memon and Stevenage.

3 *What criticisms may be made of the cognitive approach?*

Identify and explain limitations, i.e.:

- lack of agreed identity
- the mechanistic computer analogy
- ecological validity.

Glossary

Carpentered: a man-made built/structured environment of angles and straight lines that often give the illusion of space/depth i.e. Müller–Lyer

Cognitive interview: an interview technique sometimes used by the police which draws on knowledge of cognitive psychology to enhance eyewitness recall of an event

Egocentrism: viewing the world from only your point of view. Babies are egocentric and are also unaware that others have a view or perspective on the same thing

Eidetic memory: photographic memory, rare in adulthood

Gestalt: German, meaning 'whole' or 'configuration'. We perceive our world in terms of 'organised wholes'

Laws of pragnänz: Gestalt theory concerning how we organise stimuli in our world in terms of uniformity

Mediational processes: our information processes of perception, attention, language, memory and thinking. Mediational processes come between stimulus input, or what we sensorily experience, and output, our response to it

Mental representation: how we think about our world

Modes of representation: different ways of thinking about our world, e.g. Bruner's enactive, iconic and semantic modes in childhood

Schema: in the Piagetian sense, an organised body of knowledge/abilities that changes due to experience

Senile dementia: progressive wasting of brain cells or loss of brain function caused by the destruction, or atrophy, of the frontal lobes of the brain. Senile dementia, of which **Alzheimer's disease** is the most common, leads to progressive deterioration of mental functioning, with onset being slow, over years rather than months. Short-term memory is affected first, with a sufferer occasionally forgetting what happened hours or minutes ago. Sufferers have difficulty following conversations, keeping a train of thought, and making sense of what they see or read. In its early stages, a person is well aware of what is happening, and even in later stages, their confusion may be punctuated by moments of lucidity. 700,000 people are reported to have senile dementia in the UK

5

The biological approach

BY THE END OF THIS CHAPTER YOU SHOULD BE ABLE TO:

- **define and explain the biological approach with reference to its key features**
- **explain applications of the biological approach**
- **explain the limitations of the biological approach.**

Overview of the biological approach

In psychology, the biological approach gives a biological answer to the '*Who am I?*' question. It is related to the science of medicine, and consequently sometimes finds itself called the medical, or medical–biological approach. The biological approach suggests that our biology, or more precisely our physiology and genetics, cause us to think, feel and behave as we do. The biological approach believes we become ill, medically and/or psychologically, because of physiological or genetic damage, disease or accident. Because of its focus on genetics and physiology, the biological approach therefore examines thoughts, feelings and behaviours almost exclusively from a medical, biological or physical point of view. This chapter will explore the relationship between brain function and behaviour, and then examine evolution, genetics and human behaviour. Applications of the biological approach will emphasise its use of physical therapies in the control of biologically based mental disorders. Limitations of the biological approach, as being reductionist, mechanistic and deterministic, will also be considered, as will the ethics of animal research.

Key features of the biological approach

The biological approach understands us as a result of the inter-relationship between our mind, our physiology, our genetics, and our behaviours.

In Chapter 1, we came across the French philosopher, René Descartes (1596–1650). He proposed that human beings are made up of two parts, the mind and the body. In the terms of the middle ages, the mind was taken to be the human soul, and a separate entity to the body. Descartes called the relationship between our mind and body dualism. Mind interacted with body and when the body died, according to Descartes, the mind, or soul lived on. Descartes felt that the mind had some influence on the body through the pineal gland, which is a structure found at the base of the brain. Whether this is the case is debatable, but nowadays within the biological approach, great emphasis is placed on our physical internal state, in conjunction with our brain, as influencing our behaviour.

What is the biological approach?

The biological approach in psychology attempts to understand us on the basis of the interrelationship between our mind, our physiology, our genetics and our behaviours. Our physiology is our *physical* being, and consists of our bodily processes and functions. Also important to an understanding of how *physiology* affects behaviours is our brain and spinal cord, or central nervous system. The biological approach is further influenced by genetics. Genetics are those particular biological characteristics that individuals inherit from their parents, and also those common biologically based abilities or characteristics that species have evolved over time.

Physiology and genetics

The biological approach makes two important claims. The first is that all our thoughts, emotions, and behaviours can be traced to physical events in the nervous system. The second is that much human and non-human activity occurs as a consequence of our evolutionary history. Given that the biological approach understands us on the basis of the relationship between our mind, our physiology, our genetics and our behaviours, all our problems will necessarily have a physiological or genetic cause. The biological approach believes we become ill, medically and/or psychologically, because of physiological or genetic damage, disease or accident. This is why the biological approach is interested in the structure and function of our nervous system and in genetics. When someone *does* become ill, medically or psychologically, the biological approach will always look to a physiological or genetic reason as to why this has happened. Medical or psychological illness will be as a result of faulty physiology or genetics.

Physiological psychology and evolutionary psychology

These two perspectives have been given much impetus of late, and today we find them growing apart within the biological approach. One contemporary branch of psychology is physiological psychology, with its particular emphasis on brain function and behaviour. Physiological psychology investigates where behaviours occur in the brain, and looks at emotion, motivation, stress, dreams and dream states, etc. There is also the emerging area of evolutionary psychology, precipitated by the work of Charles Darwin in the nineteenth century, the discovery of DNA in the mid-twentieth century, and the human genome project of the early twenty-first century. Evolutionary psychology emphasises, perhaps not surprisingly, Darwin and evolution. This sees an interest in such issues as heredity and human sexual behaviour, aggression, intelligence and genetically influenced disorders.

Let us first turn to physiological psychology and its place in the biological approach.

Physiological psychology and the nervous system

> *'... Biopsychology's unique contribution to neuroscientific research is a knowledge of behaviour and of the methods of behavioural research ... the ultimate purpose of the nervous system is to produce and control behaviour.'*
>
> *(Pinel, 1993)*

A long-standing explanation of human behaviour within the biological approach, the physiological perspective understands us from the point of view of physical events within our nervous system. Put another way, physiological psychology believes we think, feel and behave the way we do because of our bodily processes and functions. It understands us as a result of our nervous system.

The nervous system of the human body consists of a number of divisions and subdivisions. The two interrelated divisions of the human nervous system are the central nervous system, or CNS, and the peripheral nervous system, or PNS. Before looking at the nervous system in particular, it is important to introduce a major factor to our physiology, the **neuron**. Neurons help communication in the body.

Neurons

As we discovered when we looked at the cognitive approach, we receive information about our environment via our sensory organs, which are our eyes, ears and nose. This information is transmitted to the brain, which sees us react almost instantaneously in some way. How this happens is that our nervous system gets this information to our brain, and then to the rest of the body, through an intricate network of between 10–12 billion specialised nerve cells called neurons. Neurons are the cells in our body that mostly make up our nervous system. Neurons receive, process, and/or transmit information to, and from, the brain to all parts of our body. Eighty per cent of neurons are to be found in the outer layer of the brain known as the cerebral cortex. As we may also remember from the cognitive approach, the only energy our brain and internal body understands is electrical energy. When an external energy is picked up by the physiology of our senses, be it pressure, light or sound, it is converted into electrical energy. It is the job of our neurons to convey this information to our brain to be processed, understood and acted upon.

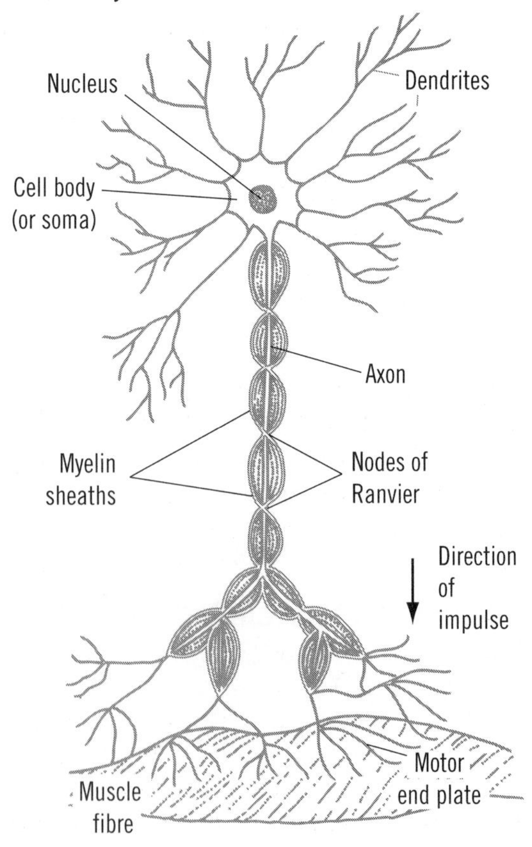

Figure 5.1 Diagram of a motor neuron

Anatomy of a neuron

The cell body, or soma, of a neuron consists of its nucleus, which houses our genetic code, and cytoplasm, from which the nucleus feeds. The dendrites help each neuron make electrochemical contact with its neighbours. The axon, a thin cylinder of protoplasm, carries signals received by dendrites to other neurons, muscles or glands. With some neurons, a white fatty substance called the myelin sheath surrounds the axon and insulates it, which helps in the transmission of electrochemical signals to the terminal buttons, or synaptic knobs. Synaptic knobs transmit neural impulses directly from the axon of one neuron to the dendrites of another.

Types of neuron

Neurons are of three main types. Our nerves are made up of bundles of neurons. Most neurons receive information from other neurons, and pass this information on.

- **Sensory neurons** (also called afferent neurons) respond directly to external stimuli from our environment. Sensory neurons carry messages from our sense organs *to* the spinal cord and brain.
- **Motor neurons** (also called efferent neurons) carry messages *from* the brain and spinal cord to our muscles and glands.
- **Interneurons** (also called connector or association neurons) link neuron to neuron, and integrate sensory and motor neurons. Only very occasionally do motor and sensory neurons connect directly.

Communication between neurons: neurotransmitters

We find a most interesting molecule in the synaptic knob called a **neurotransmitter**. Neurotransmitters are the chemical messengers of our body. It is reported that a synaptic knob can contain between 10 and 100,000 neurotransmitters. Neurotransmitters, in the form of electrochemical impulses are produced by neurons, and jump from neuron to neuron as information is passed throughout the body. The point, or junction, at which neurotransmitters cross from neuron to neuron, is called the synapse. These neurotransmitters, or electrochemical impulses, jump across from each synapse of a neuron to be received by *receptor cells* in the dendrites of other neurons.

Glial cells

What helps the passage of information from one neuron to another are our glial cells. Glial cells are a kind of glue that were once thought to fill in the spaces between our billions of neurons. Young (1994) suggests that they are much more complex than first thought. They are smaller and ten times more plentiful than neurons, and are able to pass signals to each other, receive signals from neurons, and perhaps send signals to neurons. They are thought to play a role in brain development, and provide the nutrients and building blocks for neurons themselves. One type of glial cell, the oligodendrocyte, makes up the myelin sheath, which insulates the axon of a neuron.

Motor neurone disease (MND)

As we have discovered, sensory neurons carry information to the brain from our senses, while motor neurons carry information from our brain to our muscles. With MND, these motor neurons degenerate and muscles supplied by them lose their strength. The cause of MND is unknown, but it is not infectious. It normally becomes evident in people over 40. The Scottish Motor Neurone Disease Association believes that 2.2 people per 100,000 develop MND per annum, which in real terms sees about 100 new MND sufferers per year in Scotland.

MND is of three kinds. Amyotrophic lateral sclerosis (ALS) is the most common. Symptoms of ALS include weakness and stiffness in the hands and feet, tripping when walking, and dropping things. Another type of motor neuron disease is progressive muscular atrophy (PMA), which afflicts about eight per cent of sufferers. Symptoms of PMA include weakness and wasting of muscles in one hand, which progressively spreads to other limbs. The most distressing form of MND is progressive bulbar palsy (PBP). PBP affects those muscles responsible for chewing, talking and swallowing. Eating becomes a progressive problem. Speech may deteriorate, as can mobility.

Myelin and multiple sclerosis

Myelin is the white fatty substance that insulates our neurons. Neurons pass signals, in the form of neurotransmitters from one part of the body to another.

The destruction of myelin surrounding nerves in the CNS is thought to accelerate the onset of acquired diseases such as multiple sclerosis. Multiple sclerosis (MS) affects 85,000 people in the UK from around age 20 to 50. MS sees a sufferer alternate between relapse and remission. Periods of remission unfortunately grow shorter with the passage of time. The symptoms of MS include any combination of spastic paraparesis, unsteady gait, diplopia and incontinence.

ORGANISATION OF THE NERVOUS SYSTEM

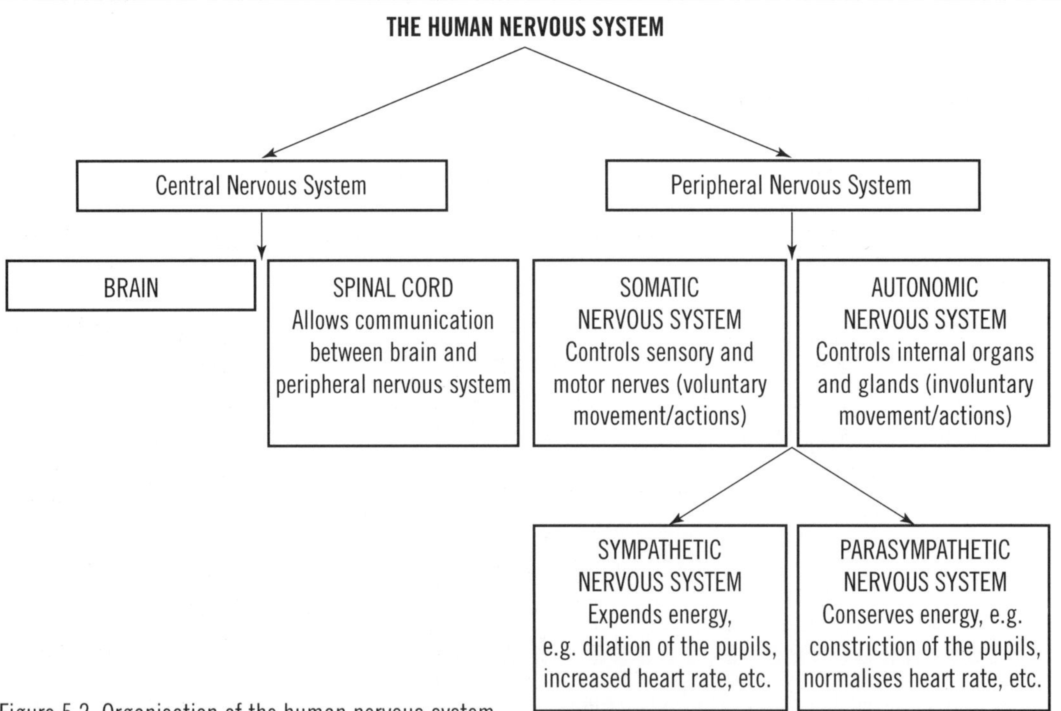

Figure 5.2 Organisation of the human nervous system

THE HUMAN NERVOUS SYSTEM

Our human nervous system consists of our central nervous system, the brain and spinal cord, and our peripheral nervous system.

The peripheral nervous system sends information about our environment, via the senses, to our central nervous system, and also assists the CNS to send information to our muscles and glands.

THE PERIPHERAL NERVOUS SYSTEM

Our peripheral nervous system consists of two subdivisions, the somatic and the autonomic nervous systems, and connects our brain to our outside world.

The somatic nervous system deals with our external environment and controls our sensory and motor nerves, which account for our voluntary movements and actions. The autonomic nervous system controls our internal world, or internal bodily environment. Together they make up the nerves in our body that connect our brain and spinal cord to our senses, our internal organs, and our glands.

The somatic nervous system

Two types of nerves are found in the somatic nervous system, sensory nerves and motor nerves. **Sensory nerves** transmit information about our external environment to our central nervous system, which make us aware of pain, pressure and temperature variation. The **motor nerves** of the somatic system carry impulses from the central nervous system to the muscles of the body, where they initiate action. All the muscles which we use to engage in voluntary actions and movements such as walking and smiling are controlled by the motor nerves of the somatic nervous system. These motor nerves also govern the involuntary movements we make to adjust our posture and balance.

The autonomic nervous system

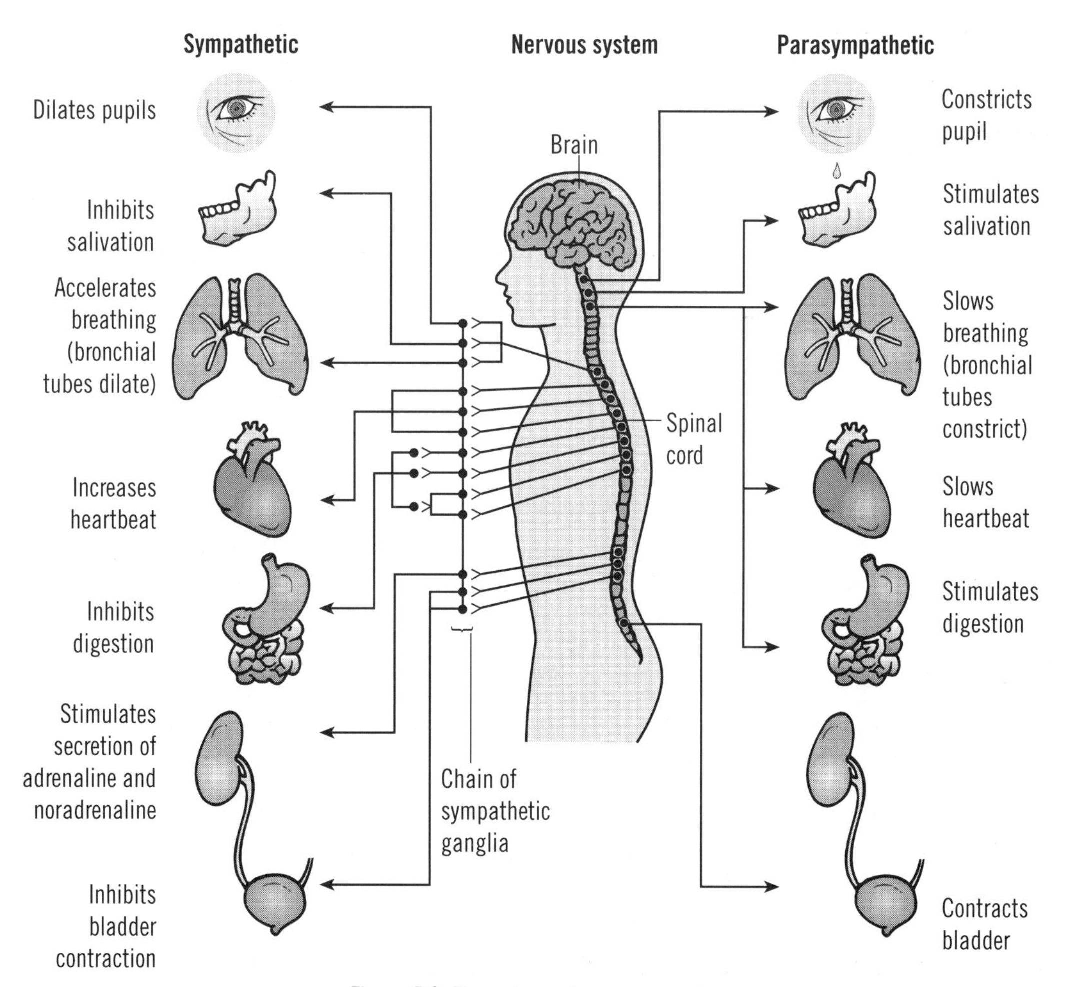

Figure 5.3 The autonomic nervous system

The autonomic nervous system or ANS (see Figure 5.3) controls our internal organs and glands over which we have little voluntary control. The function of the ANS is to regulate our internal bodily environment by sending information to our CNS, which directs any necessary adjustments. The ANS is subdivided into two branches, the sympathetic branch, and the parasympathetic branch. The sympathetic branch of our ANS moves us to action in our world. What this means is that the sympathetic branch of the ANS operates when we have to use, or expend, energy. The parasympathetic branch of our ANS operates when we have to restore this expended energy to our body. The sympathetic and parasympathetic branches of our autonomic nervous system are therefore said to be **antagonistic** to each other. Simply put, as one pulls in one direction, the other pulls in the other direction. This is to return the body to a state of **homeostasis**, or internal balance.

The sympathetic and parasympathetic branches and homeostasis

The sympathetic branch of our ANS is made up of bundles of neurons that run up either side of our spinal cord to our brain. The ANS directs and drives our bodily response to stressful environmental situations, such as emergencies (Cannon, 1927). In an emergency we can become aware of our sympathetic branch as it increases our heart rate, dilates our pupils, increases our breathing and dries our mouth. All this is necessary to focus energy outwards to deal with the situation. When the emergency has passed, the parasympathetic branch of our ANS takes over to return our body to its natural state of homeostasis. To achieve homeostasis, which is a constant, calm, comfortable internal bodily environment, the parasympathetic branch constricts the pupil, stimulates salivation, constricts our bronchial tubes, etc.

Fight or flight

The role of the sympathetic branch of the ANS

The sympathetic branch of the ANS is responsible for the *flight or fight* syndrome (Cannon, 1927). When we are startled or threatened, the sympathetic branch of our ANS reacts by quickly releasing a number of hormones. One of these hormones, epinephrine (also called adrenaline), has several effects on our body. It increases our heart and breathing rates, it changes our circulation so that more oxygen goes to the muscles needed for running or fighting, and it increases alertness and our perception. Hence the reason why our pupils dilate, or get larger, in order to maximise visual information about the threat or danger. Our senses, nerves, and muscles therefore go into *high gear* so that we can perceive any threat or danger much more quickly and accurately than normal, and respond to it faster and with more agility. On this basis we decide to take flight, or alternatively stay and fight.

Can you tell if someone fancies you?

When we are sexually attracted to someone, we unconsciously communicate our desire by dilating (enlarging) the pupils in our eyes. This is because our pupils, driven by the sympathetic branch of the ANS, *naturally* enlarge when we are sexually attracted to someone. The recipient of your desire unconsciously picks up this electrochemical signal.

The importance of the pupils to interpersonal attraction has been known for thousands of years. Women in Ancient Egypt used to wear kohl around their eyes in order to attract interest. Kohl is the forerunner of eyeshadow! Belladonna (literally, beautiful lady), an extract from the plant

Deadly Nightshade, was also long used as an eyedrop artificially to dilate women's pupils, in order to increase their sexual allure.

The endocrine system

The endocrine system is a network of glands that manufacture and secrete chemical messengers called **hormones** into the bloodstream. These powerful chemical messengers act on structures and functions throughout our body. Our endocrine system is important to our physical development and complex psychological behaviours.

Although the endocrine system is not part of the human nervous system as such, it is related to the activities of our autonomic nervous system. Our brain's **hypothalamus** and the pituitary gland, known as our *master gland*, direct the autonomic nervous system to activate the endocrine system to stimulate the release of hormones in our body. These hormones are secreted into the blood, and travel throughout the body to control a wide variety of bodily activities.

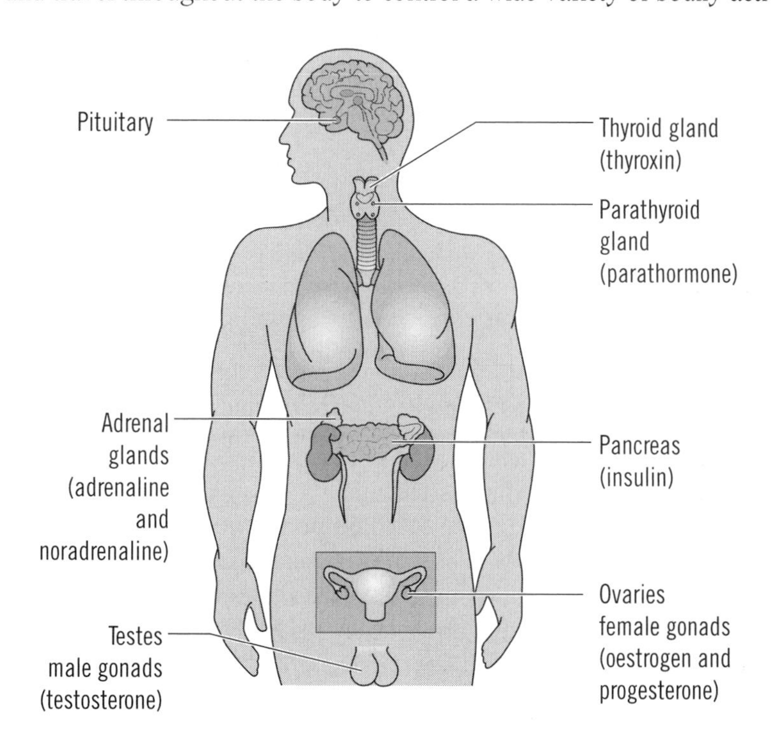

Figure 5.4 The endocrine system

The pituitary gland

The pituitary gland is our most important gland, in that it produces the largest number of hormones, and also controls the release of hormones by other endocrine glands. Gonadotrophin is a hormone, produced by the pituitary gland, which ends up at the gonads. In the gonads it stimulates the production of oestrogen, progesterone and some testosterone in females, and of testosterone in males. During puberty, oestrogen stimulates breast development and causes the vagina, uterus (womb) and fallopian tubes (that carry eggs to the womb) to mature. It also plays a role in the adolescent growth spurt and alters the distribution of fat in females, resulting in more fat being deposited around the hips, buttocks, and thighs. Oestrogen is important in preparing a female's body for childbirth. Testosterone helps to promote muscle and bone growth, and is linked to aggression.

Hormones

Probably the most common of hormones is **adrenaline**, which we came across above in relation to *flight or fight*. Adrenaline is central to emotions such as fear, anger and aggression. The ANS, hypothalamus and pituitary gland all have a role in the production of adrenaline. The effects of adrenaline include:

- increase in heart rate
- increase in oxygen intake and breathing patterns
- the release of sugar stored in the liver and muscles into the bloodstream as glycogen – this is our inner fuel or energy to help us fight or flight
- the reduction of blood supply to less important parts of the body, by the hypothalamus and ANS, to focus energy outwards towards dealing with the stimulus that has got us into this emotional state (fear, anger, aggression).

Another example is **somatotrophin**, our growth hormone. This is evident throughout infancy, childhood, adolescence, and adulthood. Somatotrophin is secreted by our pituitary gland and influences the growth of our bones and muscles, and is ultimately responsible for our adult height. Too much somatotrophin can lead to gigantism, while too little can lead to pituitary dwarfism.

Oxytocin, which is secreted by the hypothalamus, acts on the uterus, or womb, stimulating contractions during childbirth, and lactation when breast-feeding.

Insulin is produced in our pancreas to control our blood-sugar levels. Too much sugar in the bloodstream occurs in diabetes, which is potentially fatal unless treated. One new way to treat diabetes may be to use another hormone called **adiponectin**. Adiponectin is produced naturally by fat cells and encourages the body to burn up fat. Adiponectin, as a potential treatment for diabetes, came to light after teams of scientists in Japan and New York found the high blood-sugar levels of laboratory-bred diabetic mice dramatically reduced a few hours after receiving an injection of adiponectin (Scherer & Salteil, 2001). There is also some evidence to suggest that a difficulty in producing the hormone adiponectin is connected with obesity.

INTERACTIVE

Briefly describe the purpose of each of the following:

Gonadotrophin, testosterone, oestrogen, adrenaline, somatotrophin, oxytocin, insulin, adiponectin and thyroxine.

Table 5.1 The role of the endocrine glands in the production of hormones

Pituitary gland	The link between our brain and endocrine system. It is the master gland controlling many more hormones. Important in the production of the growth hormone, somatotrophin and of gonadotrophin
Thyroid gland	Controls the body's metabolism by producing the hormone, thyroxine
Testes/ovaries	Testes produce the androgen, testosterone, related to aggression. The ovaries produce oestrogen, important to childbirth
Adrenal gland	Produces adrenaline responsible for the fight or flight mechanism
Pancreas	Produces insulin, which regulates blood-sugar levels. A lack of insulin causes diabetes

The central nervous system

The central nervous system consists of our brain and spinal cord.

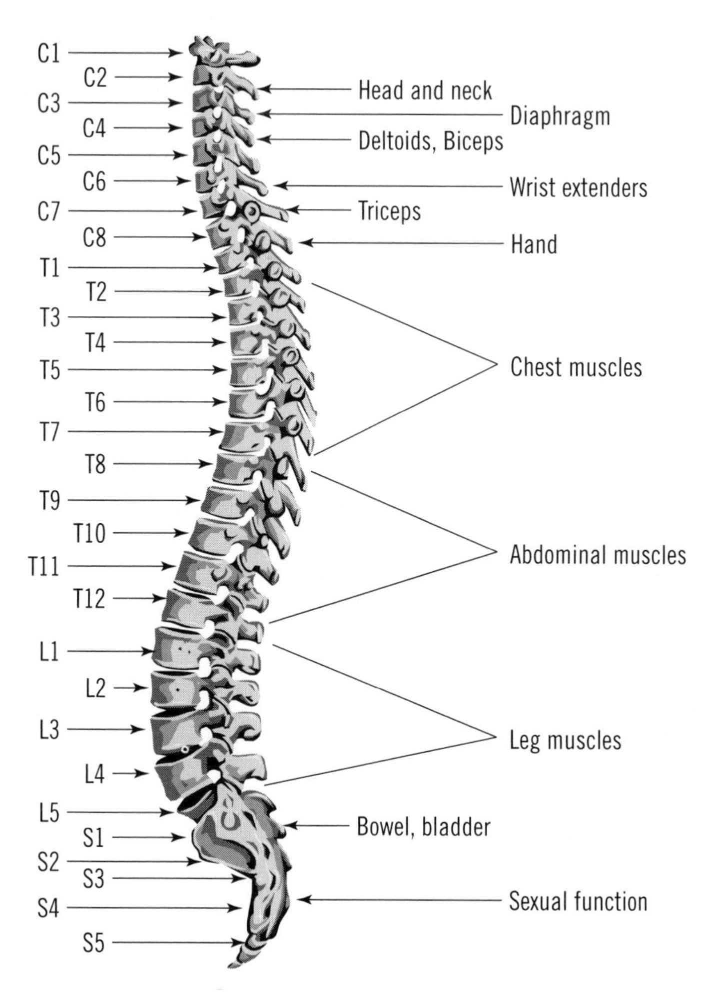

Figure 5.5 The spinal cord, the vertebrae and related body functions and structures

The spinal cord

Figure 5.6 Christopher Reeve

Our spinal cord travels all the way down our back and connects our brain with the rest of our body. Our spinal cord is like a fibre optic cable that allows communication between our central nervous system and our peripheral nervous system. Any damage or accident to the vertebrae and nerves in the spinal cord can have devastating results. Around 1000 people a year in the UK aquire a spinal cord injury, mostly through accident. In the USA, this number is tenfold.

A damaged spinal cord effectively cuts off the communication link between the brain, spinal cord, peripheral nervous system, and the muscles. The effect can be widespread paralysis. The physical effect of a spinal injury is vividly brought to mind in the case of Christopher Reeve, the actor who ironically once played *Superman*. He fell off a horse in 1995 and became extensively paralysed as a result of damage to a number of his spinal vertebrae. From a humanistic perspective (which we will turn to in the next chapter), it could be said that Reeve turned his tragic condition to his advantage. He continues to work today both as an actor, director and as a leading advocate for research into spinal cord injury. Reeve's high profile has seen much focus on the condition, with scientists getting more hopeful that damaged nerve fibres in the spinal cord will soon be able to be re-grown. This, it is thought, should restore the communication between the CNS and the PNS that may allow Reeve, and others, to walk again.

Research sponsored by the charity Action Research allowed Dr James Fawcett of the Cambridge University Centre for Brain Repair, to report in April 2001 on an exciting bacterial enzyme called chondroitinase. One reason that the nerve fibres in a damaged spinal cord do not regenerate is because of scar tissue. Chondroitinase appears to help overcome this problem. Fawcett injected the enzyme into rats with injured spinal cords. Subsequent tests proved they could walk again. This must open up the possibility of the enzyme being used in human patients with spinal injuries. At the moment, patients in the UK cannot get National Health Service treatment to promote nerve regeneration after a spinal cord injury. For Christopher Reeve and the tens of thousands worldwide who become casualties to spinal injury and paralysis, this research is seen as a priority and should be heavily resourced.

The brain

The function of our brain is threefold. It:

- takes in information, via our senses, about stimuli in our external environment
- processes and interprets this information to allow us to make sense of it, and then

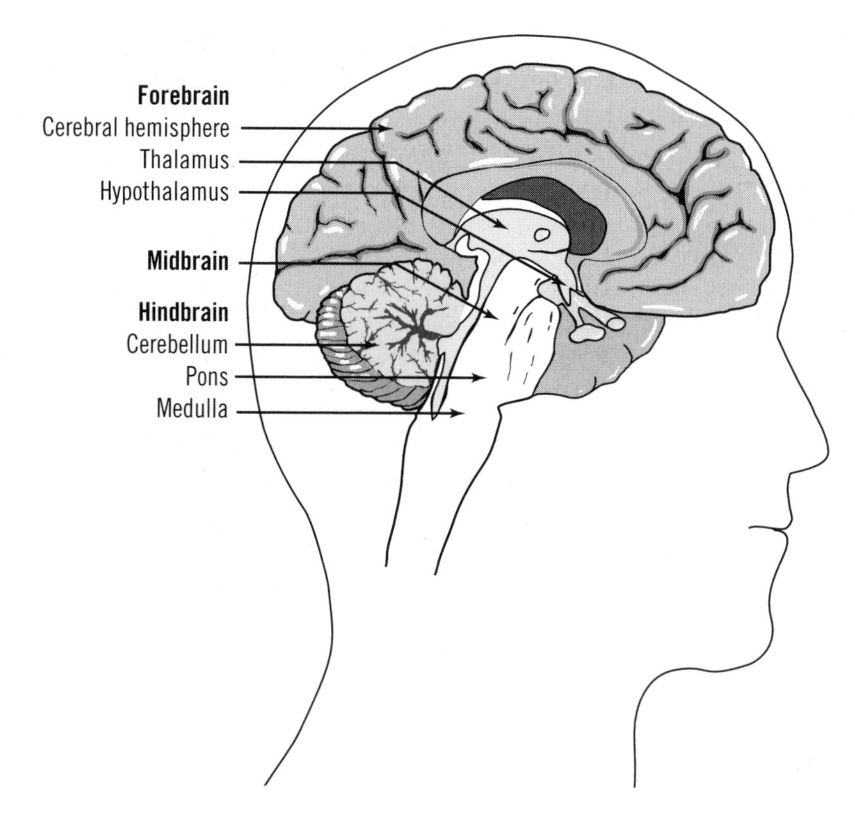

Figure 5.7 The human brain

- directs us, consciously or unconsciously, to think, feel, and/or behave in a particular way towards these stimuli.

Information received by us about our outside world, and from the rest of the body, converges at the brain to be processed, understood and acted upon. Our brain is a hugely complex information-processor. Its power is due to its make-up. It comprises between 8–12 billion neurons, each of which will have between 1,000 and 10,000 synapses connecting with other neurons. Remembering that the body communicates on the basis of neurotransmitters, or electrochemical signals, the permutations here are awesome. The number of ways neurons in a human brain can be connected and interconnected exceeds the estimated number of atoms that go to make up our universe. Via nerve impulses, communication occurs between the brain and the spinal cord, and also between the brain and twelve pairs of **cranial nerves**. Some of our cranial nerves are *mixed*, containing both sensory and motor axons. Some, like the optic and olfactory nerves, contain sensory axons only, and some contain motor axons only, an example being the cranial nerves that control the muscles of our eyeball!

The structure and functions of the brain

The human brain has three parts: the forebrain, the midbrain and the hindbrain. The forebrain is at the top of our head, the midbrain is hidden, while the hindbrain is at the bottom of our head and extends into the top of our spinal cord.

The forebrain

The **cerebrum** is the largest part of the human forebrain and is divided into two separate cerebral hemispheres: the right cerebral hemisphere and the left cerebral hemisphere (see below). The visible part of our cerebrum, or the outermost layer of our brain, is called our cerebral cortex.

The cerebral cortex

The two hemispheres of the cerebrum have numerous interconnections, especially through the hidden **corpus callosum**, a bundle of about 200 million nerve fibres that transfers information back and forth between the two hemispheres. Most of the nerve fibres connecting the brain to the various parts of the body cross from left to right, or from right to left. This means that the right cerebral hemisphere receives sensory messages from, and controls movement, on the left hand side of the body, while the left cerebral hemisphere receives sensory messages from, and controls movement on, the right hand side of the body.

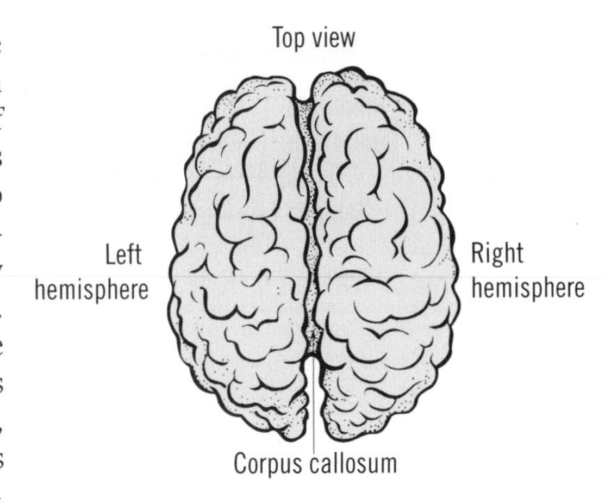

Figure 5.8 The cerebral cortex

Psychology has found that different parts of the cerebral cortex make different contributions to the same functions. Take language. In 1869, Paul Broca reported on a patient who had received a head injury and became unable to talk. He could, however, understand what was being said to him. When the patient died, a post-mortem was performed and a lesion was found on the left cerebral hemisphere. This area is now called **Broca's area** and is responsible for our ability to articulate, or produce speech. Later in 1878, Wernicke came across a patient who had an injury to a different part of the left cerebral cortex. This patient could talk, but could not understand what was being said to him. This led to the discovery of **Wernicke's area,** which allows us to comprehend, or understand speech.

THE BRAIN AND LANGUAGE

Our early infancy sees the biological maturation of those parts of our brain responsible for memory. When we looked at the cognitive approach, we discovered that our brain organises and stores different types of memory on the basis of different properties in different parts of the brain. We store and retrieve memories of/for sounds in our temporal lobe. We remember what we see using our visual cortex. We recognise and remember patterns using our parietal lobe. We store and retrieve our memories of faces in our frontal lobe. Memory is thus a whole-brain information

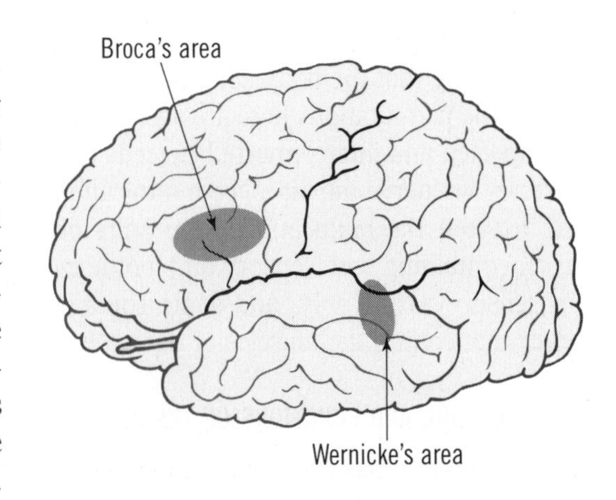

Figure 5.9 Broca's and Wernicke's areas

process. By age two, our memory structure is the same as that of an adult. This gives us the ability to remember, among other things, which combination of sounds corresponds to which given objects in our complex world. Biological maturation of the brain is therefore important to language development. We put sounds together simply, and then in a more complex fashion, to enquire about things, and to put forward our own point of view. By age two most infants can communicate in two- or three-word sentences, can think through simple problems explained to them, and have a basic understanding of the power of *language* to get what they want!

All this is related to the work of the famous psycholinguist Noam Chomsky. A psycholinguist is someone who studies the origins, development and importance of language for human beings. Chomsky (1959) argues that as human beings we are born with a biological predisposition towards acquiring language. Our brains are essentially hard-wired, or programmed, to enable us to acquire, understand and use language. Chomsky suggests we have to trigger and nurture this innate language acquisition device (LAD) in language interactions with others, otherwise we can lose the ability to vocalise. We suffer the effects of language privation as a result. Language privation is the cognitive, social and emotional effect of *never* having acquired the ability to communicate in the first place. The development of language depends to a great extent on physical/biological developments in our brain, or cerebral cortex.

INTERACTIVE

Consider the following questions.

1 Why do you think is it important to learn to talk?

2 What biological evidence is there for Chomsky's LAD?

3 Do you think infants are hard-wired and have a biological predisposition to acquire language? Give reasons for your answer.

4 At what age do you think we should start to learn foreign languages? Give reasons for your answer.

The thalamus

The **thalamus** is found at the centre of the forebrain and straddles the left and right cerebral hemispheres. The thalamus is a pivotal structure in the direction of information throughout the nervous system, and governs the flow of sensory information around our brain. It can be seen as a kind of relay station for all our senses. The thalamic nuclei also relay commands between the motor cortex and our skeletal muscles.

The hypothalamus

The **hypothalamus** is a small nucleic structure situated just below the thalamus, which plays an important role in controlling the satisfaction of our physical needs. Parts of the hypothalamus of note include the dorsal hypothalamus, concerned with pleasure-seeking, the posterior hypothalamus concerned with sex drive, and the ventromedial hypothalamus, concerned with hunger. The hypothalamus consequently influences eating, drinking and sexual activity. As indicated earlier when we considered the sympathetic and parasympathetic nervous system, the hypothalamus also governs homeostasis in the body. It does this by monitoring our bodily functions, and setting off homeostatic mechanisms if the internal environment begins to deviate from optimum

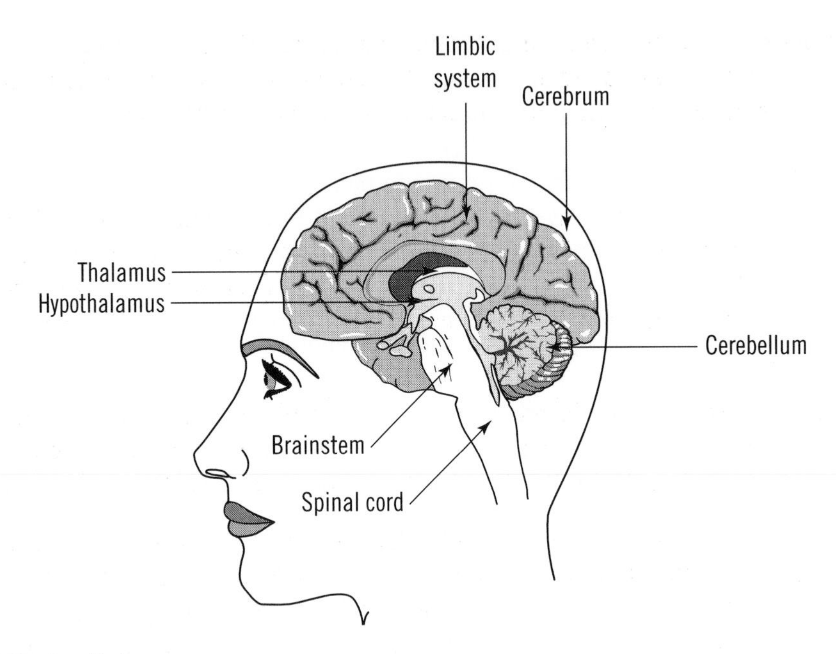

Figure 5.10 The hypothalamus

levels. For instance, if our bodies overheat, we sweat in order to cool down. Sweating is a homeostatic mechanism. The hypothalamus also plays an important role in our bodily reaction to stress. (See page 106.)

The basal ganglia

The basal ganglia are found in front of the thalamus. Their function is to control our muscle and fine bodily movements. Damage to the basal ganglia affects body posture, and muscle movement. This can be *manifested* (or seen), in jerks, tremors and twitches. The basal ganglia are also important in the production of dopamine. The deterioration of the basal ganglia is thought to be linked to Parkinson's disease.

The limbic system

The limbic system, almost at the junction of the forebrain and midbrain, consists of several structures that are important to our emotions, or how we feel. One structure in our limbic system, the **amygdala**, is often called the *window to the soul.* It is a most intriguing structure that is crucial to our ability to perceive and respond instantaneously to danger in our world. The amygdala *provokes* us to feel fear and be aggressive, important behaviours to self-survival since the beginnings of time. It is thought that damage to the amygdala is linked to psychological difficulties such as panic attacks, anxiety and depression, and sometimes, psychosis. Panic attacks, anxiety, and depression may involve feelings of overwhelming fear, while the symptoms of some psychoses may feature overwhelming aggression.

The midbrain

The midbrain occupies only a small part of the human cerebrum. The midbrain in other species is much larger. Structures in out midbrain include the reticular formation, which gathers input from higher level brain centres and passes it on to motor neurons. The substantia nigra helps coordinate our bodily movements, while the ventral tegmental area (VTA) has been discovered to be associated with our pleasure-seeking behaviour. This is because it is packed with dopamine-releasing neurons, an important hormone concerned with emotion.

The hindbrain

The **cerebellum** lies behind the *pons* underneath our two cerebral hemispheres. The cerebellum is very wrinkled, much like a cauliflower. It is responsible for muscle tone, balance, and the coordination of our voluntary movements. The cerebellum assists in controlling our physical activity. The cerebellum operates our complex motor behaviour, leaving the rest of our brain free for more conscious and deliberate activities.

The **pons** is the bridge between the midbrain and the medulla. The pons connects our spinal cord with our brain, and parts of our brain with each other. It integrates movement on both sides of our body, and is important to functions such as breathing, alertness, sleep and attention.

Finally in the hindbrain we find the **medulla**, which is part of our *brain stem*. It is around 4cm in diameter, and continues into our spinal cord. The medulla contains all the nerve fibres that connect the spinal cord to the brain. The medulla regulates our breathing, swallowing, digestion, and heartbeat. These basic bodily functions are essential to us, but for the most part we tend to be unaware of them while they are happening.

Animal research and the biological approach

Research methods used by the biological approach include experiment and observation. We have previously been looking at the structure and function of parts of our brain. How has psychology discovered such *localisation of brain function*?

Jose Delgado (1969) used observation in a laboratory setting to investigate the localisation of physical and motor functions in the brain. He used a technique called ESB, electrical stimulation of the brain, on laboratory-bred monkeys. He wanted to know what *particular* parts of the brain were responsible for *particular* physical and motor behaviours. He attached electrodes to different parts of the brains of some monkeys, and sent an electrical charge down them. By electrically stimulating particular brain areas Delgado was able to get his monkey to walk, walk in circles or run! By stimulating other areas he got his monkeys to yawn, fall asleep, or lose their appetite. In his most spectacular experiment, a 5-second electrical burst elicited a sequence of behaviour, which lasted 10–14 seconds. The monkey stopped what it was doing, changed its facial expressions, turned its head to the right, stood up on two feet, circled to the right, walked on two feet to a pole in the centre of the room, climbed up the pole, came down, growled, threatened, and attacked another monkey. It then approached the rest of the troop in a friendly manner and resumed its normal behaviour. This particular ESB stimulation was repeated 20,000 times and the monkey was observed going through exactly the same sequence of behaviour every time.

Delgado's work suggests that the cause of particular behaviours is mere electrical activity in particular parts of the brain. Evolution tells us that what is true for the brain of an animal such as a monkey, is likely to be true for human brains. It is, of course, unethical to experiment on human brains without some legitimate medical purpose. Why then, one might ask, is it not also unethical to do these experiments with laboratory animals? This disadvantage of the biological approach will be considered in due course.

continued

Another example of research using animals in biological psychology is Olds & Milner's (1954) experiment. They wanted to discover the brain's pleasure centre. Also using ESB, they attached an electrode to the hypothalamus of a rat, which the rat could self-stimulate. When the electrode was attached to one part of the hypothalamus, the rat was observed to self-stimulate the charge down the electrode 100 times a minute. It would forego food and water, seeking only the constant *buzz* to its pleasure centre. By placing the electrode in another part of the hypothalamus, Olds and Milner also discovered a pain centre. The rat sent one charge down the electrode and never went near the electrode's control mechanism again!

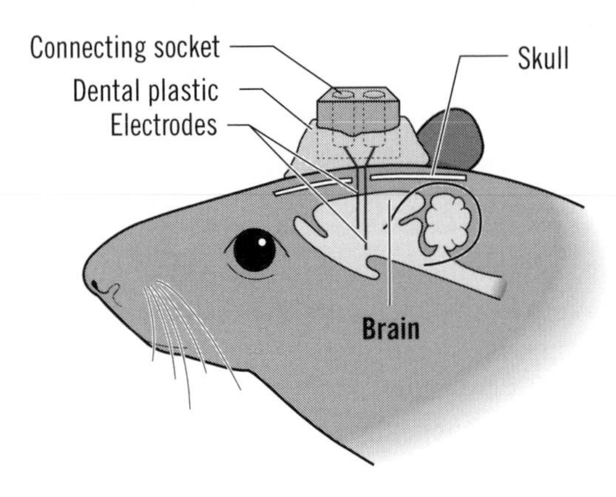

Figure 5.11 ESB – electrical stimulation of the brain

Aggression and physiology

Aggression is an important emotion recognised in us all, by us all. An emotion involves a strong internal feeling, accompanied by high physiological arousal.

Aggression is a behaviour, which is intended to cause physical or psychological harm to another. Human aggression can be accompanied by other emotions such as anger, fear or frustration. How then does the biological approach understand aggression?

Brain structure and aggression

There is evidence to show that parts of our brain are involved in aggression. Flynn (1976), on electrically stimulating the midbrain, hypothalamus and thalamus of cats, increased their aggression. Moyer (1976) further identifies the amygdala to be important to aggression. In his experiment, which involved the stimulation of the amygdala of animals, electrical stimulation of their amygdala produced aggression, and docility when unstimulated.

A surgical procedure called **psychosurgery** provides some evidence for the biological approach. This is because the biological approach always looks to a physical (physiological and/or genetic) reason for our feelings and behaviours.

Psychosurgery operates on those parts of the brain thought responsible for the production of problematic feelings and behaviours. In effect, the part of the brain thought responsible for the symptoms of the condition is cut out. The lobotomy is probably the most famous, or infamous, psychosurgical procedure known. Psychosurgery can be used to alleviate excessive aggression, clinical depression and manic depression. The effects of psychosurgery are, of course, irreversible.

INTERACTIVE

Make up your own mind about psychosurgery by reading the video *One Flew Over The Cuckoo's Nest* or read the book of the same name by Ken Kesey.

Enough said!

Hormones and aggression

Low concentrations of the hormone serotonin have been linked to irrational aggressive behaviour. Aggressive animals have been found to have lower levels of serotonin in their cerebro-spinal fluid than less aggressive species (Higley *et al.,* 1992). Lower levels of serotonin have correlated with violence in human beings.

The hormonal hypothesis concerning aggression suggests that the male sex hormone androgen (testosterone) plays its part, as do adrenaline and progesterone. Evidence for this comes from observations of male animals that have been castrated. Their testosterone level drops dramatically, as do their levels of aggression. Conversely, injecting animals with testosterone seems to increase aggressive behaviours. According to Kreuz and Rose, injecting testosterone into humans also has the same affect (Kreuz & Rose, 1972).

In considering aggression, it is, however, important to think also about the role of *environment*. Most people do not walk about with an *angry head* all the time! Something, or someone, causes us to experience *aggression*. While we all have a *biological predisposition* to be aggressive, as a result of the physiology of our brain and nervous system, we usually only become aggressive in response to environmental factors. What might these be?

The environment: alcohol and aggression

When we drink alcohol, our self-consciousness and reserve is lowered, and this can increase the probability of aggressive behaviours. There is a most definite link between alcohol consumption and crime, especially crimes of violence. The 1997 Psychiatric Morbidity among Prisoners ONS (Office of National Statistics) survey indicates that over 50 per cent of male prisoners in the UK drank hazardously in the year before coming to prison. In Scotland, of those victims of violent crime who could tell anything about their assailant, 72 per cent reported that their assailant was under the influence of alcohol (Scottish Crime Survey, 2000). In 2000, 128 people were accused of murder in Scotland. Of the 88 accused whose sobriety status was known, 61 per cent were drunk. Of those accused of culpable homicide, 67 per cent of accused in the 30+ age group were found to be drunk (Homicide in Scotland, 2000; Scottish Executive, 2001). Statistics indicate that around 75 per cent of violent crimes are committed under the influence of alcohol (Desmond, 1998; Taylor & Leonard, 1983).

It is also maybe worth knowing that, in the year 2000, there were 1,428 emergency admissions by Scottish Accident and Emergency Departments of young people aged 10–19 diagnosed with acute intoxication. Admissions were highest, at 1,036, in the 15–19 year age group. Excessive alcohol consumption is never a good idea. It can get you into lots of trouble.

Tommy Sheridan, leader of the Scottish Socialist Party and well-known Member of the Scottish Parliament, has been in prison on a few occasions for his political beliefs. When he was sent to jail for refusing to pay the poll tax, he later reported that in his view alcohol was a much bigger problem than drugs in Scotland. This was because heavy alcohol consumption figured hugely in the dysfunctional lifestyles of most of the other inmates that he met. Very much making the connection between alcohol, violence, and crime, he once told the author that, '*The only thing I've known people to attack when taking cannabis is a fridge*'. Tommy has never drunk alcohol or smoked, and is a fitness (and sunbed!) fanatic.

Our environment can further fuel our aggressive tendencies by providing stimuli that can provoke us, frustrate us, frighten us, or make us anxious. Taking alcohol can exacerbate these situations.

Excitement, adrenaline and aggression

When we are in a state of arousal brought on by an exciting situation, we naturally produce adrenaline. The presence of adrenaline in our nervous system can cause a person to overreact at the slightest provocation and frustration. Mix adrenaline, alcohol, and the cauldron of a major football match and you have an explosive mixture, both on and off the field.

The weather and aggression

It has long been thought that our weather affects our physiology, which has a knock-on effect on how we think, feel, and behave. According to Carlsmith & Anderson (1979) long hot summers have long correlated with an increase in violent behaviours.

INTERACTIVE

Watch the video *Falling Down* starring Michael Douglas.

How does the weather influence the main character's thoughts, feelings and behaviours?

Heat appears to exacerbate aggressive behaviours. Weather, and other environmental stressors, may also be associated with the phenomenon of 'road rage'.

The frustration–aggression hypothesis

Frustration is an emotion we experience when something gets in the way of us achieving a goal. According to the frustration–aggression hypothesis (Dollard *et al.* 1939), there is a far greater chance of aggression in situations where individuals think that someone/something is barring the way to them getting something. Later studies suggest that the frustration–aggression hypothesis is over-simplistic. Frustration *alone* doesn't necessarily produce aggression (Miller, 1941). Berkowitz (1989) has developed an interesting *aggressive-cue* theory on this basis. Aggressive-cue theory says that two conditions must come together to produce aggression when frustration occurs. The first condition is anticipation by the individual that aggression might be needed in their frustrating situation. The second condition is an environmental cue that precedes any aggressive behaviour. A kind of *red rag to a bull*! Both of these combine and aggression occurs

An illustration might be someone at the end of his or her tether with officialdom. Frustration at NOT getting something done may have built up over a long period. They may have tried everything but to no avail. They finally get a meeting with someone. They tell their story, but again don't seem to be getting through. Worse, the official is sending non-verbal and verbal cues that they really don't care. They've got a pressing golf game. Twenty minutes later, the official is in the hands of two paramedics, and the complainer in the hands of two policemen!

Aggression allows us to protect ourselves, and others, when in danger. Aggression is a *biological predisposition* common to us all, which sees our physiology respond in a particular way when under threat. Aggression is thus an innate, inherited biological characteristic. It is exacerbated by environmental factors, and is, as a general rule, recognised as unacceptable in modern society.

However, aggression is a biologically based characteristic common to us all. To understand why this is so, let us now examine the other emphasis within the biological approach, evolutionary psychology and evolution, genetics and behaviour.

Evolutionary psychology

Evolution, genetics and human behaviour

Evolution, genetics and related behaviour have been of interest to the biological approach in psychology since Darwin wrote his theory of evolution by natural selection in 1859. The genetic, or evolutionary, perspective is particularly interested in inherited genetic characteristics, and how they influence our thoughts, feelings and behaviours. These inherited genetic characteristics can either be common to us all, or pertinent to the individual. What this means is that a particular genetic inheritance can account for *individual differences* between individuals. This genetic inheritance can then help or hinder physical and psychological development.

What is evolution?

Evolution is the lengthy biological process through which new species emerge as a consequence of gradual alterations to the genetics of *existing* species. The environment a species finds itself in strongly influences its evolution over time.

What are genetics?

As a subject, genetics is the study of inherited biological characteristics. Inherited biological characteristics account for the colour of our eyes, our hair, our height and body shape. Genetics have been found to also influence our intelligence, personality and physical and mental health.

Our genetics further determine our physical development during the course of our life, affecting our body's anatomy (physical structure), and physiology, as already discussed. If you were to take an option in Developmental Psychology you would discover that genetics are crucial to biological maturation (physical/bodily aging) that can help or hinder cognitive, social and emotional development as we grow. A common biological ancestry is the reason why we all physically develop, or biologically mature, at approximately the same age the world over, though the onset of physical change may vary slightly from one person to another.

Chromosomes

The *normal* human baby inherits twenty-three *pairs* of **chromosomes** from its male and female biological parents. The twenty-third pairing determines its sex. During fertilisation when male chromosomes in the sperm combine with female chromosomes in the ovum, an XX twenty-third pairing will produce a female baby, and an XY, a male. Chromosomes contain genes, essential to building a molecule called protein. Our body is constructed of proteins.

It is estimated that each chromosome probably contains between 10,000 to 20,000 genes. A gene carries biological information in the form of deoxyribonucleic acid – **DNA** – to build the developing organism.

DNA

DNA contains the biological instructions to form cells necessary for any living organism to develop, grow, and function. DNA carries the body's protein-building instructions in a code, made from a four-letter string: A, T, C and G. These initials stand for four *nucleotide bases*, adenine, thymine, cytosine and guanine. Each *rung* in our DNA chain consists of these four bases, with particular bases always pairing with another: A with T, C with G, T with A, and G with C. The order of pairings differs from rung to rung. What sequence these letters take forms our *genetic code*. While we share 99.9 per cent of the same genetic code, it is the 0.1 per cent difference in our genetic code that makes us uniquely different from one another. This may seem very little, but one should note that it is estimated that the human body, or genome, consists $3 \times 1{,}000{,}000{,}000$ nucleotide base pairs!

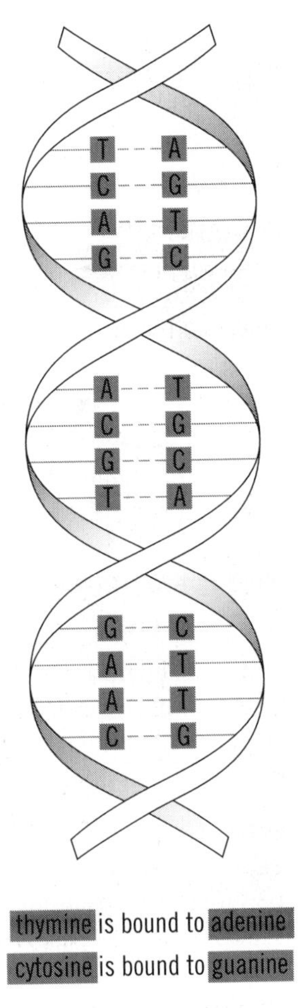

Figure 5.12 DNA

Genotype

Our genetic inheritance is a mixture of both our biological parents' genes and is called our **genotype**. Our genotype is a sort of blueprint or plan of what we will be like as we develop and grow. Our genotype is thus our inherited genetic *potential*. It accounts for the colour of our eyes, hair, height and body shape. Genetic inheritance is also an important factor to our physical and mental health, intelligence, and to some extent our personality. Whether you attain your genetic potential depends on your environment. Your biological predispositions, or genetic potential, represents the influence of *nature*, and your environment represents *nurture*. As we read in Chapter 1, the influence, and interaction, of your genetics and your environment in psychology is called the nature–nurture, or nativist–empiricist debate. The interaction of genotype and environment produces phenotype.

INTERACTIVE

ACROSS

1 Our body's 3-letter protein-building instructions
2 'Bridge' between the midbrain and medulla that connects our brain and spinal cord
4 10-12 billion of these make up our nervous system
5 Behind the pons, assists in motor movement and looks like a cauliflower!
6 Looks feline; moving X-rays
7 This area of our brain helps us understand speech
9 See 8 down
12 Three-letter system that controls our organs and glands
13 Hormone that stimulates contractions during childbirth
14 Shorthand for brain and spinal cord
15 The name given to our inherited biological characteristics
16 The other side of the nurture debate
17 Our 'fight or flight' hormone; central to our emotions

DOWN

1 Charles who? Wrote on the origin of species
2 Common name for a chemotherapy; a tablet
3 Growth hormone responsible for adult height
5 Two-word medical term for our brain and spinal cord
8 and 9 across Network of glands that manufactures and secretes hormones
9 Name for subdivision of PNS that controls our sensory and motor nerves
10 This is about 4 cm in diameter and is part of our brain stem
11 Its subdivisions are the somatic and autonomic nervous systems

Answers on page 136

Phenotype

Whether you fulfil your genotype or genetic blueprint depends upon your experiences in your environment. What we become as a result of interaction with our environment is called our **phenotype**. We may be, as a result of genotype, biologically predisposed with an extraordinary talent to play a sport or an instrument. Whether we go on to potentialise this genotype depends on the support and encouragement we get from our environment in infancy, childhood and adolescence. Our phenotype is the outcome of our genetics and our life story, or *phenomenology*. The degree to which genetic inheritance and/or environment affect intelligence, mental health, and personality is studied in the branch of psychology called individual differences.

To think that we *might* be *all genetics* as regards our intelligence, mental health and personality is quite a frightening thought. This could mean that we need not feel responsible, or be held accountable, for our actions. Our biology in general, and genetics in particular could be said to be to blame. This is why the nature–nurture debate is of such great interest in psychology. The nature–nurture, or genetics–environment debate, tries to answer the *how much* question. *How much* do our genetics, and *how much* does our environment contribute to our thoughts, feelings and behaviours?

Yet environment *can* affect genotype and the development of phenotype. We need not necessarily become what we are biologically thought predestined to become. The biological approach, and its assumption that thoughts, emotions and behaviours are solely driven by genetics and physiology, is called **biological determinism**, and will be considered later as a limitation to the biological approach.

Darwin's theory of evolution by natural selection (1859)

Environment and genetics is related to the *theory of evolution by natural selection* proposed by the famous scientist Charles Darwin in the mid-nineteenth century. Before we look at this it may be useful to remind ourselves what the biological approach is all about.

The biological approach suggests that all our cognitions, emotions and behaviours occur as a direct result of the physiological activity of our brain and nervous system. It also posits that we are genetically capable of these brain and neural activities because of our evolutionary history. Our prehistoric ancestors *Homo sapiens*, who thought, felt, and behaved as we do, were better able to survive than similar hominids called *Homo erectus*, who thought, felt and behaved in a less successful manner. *Homo sapiens* reproduced, passed on their successful brain, neural, and nervous system *hard-wiring* and evolved into the human beings of today. *Homo erectus* became extinct. How this transpired is called natural selection.

Natural selection

Charles Darwin's theory of evolution by natural selection is an attempt to explain why this happened. How does *natural selection* occur, a process that sees the survival of some species but not of others? To discover the answer we must to turn to Darwin's *The Origin of Species by Natural Selection* (1859).

The principles of natural selection

Darwin laid down that nature or the environment change over time. It is the environment that decides whether an organism survives or not.

- Successful organisms survive because they have a genetic/physical **trait** (characteristic, ability or behaviour) that allows them to adapt better to their changed environment. Having a successful **adaptation** is largely down to luck, as species can neither control their genetics nor their environment.
- Those individuals within a species that have the necessary adaptation, called a genetic **variation**, have a better ability in a changed environment to *reproduce* offspring that can themselves survive. Variations come about either as a consequence of genetic inheritance from the biological parents, or because of minor, random, genetic changes in an organism. These are called **mutations**.

Figure 5.13 Homo erectus

- Species are made up/not made up of individuals who, by chance, have this genetic variation. These individuals survive, while others don't. Variations and adaptations are therefore genetically inherited and passed from generation to generation. After a certain period of time the adapted species will appear *so* different from the original species that ultimately a new species has evolved.
- *Natural selection* best describes the process by which those species whose physical characteristics and behaviours are adapted to fit its changing/changed environment. These are the ones that survive. Hence Darwin's idea of *natural selection and the survival of the fittest*. Those who survive are those who have genetically adapted a physical characteristic or behaviour to *fit* their changed environment. It is environment that *selects* who survives, and who does not.

Empirical evidence for Darwin's theory of evolution

A famous example of natural selection was shown by Kettlewell (1955), and his observations of the peppered moth in the UK. Kettlewell looked at two variants of the peppered moth. One variation is dark, the other light, their colour being genetically inherited. Dark-peppered moths thus breed dark-coloured offspring, while light-peppered moths breed light-coloured offspring. Birds such as robins eat both types of moth – if they can see them! Before the nineteenth century, it is thought that the light-peppered moth greatly outnumbered the dark-peppered moth. This was because birds found the light-peppered moth harder to see against the lighter-coloured trees (of the time), as opposed to the darker variety, which were easier to pick out. During the nineteenth century industrial revolution in Britain, factory pollution covered our trees in soot, making them naturally darker in colour. This became a problem for the light-coloured peppered moth, as birds could now see *them* much better than their darker cousins. Kettlewell figured that if Darwin was correct, the environmental change to darker trees would favour the dark-coloured variation of peppered moth, but not be good news for the lighter coloured one. This he found to be just the case. Kettlewell (1955) reported that the number of dark-peppered moths went from being almost nil in the UK, to being over half the resident population of both types of moth in around fifty years. With concerns over industrial pollution, regulations were introduced in Britain to control factory pollution – and the amount of soot on Britain's trees declined. The number of light-coloured peppered moths has consequentially increased again.

Charles Darwin

Figure 5.14

Born in Shrewsbury in 1809, Charles Darwin developed the theory that all forms of life came about through a process of natural selection. Of a wealthy family, he went to school in Shrewsbury, and, after a brief spell at the University of Edinburgh, attended the University of Cambridge. His initial interest in medicine and the Church became overshadowed by his growing passion for life and earth sciences.

After graduating from Cambridge, the 22-year-old was taken aboard the British survey ship, the *HMS Beagle*, as a volunteer naturalist. This scientific expedition around the world was to have a major effect on both the natural and social sciences. In his observations, the young naturalist was most impressed with the effect that natural forces had on shaping the earth's surface. He observed that fossils of supposedly extinct species closely resembled living species in the same area. In the Galapagos Islands he noticed, for example, that each island supported its own form of tortoise. The various forms were closely related, but differed in structure and eating habits from island to island. He began to wonder why this had come about, and formed a theory known as the origin of species by natural selection.

This was published in *The Origin of the Species* in 1859. The essence of the theory of evolution by natural selection is that genetic variations or traits are transmitted to offspring of species. Some of these genetic variations will have survival value for the organism. They increase the probability of these species surviving long enough to reproduce and ensure future offspring. The trait is genetically inherited generation after generation. As a result the organism becomes better suited, or adapted to its environment. Eventually the (successful) genetic variation becomes so numerous a new species is born. Darwin also introduced the concept that all related organisms are descended from common ancestors.

The reaction to the *Origin* was immediate. Some biologists argued that Darwin could not prove his hypothesis. Others criticised Darwin's concept of variation, arguing that he could explain neither the origin of variations, nor how they were passed to succeeding generations. This particular criticism was not answered until the discovery of DNA in the middle of the twentieth century. The church was most vigorous in its attack. Bishop Wilberforce, in a famous debate at Oxford University denounced the theory as atheistic, and famously mocked the whole idea by asking Thomas Henry Huxley, a supporter of Darwin, whether he was descended from a monkey on his grandfather or grandmother's side. It was however the church that had to develop an adaptive ability!

Darwin was elected to the Royal Society in 1839 and the French Academy of Sciences in 1878. He was also honoured by burial in Westminster Abbey after he died in Downe, Kent, on 19 April 1882.

Darwin's publications include: *The Variation of Animals and Plants Under Domestication* (1868), *The Descent of Man* (1871), and *The Expression of Emotions in Man and Animals* (1872).

Darwin, James and emotions

In a later book *The Expression of the Emotions in Man and Animals* (1872), Charles Darwin said that humans have evolved physically *and* psychologically. On the basis of his observations of different peoples on the voyage of the Beagle, Darwin thought that we have evolved, and therefore share and recognise the same emotions, such as happiness, sadness, anger, disgust, etc. He said these emotions were innate, unlearned responses, comprising a complex set of facial movements and expressions. The expression of emotion is as a result of our genetics, which construct our physiology.

In the biological sense our emotions are understood from the point of view of physical structures and processes in our cerebral cortex and nervous system.

The American psychologist William James in his work the *Principles of Psychology* (1890), was later to agree with Darwin. James, considered by many to be the father of American psychology, said, 'we feel sorry because we cry, angry because we strike, afraid because we tremble'. What he meant by this is that a stimulus from our environment, i.e. a snarling dog will automatically trigger an innate bodily response in us, i.e. sweating, faster heart rate, trembling etc. It is these bodily responses that give us our *feelings* of fear. This is called the *peripheric* theory of emotion, better known as the *James–Lange theory*. James–Lange suggests we feel fear, etc. because of feedback got from internal bodily changes that have been triggered automatically by a stimulus in our environment. Their idea, then, rather counter-intuitively, is that we feel sad *because we cry*, rather than we cry because we feel sad. It should be noted that the James–Lange theory has since been overcome by other theories about our emotions, such as those of Canon (1929), Schacter & Singer (1962) and Pinel (1993). However James–Lange is important because the theory gave impetus to investigation into the biological basis to our emotions and behaviours. The biological approach consequentially explains us, physically and psychologically, as a result of genetically inherited biological characteristics. We are as we are because of our physiology and genetics. It is *nature*, largely, that gives rise to why we think, feel and behave as we do.

We will now briefly look at three areas in psychology where our biology, or genetics and physiology are, or were, thought to play an important role: personality, intelligence, and genetically influenced behaviours.

INTERACTIVE

Emotions are subjective feelings accompanied by physiological arousal that moves us to action. In the tradition of Darwin, Robert Plutchik (1994) categorised eight emotions, common to us all. They are called our primary emotions and are grouped in four pairs of opposites: expectation and surprise; anger and fear; acceptance and disgust; and joy and sadness. Identify these individual emotions in the photos below. Compare your answer with others. You should find that you mostly agree on most. You confirm Darwin's theory that we have evolved common emotions.

Figure 5.15 Emotions

Personality

'Where does our personality come from?' This is a question often asked by students of psychology. The answer was once thought to be nature – our biology. The Ancient Greek, Galen, 2,500 years ago, thought we behaved the way we do because of an excess of one of four bodily fluids in our body blood, phlegm, black bile and yellow bile. An excess of one of these fluids or *humours* gave rise to a particular **temperament** or general personality. Thus, excess blood would lead to a sanguine personality according to Galen; excess phlegm – a phlegmatic personality; excess black bile – a melancholic personality, or excess yellow bile – a choleric personality. Galen's personality temperaments live on today in **Eysenck's Personality Inventory** (EPI). The EPI has four personality types into which we all fit. Eysenck's stable extrovert reflects the traits of a sanguine personality; unstable–extrovert, Galen's choleric traits; unstable–introvert, Galen's melancholic traits and stable–introvert, Galen's phlegmatic personality traits.

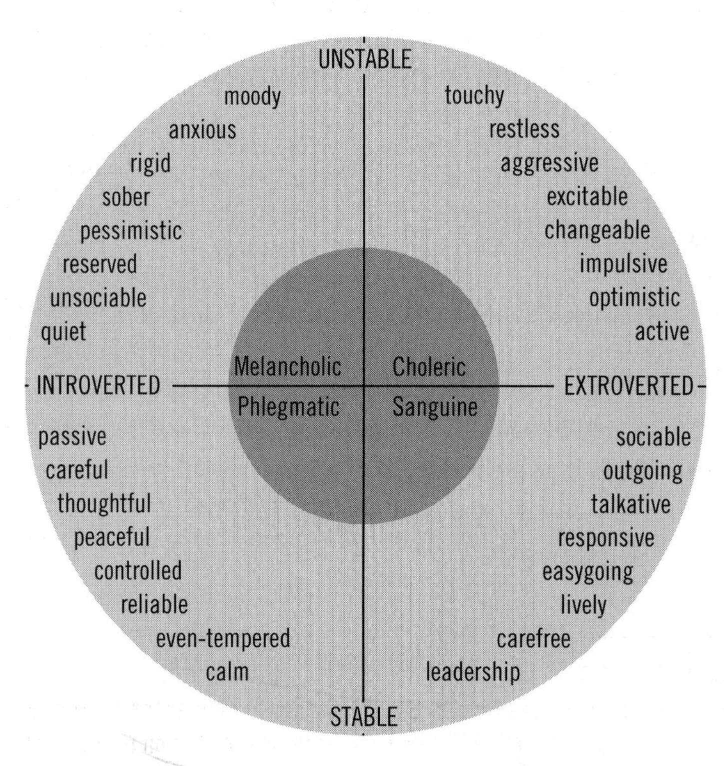

Figure 5.16 Dimensions of personality (from Eysenck, 1965)

Temperaments

We may well inherit such temperaments or general personality traits, not, of course, on the basis of excess bodily fluids, but because of our genetics. Temperament is the building block of our personality, which is thereafter greatly influenced by our experiences in our environment. Nature plays some part in the formation of our personality, but *nurture* has its influence as well. Otherwise, as a result of similar genetic inheritance we could have the same personality as a brother or sister, or worse – a parent!

Intelligence

The study of intelligence from a biological point of view was greatly influenced by family genetics themselves. This was because Darwin had a cousin Francis Galton who became intrigued with his work, and consequently developed the idea that intelligence could be genetically inherited. Galton is best known for his studies of heredity and intelligence published in *Hereditary Genius* (1869), which led to the founding of the controversial **eugenics** movement. Eugenics became particularly popular with the Nazis around seventy years later in their drive for racial purity and an Aryan master race: this was because eugenics advocated that in order to preserve desired genetic characteristics, selective breeding must occur within a population. Put simply, to create a very intelligent child, it is a good idea that a very intelligent male and female be its biological parents. This ultimately influenced the deaths of millions of Germans and non-Germans alike whose genetic characteristics did not fit the Nazi profile of a member of their abhorrent *master race*.

Galton's importance to the study of intelligence is twofold, both as a historical figure and in suggesting that intelligence could be measured. His work precipitated interest in the development of psychometric tests of intelligence. Psychometric essentially means *measurable*.

Psychometric tests of intelligence all see some kind of biological inheritance/maturation as their base. Because we share a common biology, intelligence tests have established that there is a common or average IQ (intelligence quotient) in a normal population of people. This has been set at 100, so that if general intelligence were measured in a community, most would get an IQ score of around 100, with a few scoring much higher, and some much lower. Those whose score is far from the average, whether higher or lower, would be said to be reflecting individual differences in intelligence in comparison to the bulk of the *population*. These individual differences can be greatly influenced by our biology, genetics, and physiology.

It is not intended here to debate the issue of *intelligence*. By way of introduction however, it may be useful to try to get a general idea of what intelligence might be, and more importantly, what influences the maximisation of whatever intellectual potential we have. This sees a return to the nature–nurture debate, or the influence our genetics and environment play in the unfolding of intellectual ability and potential.

Do eugenics still exist today?

In the USA, men can donate their sperm to clinics, which then sell the sperm to women wanting babies by Artificial Insemination by Donor (AID). AID is very popular. Male sperm sells on the basis of the characteristics of the male donor. The sperm of a concert pianist is far more valuable than that of a refuse collector. What does this suggest?

Intelligence: the genetics–environment debate

The nature of intelligence has perplexed psychology since its early days. In a general sense, '*Intelligent activity consists of grasping the essentials in a situation and responding appropriately to them*' (Heim, 1970). The ability to do this is a result of our genetic inheritance from our biological parents *and* our own learning experiences in our environment. Debate has raged as to *how much* genetics, and *how much* environment each contribute to our overall *intelligence*. Psychologists like Eysenck and Jensen have argued that genetics contributes over 90 per cent to our *intelligence*, while others like Kamin would argue the opposite – that environment makes a 90 per cent plus contribution towards intellectual ability. Who is the more correct? Whatever intelligence is, it is neither *all* genetics nor *all* environment, but a mixture of both.

Nowadays, there is a strong belief in psychology that biological/genetic inheritance does play a part in overall intellectual growth, contributing towards 60–70 per cent of our IQ. Therefore environment contributes 30–40 per cent (Bouchard & Segal, 1988). As most of us share the same IQ of around 100, the genetics–environment debate about intelligence is a bit pointless. Psychology is maybe better occupied concerning itself with the outcome of the interaction of genetics and environment, and discovering more about how it can help maximise all peoples' *intelligence(s)*, whatever these may be.

This is because environment is *the* factor that makes the difference between one person developing whatever intellect they have to the maximum, and another not being able to do so. As regards genotype, phenotype and intelligence, the social setting, or environment, in which we find ourselves, is of immense importance to the maximisation of whatever abilities we have in the first place (Plomin & DeFries, 1998).

Genetically influenced behaviours: schizophrenia and depression

The International Classification of Diseases manual, ICD–10, which is used by psychiatrists in the UK, defines schizophrenia and depression as mental disorders. As we will see when we look at applications of the biological approach, the diagnosis and treatment of mental disorders is hugely influenced by the biological approach. This is because the biological approach suggests that the causes of our cognitions, emotions and behaviours, normal and abnormal, are *physical* in origin. We become ill, mentally and physically, as a consequence of our *biology*. Our *genetics* and *physiology* are faulty in some way, possibly as a result of disease, accident, injury or genetic inheritance.

Schizophrenia

According to the National Schizophrenic Fellowship (NSF), 1:100 people will experience schizophrenia at some point in their lives, the onset usually being in a person's late teens or early twenties. It should be noted that schizophrenia can be treated, and that the majority of people with schizophrenia lead ordinary lives. Symptoms of schizophrenia are twofold; positive and negative. Positive symptoms develop gradually and include exaggeration or distortion of normal thoughts, emotions and behaviour. Negative symptoms refers to the loss of social characteristics normally associated with our everyday interactions with one another. Both positive and negative symptoms may occur together. A person affected by schizophrenia may also experience secondary symptoms such as depression. Secondary symptoms result from the difficulties they may be having in learning to cope with the onset of their disorder.

Positive symptoms: hallucinations and delusions

While visual, olfactory and tactile hallucinations are reported, most commonly, a person with schizophrenia hears thoughts spoken aloud in their head. These *auditory hallucinations* may take the form of an uncontrollable running commentary about what they are doing, and appear to come from an external source. MRI (magnetic resonance imagery) techniques have shown neurotransmitters firing off in speech areas of the brain when someone is reporting *voice hearing*. It is thus a real neurological experience for the individual, and is not *imaginary*.

The NSF sees delusions as logical for the schizophrenic. The schizophrenic realises these voices are abnormal, and tries to find a reason for them. They come to believe they are coming from the television, the Martians, the government, God, the devil, and so on. Two types of delusion deserve mention. Delusions of grandeur occur where the sufferer comes to believe they are a very important person such as Jesus Christ or Napoleon. The other is delusion of persecution, where the sufferer believes they are being persecuted by an external source such as the government. These convictions can become overwhelming and all-consuming for the person, and account for the person's strange behaviours.

Negative symptoms: loss of motivation

Negative symptoms emerge over time and eventually become everyday social (anti-social) or behaviours. A schizophrenic person gradually becomes slow to think, talk and move. They withdraw from their former social world and become socially isolated. Their sleeping pattern can change and they may stay up all night, and sleep all day. From a psychological point of view, *motivation* becomes seriously affected. They show a lack of *volition*, where they become indecisive, give up easily on things, and seem unaffected by concern shown by friends and family. These they can eventually lose.

INTERACTIVE

Visit http://www.mentalhealth.com/icd/p22-ps01.html and outline the symptoms of:

1 simple schizophrenia
2 hebephrenic schizophrenia
3 catatonic schizophrenia
4 paranoid schizophrenia.

A biological explanation for schizophrenia

Schizophrenia was not recognised as a major mental disorder until Kraepelin (1896) identified some of its symptoms as *senility of youth* or *dementia praecox*. Until the 1970s the cause of schizophrenia was unknown. Then a moving X-ray beam technology, called computerised axial tomography, or CAT scan, was invented. Using such technology, Johnstone *et al.* (1978) were able to reveal that chronic schizophrenics had slightly abnormal brains in comparison with non-schizophrenics. Their lateral cerebral ventricles, the fluid-filled spaces in the middle of the brain, were larger, and they had less tissue in the medial temporal lobe. Post-mortems also began to produce evidence that the hippocampi and limbic system of the schizophrenic are smaller in comparison to the non-schizophrenic. CAT, MRI and post-mortem evidence further reveals that schizophrenics suffer from a reduced blood flow in the frontal cortex (Gershon & Rieder, 1992).

The dopamine hypothesis

The most direct biological explanation of schizophrenia is the dopamine hypothesis. Dopamine is a chemical neurotransmitter produced in the brain. Schizophrenics have been found to show abnormal production of dopamine. They produce too much of it, which is thought to produce their symptoms (Iverson, 1979).

One way to try to confirm whether the dopamine hypothesis is correct is to use twin-studies. There are two types of twins: Dz or dizygotic non-identical twins, and Mz, monozygotic identical twins. Monozygotic twins have the same genetic code, and inherit exactly the same biological characteristics. If one identical twin has schizophrenia, the other should also have the condition if the condition were hereditary. There should be 100 per cent **concordance** of schizophrenia between identical twins. However, according to Frith & Cahill (1995), 100 per cent concordance is not found. Schizophrenia may not be entirely biological in origin; environment may also be a factor.

Lloyd *et al.* (1984) make the interesting observation that dopamine may be only an indirect cause of schizophrenia. Their research indicated that abnormal family circumstances could produce abnormal levels of dopamine, which then goes on to trigger the symptoms illustrated above.

While biology alone cannot fully account for schizophrenia, studies comparing the occurrence of schizophrenia in Mz and Dz twins throw up strong statistical indicators that genes do play their part. The concordance rate for schizophrenia in Mz twins is five times higher than in Dz twins, at 50 per cent and 10 per cent respectively (Shields, 1976, 1978).

Depression

ICD–10 classifies depression as a mood, or *affective*, disorder. Depression is reported to affect between 20–30 men, and 40–90 women per 1,000 in the UK. The effects of clinical depression can be devastating. Gelder *et al.* (1999) indicate that around 10 per cent of patients commit suicide. Symptoms of depression include:

- irritability
- sadness
- exhaustion
- low self-esteem
- irrational self-criticism
- shame
- guilt
- mood and behavioural swings
- suicidal thoughts and actions.

Depression is *not* just sadness, a sign of personal weakness, or grief. It is more than this, and a most debilitating condition that can last anything between three months and a lifetime.

A biological explanation for depression

It is thought that an inability to produce the neurotransmitter **serotonin** is related to depression (Gelder *at al.*, 1999). Serotonin is one of the key mood regulators in the human brain. Too little serotonin production leads to depression, while irregular serotonin production levels contribute to the *bipolar disorder*, manic depression.

Tebartz *et al.* (2000) points to the amygdala also having something to do with depression. They found that depressed patients have enlarged amygdala, and that the amygdala in their female patients was significantly larger than those of males.

Schizophrenia and depression are then genetically influenced conditions. In both instances some aspect of our physiology is affected. It would now be appropriate to consider applications of the biological approach in its treatment of these conditions.

Are you a SAD person?

SAD (Seasonal Affective Disorder) is a type of winter depression that affects an estimated half a million people in the UK every year, particularly during December, January and February. Symptoms include lethargy, overeating, depression, social problems, anxiety, mood swings and loss of sex drive. For many sufferers SAD is a serious condition, preventing them from functioning normally without medical treatment.

The root cause of SAD is unknown. Scientists believe it is caused by a biochemical imbalance in the hypothalamus triggered by the shortening of daylight hours and the lack of sunlight in winter. During the summer, bright light at dawn suppresses the body's production of melatonin, which makes us drowsy. Lack of bright light during the winter months could mean that the brain is not stimulated into waking up. This, and other chemical reactions in the brain, can trigger SAD.

The most popular treatment uses a special highly fluorescent light bulb plugged in to a socket at home and turned on when it is dark. This appears to alleviate the symptoms, presumably by artifically suppressing the production of melatonin. The UK Seasonal Affective Disorder Association suggests that this is much more useful than a prescription for anti-depressants. Interestingly, SADA highly recommend psychotherapy for SAD sufferers.

Applications of the biological approach

Applying the biological approach is relatively easy, if only because we know that the approach looks for a physical cause behind our thoughts, feelings and behaviour. *Physical cause* concerns a bodily process or function that has suffered damage, disease, accident or been genetically influenced in some way. If something has a *physical* cause, it is treated with a *physical* therapy, from a *physical* point of view. How then does this apply to schizophrenia and depression?

Applications to mental health: schizophrenia

We have seen that one biological approach to the understanding of schizophrenia concentrates on the dopamine hypothesis. An overproduction of the neurotransmitter dopamine has been found to trigger the aforementioned symptoms of schizophrenia. One of the main medical treatments for schizophrenia is to use a range of drugs called **neuroleptics**.

Neuroleptics and schizophrenia

The use of drugs in medicine is called chemotherapy. Neuroleptics like *Largactil*, *Stelazine* and *Modecate* moderate the production of dopamine, and try to normalise the positive and negative symptoms of hallucinations, delusions, and/or loss of motivation. Neuroleptics can be administered by tablet, liquid or injection.

Prescribing neuroleptics is controversial. Each patient responds differently to his or her medication. Finding the right neuroleptic and the right dosage can take some time. Even then, distressing adverse side effects have been reported. These include unusual body movements, such as tremor, which resemble the symptoms of Parkinson's disease. Another side effect is tardive dyskinesia, which sees unusual and repetitive movements of the tongue, face, and neck muscles and sometimes of the arms and legs. Other side effects are feeling drowsy and sedated, the overproduction of the hormone prolactin, reduced sexual desire, weight-gain, blurred vision and dizziness. These side effects are controlled by the prescription of more drugs.

Applications to mental health: depression

Ben Green, editor of *Psychiatry On-Line* at http://www.priory.com/treatmen.htm believes the treatment of depression currently costs the UK anything between £220 million and £417 million per annum. The World Health Organisation (WHO) thinks that by 2010, one in three people will be affected by depression at some point in their life. In British terms this will mean an incredible 18 million people could become medically depressed by the end of the first decade of the twenty-first century (Munro, 2000b).

Depression and antidepressants

The biological cause of depression is thought to be due to changes in neural receptors, sensitive to the 5–HT hydroxytryptamine neurotransmitter, serotonin and others like **noradrenaline** and **dopamine**. Serotonin helps control appetite, sleep and sexual activity. Noradrenaline regulates mood and motivation, while dopamine is thought to be involved in our ability to experience pleasure. Depression is treated mainly through the prescription of antidepressants. These act on the sensitivity of the dulled neuron receptor cells to serotonin, noradrenaline and dopamine. As a consequence the depressed person's mood state is altered.

The main difference for the patient regarding the different varieties of antidepressants is their side effects (Gelder *et al.,* 1999). Most antidepressants take between 10–14 days to begin to have any effect. The *safest* nowadays are specific serotonin reuptake inhibitors (SSRIs), such as *paroxetine* and *fluoxetine*, better known as *Prozac*. Prozac is by far the most popular chemotherapy for those with depression. Since its introduction in 1988, more than 38 million people worldwide have been prescribed it (Costello *et al.,* 1995; Bosley, 1999).

INTERACTIVE

Read http://www.guardian.co.uk/Archive/Article/0,4273,4341235,00.html and the site's related articles. Summarise those side effects associated with anti-depressants such as *Prozac*.

The biological approach controls the symptoms ...

The biological approach believes the cause of both disorders to be physical in origin. Schizophrenia is caused by the overproduction of the neurotransmitter, dopamine. Depression occurs due to physical changes to neural receptors, which frustrate the normal workings of serotonin, noradrenaline and dopamine. To solve the problem, or more precisely, alleviate the *symptoms*, the biological approach recommends chemotherapy, or the use of drugs, like *Largactil* and *Prozac*. These help to control the symptoms for the sufferer ....

... BUT MAYBE NOT THE CAUSE?

The final emphasis must be the impact nurture, or *environment*, has on schizophrenia and depression. There is, as we have read, some evidence to suggest that environment plays its part in the onset of both conditions. We cannot conclude from twin studies that schizophrenia is entirely biological in origin. In the case of depression, *something* has influenced changes to our physiology that affects serotonin. That *something* is environmental. Simply put, depression can be caused by the overwhelming pressures, stresses and strains of everyday living for, soon to be one-third of us, according to the WHO.

The biological approach takes an over-simplistic view of such complex psychological issues. In ignoring environment, it is reductionist, mechanistic and deterministic in outlook, and it is to these limitations of the biological approach that we now turn.

Limitations of the biological approach

The biological approach has much to offer, in the form of physiological and genetic explanations of our thoughts, feelings and behaviours. It has been most useful when applied to health and the development of chemotherapies to relieve symptoms of numerous physical and mental conditions, which have arisen from damage, disease, or accident. Often this damage is genetic, and as a result of biological inheritance.

The biological approach, we can now agree, explains and understands us from the point of view of our biology, or physiology and genetics. It believes that we are as we are, as a result of our inherited genetic characteristics and physiological processes and functions. It has been criticised as being reductionist, mechanistic and deterministic. It also attracts some attention in its research with non-human animals.

REDUCTIONIST, MECHANISTIC AND DETERMINISTIC

The biological approach is reductionist and mechanistic because it explains us in terms of our genetically inherited physiological structures, their functions and processes. If we behave in a particular way, the biological approach points to the workings of our nervous system. We are our brain chemistry. It reduces explanations of human beings to the level of neurons, our autonomic, peripheral and endocrine systems, hormones, and so on. As a result the biological approach can also be criticised as being deterministic, since it sees us in terms of *biological inevitability*. Our genetics and physiology will determine who we are, and what we can and will become.

Other approaches in psychology remind us that there is more to our thoughts, feelings and behaviours than just bodily processes and functions. In considering nurture, or environment, the psychoanalytic approach emphasises the role of early environmental experiences. Behaviourism believes learning in our environment to be important, while the cognitive approach understands us from the point of view of subjective experience in our environment, and the influence this can have on our mediational processes.

All of these approaches must be considered alongside our physiology and genetics to appreciate why we are as we are. In our next chapter we will read about a final contribution to our psychological understanding of humankind, the humanistic approach and the role of personal experience.

Animal research as a limitation of the biological approach

The use of animals as research subjects is not exclusive to the biological approach. Behaviourism is an obvious example of this. We *all* should take the issues that concern animal research on board, but let us first consider the question, 'Why does science experiment on animals at all?'

The reasoning behind animal experimentation across many sciences is twofold – the pursuit of scientific knowledge and the advancement of science (Gray, 1987). The reasons given for using animals in *psychological* research are:

- the behavioural continuity of animals and humans, which allows species-species comparisons to be made
- their simpler biological form
- fewer emotive implications which helps objective academic debate
- the ability in an experiment to give a clearer cause–effect relationship between an independent and dependent variable.

Cross-comparative species–species research has its origins in Darwin's (1859) *Origin of Species*. The study of simpler life forms from our evolutionary history can give us a greater insight into why we think, feel and behave as we do. Coolican (1994) believes that species–species comparisons across the **phylogenic** (evolutionary) scale can indicate what we as humans have lost or gained in our evolutionary history when compared with animals.

Saying this, two major concerns are raised by the use of animals in psychological research. The first are the ethical questions relating to the pain or suffering which may be inflicted on laboratory animals. The second is the ecological validity of whatever conclusions the experiment reaches. There is a wide-ranging debate about what animal studies can, in theory, reveal about human behaviour. The early behaviourists believed that their principles of learning were applicable to both human and non-human alike, and that their theories of conditioning applied equally to rats and man. This belief is no longer accepted, with species–species comparisons and generalisations about animal–human behaviours being regarded with a deal of suspicion. There are, as we have discovered, other variables involved in why or why not, we human beings behave as we do in our world.

Ethics and non-human research in psychology

Decisions about whether or not to use animals in experimentation can be made using the Bateson Decision Cube (1986, 1992). The three dimensions upon which the researchers base their decision to use animals are:

- the quality of research
- the certainty of benefit to humankind
- the degree of animal suffering.

Bateson believes that animal suffering can only be justified if the quality of scientific research and the medical benefit are deemed high. Experimentation on animals should not be undertaken for its own sake.

In order to try to help psychologists in their decision the British Psychological Society (BPS) have a code of conduct applying to animal research. This is called The *Guidelines for the Use of Animals in Research* (BPS and Committee of the Experimental Psychological Society, 1985) and should be read in conjunction with *The Code of Conduct for Psychologists* (BPS, 1983), and *The Ethical Principles for Conducting Research with Human Participants* (BPS, 1990, 1993).

INTERACTIVE

Under what circumstances would you allow experimentation on animals? Give reasons for your answer.

Conclusion

The biological approach is concerned with the relationship between our physiology and genetics, and our thoughts, feelings and behaviours. It examines us from the point of view of our bodily processes and systems, and how evolution and genetics accounts for those things that we have in common, and those things that make us different. As an approach it is influential in all other approaches bar behaviourism. The biological approach is evident in psychoanalysis, with its emphasis on the patient. The cognitive approach understands there to be a biological basis to our information processes, as was most apparent when we looked at the senses and gestalten, the biological basis of language, memory storage areas in the brain. Chapter 6 will see us look at the humanistic approach. It too has strong biological undertones, in that it believes we have a biological predisposition to *be all that we can be*. This, as we will see, can be frustrated by experiences in our social world, which has an impact on our personality and can make us psychologically healthy or otherwise.

Summary

The biological approach sees us as the sum of our genetics and physiology. We become ill, medically and/or psychologically, because of physiological or genetic damage, disease, or accident. It is the only approach in psychology that examines thoughts, feelings and behaviours from a *physical* point of view. Thus for the biological approach, psychologically we are the result of our genetics and the workings of our central nervous system, peripheral nervous system and endocrine system. The influence of Charles Darwin introduces the notion that we have evolved both physically *and* psychologically in response to our environment. Our genetics account for our shared physique and emotions. Common emotions, such as aggression, are understood as a result of our physiology and genetics. Our genetics also influence our individual development, physically and psychologically. Because of the emphasis on a physical/biological cause to psychological difficulties, the approach has been very influential in the use of physical therapies, or chemotherapy, as a treatment for a variety of mental disorders. Schizophrenia is understood to be caused by the overproduction of the neurotransmitter dopamine. Depression comes from physiological changes to neurons that dull them to serotonin. Both disorders are treated with drugs. The symptoms of schizophrenia are controlled by neuroleptics, which have side effects. The symptoms of depression are controlled by antidepressants such as Prozac, a chemotherapy also not without controversy. In both instances there is thought to be an environmental influence to the onset of the disorder, something the biological approach does not explore too well. In its influence into the study of individual differences, the biological approach also suggests genetics plays its part. In consideration of the likes of personality and intelligence, again however, the biological approach plays down the influence of environment on genotype and phenotype. The biological approach finds itself firmly on the nativist side of the 'nature–nurture' debate on these issues. Its understanding of us as neurons, structures and functions in the brain, hormones, our genome, etc. has seen it accused of being reductionist, mechanistic and deterministic. The biological approach has also attracted some attention because of its use of non-human subjects in experimental research.

INTERACTIVE

1. Electrically stimulate a human brain at http://www.pbs.org/wgbh/aso/tryit/brain/probe-nojs.html. (You may need to download Macromedia Shockwave to support this activity.)
2. Go to http://www.headinjury.org/brainmap.htm. What impairments might a victim of a head injury suffer as a result of accident to their a) frontal lobe b) parietal lobe c) temporal lobe and d) occipital lobe?
3. Go to http://www.thirteen.org/closetohome/animation/ingestion/main.html and using the animations see how alcohol, nicotine, cannabis, etc. reach the cerebral cortex.
4. Investigate BBC Biotopia @ http://www.bbc.co.uk/education/darwin/alife/instr.htm

   Create your own virtual life forms and observe them interact and mutate in real time.

Structured questions with answer guidelines

1 *Define and explain the biological approach in psychology.*

With reference to the preceding chapter, structure your answer around the following model:

Define the biological approach as one that understands us as an interrelationship between our mind, our physiology, our genetics, and our behaviours. Identify the two emerging perspectives of physiological and evolutionary psychology, and then go on to explain

- Physiological psychology. Definition.
  - Anatomy of a neuron, glial cells, neurotransmitters. Influence on MND and MS
  - Human nervous system. PNS. Homeostasis
  - The endocrine system. Pituitary gland. Hormones
  - Central nervous system. Some structures and functions of the brain, e.g. Broca and Wernicke's areas. Language.
- Evolutionary psychology. Definition.
  - What is evolution? What are genetics? DNA. Genotype and phenotype
  - Darwin and natural selection
  - Genetics and aggression/personality/intelligence/atypical behaviours (discuss at least two)
  - Nature and nurture in the light of your discussion above.

2 *How is the biological approach applied in practice?*

Structure your answer as follows:

- Identify the application of the approach as a physical therapy, i.e. chemotherapy. Explain the relationship between chemotherapy and cause in the biological approach, and then go on to discuss it in relation to
  - Schizophrenia
  - Depression.

Evaluate chemotherapy as a treatment in relation to schizophrenia and depression.

3 *What criticisms may be made of the biological approach?*

Identify and explain limitations, i.e.

- Reductionist and mechanistic.
  - Explain with some reference to neurons, neurotransmitters, structures and functions of the brain, bodily systems, hormones, etc.
- Deterministic.
  - Over-emphasis on 'nature' in the genetics-environment debate
  - Give some examples to explain what you mean e.g. in relation to aggression, personality, intelligence, and atypical behaviours.
- Ethics of experiments on non-human subjects.
  - BPS Guidelines.

Glossary

Adaptation: a modification that an organism develops that makes it better suited to survive and reproduce in its environment

Biological determinism: the idea that it is our biology that determines, or makes us what we are/will become. We are the result of our genetics and physiology

Cerebrum: name given to the anterior (the front) portion of the brain made up of two lateral hemispheres

Chromosomes: cells of nucleoprotein that form genes, which are responsible for the transmission of hereditary characteristics in species

Concordance: the agreement of one thing with another. Concordance studies with identical Mz twins are common in psychology. They are used to assess the influence of genetics, or nature, on an aspect of personality, intelligence, or atypical behaviour. If both Mz twins share a particular problem, this concordance would suggest that the characteristic, e.g. schizophrenia, is genetically inherited

DNA: deoxyribonucleic acid, which is the main ingredient of chromosomes, or genes

Dopamine: a chemical neurotransmitter found in the brain

Eugenics: the study of selective breeding (in human populations)

Eysenck's Personality Inventory: a general personality 'test' made famous by the late Professor Hans Eysenck, one of the UK's leading psychologists

Hormone: chemical substances produced by the endocrine system, which are transported in our bloodstream and affect bodily tissues in some way

Hypothalamus: small structure at the bottom of the forebrain that regulates our autonomic nervous system and controls the secretion of hormones responsible for a number of our behaviours into our bloodstream via the pituitary gland

Mutation: a sudden change in the genetic make-up of an organism that alters it in some way from others of the same species

Neuroleptics: medication used in the treatment of mental illness

Neurotransmitter: a chemical released by a neuron that transmits across a synapse to another neuron

Phenotype: the outcome of interaction between our genotype and our environment

Phylogenic: the evolution of a species

Psychosurgery: controversial surgery that involves the destruction of neural tissue in our brain

Serotonin: a neurotransmitter that appears to play a role in mood state

Temperament: a disposition towards a particular personality

Trait: in genetics, an inherited characteristic. Also, it is a name given to aspects of our personality

Variation: the genetic adaptation necessary for a species to survive and reproduce

Crossword answers

Across 1 DNA, 2 Pons, 4 Neuron, 5 Cerebellum, 6 CAT, 7 Wernicke's area, 9 System, 12 ANS, 13 Oxytocin, 14 CNS, 15 Genotype, 16 Nature, 17 Adrenaline.

Down 1 Darwin, 2 Pill, 3 Somatotrophin, 5 Cerebral cortex, 8 Endocrine, 9 Somatic, 10 Medulla, 11 PNS.

6

The humanistic approach

BY THE END OF THIS CHAPTER YOU SHOULD BE ABLE TO:

- **define and explain the humanistic approach with reference to its key features**
- **explain applications of the humanistic approach**
- **explain the limitations of the humanistic approach.**

Overview of the humanistic approach

The humanistic approach is an approach in psychology that emphasises the whole person. It began in the 1950s in America, gathered momentum in the 1960s, and by the 1970s had become an approach in its own right across the world. It is a perspective that is concerned with the study of personality, motivation, atypical behaviour and counselling, and states that we have a biological predisposition towards self-actualisation. Self-actualisation is where we try as individuals to fulfil all the potentials we have, and is, according to an important contributor, Abraham Maslow, the peak of human personality development. The idea of personal growth is important to self-actualisation, in that frustration of personal growth may lead to an inability for a person to self-actualise, or to become all that they might become. The humanistic approach stresses the uniqueness of the individual and says we have a right to interpret life as it affects us. It sees a connection between our personal interpretation of life's experiences and our inner personality, which the approach calls the self. In this chapter the humanistic concept of self will be looked at in relation to personality. Personal growth will be examined in the light of Abraham Maslow's hierarchy of needs, and growth and deficiency needs explained in relation to self-actualisation. Carl Rogers' contribution to the application of the humanistic approach will see us highlight humanistic psychotherapy and counselling. Finally, we will consider the limitations of the humanistic approach, such as doubts over the validity of its constructs and methodology, and its over-optimistic view of our ability to exercise free will.

Key features of the humanistic approach

The humanistic approach is concerned with personality, formed by an individual's personal view of themselves in their world, and how this influences their thoughts, feelings and behaviour.

The humanistic approach came about as a reaction to the earlier approaches of psychoanalysis and behaviourism. Early humanistic psychologists rejected these two approaches as being reductionist and deterministic. According to the humanistic approach, psychoanalysis is reductionist because it explains us *solely* from the point of view of the unconscious. Behaviourism is reductionist because it sees us as *merely* stimulus–response units of learned behaviours. Humanistic psychology believes that we are more complex and should, therefore, be understood as *more* than just our unconscious and/or S–R units of learned behaviour.

Humanistic psychology further criticised psychoanalysis and behaviourism for being deterministic. **Determinism** in psychology means we become what we become because of factors *other* than ourselves. Forces outside our control make us what we are. Psychoanalysis thinks these forces are early childhood experiences, over which we as children have little control. Behaviourism, on the other hand, thinks it is our environment that entirely determines what we become. As we read earlier, we form stimulus–response units of learned behaviour as we interact with our environment. We do not, according to behaviourism, have much control over our environment, and respond to it as opposed to acting upon it. As a result, both psychoanalysis and behaviourism say things happen, external to us, that determine why we think, feel and behave as we do. Psychoanalysis and behaviourism take a reductionist, deterministic and thus passive view of human beings in their ability to control and shape their own destiny.

Third force psychology

Humanistic or 'Third Force' psychology takes an alternative view. It sees us as active beings that can be more in control of what we become. We are not just the products of our unconscious or of learned units of behaviour. We are as individual personalities also the result of personal experience. It rejects behaviourism and its findings as being humanly insignificant. For humanistic psychology, Pavlov's dogs and Skinner's rats lack psychological validity. This means that the humanistic approach thinks that behaviourist findings do not reflect real-life human affairs. It thinks behaviourist theory, because it is based on animal research in a laboratory, is not appropriate to humans. In its criticism of psychoanalysis and behaviourism, the humanistic approach sets out to tell us what it believes psychology to be about: the promotion of psychological good health and the welfare of the individual.

In the application of the humanistic approach in humanistic psychotherapy, the aim of therapy is to move the client towards psychological good health. Poor mental health comes from an individual's negative perception of himself or herself, which is a consequence of their experiences in life. Important to humanistic psychotherapy and counselling is the client. Humanistic psychotherapy and counselling emphasise a person-centred model of therapy in that 'the client knows what hurts, what directions to go, what problems are crucial, what experiences have been buried' (Rogers, 1961).

The self

The humanistic approach concerns the study of personality formed by an individual's personal view of themselves in their world. Our personality – called the *self* – is influenced by the experiences, and interpretation of the experiences, we as individuals have in life. Our self-concept is our inner being, or who it is we come to perceive we are as individuals. The humanistic approach says the self is composed of concepts we view as unique, particular, and peculiar to ourselves. These include self-image, self-esteem and ideal self.

Self-image

The self is our inner personality and is influenced by our interpretation of the experiences we have in life. Self consists of self-image, self-esteem and ideal self.

Self-image is how we see ourselves, which is important to our good psychological health. Self-image includes the influence of our body image on inner personality. At a simple level, we might perceive ourselves as a good or a bad person, beautiful or ugly. Self-image, and how it comes about, has an effect on how we as individuals think, feel and behave in relation to our world.

Self-esteem

Self-esteem, which will be looked at in more detail when we examine Maslow's hierarchy of needs, concerns how much an individual comes to regard, or value, him- or herself as a person. Self-esteem is influenced by the reaction of others to us, and the comparisons made of us by other people (Argyle, 1983).

Ideal self

Ideal self is the personality we would like to be. It consists of our goals and ambitions and is, according to Maslow, dynamic in nature. What he means by this is that ideal self is forever changing. The ideal self of our childhood is not the same as the ideal self of our late teens or our late twenties, etc. As we shall discover in our look at applications of the humanistic approach, humanistic psychotherapy helps many people uncover their ideal self. Knowing who you would ideally like to be sees the humanistic psychotherapist move the client from a poor perception of self to a more psychologically healthy ideal self.

How the self is formed comes about as a result of phenomenology, personal agency, existentialism and gestalten. All interlinked, the humanistic approach says these influence self for good or ill. The humanistic approach emphasises that a healthy self should be seen particularly in terms of personal growth and self-actualisation.

Phenomenology and the self

Phenomenology concerns our personal, subjective interpretation of the experiences we have in life that mould us as an individual personality. These experiences come to us from our outside world, which is called our **phenomenological field**. Phenomenology is an element of personality that contributes towards why we think, feel and behave the way we do. Put simply, if a person's experiences in life have been negative, their interpretation of these experiences, their **phenomenology**, may result in that person thinking, feeling and behaving in a negative and often destructive way.

The humanistic approach consequently sees the self as fashioned by our phenomenology, or personal interpretation of experiences. Our phenomenology helps to form our inner personality of self and our personal perception of who we are, or think we are. Try the following.

INTERACTIVE

PHENOMENOLOGY

Phenomenology is your personal subjective view of the world. Not surprisingly, as it is based upon your own life experiences. Read the following scenario. Two friends go to see an Old Firm Cup Final at Hampden Park. They each go to their designated parts of the ground. The Celtic fan to the Celtic end, the Rangers' fan to the Rangers' end. Both at an objective sensory level 'see' the exact same 90 minutes of football. At the end of the game they meet up and discuss the game. One reports it as the best game he has ever seen. The other claims it the worst!

Despite seeing the same game, why are their views different? Write a 500-word report using your knowledge of their phenomenology to help you. You can be as imaginative as you like!

R.D. Laing

This textbook would be lacking without mention of Ronnie Laing. Born in 1927 in Govan, Glasgow, he went on to become hugely important to 1960s psychiatry. After studying medicine at Glasgow University he was called up in 1951 to work as an Army psychiatrist. On his demobilisation in 1953 he returned to Glasgow University to teach. He later moved to the Tavistock Clinic and Institute for Human Relations in London, where he remained until his death in 1989. His particular contribution to psychiatry was in his use of phenomenology to the understanding of schizophrenia. He thought schizophrenia was exacerbated by how the schizophrenic perceived their 'self', and how others perceived the schizophrenic. Very much against traditional psychiatric treatments such as drugs, electro-convulsive therapy and psychosurgery he set up asylums (safe houses). Here the schizophrenic client could explore their perception of self in art, drama and music therapy. Sympathetic psychiatrists, psychologists and social workers used paintings, for example, to focus in on how the schizophrenic saw *their* condition. This helped them as professionals understand the client and their condition better. A most humane psychiatrist, R.D. Laing died on 3 August 1989.

Figure 6.1 R.D. Laing

PERSONAL AGENCY AND EXISTENTIALISM

Also important to the formation of self, is the exercise of individual free will. The importance of free will, and how it can affect you, came to the humanistic approach from the writings of philosophers and writers such as Albert Camus (1913–60), Søren Kierkegaard (1813–55) and Jean-Paul Sartre (1905–80). These existentialist writers emphasised that people make choices in life, and that with choice comes the personal responsibility for what follows. They wrote about people's individual destinies as a result of their exercise of free will and how this influenced their existence for good or bad at the end of the day. The impact our existence, or everyday environments, can have on the formation of personality is called existentialism. **Existentialism**, the environment we find ourselves in, is affected by the choices we make in life.

The humanistic approach says that when we make choices in life and exercise free will we are using **personal agency**. Personal agency can be destructive if we make negative choices, or constructive if we make positive choices. Personal agency, which is the exercise of free will, affects your self, your phenomenology and your existentialism. One need only consider the very slippery slope a person may be embarking upon if they decide by the use of personal agency that the drug heroin is for them.

INTERACTIVE

TRAINSPOTTING

Watch the video *Trainspotting*, or read the book by the same name written by Irvine Welsh, and consider the following questions.

1 Whose phenomenology does this film concern?

2 How does the idea of personal agency apply in this film?

3 Outline the phenomenological field of the central characters.

4 How does the central character's self, or inner personality, become influenced by his existentialism? Give reasons for your answer.

5 What exercise of personal agency does the central character employ to change his existentialism?

As we shall see when we look at the limitations of the humanistic approach, we are never entirely free to exercise complete personal agency and choose our own paths in life – but the *degree* to which we are able to exercise personal agency to influence our own destiny is important to how we feel about ourselves. Free will is related to self. The good and bad choices we make in life influence our phenomenology, which affects self – for good or ill.

Another important strand to self comes from gestalt psychology with its influence on the humanistic concept of the whole person.

GESTALT PSYCHOLOGY AND THE WHOLE PERSON

Gestalt psychology contributed to the humanistic approach with their idea that we respond holistically – *from the experiences of our whole person* – to our world. Because the humanistic approach is interested in promoting the psychological good health of the *whole* person, a clear *total* perception of all the elements that go to make up our self is thought useful. Our self – our inner personality that influences how we think, feel and behave in our world – is as it is, because of our phenomenology and use of personal agency. Being aware of these personality-shaping life events, and the significance of some of our choices, helps us achieve what is called 'good gestalt'. For the humanistic approach good gestalt means that you are aware, or helped to become aware, of all the elements that go to make up self or personality. As a result you understand your whole person better, why you are as you are, and why you respond and behave as you do.

If you are unhappy about aspects of your thoughts, feelings and behaviours, good gestalt can see you deliberately decide to make positive changes, which gives rise to a psychologically healthier personality. The humanistic approach says good gestalt makes us psychologically better able to respond to our world from the point of view of being a healthier whole person. You are aware of all the elements of your personality.

The humanistic approach measures the psychologically healthy whole person in terms of **personal growth**. Personal growth is a concept the humanistic approach believes we are all driven to achieve as individuals. A greater awareness of all the issues that frustrate personal growth, and thus a psychologically healthier self, is helped by good gestalt.

Self-actualisation and personal growth

Humanistic psychology did not begin to achieve world prominence until the 1960s when, as we read, Abraham Maslow began to criticise behaviourism and psychoanalysis as promoting the idea that we are *inevitably* psychologically ill or average. He put forward an alternative view, which is that we are naturally motivated towards psychological good health because we are born with an innate need to be psychologically healthy. This is called personal growth, the peak of which Maslow called *self-actualisation*.

Self-actualisation is our natural predisposition to develop and grow as human beings. Often, however, personal growth towards self-actualisation is hampered by other factors. When self-actualisation is frustrated, the humanistic approach would say the individual is inevitably psychologically unwell. This is because before we can achieve self-actualisation, we have to first satisfy certain other innate needs. These are identified in Maslow's hierarchy of needs (Figure 6.2) as *physiological* needs; *safety* needs; *love and belongingness* needs; *esteem*; *knowledge and understanding* – or cognitive – needs; and, ultimately, *self-actualisation* needs. The achievement of each of these by us is seen in terms of personal growth. Personal growth makes us feel good about ourselves, within ourselves and towards others.

Maslow's hierarchy of needs

Self-actualisation
Realising one's full potential 'becoming everything one is capable of becoming'.

Aesthetic needs
Beauty – in art and nature – symmetry, balance, order, form.

Cognitive needs
Knowledge and understanding, curiosity, exploration, need for meaning and predictability.

Esteem needs
The esteem and respect of others, and self-esteem and self-respect. A sense of competence.

Love and belongingness
Receiving and giving love, affection,trust and acceptance. Affiliating, being part of a group (family, friends, work).

Safety needs
Protection from potentially dangerous objects or situations, (e.g. the elements, physical illness). The threat is both physical and psychological (e.g. 'fear of the unknown'). Importance of routine and familiarity.

Physiological needs
Food, drink, oxygen, temperature regulation, elimination, rest, activity, sex.

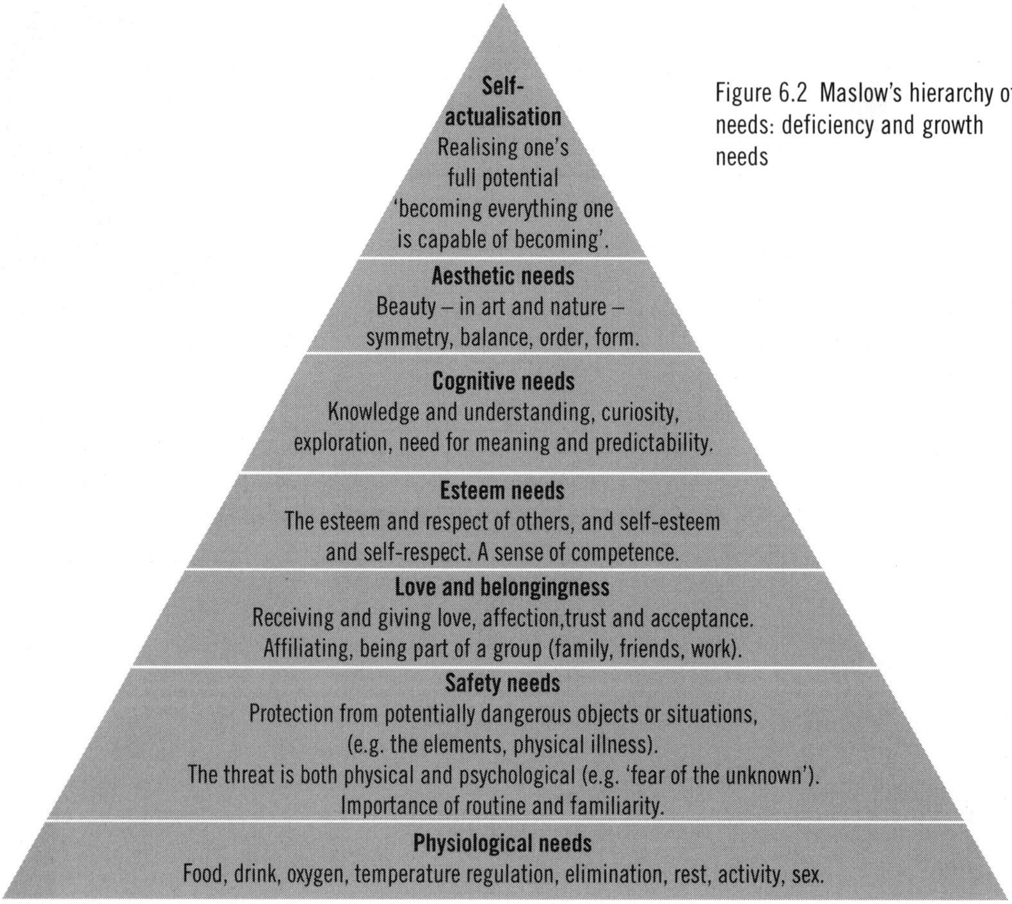

Figure 6.2 Maslow's hierarchy of needs: deficiency and growth needs

Maslow says we need to first satisfy lower-order **deficiency needs** to experience personal growth and thus move towards self-actualisation. When deficiency needs are frustrated we behave in ways to safeguard ourselves. Essential to personal survival, the satisfaction of deficiency needs might see us lie, cheat, steal and be prone to violence in order to get them satisfied. Deficiency needs, as we shall see, are *physiological*, *safety*, *love* and *esteem*-orientated. Deficiency needs are, as a consequence, **prepotent**. Prepotent means that the satisfaction of one or more of these lower order needs can occupy an individual's mind all the time. An unemployed homeless person's life is *wholly* preoccupied with meeting physiological and safety needs such as finding food, warmth and secure shelter. They have little time for anything else. They may, as alluded to earlier, be necessarily criminal in their behaviours in order to get their prepotent needs met. This is because if they don't satisfy them, they could die.

Prepotent needs are natural, and often very obvious in the behaviours of the person trying to get them satisfied. We all need to have enough to eat and drink in order to stay alive. We all need to feel comfortable and safe in our homes. We all need to be loved. We all need to be accepted for who we are by our peer group. If one, or more, of these needs are hampered, humanistic psychology thinks a psychologically unhealthy person, or self, will emerge.

Abraham Maslow

Best known for his theory of self-actualisation, Maslow was born in New York on 1 April 1908 and died in 1970. He initially studied psychology at the University of Wisconsin and later returned to New York where he studied gestalt psychology at the New School for Social Research. This experience was to have a profound effect on his thinking. A lifetime of teaching and research began when he joined the faculty of psychology at Brooklyn University in 1937. He left Brooklyn in 1951 to become head of the psychology department at Brandeis University in Massachusetts where he stayed until retirement in 1969.

Figure 6.3 Abraham Maslow

He believed that we all have within our being a hierarchy of needs concerning our bodies, our need to love and be loved by others, the way we feel about ourselves, and the fulfilment of all the potentials we may have. These deficiency and growth needs have to be met in that we are biologically motivated to satisfy them. The more we achieve the satisfaction of physiological, safety, esteem, cognitive and self-actualisation needs, the more psychologically healthier and happier Maslow believed we would be. Maslow's major works include *Motivation and Personality* (1954), *Towards A Psychology of Being* (1962) and *The Further Reaches of Human Nature* (1971).

Deficiency needs

Within Maslow's hierarchy of needs, physiological, safety, love and belongingness and esteem needs are called deficiency needs.

Physiological needs

Physiological, or bodily, needs are essential to individual survival and include air, water, food and sleep. If these are not satisfied, we die. In the developing world, the major physiological need of getting enough to eat preoccupies the majority of the population most of the time.

Safety needs

Safety needs concern our need to feel secure. They are best met when we find ourselves brought up in a safe and stable family-type environment. Safety needs are about how safe we feel in relation to our world. If you feel safe and secure in your home environment, this helps you feel safe and secure in relation to your world and the people in it. As a result you feel more confident in your self, and in your world.

Figure 6.4 The satisfaction of deficiency needs is essential to survival

In our society tragic cases of child neglect make us very aware that not everyone has a safe and secure home environment. If safety needs are not met, this affects phenomenology, the self-concept and personal growth. If you had the type of background that unfortunately saw you hit or abused in childhood, this would very likely make you wary of your home environment. In the broader world your experiences would make you very unsure, and insecure, in relation to other people. You would tend to have difficulty trusting others. As a consequence, you could find personal growth and the journey to self-actualisation difficult. According to Maslow, this is because we need to have lower-order needs satisfied before we can address subsequent needs in the hierarchy.

Love and belongingness needs

Our love need is our inborn need for *belongingness*. We have all been, or are, members of a family, peer group, gang, club, organisation, work group, social group or religious group.

Figure 6.5 Membership of a peer group can satisfy our need for belongingness

Membership of such groups gives us a sense of being needed, wanted and loved. Membership of groups fulfils a need within us to feel that we are valued. We have a need to know that we belong and when an ability to 'belong' eludes us, we feel less of a person. Essentially we value our self less. Very often people with whom we want to be friends exclude us from belonging – as is often evident in childhood and adolescence. Those who are in groups often marginalise other children and teenagers who are seen as *different*. All *they* however want to do is *belong*. Rejecting others is very hurtful to them. It can be psychologically damaging in that when love and belongingness needs are met, we value ourselves more. If they are not – and this is very often in other people's hands – we value our self less.

Esteem needs

Esteem needs involve our self-esteem and self-respect.

Self-esteem comes to us when we master a particular skill or task and feel good about ourselves as a result. Your self-esteem will inevitably soar when you pass an exam, or your driving test, etc.

Self-esteem, an important aspect of self, concerns how much an individual values himself or herself as a person. It is influenced by the reaction of others to us and others' comparison of us with others.

If an individual goes through life being told by others that they are not very good at something, this can produce a person with low self-esteem. If, on the other hand, others encourage an individual in a positive fashion in the things they do, this can result in them having a self-concept that is high in self-esteem.

Comparison with others can also have an effect on self-esteem. Whether we like it or not, we need others around us to measure ourselves against to establish our own self-esteem. Put simply, if you see others around you getting on and you are not, your self-esteem will diminish. This can be exacerbated if parents constantly compare how their child is doing with the performance of another person. If they let their child know that they view the other person's performance as better, the child can view their parents as valuing them less in this comparison to others. Comparison with others is related to conditional regard in the humanistic approach and is as we shall explore later another important factor to the humanistic understanding of personality.

Self-respect is different. Self-respect comes from the relationship given to you by others because of the things *they* value in you. Respect is earned. Respect cannot be bullied or bought from people. Examples of respect might be the classroom relationship between you, and your psychology teacher or lecturer. Another example of respect is the relationship between the older and younger generations in China. In China, and other cultures like Japan and the Russian Federation, the older generation is respected as a consequence of the wisdom that the younger generation perceive old age brings. The older person, because of the respect given them, has a greater self-esteem. They feel better about themselves. The respect you get from others allows you to value yourself more. Your self-respect is high, and as a consequence you experience personal growth in terms of esteem needs.

STUDY

S. Coopersmith (1967) *The Antecedents of Self-esteem*. San Francisco, Freeman

Self-esteem is '... the evaluation the individual makes and customarily maintains with regard to himself ... and indicates the extent to which the individual believes himself capable, significant, successful and worthy.' (Coopersmith, 1967, pp. 4–5).

Aim: Coopersmith (1967) endeavoured to assess the origins and effects of levels of self-esteem in children.

Method/procedure: Coopersmith studied several hundred 9–10-year-old white middle-class boys. He measured their self-esteem using the Self-esteem Inventory, teachers' ratings as to how each boy reacted to failure, the Thematic Apperception Test and an assessment of their confidence when in strange surroundings. On the basis of what he found, he then divided the boys into high-, middle- and low-esteem groups and examined the personality characteristics of the boys in each group via questionnaires and interviews. He also questioned and interviewed the boys and their mothers about their upbringing.

Results: The results indicated that 'external indicators of prestige [measurements of the parents' status] such as wealth, amount of education, and job title did not have as overwhelming and as significant an effect on self-esteem as is often assumed' (Pervin, 1993). Parental attitudes and behaviours including acceptance of their children, giving them clear and well-enforced behavioural boundaries and giving them respect for their actions all contributed to the children's sense of self-esteem or self-worth (Pervin, 1993). Coopersmith found that of the three self-esteem groups, the high self-esteem group were more expressive, active, confident and successful (academically and socially) than the middle- and low-esteem groups. The middle self-esteem group were the most conforming. The low self-esteem group were underachievers and did not rate themselves too much at all. They were social isolates, shy and hurt by criticism.

Coopersmith followed his participants into adulthood and found that those identified as having high self-esteem in childhood were more successful in both work and in their relationships than participants in the other two groups.

Conclusions: Self-esteem is formed from childhood. It does not depend on family wealth or background. Important to self-esteem is upbringing. Parents who give unconditional positive regard and bring children up within firm boundaries are more likely to produce children with high self-esteem. Low self-esteem children are from overly strict, overly lax or unloving family environments. Self-esteem can have a long-lasting influence on work and social relationships in adulthood.

INTERACTIVE

1. What do you understand by the term self-esteem?
2. What was the aim of the Coopersmith study?
3. Explain the method and procedure Coopersmith used.
4. What were the results of his study?
5. What conclusions can we draw from Coopersmith (1967)?
6. What criticisms might be made about this study?

Growth needs

Within Maslow's hierarchy our quest for knowledge and understanding, and self-actualisation are called growth needs.

Knowledge and understanding needs

When our lower-order deficiency needs (physiological, safety, love and esteem) are satisfied, we then have the time and motivation to turn our attention to understanding our lives better. Knowledge and understanding of our lives gives us a better idea of what it means to be human. According to Maslow, once lower-order deficiency needs are met, pursuing our knowledge and understanding need is the first important *growth* need we must satisfy. This is because knowledge and understanding lead to better psychological health for the individual. Their pursuit allows you to understand yourself, your world, and yourself in relation to your world that much better.

Figure 6.6 These students are satisfying their need for knowledge and understanding. Well mostly!

We satisfy our cognitive, or knowledge and understanding, needs in all sorts of ways – depending upon what we see as important *knowledge and understanding* for us at the time. This might be by taking up a series of night classes in psychology, art or literature just because we want to understand ourselves and aspects of our world better. The pursuit of personally relevant knowledge and understanding needs might equally result in someone learning Spanish because they go to Spain every year for a holiday. Learning Spanish makes an important aspect of their life more meaningful. The person feels the better for it. We experience personal growth as our knowledge and understanding of our world grows. We have a clearer picture of what our life is all about. Fulfilling knowledge and understanding needs can be an almost endless quest because our existence is so complex. It is rightly called a growth need.

Self-actualisation

Self-actualisation is:

> *'the desire to become more and more what one is, to become everything that one is capable of becoming'.*
>
> *(Maslow, 1955)*

Self-actualisation is the epitome of personal growth. Originally, Maslow said that only the most eminent of people, such as Abraham Lincoln and Albert Einstein, had *self-actualised*. This he later revised in *Towards a Psychology of Being* (1968), and today it is accepted that self-actualisation is available to *all* who strive for it. Self-actualisation is embodied by what Maslow calls **episodic peak experiences**. An episodic peak experience is sometimes referred to as transcendence.

Episodic peak experiences

An episodic peak experience occurs when we get an insight into what it means to be human. Episodic peak experiences are mystical, and varied in substance. It can be that feeling we get when you put down our pen in our final exam and gain a momentary insight into what has been, and what might be in the future; it can be the experience of one day looking at our baby in that one-off way and realising what being human is *really* all about. An episodic peak experience might also be the personal triumph and insight gained into ourself by coming through something when all the odds seemed against us. Self-actualisation and episodic peak experiences are available to us all. When achieved, our perception of ourselves and our world is never quite the same again. We understand more fully what it means to be human. A person who has achieved knowledge and understanding and self-actualisation, and thus fulfilled their growth needs would be said to have achieved the optimum in personal growth. They are a **fully functioning person** according to the humanistic approach.

A syndrome of decay

Someone who has fulfilled their lower-order deficiency needs (physiological, safety, love and esteem) and then does not go on to achieve their growth needs (knowledge and understanding and self-actualisation) would, for Maslow, fall into a syndrome of decay. Symptoms include despair, despondency, boredom and apathy. On the other hand, Maslow thinks a person who successfully fulfils their growth needs and achieves episodic peak experiences and self-actualisation would exhibit certain characteristics of personality. The self-actualising person:

- holds high values
- is self-sufficient
- gives an objective factual account of what they see as truth
- is uniquely individual and at ease with who they are
- has a notion of beauty and form
- is spontaneous in action
- enjoys simplicity in life
- has a richness and complexity of character

- has a keen sense of fairness and justice
- shows a balance and unity of spirit while realising there is an inevitable ending to life.

These personality characteristics of the self-actualising person are known as meta-characteristics. Do you recognise the personality of anyone you know?

Carl Rogers' contribution to a humanistic theory of personality

While Rogers' main contribution to the humanistic approach is considered later in the application of humanistic theory to humanistic psychotherapy and counselling, Rogers did make a number of valuable contributions to the theory of the formation of the self, or personality.

Carl Rogers

Figure 6.7 Carl Rogers

Important for his non-directive person-centred therapy, Rogers was born on 8 January 1902, in Illinois, USA. Like Maslow he went to the University of Wisconsin. His interest in psychology was sparked when he later studied for the ministry at the Union Theological College in New York. His growing passion for psychology saw him leave UTC and go to Columbia University to complete an MA in 1928. This was followed by a doctorate, PhD, in 1931. His first job was as Director of the Society for the Prevention of Cruelty to Children in Rochester, New York. From 1935–40 he lectured at the University of Rochester. He was elected professor of clinical psychology at Ohio State in 1940 where he first proposed non-directive counselling as a means of facilitating the client towards psychological good health. He then moved as professor of psychology to the University of Chicago in 1945 where he remained until 1957. It was here he pioneered a Counselling Centre where he was able to conduct investigations into the usefulness and effectiveness of his methods. His conditions for growth in the counselling situation, he extended, refined and promoted from 1957–63 at the University of Wisconsin, Madison, and at the Centre for the Study of the Person in La Jolla California. Rogers died on 4 February 1947. His major works include *The Clinical Treatment of the Problem Child* (1939): *Counselling and Psychotherapy* (1942); *Client-Centred Therapy* (1951); *Psychotherapy and Personality Change* (1954); *On Becoming A Person* (1961); *Carl Rogers on Personal Power* (1977) *and Freedom to Learn for the 80s* (1983).

Rogers' theory of personality: on becoming a fully functioning person

Rogers and Maslow agreed that we are all born with a biological predisposition towards self-actualisation. Self-actualisation, becoming all that you can become, can be either frustrated or nurtured by environmental forces.

The actualising tendency

Rogers (1959) maintains that we have a natural and innate actualising tendency which urges us to develop all our capacities. This fulfilment, or otherwise, of our actualising tendency helps make us feel the way we do about ourselves. If it becomes frustrated, we can become psychologically unwell. The actualising tendency is thought to be a '*biological pressure to fulfil the genetic blueprint*' (Maddi, 1996). Rogers then believes us to be biologically predisposed to self-actualisation, in much in same way as we are biologically predisposed to the onset of puberty.

The role of this actualising tendency is '*to confirm who we think we are*'. Our actualising tendency is for Rogers '*the most profound truth about man*'. If, for example you believe yourself to be a seeker after knowledge, you will involve yourself in knowledge-driven pursuits. You will inadvertently push yourself towards experiencing yourself in ways that are consistent with your self, and consequentially confirm who you think you are.

Rogers and the self

> *Self is 'the organised set of characteristics that the individual perceives as peculiar to her/himself'.*
>
> *(Ryckman, 1993)*

Self is your awareness of who you are based upon your conscious and unconscious experiences. As mentioned earlier, self develops as a consequence of an individual's interpretation of their experiences as they interact with their environment. Self is our unique personal evaluation of past experience as it has influenced us to think, feel and behave in our world. Rogers suggests that self ultimately shapes each individual's particular behavioural and psychological response to whatever life throws at them. An unhealthy self will think, feel and behave in a dysfunctional manner. For Rogers, a person being made aware of self is important. In the example above the humanistic approach would try to make the client aware of why their unhealthy self has come about, and, consequently why they think, feel, and behave as they do. Rogers considers that a major step towards **self-awareness** is self-acceptance.

Self-acceptance

Rogers' theory of personality in *Towards Being a Fully Functioning Person*, initially attracted criticism because it suggested that only the very few were able to become fully functioning persons. By 1961 Rogers' position had become more open. Complementing Maslow's revision of self-actualisation, Rogers' theory now also advocates that becoming a fully functioning person is available to us all, especially if we show self-acceptance of whatever we have become.

Self-acceptance means that past experiences, good and bad, are accepted as just that. We examine and use past experiences in a constructive way to help us move forward (and upwards through Maslow's hierarchy of needs). This restores us to Rogers' natural (biological) state of psychological balance, and well-being.

Self-actualisation is impossible without self-acceptance, or acceptance of (your) self. We can decide to be self-accepting ourselves, or seek help to understand why we are as we are through humanistic psychotherapy, or humanistic counselling.

Conditions of worth

Central to Rogers' theory of personality, conditions of worth concern how we go about valuing, or 'seeing' ourselves. Conditions of worth, or the degree to which we value ourselves, come to us from birth. These conditions are twofold, unconditional positive regard and conditional positive regard, which either help or hinder us in the attainment of esteem needs.

Unconditional positive regard

Unconditional positive regard is given when parents or primary caregivers offer their *unreserved* support, love and acceptance for the things we do. We can see this in those adults who would say

'Well done' to a child who had come a valiant last in a primary school race. Unconditional positive regard is full acceptance by others of who we are as a person.

Conditional positive regard

Conditional positive regard is when parents or primary caregivers place *conditions* on the value, or worth, of something we do. An example might be when others, whom we love and/or hold in very high regard, criticise our performance by comparing it to those whose performance they see as better. As a consequence we feel our performance, and our self, to be less valued by them. Our self is shaped by the perceptions of others – whether these perceptions are right or wrong. Conditional positive regard can result in an individual being unable to know their true self (who they actually are), which can lead to confusion, tension and maladaptive behaviour (Rogers, 1959).

ROGERS, THE FULLY FUNCTIONING PERSON, AND THE SELF

A fully functioning person is the ultimate and natural state of being for Rogers and the humanistic approach. A fully functioning person displays personal growth as illustrated by the meta-characteristics of the self-actualising person (page 148).

According to Maslow, a fully functioning person is one who is open to experience, past and present, and who uses what they have learned to live as free a life as possible. They would also be trusting in themselves, be able to express feelings freely, be able to act independently, and be creative in thought and action. For many who want to be fully functioning, self-application of humanistic theory is rewarding. Some however may want help. This is where humanistic person-centred psychotherapy and counselling is useful, and is the area where Rogers has been most influential.

Applications of the humanistic approach

HUMANISTIC PSYCHOTHERAPY AND COUNSELLING: PERSON-CENTRED THERAPY

'Delirium on helium, I am my own experience.' Manic Street Preachers, *'I'm Not Working.'*

Some people need assistance to unlock obstacles to becoming a fully functioning person. To assist them we find the practical application of Maslow's theory of self-actualisation within Rogerian person-centred psychotherapy and counselling; a combination of theory in clinical practice that helps the client become a fully functioning person.

The people involved in the application of humanistic psychological theory are not necessarily psychologists. What Rogers emphasises is applicable to other counselling situations as well as humanistic psychotherapy. Psychologists, psychiatrists, counsellors and others would apply humanistic theory to practice, if, in their work situation they show **genuineness**, **unconditional positive regard** and **empathy** towards people.

Conditions of growth

The use of genuineness, unconditional positive regard, and empathy by a facilitator (a person-centred humanistic psychologist, psychiatrist or counsellor) helps create essential *conditions of growth* within therapy to unlock difficulties for a client trying to become a more fully functioning person. Genuineness, empathy and unconditional positive regard become fused to create a focused, non-judgemental, open and honest counselling environment in which the client can examine self. Genuineness, empathy and unconditional positive regard help towards self-acceptance and personal growth. The summit of the client's journey is self-actualisation, episodic peak experiences and psychological good health. This is for Maslow and Rogers a natural, biological state *now* available to us all.

Genuineness, empathy and unconditional positive regard

GENUINENESS

Genuineness sees the counsellor, or facilitator, attempt to create the best conditions in therapy to nurture their client's journey towards self-actualisation. The facilitator should try to be relaxed, open and at ease about *themselves*. This genuineness is picked upon by the client hopefully making them think, 'If he or she can be honest, open and genuine, so can I'. The humanistic psychotherapy or counselling session is enriched and is more beneficial to the client as they seek to become more fully functioning.

Figure 6.8 A counselling session is enriched by the genuineness of the counsellor

EMPATHY

Empathy is where the facilitator tries to enter, and gain insight into, the client's world. They try to see the client's understanding of their situation from the *client's* point of view. They respond to the client using the 'reference points' the client uses. Empathy is an appreciation of where the client is coming from in humanistic psychotherapy and counselling.

UNCONDITIONAL POSITIVE REGARD

Here, unconditional positive regard is the facilitator accepting the client unreservedly. A humanistic practitioner avoids making any value judgements about their clients in case they perceive the value judgement as a 'condition of worth' – conditional positive regard. This is avoided by the use of unconditional positive regard, which is acceptance of the client as a person and gives the client confidence to better, and more honestly, express thoughts, feelings and behaviours. They reveal more of themselves and self. Unconditional positive regard helps the client achieve a greater personal insight into their self and why they are as they are, which contributes towards personal growth and a more fully functioning person. The facilitator must be neutral, showing neither approval nor disapproval of anything revealed by the client, even though it may be illegal, unethical or immoral.

A decision to change

The purpose of genuineness, empathy and unconditional positive regard is to allow the client room to explore who they believe they are. The use of these three conditions for growth nurtures a developing awareness of self and helps lead the client to self-acceptance and a *decision to change*, as a result of which the client begins personal growth. Clients are, for the humanistic approach, satisfying their biological predisposition to be in a state of psychological good health. The decision to change will vary from client to client depending on why their self is as it is. For an alcoholic this might be 'to stop drinking'; for an abused woman this might be 'to leave the violent relationship' and so on.

Counselling

'Counselling' is often quoted as a reason why many students are attracted to psychology in the first place. Many know of people who have been 'counselled', have been 'counselled' themselves, or think they want to be 'counsellors'. The desire to counsel is maybe indicative of something within us all. This, the humanistic approach would recognise, is the desire to give to others something of ourselves – from which we *both* benefit from the perspective of self.

However, psychology is not *all* about counselling and counselling *need not* involve psychology. An understanding of psychology is desirable for those who would like to offer counselling services but is also very relevant to those who don't! If you are one of the two million people the Department of Trade and Industry say are involved in 'counselling services' in the UK today and use *empathy, unconditional positive regard and genuineness* within your work situation, you would be said to be using the humanistic person-centred approach. You are not however a 'counsellor' – you are a facilitator. There are 'counselling psychologists' in the UK who have a psychology degree, have undergone post-graduate training as clinical psychologists and are members of the British Psychological Society.

THE *Q*-SORT TECHNIQUE: THE HUMANISTIC APPLICATION OF THE CORRELATION IN THERAPY

The *Q*-sort, first popularised by Stephenson (1953), is a statistical measure that allows for comparisons and relationships to be made between two factors known as covariates. Generally, a researcher using a *Q*-sort gives a participant a pack of cards, each containing a statement concerning a personality characteristic such as 'sociable and outgoing' or 'irritable'. The participant would be asked to read the cards and sort them into piles according to which ones best describe them and which ones least.

Very like me, more like me, not like me

Rogers used the *Q*-sort technique to judge self-esteem and personal growth in therapy. The *Q*-sort is still used in humanistic psychotherapy and counselling today. It involves giving the client a pack of self-assessment cards. Each card has a 'me' statement on it reflecting aspects of self or personality such as 'I am a domineering person'. The client is asked to sort the statements on the cards into piles entitled 'very like me', 'more like me', 'not like me' and so on. The client in humanistic psychotherapy or counselling would initially put a lot of negative statements about themselves in the 'very like me' category. These reflect what is called their perceived self. They are given the pack again and asked to put into piles those statements that they would like to apply to themselves. This produces ideal self.

Figure 6.9 The *Q*-sort

Perceived self

The Q-sort helps move the client from incongruent perceived self to a more congruent ideal self.

The *incongruent* perceived self is explored first in therapy. As the sessions go on the client is asked to do the *Q*-Sort again. The instruction is 'What statements apply to you now?' This should see the client now putting more positive statements about themselves into the 'very like me' and 'more like me' categories. The facilitator compares this with the previous one. Changes in the person's original incongruent perceived self will be evident. This change in their self-image, or movement from an incongruent perceived self to a more *congruent* ideal self, can be statistically measured using a **correlation**. Rogers & Dymond (1954) in applying the *Q*-Sort to correlation found evidence to support the technique's worth in humanistic psychotherapy. The use of the *Q*-sort identified perceived self and ideal self. Correlations, or relationships, were found between perceived/ideal self and improved psychological health. The, now measurable, change in their client's self-image allowed them to become more fully functioning.

Personal growth towards ideal self

The aim of the *Q*-sort is thus to identify perceived self and ideal self: who, and where, you presently are, and who, and where, you ideally would like to be. The counselling parameters are also identified to assist the client move from perceived to ideal self. Doing the *Q*-sort in a future session, and comparing it with a previous one, can further measure personal growth. It allows the client to see that they are becoming a more fully functioning person. This is the goal of person-centred humanistic psychotherapy and counselling. Research by Truax (1966) discovered that if the therapist gave positive feedback on some of the things a client said, this seemed to affect their progress towards psychological good health even more. Nowadays as a result, person-centred humanistic psychotherapy and counselling is liable to be *directive* in nature. Previously, it had been non-directive which meant the client led the pace and progress of facilitator-client meetings. Directive positive feedback by the facilitator gets better results quicker.

HEALTH EDUCATION

Applications of the approach are not just found in humanistic psychotherapy and counselling. Health educators use the links between personal agency, the self, phenomenology, existentialism, personal growth and self-actualisation in health campaigns particularly aimed at the young. Their campaigns avoid preaching to people and instead show the effect personal agency – a person's right to exercise free will or choice – can have on our lives.

Health Education Board for Scotland

An excellent example of this is Health Education Board for Scotland (HEBS) *Think About It* message contained in their drugs' awareness campaign of recent years. Accepting that teenagers in Scotland are surrounded by the temptation to take drugs, it used a television advertisement that captures the journey into adulthood of a fourteen-year-old who has to make a choice between taking heroin or not. One part of the advert sees the boy choosing to take the drug. His life spirals downwards and he is shown addicted, homeless and unemployed. The other part of the advert shows the same boy make the alternative choice and reject heroin. He is shown to turn to football and other healthy pursuits. He emerges into adulthood fit, healthy and with a job. The last scene sees *this* boy with a girlfriend on his arm, his arms laden with desirable things from the shops, look down on his other self begging in the street.

The HEBS campaign makes no value judgement on the fourteen-year-old's right to exercise personal agency. In showing both options it allows him to make whichever choice he wants. This is unconditional positive regard. In capturing the humanistic idea of personal agency it then allows the fourteen-year-old, and the rest of us, to explore the outcome of the particular choice made. Each choice is examined and shown to influence phenomenology in either a positive or a negative way. Self, in the form of self-esteem and self-respect, is also seen to either spiral downward or soar upwards. Choices made at fourteen are vividly portrayed in relation to inevitable existentialism and what this brings with it. The life of a homeless, unemployed heroin addict is not a happy one. Personal agency is linked with personal growth and becoming a fully functioning person, or otherwise. The exercise of personal agency at age fourteen has one *persona* experience difficulty satisfying basic lower-order deficiency needs in early adulthood. The alternative healthier choice made by his other *persona* sees *him* strive towards self-actualisation. By early adulthood he is on the way to becoming all that he can become. Personal agency, the right to exercise choice or free will in life, can inevitably cause you to be psychologically healthy, or psychologically unwell.

Limitations of the humanistic approach

The humanistic approach is just one of five ways we study behaviour and mental processes in psychology. No one approach is pre-eminent at any one time. There is no particular approach that is 'first among equals'. The study of psychology promotes a holistic understanding of all approaches (biological, psychodynamic, behaviourist, cognitive and humanistic). Further, psychology encourages an eclectic view in the application of an approach as a treatment or therapy. 'Eclectic' means using a wide range of sources and therefore the most appropriate treatment pertinent to the problem. As we have seen, the types of behaviour and mental processes studied in psychology get each of the different approaches interested in different aspects of the human condition. As a consequence, each has a particular contribution to make to the understanding and treatment of psychological issues. The humanistic approach is no exception with its unique and thought-provoking view of personality.

Very often different therapies from different approaches will be used together in the clinical situation. For example, someone suffering from an eating disorder might initially benefit from the application of the biological approach with the use of drugs to first stabilise their medical condition. Food supplements might also be used to bring about weight gain. They may then benefit from the application of the behaviourist approach to learn better ways to respond to the stimulus of food. Finally they may utilise the humanistic approach in person-centred therapy or counselling to explore their poor self-image. It may be the self has impeded both physical and psychological health. This is an eclectic view at work within a holistic psychology.

Construct validity

Like the psychoanalytic approach, the humanistic approach can be criticised for its use of hypothetical constructs such as self, episodic peak experiences and self-actualisation. These, as we know, are terms given to things in psychology that do not exist in reality. Support in a scientific sense for such hypothetical constructs is weak. As a consequence of this lack of scientific evidence to support such concepts, the humanistic approach can be said to lack construct validity. However, while scientific proof concerning self, episodic peak experiences and self-actualisation, etc. is absent, there is some empirical evidence to support the benefits of empathy, unconditional positive regard and genuineness in humanistic psychotherapy and counselling (Rogers & Dymond, 1954).

Within psychology, the humanistic approach is not as scientifically rigorous as its biological, behaviourist or cognitive cousins – but maybe doesn't see that it needs to be. If a more scientifically sound method of enquiry was available to the humanistic approach, practitioners would probably not shy away from using it. It is, at the end of the day, an approach that seems to be instinctively sympathetic to new methods of research to understand what it means to be human.

Methodological criticisms

The theory originated from the examination by Maslow of case studies of those he thought to be psychologically unwell, in contrast to the lives of eminent individuals such as Abraham Lincoln and Albert Einstein whom he thought had achieved self-actualisation. Case studies themselves attract a degree of criticism in that they do not give a theory much, if any, objective research evidence. Further, there is a methodological problem in generalising findings from individual case studies to the public at large. What evidence does exist to support humanistic theory and therapy is in the form of correlations. Correlations are not, however, conclusive scientific evidence for many in the broader psychological community.

Culture-bound

The humanistic approach is culture-bound. What this means is that it is more at home in American culture than anywhere else. Self-actualisation – striving to be all you can be – is part of the American dream, and is more at home in a society that likes to think it enables individuals from humble beginnings to rise to become their President in the White House. For the millions that exist below the poverty line in the USA humanistic ideas like self-actualisation are not important. They may feel insulted with the humanistic label of being 'psychologically unwell' because of their *necessary* everyday preoccupation to get basic physiological and safety needs satisfied. The same culture-bound criticism of the humanistic approach could apply from the point of view of people in any other culture who have difficulty getting by from day to day. Further, its emphasis on the individual ignores cultures that promote a more collective approach to life. For example, are those who opt to live collectively on Israeli kibbutzim to be similarly considered psychologically unwell because they sacrifice the exercise of individual free will for the good of their community as a whole?

Free will versus determinism

The exercise of free will in the humanistic approach is called personal agency. The humanistic approach takes a very optimistic view of our ability to exercise personal agency and seems to ignore the realities of life. These realities influence what real choices people have in the exercise of personal agency. This is because very often our destinies are chosen for us, or determined, by our environment. Up until the 1960s it was most unusual for women to attend university in any great numbers. One of the reasons for this was that women were at this time destined to become wives and mothers, roles for which higher education was felt unnecessary. Working-class students were not in great abundance either. Working class people worked. They may have wanted to go to university, and were perfectly capable of doing so, but their environment made going out to work at the earliest opportunity in order to support the family essential. An impoverished environment restricted the choices they could make. A person's ability to use free will to their benefit, to become all they can become, to be a fully-functioning person, is greatly determined by the practical realities of their current lives: social, economic, educational and health.

INTERACTIVE

Al Capone

Please read the following and answer the questions that follow.

In 1929 the United States of America was hit by an economic catastrophe known as the Wall Street Crash. By 1933 there were thirteen million people unemployed in the USA. In 1920 there had been 1.5 million people unemployed. Three successive Presidents – Harding, Coolidge and Hoover – apparently did little to prevent or alleviate the situation. President Hoover in the 1930s could only offer the 13 million victims 'rugged individualism', which was where his Federal government advised them they could only 'help themselves'. Suicides, homelessness, poverty and ill health abounded. Charities were the only organisations to offer help. The Chicago gangster Al Capone gave $2,500 dollars a week to a charity that fed many thousands who were starving. He was later jailed for eleven years by the Federal government on tax evasion charges concerning bootleg liquor.

1. In the light of the above how might a victim's self have been influenced by the Wall Street crash? Give reasons for your answer.
2. Do you think Al Capone exercised personal agency in his career choice? How did it affect his existentialism?
3. Do you think the thirteen million victims of the crash exercised personal agency?
4. What needs were the beneficiaries of Capone's generosity trying to fulfil? What type of needs are these?
5. What needs was Al Capone possibly fulfilling? Give reasons for your answer.
6. How does the above scenario illustrate the limitations of the humanistic approach?

Conclusion

As a theory, the humanistic approach explains personality from the perspective of self, and gives great insight into how self is formed, but gives little clue as to the origins of personality. This aside, there is valid empirical research, which lends authority to some of what the approach claims. Chodorkoff (1954) found justification that the facilitator's genuineness and experience helped the client towards becoming more psychologically healthy. Butler & Haigh (1954) confirmed that the person-centred approach in a therapy situation is beneficial in helping clients resolve difficulties that inhibit their development as a fully functioning and psychologically healthier person.

Maslow gave to the humanistic approach a psychological understanding of the importance of self and healthy psychological functioning. Rogers extended and applied this in, and to, the field of person-centred humanistic psychotherapy and counselling. The humanistic approach has had an impact within and outside psychology. The humanistic approach is an approach in psychology that encourages a humane and ethical view of human beings and has the psychological welfare and well-being of the individual at its core.

Summary

The humanistic approach, or Third Force psychology, explains an individual's past and current thoughts, feelings and behaviour from the perspective of the individual's subjective interpretation of their past experience. It is an approach in psychology that is interested in what it means to be human. It came about as a reaction to the behaviourist and psychoanalytic approaches. It believes we have an inbuilt biological drive that motivates us towards personal growth and the healthy psychological state of self-actualisation. It emphasises the importance of 'self'. The self is who you think you are as a person; it is your personality. Influential figures in the development of the approach include Abraham Maslow and Carl Rogers. Maslow gave the humanistic approach a theory of self-actualisation as illustrated by his hierarchy of needs. Rogers extended Maslow's work into the field of humanistic person-centred psychotherapy with his emphasis on empathy, unconditional positive regard and genuineness. Creating these conditions of growth in therapy facilitates an environment that helps the client become a more fully functioning person. Their application moves the person from incongruence to **congruence**, or from perceived self to ideal self. The ultimate is a fully functioning person who has achieved self-actualisation. The notion of self-actualisation lacks empirical support, but correlations have been generated to help validate the effectiveness of theory to practice in humanistic psychotherapy and counselling. The humanistic approach has had a worldwide impact within, and outside, psychology, especially in the areas of therapy and counselling. Its popularity with clients would appear to suggest that they do not view the lack of scientific support for the approach as problematic.

Table 6.1 Approaches and methods at a glance

	Psychoanalytic approach	Behaviourist approach	Cognitive approach	Biological approach	Humanistic approach
Cause of dysfunction	Unconscious and early childhood experience	Faulty learning in environment	Faulty information processes	Damage to our physiology/ genetics	Dysfunctional self (self-image) as a result of experience
Features	The unconscious Id, ego and superego Ego-defence mechanisms Psychosexual theory of adult personality development	S–R Pavlov and classical conditioning Skinner and operant conditioning	Computer analogy and S–X–R Perception Memory Thinking	Physiological psychology Evolutionary psychology	Self, phenomenology, existentialism, gestalten, and whole person Maslow's hierarchy of needs – growth needs and deficiency needs Rogers – actualising tendency
Limitations	Methodology: biased sample Use of case study Hypothetical constructs Over-emphasis on sexual, rather than social world (psychodynamic approach)	Reductionist Mechanistic Deterministic	Identity Mechanistic: computer analogy Ecological validity	Reductionist Mechanistic Deterministic Ethics	Hypothetical constructs/lack of scientific support Methodology Culture-bound Naïve
Applications	Psychoanalytic psychotherapy, purpose to access the unconscious. Features – the interpretation of dreams, free association, hypnosis/regression. Play therapy	Behaviourist psychotherapies Behaviour therapy i.e. SD, IT and AV Behaviour modification i.e. TE and PL.	Perception and advertising, marketing, etc. Memory and the CIT	Chemotherapy Schizophrenia Depression	Humanistic psychotherapy, purpose to help create ideal self Features – genuineness, empathy, positive regard Conditions of growth HEBS campaign
Associated research method/ technique	Case study Interview	Experiment	Experiment	Experiment	*Q*-sort correlation, interview, case study

INTERACTIVE

1. Using the Internet, find alternative definitions for phenomenology, gestalt psychology, self, self-concept and self-actualisation. Please give http references for these.
2. Imagine you are a journalist. Using websites such as http://chiron.valdosta.edu/whuitt/col/regsys/maslow.html design and write a front-page exclusive explaining 'Maslow's hierarchy of needs'.
3. Find the Carl R. Rogers Collection, 1902–90 at http://www.oac.cdlib.org/dynaweb/ead/ucsb/rogers. Use the biography and answer the following questions:
   - ☐ What was Rogers' second name?
   - ☐ What is first and second force psychology?
   - ☐ What job did Rogers have with the RSPPC?
   - ☐ What is the essential difference between Rogers' approach and psychoanalysis?
   - ☐ What factors led to Rogers' death in 1987?
4. Go to http://www.docdreyfus.com/therapy.html. In around 500 words discuss whether this psychotherapist takes an eclectic view of therapy? Give reasons for your answers.

Structured questions with answer guidelines

1 *Define and explain the humanistic approach in psychology.*

With reference to the preceding chapter, structure your answer around the following model:

- Define the humanistic approach. Explain why it came about. State the aim of its therapy.
- Explain what the self is, and with reference to the following, how it is formed:
  - phenomenology
  - existentialism
  - gestalten and the whole person.
- Discuss Maslow's hierarchy of needs with reference to growth and deficiency needs.
- Discuss some of Rogers' contribution to humanistic personality theory, e.g. the actualising tendency, self, self-acceptance and conditions of worth.
- Mention that Rogers' main contribution is in the application of theory to clinical practice (humanistic psychotherapy and counselling).

2 *How is the humanistic approach applied in practice?*

Structure your answer as follows:

- Identify the application of the approach as a treatment, i.e. humanistic psychotherapy and counselling. Explain what humanistic psychotherapy attempts to do. Explain what aspects of the approach are applicable in the broader counselling industry. This is because of the wide use of:
  - genuineness
  - empathy
  - unconditional positive regard.

  Explain these 'conditions for growth'. To what does each contribute?
- Explain the Q-sort as used in humanistic psychotherapy and counselling.
- Discuss personal agency in the light of health campaigns.

3 *What criticisms may be made of the humanistic approach?*

Structure your answer as follows:

- Discuss its use of hypothetical constructs, and lack of scientific validity.
- Give methodological criticisms.
- Explain why it could be said to be a 'culture-bound' approach.
- Discuss the exercise of personal agency in everyday reality. Give examples. Consider the influence determinism in/from our environment has on the real exercise of personal agency.

Glossary

Congruence: the creation of the humanistic counselling environment using empathy, genuineness and unconditional positive regard towards the client

Correlation: the strength and direction of a statistical relationship between two variates

Deficiency needs: physiological, safety, love and esteem needs are deficiency needs. We need to achieve these before we can move on to our growth needs

Determinism/deterministic: behaviourists think the S–R units of learned responses we have accumulated as a consequence of learning determine our behaviour in our environment. Behaviourism is 'First Force' psychology. We react to stimuli in our world on the basis of previously learnt responses to it. Alternatively, in psychoanalysis, unconscious forces direct individual behaviour. We are unaware of this 'Second Force' behind our behaviours, unless the source of the behaviour is retrieved from our unconscious in the course of psychoanalytic therapy. For behaviourism and psychoanalysis, what we become is determined by forces outside our control/conscious awareness

Existentialism: how our personal experience in our environment influences us as a person

Free will: an individual's ability to act free from external influence

Fully functioning person: someone achieving personal growth. A person in psychological good health

Personal agency: our exercise of free will

Personal growth: achieving deficiency and growth needs. In the humanistic sense, personal growth is psychological good health

Phenomenology: our 'life story'

Phenomenological field: the environments in which our phenomenology, or life story, is formed

Prepotent: before all others

Respect: the regard given to you by others for what they admire in you

Self-awareness: the degree to which an individual is aware of his or her self

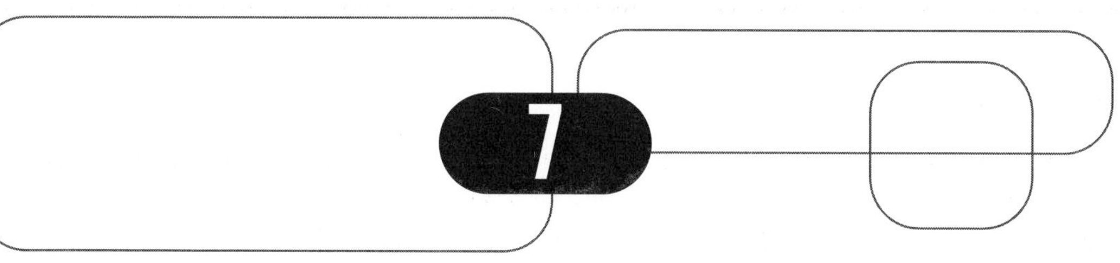

Research methods and the correlational technique

BY THE END OF THIS CHAPTER YOU SHOULD BE ABLE TO:

- identify by example the correlational technique
- define and explain the correlational technique with reference to its key features
- explain and evaluate the correlational technique in terms of its advantages and disadvantages.

Overview of research methods and the correlational technique

The purpose of this chapter is to introduce you to the topic of research methods in psychology and the correlational technique. You will have guessed by now that psychologists do quite a bit of research, if only because psychology regards itself as a science. Any science must produce evidence to support its theories and psychology is no different. Psychologists, and students of psychology, thus conduct research; something this chapter will begin to explore. As you will find in psychology, research methods fall into two categories. Some research methods are experimental in design and others are non-experimental. This chapter will explain the difference, with each method in each design category being more fully explored in later chapters. Some general research terms pertinent to research methods will be introduced. Lastly, this chapter will consider correlation as a research technique, illustrating its key features, applications, advantages and disadvantages.

Psychology and research

How we go about doing research, or our **research methodology**, is what makes psychology different from other social sciences such as history, philosophy, politics, sociology, etc. They do not claim to be sciences in the same sense as psychology and therefore don't need to adopt a rigorous scientific approach.

Psychology concerns itself with individuals, their environment, and the interaction of both. As you will discover, its main *scientific* research method is the experiment. However, because of what we are interested in – people, and their behaviours in their world – the experimental method is often not the most appropriate method of enquiry to use. Put simply, experiments can be too artificial. Any experimental research which doesn't reflect our real-life behaviours is said in psychology to lack **ecological validity**. This is something we will return to quite frequently, when we think about the advantages and disadvantages our different research methods attract. At this juncture it is enough to say that if an experiment, or any other research method, lacks ecological validity, this means that we are having difficulty in accepting that its results and conclusions can be generalised to real-life situations.

It is clear that psychology encourages research and indeed, all our approaches have strongly emphasised this fact. It is very likely you yourself will conduct research for a practical investigation. What all students of psychology have in common is that they use a research *method* in the carrying out of any practical work that they do. They are *methodical* in investigating phenomena, whatever research method they use. This is because a method gives your research purpose, and a route to achieve an aim. Each has a recognisable procedure, which is important, as data needs to be collected.

Qualitative and quantitative data

Data can be of two kinds, qualitative or quantitative. **Qualitative data** is descriptive detail about an issue. An example of qualitative data would be detail about what people thought of the Chancellor's Budget Speech. It is thus opinionated and personal.

Quantitative data is factual and objective, and will be a count or measurement of some kind concerning the behaviour under investigation. An example of quantitative data would be the number of times a rat electrically stimulated its brain within a particular time period. In psychology, quantitative data is often also called **empirical data**, i.e. those facts about our world achieved through sensory experience. According to the seventeenth and eighteenth century philosophers Locke, Hume and Berkeley, sensory experience is the only true knowledge which exists.

An ability to gather empirical data is central to the traditional sciences of physics and chemistry. A *true* science steers clear of qualitative data. How then does our claim to be the *scientific* study of behaviour and mental processes *now* square with the fact that not all research methods give rise to quantitative empirical data? Research methods are a political hot potato in psychology, with implications for psychology's very identity. By the end of this book you may want to return to the definition of psychology as the science of mind and behaviour and ask whether psychology is a science, a non-science, or a bit of both. And should we care?

Validity and reliability

Any type of data collected for psychology must be scrutinised for validity and reliability. This is because data is used to back up hypotheses and theories. As psychology is a subject that tries to be as scientific as possible, psychologists are instinctively wary of accepting the results, explanations and conclusions of *any* research. We are not being awkward. It is because psychology has the welfare of society at heart. It does not accept any research, of any design, without first holding it up to the light for examination. This is *good science*.

Validity in psychology thus asks the question, *Is the criterion in this research measuring the psychological phenomena it claims to evaluate?* **Reliability** is slightly different and concerns the question, '*Is the criterion in this research consistently measuring the psychological phenomena it claims to evaluate?*' As you will discover, some research methods are more valid and reliable than others. This can strongly influence the value of what they discover, and whether or not a researcher can generalise their conclusions to a wider population.

Participants and subjects

Human beings who help us in our research are called participants, while non-human animals are called subjects. Often in research reports, etc. participants are abbreviated to *P*s, and animals, *S*s.

*P*s particularly plague research in psychology! This is because they bring things you don't really want into a research situation. *P*s can muddy the water in any results you get, and thus any conclusions you may reach. These 'flies in the ointment' are referred to as **participant variables**. Participant variables are the individual peculiarities participants bring into a research environment. Participant variables can give rise to alternative explanations for your results and conclusions, and should be avoided. Participant variables *can* be controlled with careful thought. How this is done is considered in our next chapter on the experimental method.

Samples and populations

Whether a *P* or an *S*, each individual in our research forms part of a research **sample**. A research sample should be representative of the **target population** onto whom you want to generalise your results. A representative sample is thus one that reflects the characteristics of the target population. If it were representative, it would then not reflect **sampling bias**. When we turn to the survey method in particular, we will consider sampling bias, and examine how a representative sample is obtained using a variety of sampling techniques.

If a sample is not representative of the target population, another reason might be **volunteer bias**. A lot of research in psychology takes place in universities, and very often the participants who take part are students. Indeed, they are usually psychology students, and as participants they illustrate volunteer bias. Psychology students who volunteer for psychological research are not representative of the general student population and neither are their teachers and lecturers. Volunteer bias is a further consideration in whether you can generalise your results and conclusions to a wider population.

Extraneous variables

Participant variables, sampling bias and volunteer bias are examples of extraneous variables in psychological research. **Extraneous variables** are *variables from the outside* that can creep into any research investigation and pollute results. Alongside validity and reliability, extraneous variables are factors to be considered in the examination of any research done in psychology, by whatever method.

Approaches and methods

The two topics of approaches and methods in psychology are very much interlinked. Our five approaches tend to use one or two types of research method in preference to others.

The psychoanalytic approach explains thoughts, feelings and behaviours in terms of our unconscious. The approach puts particular emphasis on the individual, and past experience. Similarly, the humanistic approach stresses the individual and their unique potential to change in a positive direction. Both the psychoanalytic and humanistic approaches use case studies and interviews as their main methods of research because these methods are more suitable to the personal and individualised approach.

Behaviourists focus on the study of behaviours, which they control, observe and measure using an experimental design, due to their early wish that psychology be a science. Scientists conduct experiments, which behaviourists favour as they are the most controlled of all research methods. The observational method is also associated with the behaviourist approach because of this method's emphasis on the *controlled observing, recording and measurement* of behaviour.

The biological approach explains thoughts, feelings and behaviours in terms of biology, or physiology and genetics. The biological approach has its roots in both these sciences, and in medicine. No surprise then that the biological approach relies mainly on the experimental method in its investigations of human and non-human behaviour.

The cognitive approach is concerned with cognitions: perception, attention, language, memory, and thinking or problem solving. As we read earlier, the cognitive approach understands the person as an information processor, with a brain that selects, organises, stores and uses sensory information. Like the biological approach, the cognitive approach relies mainly on the experimental method as its main avenue of enquiry. In cognitive psychology the experimental method is used to make *inferences* about our cognitions, rather than measure and record directly observable behaviour.

Research design and research methods

As indicated in our overview, our different research methods fall into two categories. The laboratory experiment, field experiment and quasi-experiment are experimental in design. The observational, interview, case study and survey methods are non-experimental in design. What determines whether a research method is experimental, or non-experimental, is just how scientific it is thought to be. Does the research method follow what is called the **experimental method**? The experimental method is the topic of our next chapter.

Table 7.1 Research designs

Experimental designs	Non-experimental designs
Laboratory experiment	The observational method
Field experiment	The interview method
Quasi-experiment	The case study method
	The survey method

The scientific method

The key element of any form of research is that the methodology, or research method, should be as rigorous and as objective as possible. The main way to do this is to adhere to what is called the scientific method, in which:

- Researchers make observations to produce factual data about behaviour.
- This data forms a theory to explain the behaviour.
- From the theory a prediction, called a hypothesis, is made about the behaviour.
- The hypothesis is then tested which generates more data.
- In the light of this new data the explanation of the behaviour, or theory, is supported or adjusted. Major adjustments often lead to a brand new theory.

The scientific method, and the cyclical nature of how science progresses, is back to square 2!

A bit more on hypothesis testing

A hypothesis is a testable statement derived from a theory. A hypothesis makes a specific prediction about what is expected to happen under certain circumstances. All sciences test such hypotheses under controlled conditions. To discover whether the prediction is correct, measurements of the extent of their prediction are taken. This factual data helps to support the hypothesis or otherwise. If the hypothesis *has* generated supporting evidence, this gives a measure of confidence in accepting any theory from which the hypothesis came.

There are two types of **research hypothesis** used in psychology, the experimental hypothesis and the correlational hypothesis. You will meet the experimental hypothesis in our next chapter, but now let us turn to the correlational hypothesis, a feature of the correlational research technique in psychology.

Variables

To test a hypothesis underlying a theory you have to first identify the **variables** to be investigated. According to Mike Cardwell a variable '*is literally anything whose value is free to change*'. Variables, then, include intelligence, depression and aggression. The next stage is to operationalise these variables. The **operationalisation** of variables means finding a physical objective measure to observe and record their occurrence. The variable of intelligence could be measured by way of an IQ test. An IQ test gives you a quantifiable score. Depression could be measured using the BDI (Beck's Depression Inventory) also giving you a quantifiable score.

The operationalisation of hypothetical constructs is particularly difficult. This is because the construct itself doesn't exist in reality. Difficulties abound in finding an agreed definition of constructs from which we can identify variables to then operationalise.

THE CORRELATIONAL TECHNIQUE

Correlation is a statistical technique used to indicate the degree of relationship between two covariates.

Correlation is not a research method but a statistical technique used to discover the degree of relationship between two covariates, or **covariables**. A covariate could be an individual or group behaviour, an event, or a situation that is itself free to vary. Examples would be hours spent studying, hours spent watching TV, levels of aggression, delinquent behaviours, etc.

Correlations and hypotheses

As with an experiment, a correlational study will have a **null hypothesis**. The null hypothesis is more fully explored in our next chapter on the experimental method.

In a correlational study the null hypothesis (H_0) would predict that there is *no relationship* between two covariates. If a correlation coefficient were being used, the level of significance (*p* value) would also be stated.

Further, as with an experimental hypothesis, a correlational *research* or *alternative* hypothesis (H_A or H_R) would indicate whether the hypothesis was either one- or two-tailed. In a correlation a one-tailed hypothesis predicts the direction the relationship between the covariates is expected to go. A two-tailed hypothesis does not predict the expected direction. A one-tailed H_R would predict that there was a positive **or** negative relationship expected between the covariates. A two-tailed H_R would predict a relationship, but not its direction.

Correlations are widely used in psychology to discover the extent to which two independent behaviours might be related. If you find you *do* have a correlation, this allows you to make a prediction about a behaviour/event/situation in the future. We will discover that a correlation can establish a relationship between one covariate and another and this allows predictions to be made.

Examples of correlations, or relationships between two covariates, could be: hours spent studying, and examination performance; amount of violent TV programmes watched, and levels of aggression; physical punishment in the home, and delinquency; finger length, depression, and fertility; and even levitation and crime levels! Let us take an example of a possible correlation between the number of hours studied by ten students, and their subsequent scores in a psychology assessment.

To get a correlation you obtain a measurement of each covariate from the individuals/groups in your sample. You then tabulate this paired data as shown below.

Table 7.2 Covariate measurements

Participant	1	2	3	4	5	6	7	8	9	10
Hours studied (*x*)	8	3	2	5	9	2	1	4	6	8
Psychology assessment score (*y*)	83	34	32	48	76	40	27	36	56	81

To discover whether there is a correlation between the number of hours studied and scores in an assessment, we would tabulate our data as above, and then plot our pairings onto a **scattergram**. A scattergram is a *descriptive* statistic that helps *illustrate* a statistical relationship, such as a correlation. The patterns our plots form indicate whether a correlation exists. Number of hours studied is the *x*-axis value, plotted on the horizontal, and score in the assessment, is the *y*-axis value, plotted on the vertical.

Positive correlations

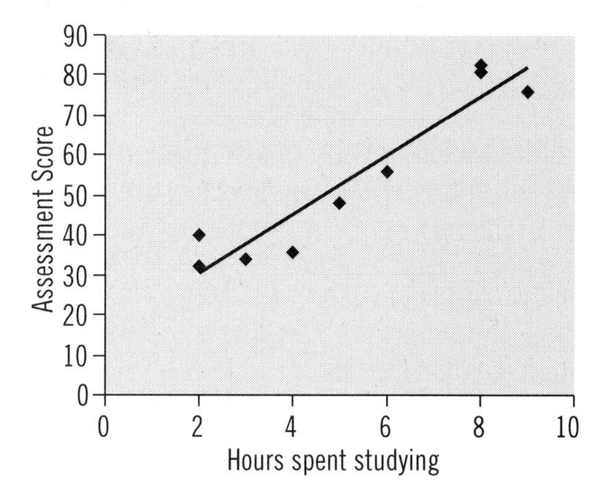

Figure 7.1 Scattergram illustrating a near perfect positive correlation

We can see from the plots on the scattergram that as the number of hours spent studying increases, the student's assessment score increases. When, as here, one covariate *increases*, and the other similarly *increases*, we have a **positive correlation**. This is because there is a *positive* relationship between hours spent studying and assessment scores. We can tell this from the pattern our plots make. Our plots are going in an upward, positive direction, as indicated by the **trend line**, which you will note in a scattergram, does not 'join the dots'! It runs through them as a 'line of best fit'. The direction, and the degree of elevation in our trend line, indicate the strength and degree of correlation between our two covariates. Here we have a *picture* of a **near perfect positive correlation** between the two covariates on our x and y axes; hours spent studying, and assessment scores.

From our scattergram we are able to predict future assessment performance by suggesting, on the basis of our trend line, that a student who puts in two hours studying will do less well than a student who works for ten hours. We are also able to project our line of best fit to accommodate a prediction of results based on more/fewer hours studied by individuals. If someone studied for twenty minutes their predicted score would be less than twenty. If someone studied for between eleven and twelve hours their predicted result would be over ninety.

The correlation coefficient

We can also take our correlational data one step further and use a statistical sum such as Spearman's rho to calculate a **correlation coefficient**. A correlation coefficient is a mathematical calculation, and representation of the degree of relationship between two covariates. A Spearman's rho calculation would give you a correlation coefficient answer of between –1 and +1, somewhere along the following range:

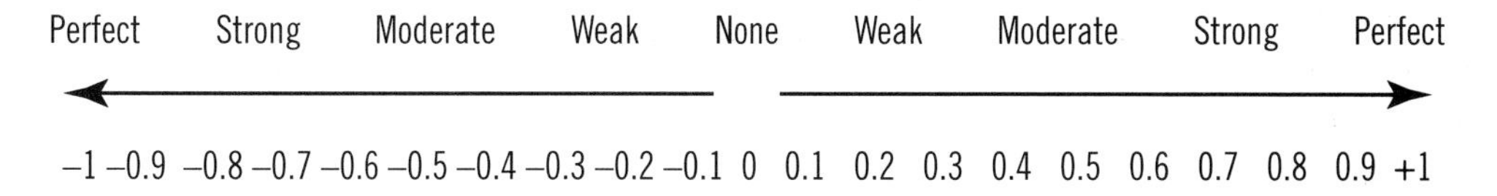

Figure 7.2 Spearman's rho calculations

The nearer rho (ρ) is to +1, the more perfect the correlation you have, and thus the more certain you are that there is a positive relationship between your two covariates. You can infer that one is positively related to the other. A correlation coefficient of around +1 is diagrammatically represented in our scattergram above. If a Spearman's rho was calculated on the basis of our data, ρ would be somewhere between 0.8 and +1 (see Spearman's rho, page 172). This would be confirmation of our strong positive correlation pattern as seen above. Absolutely perfect positive correlations, having a calculated correlation coefficient of $\rho = +1$, are rare in psychological research.

Another useful property of a correlation coefficient is that it allows you to test the significance of your results. Levels of significance are more fully explored in our next chapter on the experimental method.

The nearer ρ is to 0, the less likely there is to be any correlation between your covariables.

Negative correlations

We can also generate a negative correlation between two covariates. What this means is that as one covariate increases, the other decreases. There is thus a negative relationship between the two covariates. Again a negative correlation can be represented by a scattergram, and also calculated using Spearman's rho. Let us take our example above of hours spent studying and assessment scores. Our data could be:

Table 7.3

Hours	1	2	3	4	5	6	7	8	9	10
Score	83	76	74	67	56	48	36	34	32	27

Our scattergram would then look like Figure 7.3:

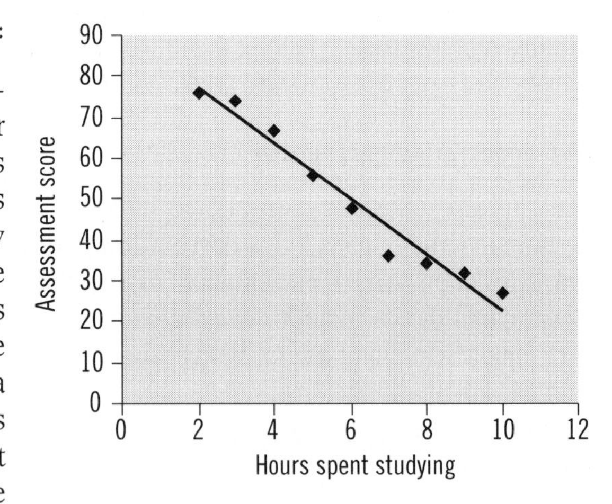

Figure 7.3 A negative correlation as illustrated by a scattergram

The pattern got with our plots in the scattergram Figure 7.3 is an example of a near **perfect negative correlation**. This is because as one covariate *increases* (hours spent studying), the other consequently *decreases* (assessment scores). In a negative correlation, as in Figure 7.3, the trend line is going in a downward, negative direction. We can say that our scattergram here illustrates a strong negative correlation between hours spent studying, and scores in a subsequent assessment. On the basis of this trend line you could predict that someone who studied a lot would not do as well as someone who did not! If we were to apply Spearman's rho to this data it would give rise to a negative correlation coefficient of ρ being between –0.8 and –1.0.

A negative correlation like the above does not sound as absurd as it might seem. It would be true to say that the author was not known for his academic ability in S5 and S6 at Holyrood

Secondary School, Glasgow. His mother would say this was an understatement. His mother would be right. Studying was for swots, and aged seventeen or so he did not want this tag. No chance. The night before his Higher Modern Studies examination in 1974, when others were hard at work in their bedrooms, he was watching TV! Panorama ran a documentary entitled '*The Social, Political and Economic Effects of Scottish Oil.*' The first question your author saw in his Higher paper the next day was '*Discuss the social, political, and economic effects of Scottish oil.*' The invigilator had to get a bucket of water in case his script burst into flames, because of the fury and speed at which he wrote. He got an A band 1, the *only* thing that impressed at his university interview for social sciences, and his introduction to the subject of psychology. This book is a result of a negative correlation!

The point to this story is that you can get correlations between almost anything. There could be other factors, as identified earlier, called extraneous variables that might influence your results, which you have not taken into account. Hours spent studying and assessment performance may indeed be related, but our positive/negative relationships could have arisen because of other factors. Our negative correlation may have arisen because the students who put in a lot of hours 'studying' could just have been dossing on their bed for hours 'reading' pages of notes from their big fat psychology folder. Cognitive psychology would tell you why these students didn't do as well as others, who did not study (badly) like this, but instead watched dedicated TV programmes, building upon, and enriching, their previously learned knowledge of psychology. The study of cognitive psychology can improve your examination performance. Definitely.

Correlations should then never be taken as scientific 'truths'. They can only indicate that there *might* be a positive or negative relationship between two behaviours or situations. They cannot ever show that one covariate *causes* another. Very often the general public can be lulled into believing a correlation is scientific 'proof' that one thing causes another.

Any cause–effect relationship in psychology can *only* be established using the experimental method. Correlation is a statistical technique that can only be used to establish the degree and strength of a relationship between two things; *never* that one covariate causes another.

Later we will look at a good, and a circumspect, or dodgy correlation; for the moment please see below an illustration of a 'no correlation' situation using our 'hours studied/assessment performance' example.

Table 7.4

Hours	1	2	3	4	5	6	7	8	9	10
Score	83	32	34	56	67	48	36	74	76	27

In Figure 7.4, there is no correlation. We cannot establish a trend line, or line of best fit between the paired covariate data. An interpretation of this scattergram pattern would be that no relationship exists between hours spent studying, and assessment performance.

Spearman's rho

To recap, Spearman's rho allows you to calculate the strength and degree of relationship, or correlation, between sets/pairs of ranked data. It produces a correlation coefficient of between –1 and +1, from which you can tell the degree of positive or negative relationship. The nearer your answer is to +1, the more positive the relationship between the covariates. They are each increasing in a positive direction. The nearer your answer is to 0, the less chance of a relationship, while the nearer it is to –1, the more negative the relationship that exists between the covariates. As one goes in one direction, the other goes in the other.

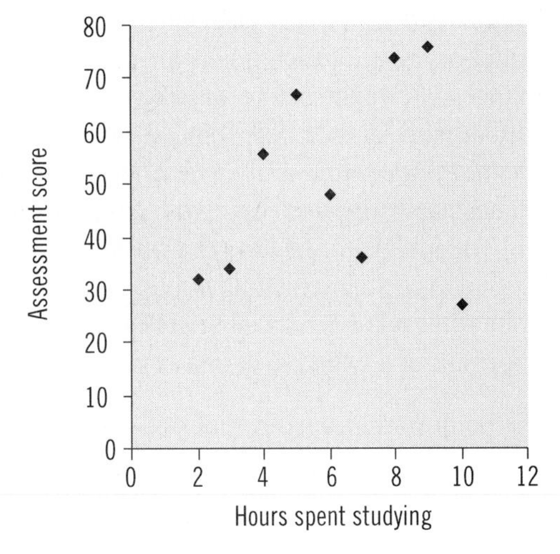

Figure 7.4 Scattergram illustrating no correlation

Using rho also allows you to test your null hypothesis (H_0) for significance. We use levels of significance to test the **probability** that our results happened by chance or random factors. Levels of significance are highlighted in our next chapter on the experimental method, where the null hypothesis and probability are more fully explored. Let us here however try to work out a correlation coefficient for the above data based upon the following correlational hypotheses.

Alternative hypothesis H_A: 'That there is a positive relationship between the number of hours a student studies and their subsequent assessment score.'

Null hypothesis H_0: 'That there is not a positive relationship between the number of hours a student studies and their assessment score at the 0.05 level of significance.'

Our alternative (or research) hypothesis, H_A, is one-tailed. This is because it is predicting the direction of expected relationship, i.e. as the number of hours spent studying increases, a student's assessment score should similarly increase. It is predicting a positive correlation, or relationship.

Our H_0 predicts that there will be no relationship. If the data, when applied to Spearman's rho, does produce a calculation to support a relationship, testing to a level of significance of 0.05 indicates that the researcher is willing to accept that there is a 1:20 likelihood that any statistically supported relationship has happened because of chance or random factors.

Using our original data (from page 168) that produced our first scattergram, you calculate rho as follows.

Table 7.5

Hours studied	1	2	2	3	4	5	6	8	8	9
Score	27	40	32	34	36	48	56	81	83	76

How to do a Spearman's rho

Lay out the data in the following way:

Table 7.6

Column 1 Participant	Column 2 Hours studied *x* value	Column 3 Psychology Assessment Score *y* value	Column 4 Rank *x*	Column 5 Rank *y*	Column 6 Difference *d* (between values in columns 4 & 5)	Column 7 Difference multiplied by the power 2 d^2
1	8	83	8	10	–2	4
2	3	34	4	3	1	1
3	2	32	2	2	0	0
4	5	48	6	6	0	0
5	9	76	10	8	2	4
6	2	40	2	5	–3	9
7	1	27	1	1	0	0
8	4	36	5	4	1	1
9	6	56	7	7	0	0
10	8	81	8	9	–1	1
						$\Sigma d^2=20$

Then

1. Enter participants, e.g. 1–10 in column 1.
2. Enter in your x values in column 2 (number of hours each studied), e.g. participant 7, 1 hour, etc.
3. Enter in your y values in column 3 (psychology assessment scores), e.g. participant 7, 27, etc.
4. Rank order your x values in column 4. Rank the smallest score 1 (first), etc.
5. Rank order your y values in column 5. Rank the smallest score 1 (first), etc.
6. Subtract each y value from each x value, as in column 6, e.g. participant number 2, $4 - 3 = 1$.
7. Find the difference 'squared' for each $(x - y)$ value, as in column 7, e.g. participant number 2, $1 \times 1 = 1$.
8. Add up all the values in the d^2 column to get Σd^2. The symbol Σ (sigma) means 'sum of'. So Σd^2 means that you add up all the figures in the d^2 column. In this instance in column 7, $\Sigma d^2 = 20$.

You now have all the necessary data to 'plug' into the Spearman's rho formula, which is:

$$r_S = 1 - \frac{6(\Sigma d^2)}{N(N^2 - 1)}$$

where

r_S = Spearman's rho
Σ = sum of
d^2 = difference $(x - y)$ squared
N = number of participants
N^2 = number of participants squared

$$r_S = 1 - \frac{6(20)}{10(100 - 1)}$$

$$r_S = 1 - 0.12$$

Calculated $r_S = 0.88$

This is your calculated rho. One last step is to find critical rho. Consult the Spearman's rho critical value table shown on page 175. Run your finger down the n column – n means the number of participants in your correlation. So here, $n = 10$

Remember our null hypothesis H_0: 'That there will not be a positive relationship between the number of hours a student studies and their assessment score at the 0.05 level of significance.'

You then run your finger along until you find the 0.05 level of significance for a one-tailed test. Here you find critical rho. Critical rho at the 0.05 level of significance for a one-tailed test, where $n = 10$ is 0.564.

Then merely follow the instruction at the bottom of the table, which is:

'Calculated r_S, must EQUAL OR EXCEED the tabled (critical) value of significance at the level shown.'

Our r_S of 0.88 does indeed 'equal or exceed' the critical value of 0.564 at the level of significance shown in our null hypothesis (0.05) for a one-tailed test. As a result we can reject the null hypothesis, and accept the alternative hypothesis H_A: 'That there is a positive relationship between the number of hours a student studies and their subsequent assessment score.'

Our Spearman's rho correlation coefficient calculation of 0.88 now clearly supports this conclusion. Remembering that our null hypothesis has a probability (p) value of 0.05, please appreciate that while being able to reject the H_0 and accept the H_A we must accept that there is a 1:20 likelihood that this positive correlation has arisen because of chance or random factors.

Table 7.7 Spearman's rho table of critical values

	Level of significance for a two-tailed test			
	0.10	0.05	0.02	0.01
	Level of significance for a one-tailed test			
	0.05	0.025	0.01	0.005
$n = 4$	1.000			
5	0.900	1.000	1.000	
6	0.829	0.886	0.943	1.000
7	0.714	0.786	0.893	0.929
8	0.643	0.738	0.833	0.881
9	0.600	0.700	0.783	0.833
10	0.564	0.648	0.745	0.794
11	0.536	0.618	0.709	0.755
12	0.503	0.587	0.671	0.727
13	0.484	0.560	0.648	0.703
14	0.464	0.538	0.622	0.675
15	0.443	0.521	0.604	0.654
16	0.429	0.503	0.582	0.635
17	0.414	0.485	0.566	0.615
18	0.401	0.472	0.550	0.600
19	0.391	0.460	0.535	0.584
20	0.380	0.447	0.520	0.570
21	0.370	0.435	0.508	0.556
22	0.361	0.425	0.496	0.544
23	0.353	0.415	0.486	0.532
24	0.344	0.406	0.476	0.521
25	0.337	0.398	0.466	0.511
26	0.331	0.390	0.457	0.501
27	0.324	0.382	0.448	0.491
28	0.317	0.375	0.440	0.483
29	0.312	0.368	0.433	0.475
30	0.306	0.362	0.425	0.467

Calculated r_S must EQUAL or EXCEED the table (critical) value for significance at the level shown.

Source: J.H. Zhar, 'Significance testing of the Spearman Rank Correlation Coefficient', *Journal of the American Statistical Association*, 67, 578–80. With the kind permission of the publishers.

Depression, fertility and fingers

Figure 7.5 Dr John Manning

On 13 March 2002, the BBC TV programme 'Tomorrow's World' celebrated National Science Week. It reported on some very interesting research based upon correlations done by Dr John Manning of the School of Biological Sciences at the University of Liverpool. Manning had discovered a relationship between the length of our fingers, depression, and also fertility rates.

Manning, Martin & Dorwick (2001) studied 50 men and 52 women from different socio-economic backgrounds. They took a number of physical measurements such as wrist size, ear size, height, and the length of their fingers. The also gave each participant the Beck Depression Inventory (BDI), widely used in the clinical diagnosis of depression.

With men, the results showed that the length of their ring finger (fourth digit) positively correlated with a high BDI score. Dividing finger length by height, to control for the fact that tall men have longer limbs, fingers and feet, gave an even stronger basis for predicting that male participants with long ring fingers would score highly on the depression inventory. The 50 male participants on average scored 5 on the BDI. The ten male participants with the shortest ring fingers had a mean score of 1.56, while the 10 longest-fingered males averaged 8.5. (The BDI 'depressed' range starts at 10.)

The key to this strange relationship appears to be prenatal testosterone, which is produced from the eighth week of pregnancy. According to Dr Manning: 'Foetal testosterone plays a key role in the development of the male genital system. It also impacts on the development of fingers and thumbs, and the central nervous system. Men who experienced high concentrations of foetal testosterone have relatively long fingers – in particular, fourth digits, which are longer than their second digits. Conversely, men who experienced low concentrations of foetal testosterone have shorter fourth digits than their second digits ... Interestingly, the study's results suggest that depression in women has a different, and as yet undetermined origin.'

What this work suggests is that high foetal testosterone levels in males (as indicated by the length of the ring finger) biologically predisposes them to be more susceptible to depression than males with low foetal testosterone levels (who have short ring fingers).

It isn't all bad news for long-ring-fingered males however. Men with long ring fingers have higher fertility levels than their shorter ring-fingered male counterparts. So, if having lots of babies is important to you, you might consider the length of fingers from now on! Please note however that Dr Manning warns that much more research is needed in order to be more confident in any relationships suggested by his amazing correlations.

Circumspect correlations

Followers of the Maharishi Mahesh Yogi in the UK have established the transcendental meditation TM–Sidhis programme. It is more commonly known as yogic flying, first brought to the

British public's attention by the not unrelated, and now defunct, Natural Law Party in the mid-late 1990s. Yogic flying is attempting to levitate, or jump, into the air from a squat position. Yogic flying is thought to bring 'bubbling bliss for the individual' and 'positivity and harmony in the environment'. T–m.org.uk suggests that when yogic flying is practised in groups, it produces a 'field effect on the level of human consciousness'. Through this field effect apparent 'coherence radiates throughout the environment, dissolving stress, reducing negativity and creating a positive and harmonious influence in society'. This has seen them allege something called the 'Maharishi effect'. A graphical representation of the 'effect' is reproduced here.

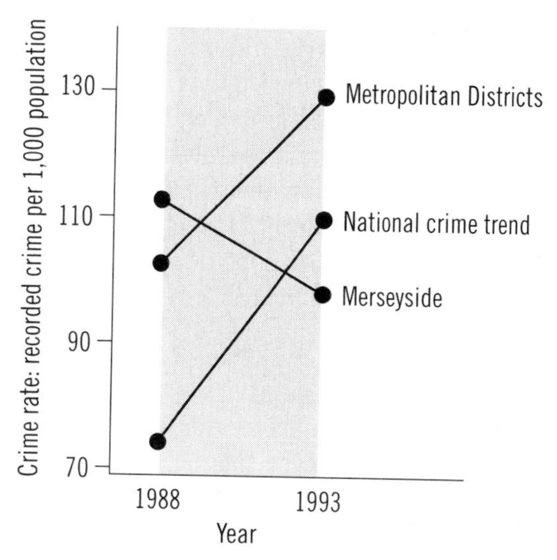

Figure 7.6 Maharishi effect

The organisation claims that during a five-year period into a study of the Maharishi effect, crime in Merseyside 'fell by 15 per cent while crime in the rest of the country rose by 45 per cent, a relative decrease of 60 per cent'.

The reason for the fall in crime in the Merseyside area, t–m.org.uk says, was down to the transcendental influence of a group of 200 yogic flyers. This was because they had been yogic flying in nearby Skelmersdale from 1998, at around the same time the fall in crime rate on Merseyside began (see Figure 7.6). According to the Natural Law Party at http://www.natural-law-party.org.uk/pressreleases/UK-20000529-nlp-fact-sheet.htm this negative correlation between yogic flying and the crime rate known as the Maharishi Effect, is the best established of all findings in the social sciences.

Figure 7.7 Yogic flyer

The Maharishi effect

This is an excellent example of why we should be wary of correlations. While yogic flying may indeed bring bubbling bliss, it cannot claim to cause a fall in crime rate just because people were jumping up and down from a squat position at the time the crime rate began to fall. There are just far too many other extraneous variables.

The variable that precipitated the fall in crime rate in Merseyside during this time happened a few years earlier. This was the Toxteth riot that erupted during a very hot summer spell in 1981 in an area of Liverpool known as Liverpool 8. The Toxteth riot sparked similar riots in Moss Side, Manchester and Brixton in London. The Conservative government was so concerned that all police leave throughout the UK was cancelled during the summer of 1981. The author was in Sheffield and Brixton at the time, and can guarantee that revolt was in the air. Thousands spilled onto the streets of major cities in Britain 'waiting', and/or posturing aggressively towards the hundreds of riot police opposite, themselves 'waiting', and/or posturing back. A heady cocktail for someone with an interest in social psychology!

Toxteth led to the then Home Secretary Michael Heseltine setting up the Scarman Enquiry, which consequently saw a massive sea change in police–community relations in Merseyside. There was a vast increase in financial investment in police–community affairs in Merseyside from the mid-1980s onwards. Maybe this better explains the drop in crime rate, as opposed to the alleged negative correlation called the Maharishi effect. You can make up your own mind.

Figure 7.8 The Toxteth riots

INTERACTIVE

The reference given for all the above is Deans, G.D.A., Cavanaugh, K.L. and Orme-Johnson, D.W. (1996) 'The Maharishi effect: A model for social improvement. Time series analysis of a phase transition to reduced crime in Merseyside metropolitan area'. Psychology, Crime and Law, 2(3). G.D. Hatchard, 2000, Vedic Economy. PhD dissertation, Maharishi University of Management.

Looks impressive, doesn't it? Spot any small snags with this?

Advantages of the correlational technique

The correlational technique is useful in situations where an experiment would be impractical. This is because no manipulations of behaviour are required. The behaviour, over which you as a researcher have no control, is already occurring/has just occurred. This is why the correlation is an *ex post facto* research technique. *Ex post facto* means *after the fact*, the fact being the covariates you are now measuring in retrospect.

Correlation is also used in situations where other research methods would be unethical. It is correlations, for example, that have established the relationship between cancers and smoking. To conduct an experiment in which one group was encouraged to smoke, and another not, and then to measure any effect on health would be unethical.

Correlations are a good basis for more rigorous experimental investigations to be carried out later on. Strong relationships between behaviours are always worth exploring in a more scientific fashion. We could conduct an experiment to discover what the *cause* might be behind any strong relationship suggested by a correlation. Using a correlation coefficient can also indicate and help you decide whether it is worth exploring the phenomenon further using the more controlled experimental method.

This is because techniques like Spearman's rho give you a *numerical* indication of the type and strength of relationship between two covariates (–1.0/+1.0). Inferential statistics like rho turn the descriptive data on your scattergram into *quantifiable* data, in the form of a correlation coefficient. This gives you more precise information to decide what to do next. A coefficient of near –1 or +1 would be worth investigating further, while a coefficient of say –0.2, or 0.3 would not.

Disadvantages of the correlational technique

The main disadvantage of the correlational technique is that it lacks the power and rigour of the experimental method in that it establishes *only* a relationship. It is a statistical technique that can never specify a cause and effect relationship between its covariates. This is in contrast to the experimental method, which as we will shortly discover does allow cause–effect conclusions to be reached – if they are scientifically justified.

Consequently, in a correlational study any apparent relationship that is suggested may well be due to factors *other* than those being claimed, as with our yogic flying/crime rate example earlier.

Summary

'Research methods' fall into two categories, called designs in psychology. Research methods that are experimental in design include the laboratory, field and quasi-experiment. Non-experimental methods include the observational, survey, interview and case study methods. The correlation is not a research method, but a research technique. It endeavours to find relationships between two covariates, or independent behaviours, situations or events. A correlation can be positive or negative. A positive correlation means that there is a positive relationship between the two independent covariates, such that as one increases, so does the other. A negative correlation means that there is a negative relationship between the two independent covariates, where here an increase in one covariate is related to a decrease in the other. The degree of relationship can be illustrated using a descriptive statistic called a scattergram. The scattergram's trend line illustrates the strength, direction, and degree of positive or negative correlation. It may also indicate no correlation at all. The strength of correlation can be further tested using an inferential statistic called a correlation coefficient. Using the likes of Spearman's rho, the nearer rho is to +1, the more positive the relationship is said to be, while the nearer rho is to −1, the more negative the relationship between covariates. A rho of near 0 indicates no relationship between the covariates. The correlational technique is useful in situations where an experiment would be unethical or impractical. This can help decide whether a more rigorous scientific investigation into the apparent relationship is justified. This is enhanced by the correlational technique's ability to produce quantifiable data in the form of a coefficient. However, even with a coefficient, be wary of correlations. Remember the Maharishi effect! Correlations can only infer a positive or negative relationship between its covariates. No cause–effect conclusions can be reached. This is the province of the experimental method, to which we now turn.

INTERACTIVE

1 Examine the scattergrams below. Draw in a trend line (in pencil!). What type of correlation does each indicate? Give reasons for your answer. Estimate a Spearman's rho for each.

2 On the basis of the data in Table 7.8 for a one-tailed hypothesis tested at the 0.05 level of significance, follow the steps described on page 173 and calculate a Spearman's rho.

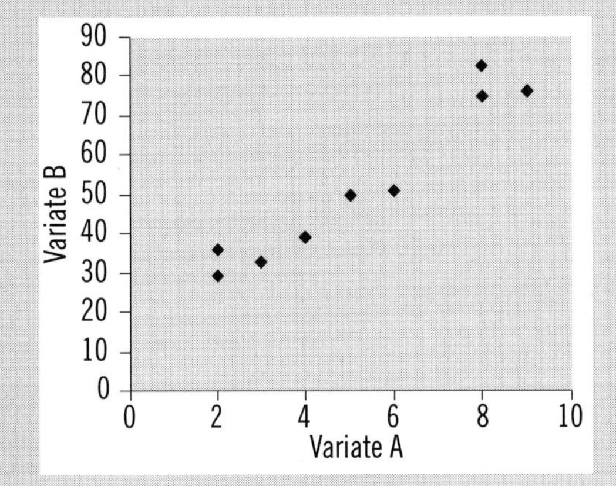

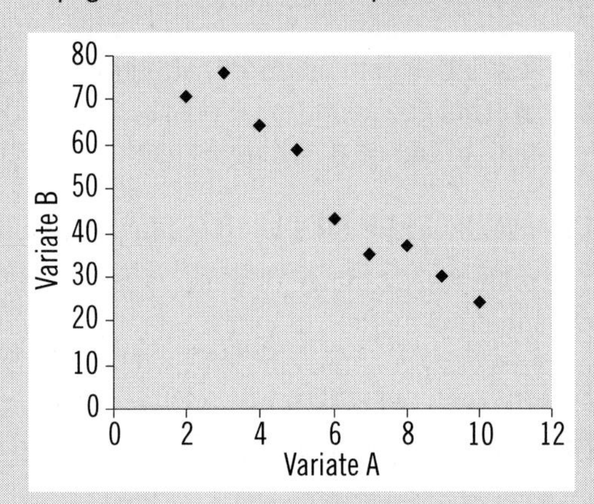

Figure 7.9

Table 7.8

Variate A	1	2	2	3	4	5	6	8	8	9
Variate B	24	36	29	33	39	50	51	75	83	76

Structured questions with answer guidelines

1 *Describe and explain the correlational technique.*

With reference to the preceding chapter, structure your answer as follows:

- Define the correlation as a statistical technique used to indicate the degree of relationship between two covariates. Explain what a covariate is, and give some examples. Then go on to identify and explain the following features of the correlational technique:
  - scattergrams and their purpose
  - positive correlations
  - negative correlations
  - the correlation coefficient and its purpose (e.g. Spearman's rho)
  - examples of correlations
  - circumspect correlations.

2 *Evaluate the correlational technique in terms of its advantages and disadvantages.*

Structure your answer as follows:

- Define the correlational technique. Explain its purpose.
- Identify and explain the advantages of the correlational technique, i.e.
  - when, and in what circumstances it is used. Give examples.
  - usefulness in its ability to generate quantitative data. Why is this important to science?
- Identify and explain the disadvantages of the correlational technique, i.e.
  - relationships only, no cause and effect.
  - circumspect correlations, e.g. the Maharishi effect
  - extraneous variables. Give example(s).
- *Describe and explain the null hypothesis.*

With reference to this chapter, and the one that follows:

- define the null hypothesis
- discuss the purpose of the null hypothesis in the light of the scientific method. Use an example to help you discuss falsification, H_0 and H_A.

Glossary

Correlation coefficient: a statistical sum that calculates the strength and degree of relationship between two seemingly unconnected events

Covariables: also known as covariates, these are the independent behaviours etc. studied by the correlational technique

Experimental method: the method of *scientific* enquiry in psychology, the experimental method involves the strict control, observation and measurement of variables

Extraneous variables: variables, or things from the outside that can contaminate a piece of research. Extraneous variables give rise to alternative explanations for your results

Null hypothsis: a research statement of no observed effect between two variables or covariates, used in the experimental method and correlational technique

Operationalisation: concerns agreeing a precise definition of our variables in research, and then finding a suitable measure of their occurrence. This can be difficult. Consider the concept of 'intelligence'. What is intelligence? Can intelligence be measured?

Participant variables: peculiarities individuals bring to the research situation that can give rise to alternative explanations for your results and conclusions

Positive correlation: as one covariate increases in one direction, so does the other, e.g. number of hours studied/examination mark

Probability: the likelihood of events occurring by chance or random factor

Qualitative data: descriptive information

Quantitative data: numerical information

Reliability: a major question of research, which asks if the research is investigating what it claims it is investigating

Research hypothesis: a research prediction or statement

Sample: participants/subjects who take part in an investigation got from a target population

Sampling bias: where participants/subjects who make up a research sample don't mirror the target population. This makes generalisation of results onto the target population questionable

Scattergram: a graphical representation of a correlation between two covariates

Target population: the wider population from which a research sample is drawn and onto which one can then generalise any results

Validity: another question of research, which asks if the research is consistently investigating what it claims to be investigating

Variables: literally anything whose value can change e.g. temperature, heart rate, score on an IQ test, etc. There are three main kinds of variable in experimental research, i.e. independent, dependent and extraneous variables

Volunteer bias: an interesting extraneous variable. Volunteers in psychological research have personal characteristics that set them apart from individuals in the general population. Thus they are not representative of the population upon whom you may wish to generalise your results (see also page 235)

8

The experimental method

BY THE END OF THIS CHAPTER YOU SHOULD BE ABLE TO:

- **identify by example the experimental method of research**
- **define and explain the experimental method of research with reference to its key features**
- **explain and evaluate the experimental method of research in terms of its advantages and disadvantages.**

Overview of the experimental method

The experimental method is a research procedure well-known to traditional sciences such as physics and chemistry. In this chapter the experimental method will be presented as *the* most powerful and scientifically vigorous method of investigation used in psychology. In using the experimental method you are adhering to its essential principles: the manipulation of an **independent variable**; the observation of any effect this has on a **dependent variable**; and the control of extraneous variables. Importantly, the experimental method allows us to generate data that gives scientific support to the *experimental hypothesis* being tested. An experimental hypothesis is a testable prediction of a cause and effect relationship between an independent and dependent variable. This shall be examined in detail. We will further discover that there are three types of experiment – laboratory, field, and quasi – that reflect the experimental method. These will be illustrated, as will their advantages and disadvantages.

What is the experimental method?

The experimental method of research is a controlled procedure involving the manipulation of an independent variable (IV) to observe and measure its effect on a dependent variable (DV).

The experimental method of research is *the* major method of enquiry in psychology. As we read earlier, the behaviourist, cognitive and biological approaches particularly favour the experimental method. The experimental method generates all-important empirical data upon which these approaches base a lot of their theories and ideas. Theories or ideas can be converted into an *experimental hypothesis,* a claim that one thing causes another. The experimental method tests this in a scientifically rigorous fashion.

Generalisation, replication and validity

The experimental method sets three standards. These include the ability to *generalise* your results to a wider population: the procedure you follow should be *standardised* (set down step-by-step) allowing others to *replicate* the experiment and get the same results; finally any measure you use to record the behaviour under investigation should be *valid.* This means that your measure must be related to the behaviour under investigation. Using 'kilograms' would not be an appropriate measure of running ability! Neither would the use of the Weschler Intelligence Scale for Children (WISC) (a measure of intelligence) to investigate the capacity of short-term memory – WISC would just not be valid.

A variable is anything that can vary in its quantity or quality. It is any measurable characteristic, such as a type of behaviour, a physical entity, a way of thinking, feeling, or anything else that can be counted.

The experimental hypothesis is tested by the experimental method by manipulating something called an *independent variable* (IV). This is to measure or observe the effect this manipulation might have on a *dependent variable* (DV). The experimental method further requires us to control all other factors which might influence the effect of any manipulation of the IV on the DV. These other factors are called *extraneous variables*. One way to control for extraneous variables is to use a particular *experimental design*.

Experiments are of three main types: *laboratory; field; and quasi-experiment*. The difference between the three is their *location*. Location, or where the experiment takes place, also affects the degree of *control* the researcher has over extraneous variables.

Key features of the experimental method

The independent variable and the dependent variable

In an experiment, the researcher manipulates or changes one factor to measure or observe any effect this has on another factor. What is changed or manipulated is called the independent variable. What is observed or measured as a result is called the dependent variable. Take the following example.

Imagine the government were interested in a total ban on alcohol consumption for all drivers. This would not be a popular move, despite the dangers associated with drinking and driving. The government would need to come up with convincing scientific evidence to support a ban, and would fund some research to help their case. The researchers would be asked to investigate what effect drinking alcohol has on driving ability. They could set up an experiment where alcohol is given to participants. Participants would then sit a driving simulation test to measure the effect alcohol has on driving ability. The *manipulation* – of giving alcohol to participants – is the independent variable. The *effect* of this manipulation – measured by the number of errors made on the driving simulation test – is *the dependent variable*.

Control group and experimental group

The researchers would want to be sure that any observed effect on driving ability is caused by alcohol and no other factor. To be confident that it is alcohol alone that influenced driver ability they could set up a situation where they have a **control group** and an **experimental group**. Volunteers would be randomly allocated to each group. The control group and the experimental group would then undergo different **conditions** of the independent variable. The control group would get the no-alcohol treatment and take the simulation test. The experimental group would get the alcohol treatment and likewise take the simulation test. The **treatment**, or condition of the independent variable, is here the giving/not giving of alcohol.

INTERACTIVE

Identify the independent and dependent variable in the experimental hypothesis to the right. The independent variable is the one you manipulate or change. The dependent variable you observe or measure as a result. Libido is a free-floating sexual energy identified by Freud.

H_1: 'That Viagra will have a significant influence on libido'.

THE DEPENDENT VARIABLE: AN OBSERVED EFFECT

A key feature of the experimental method is the observation and measurement of the dependent variable. In an experiment the experimenter controls any manipulation of the independent variable and has no control over the dependent variable.

The dependent variable is always a *measurable* aspect of a human's or an animal's behaviour. We observe and measure the effect of a manipulation of the independent variable using whatever measure is most appropriate. In our example the dependent variable would be measurable in terms of errors made on a driving simulation test.

It is important that what you want to observe should be measurable in terms of number or category. Number or counts in a category later allow you to use statistics to discover if your results mean anything. Let's say in our example that the average number, or **mean**, of driver errors in the non-alcohol condition was 6.5, and in the alcohol condition 16.5.

With a mean error difference of 10 there has clearly been some kind of effect. Measurement of any observed effect is important to the experimental method. It allows you to draw conclusions that your manipulation is the cause of the observed effect. We shall return to the measurement of the dependent variable when we look shortly at the null hypothesis, probability and significance.

It is worth noting that it would be ethically wrong to conduct this type of experiment in a real-life situation. You could not give a group of drivers alcohol, let them loose in public, and observe them breaking the law! The use of simulation ensures safety in a controlled environment in the investigation of a serious issue.

INTERACTIVE

Your school/college thinks drinking water during examinations has a positive influence on examination performance. They have asked you to write up an experimental procedure to test this idea. Include in your report reference to your independent variable, dependent variable, the different conditions of the independent variable and treatment.

The experimental hypothesis

Experimental hypothesis: a testable scientific prediction of cause and effect between an independent and a dependent variable.

An experimental hypothesis has two features. It must be a prediction, and this prediction must be testable.

Any experimental hypothesis will *predict* that the manipulation of an independent variable will have a *measurable effect* on a dependent variable.

Taking our example of alcohol and driving ability, our experimental hypothesis could be.

H_1: Alcohol affects driving ability.

The giving/not giving of alcohol to our participants is the treatment, or manipulation of the independent variable. Driving ability, as measured by the number of errors made on the driver simulation test, is our dependent variable. As an experimental hypothesis, or cause and effect prediction, it is ready to be tested.

We should note that an experimental hypothesis is also called a research hypothesis or alternative hypothesis. While psychologists using non-experimental methods would have a research hypothesis, the only procedure where you can say you are using an *experimental hypothesis* is in an experiment. An experimental/alternative/research hypothesis in a true experiment must predict some relationship between a dependent variable and an independent variable. This is the experimental method in essence.

The IV and the DV: a cause and effect prediction

Since an experimental hypothesis predicts a cause and effect relationship between an independent and dependent variable, the experimental method emphasises that all other aspects of the investigation be kept constant, to ensure that an identifiable cause did indeed create the effect. This will be more fully explored when we turn to *extraneous variables*.

To establish cause and effect in our example we would give participants differing levels of alcohol (the IV) and measure their performance on the driving simulation test (the DV). The independent variable which we control is 'cause' and the dependent variable is 'effect'. If a significant number of errors were made on the driver simulation test, levels of alcohol would be our IV, or cause; errors made on the simulation, our DV, or effect.

The independent variable is the one the experimenter controls or manipulates. The independent variable or IV is the cause in an experimental hypothesis.

The dependent variable, or DV, is the one the experimenter measures or observes as a result of the manipulating the IV. The DV is the measurable effect in an experimental hypothesis.

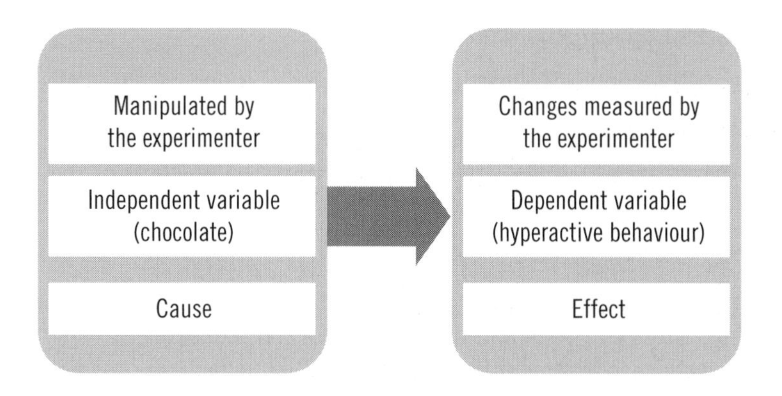

Figure 8.1 The independent and dependent variable and the experimental method

STUDY

Asch (1955) 'Opinions and social pressure.' *Scientific American*, 193, 31 –35.

Aim: To test how we conform to others' points of view when we find our judgement is questioned.

Method: Participants were individually taken into a psychology laboratory and shown a straight line drawn on a card. They were then shown another card with three straight lines drawn on it. They were asked which of the second three was the same length as the first single line. All got the answer correct.

The same participants were then put into a room with a number of other people who were confederates of the experimenter. The same question was asked again of the participants, but the confederates, who were to answer first, were instructed to give wrong answers.

Results: Seventy-four per cent of the original participants (who had as individuals previously given correct answers) changed their answers in the group situation. When asked why, they said they knew they had given incorrect answers.

Conclusions: Social pressure from others influences conformity in that here each individual bowed to group pressure and gave incorrect answers they clearly knew were wrong. The issue was completely unimportant, i.e. the length of lines. Asch is horrifyingly reminiscent of the famous Pastor Martin Niemöller quotation: '*First they came for the Jews and I did not speak out because I was not a Jew. Then they came for the Communists and I did not speak out because I was not a Communist. Then they came for the trade unionists and I did not speak out because I was not a trade unionist. Then they came for me and there was no one left to speak out.*' Martin Niemöller was held in Sachsenhausen and Dachau concentration camps from 1937 until 1945.

INTERACTIVE

1. What type of experiment is this?
2. Construct a hypothesis for Asch (1955).
3. What were the two conditions of the independent variable in this experiment?
4. What lessons can we learn from Asch (1955)?

One- and two-tailed experimental hypotheses

In the framing of an experimental hypothesis we can make it one- or two-tailed.

A *one-tailed experimental hypothesis* predicts the *direction* of the result, or effect. Generally a one-tailed hypothesis would state that one condition or manipulation of the IV is *better* than another condition or manipulation of it; or, that there is a *positive* or *negative* relationship between the IV and the DV.

A *two-tailed experimental hypothesis* simply predicts that there will be an effect. This can be a predicted difference between our different conditions of the independent variable. It can also be stated in terms of a cause–effect relationship between the independent and dependent variable.

In our example we could have H_1: *Alcohol will have an negative effect on driving ability*. This experimental hypothesis indicates the predicted direction of the results (a negative effect) and is therefore a one-tailed hypothesis.

Alternatively we could have H_1: *Alcohol will affect driving ability*. This is a two-tailed experimental hypothesis. We are predicting that there will be an effect, but not indicating the direction, i.e. whether it is going to be positive or negative.

INTERACTIVE

Which of the following are examples of a one- and a two-tailed hypothesis? Give reasons for your answer.

1 H_1: Alcohol will have a positive effect on reaction time.

2 H_1: Those in the no-alcohol condition will do better on reaction time tests than those in the alcohol condition.

3 H_1: There will be a difference in reaction time between the non-alcohol condition and the alcohol condition.

The null hypothesis

Another feature of the experimental method is the null hypothesis. The null hypothesis is important from the point of view of statistics. In an experiment we have *both* an experimental and a null hypothesis. Remember that an experimental hypothesis is a prediction of an effect due to the manipulation of an independent variable. A *null hypothesis* states there is *no observable effect* with regard to the IV and the DV. Taking our example, our null hypothesis would therefore be:

H_0: Alcohol will not have an effect on driving ability.

A null hypothesis is an assumption that the experimenter takes to be true. If the experimenter comes up with evidence that contradicts this assumption, i.e. our data indicates that the null hypothesis is untrue, this allows the experimenter to do a very clever thing. They can take it that because the null hypothesis is false, the experimental hypothesis must be 'true'.

To use the jargon, if you find evidence to *reject* your null hypothesis, this allows you to *accept* or *support* your experimental hypothesis. If, on the other hand, you find evidence to support your null hypothesis, you must accept this and reject your experimental hypothesis. By attempting to prove a null hypothesis you also show that your experiment is unbiased, which improves the **validity** of your experimental conclusions.

If, in our experiment, we found evidence to say that alcohol had an adverse effect on driving ability we could conclude our research by saying: *On the basis of the supporting evidence, the null hypothesis,* H_0*: 'Alcohol does not have an effect on driving ability' is rejected, and the experimental hypothesis* H_1*: 'Alcohol affects driving ability' is accepted.*

If we found that the group in the alcohol condition performed better than the no-alcohol group you would however have to conclude: On the basis of the supporting evidence, the null hypothesis, H_0: *'Alcohol does not have an effect on driving ability' is accepted and the experimental hypothesis* H_1*: 'Alcohol affects driving ability' is rejected.'*

If you did get this highly unlikely result, it is possible that it could have been caused by other factors you did not take into account when you were designing your experiment. As indicated in Chapter 7, other factors that could account for any results you get are called extraneous variables. Before we turn to this, let us consider the $64 000 question. If you reject your null hypothesis, is your now accepted experimental hypothesis significant? Does your cause and effect relationship really mean anything?

Probability and significance

A null hypothesis, as was said earlier, is always assumed primarily to be true. It is a testable statement about a belief i.e. H_0: *Alcohol does not affect driving ability*. If you came up with evidence to reject this H_0: and consequentially accepted the experimental hypothesis, H_1: *Alcohol affects driving ability*, how sure could you be of your results and conclusions?

To have confidence in your conclusions you would place a bet on yourself that your results were not down to chance factors. Chance factors are referred to as *probability*. Probability is the likelihood of an event happening – like Scotland getting through to the second round of the World Cup, or even the first (!), or it snowing on Christmas Day, etc. If you went to a bookies you could get odds on the likelihood of these events happening. If they do, you've won some money. If you are over eighteen of course!

The likelihood of results in a psychological experiment being due to chance factors other than the manipulation of the IV, are expressed in terms of levels of significance. Levels of significance indicate the probability level (p value) of chance factors being the cause of your results. *You* choose your p value, or level of significance. It is normal in psychological experiments to set a p value, or level of significance, at $p = 0.05$. This means that you accept that there is a 1:20 chance that any result you get is due to factors other than the manipulation of your IV. Our null hypothesis would thus be written:

> H_0: Alcohol will have no effect on driving ability at the 0.05 level of significance.

Having a level of significance also allows you to use powerful inferential statistics to test the results that you generate. If you found evidence to reject the above null hypothesis and thus support the experimental H_1: *Alcohol affects driving ability*, with a 0.05 level of significance in your null hypothesis, you are accepting that there is a 5 per cent, or 1 chance in 20 that your results are wrong. You are also, however, accepting that there is 0.95, 95 per cent or 95 chance in 100 that your results are correct.

INTERACTIVE

Indicate the percentage and chance factor associated with the levels of significance below:

Table 8.1

Level of significance	Chance factor	Percentage
0.05	1:20	5%
0.01		
0.005		
0.001		

If your doctor prescribed you a new drug, what would be the highest level of significance you would want it to have been tested at? Give reasons for your answer.

Extraneous variables

An *extraneous variable* is, as we read in Chapter 7, something that can creep in and give rise to an alternative explanation for your results. An extraneous variable can be the cause of any effect that might result from your experimental procedure. Extraneous variables also influence the outcome of correlations and structured observation, both of which are non-experimental methods of research. Extraneous variables (*coming from the outside*) are of two main types – random and confounding.

Random variables

Random variables are extremely difficult to control. Using our alcohol/driving ability example, a random variable would occur if a participant were feeling unwell on the day and didn't perform as they might. You have little control over this. Random variables just happen. Another example of a random variable would be if, during our driving simulation test, a radiator in the room starting making strange noises – so strange that people were distracted. Random variables like these are almost impossible to anticipate; they can, however, give rise to an alternative reason for any cause–effect conclusion that the manipulation of your IV gives you.

Confounding variables

Confounding variables are variables that *can* be anticipated, and controlled. Let us look at three types of confounding variable that occur when using the experimental method.

Situational variables

Situational variables refer to *the experimental situation* itself. The environment, or where the experiment takes place, may influence our results. This is especially the case with laboratory experiments. Situational variables concern the physical environment of the experiment. In order to control situational variables, all taking part in our alcohol/driving ability experiment should experience the *same* environmental situation. Temperature, lighting, background noise, etc. would therefore be kept *constant* throughout our experimental procedure.

Experimenter variables

Experimenter variables unsurprisingly refer to the experimenter(s) themselves. You, the experimenter can be a confounding variable. One experimenter variable known as the **experimenter effect** has suggested that experimenter characteristics such as age, sex and general behaviour may have subtle effects on participants' performance (Eagly & Carli, 1983).

Experimenter bias is a more common confounding variable in experimental research. Experimenter bias happens when the expectations of the experimenter influence the participants' behaviours. A classic example of experimenter bias is the **expectancy effect** discovered by Rosenthal & Fode (1963).

Rosenthal & Fode (1963) asked students to train rats to run through a maze. They told one group of students that they had been given particularly smart rats that would learn to run the maze quickly. The other group were told that they had dull rats that would be slow to learn to run the maze. Rosenthal and Fode actually had no idea how clever or otherwise their rats were.

The group who were told they had smart rats later reported that they had quickly learned to run through the maze, while those who had been told their rats were dull reported theirs to be slow. The smart rat group produced data showing a better maze running performance in comparison to the dull rat group.

Rosenthal & Fode (1963) say that the students' (false) expectations about whether a rat was smart or dull had had an effect on the results. The group with the smart rats got the result they did, either because they put more effort into training their rats to run the maze, or because their recording of the rats maze running abilities was affected by expectations.

In order to control for experimenter variables many experiments first do a **pilot study**, or a rehearsal of the experiment. A pilot study, which can involve the researchers as the 'participants', helps iron out confounding variables such as the experimenter and expectancy effect. Pilot studies give you an opportunity to develop an even more controlled experimental procedure, which we generally refer to as standardisation.

Participant variables

Remember that a confounding variable concerns other factors that could account for your result.

A participant variable could then be the cause of any observed effect on your dependent variable, other than the manipulation of your independent variable.

Participant variables are confounding variables that come from the participants themselves. In our alcohol/driving ability example participant variables include whether participants were male or female. This is because men and women have different metabolic rates and break down alcohol differently. Other participant variables that could interfere with our results are body fat, which influences the breakdown of alcohol, drinking experience, or lack of it, etc.

We can control for such participant variables using a standardised experimental procedure called an **experimental design**. Experimental designs help control for confounding variables.

At this juncture two participant variables deserve explanation: the Hawthorne Effect, or participant expectancy; and demand characteristics.

THE HAWTHORNE EFFECT: PARTICIPANT EXPECTANCY

Participant expectancy was discovered in 1939 by probably the world's first occupational psychologists, Roethlisberger and Dickson. Their study is better known as the Hawthorne Effect. They were interested in the relationship between factory pollution and productivity levels at the Hawthorne electrical generating plant in America. Their independent variables included changing the lighting conditions in the factory and the times the workers could take their breaks. They assessed the output of five female workers under differing working conditions for two years. Much to Roethlisberger and Dickson's surprise productivity increased, rather than decreased, when they manipulated their IV of worsening working conditions. They discovered the women had worked harder because they wanted to please the psychologists. It was this 'wanting to please the psychologist' that produced their strange results. Knowing that you are taking part in an experiment, and wanting to please, can create the Hawthorne Effect. The Hawthorne Effect sees participants behave in an unnatural way.

DEMAND CHARACTERISTICS

Demand characteristics are any features of an experiment, which help participants work out what is expected of them, and consequently lead them to behave in artificial ways. These features 'demand' a certain response. Participants search for cues in the experimental environment about how to behave and what (might) be expected of them.

How did the workers in the electricity generating factory work out they were taking part in an experiment? Psychology tells us they most likely picked up *cues* that gave the game away. Cues that give away the nature of an experiment are called **demand characteristics**, a term first coined by Orne in 1962.

INTERACTIVE

Please now go to the British Psychological Society at http://www.bps.org.uk/about/rules5.cfm and print off The Psychologists Code of Conduct.

Demand characteristics, or giving participants too many clues about what we are interested in, are some of the main reasons why psychologists are never entirely truthful with participants who take part in our research! If you tell someone, consciously or unconsciously, about what you are *really* after, you can never be sure of your results; they might be caused by demand characteristics. As a result we very often use deception in experimental work – we do not tell participants the true nature of our research. This raises ethical issues, which should not be avoided. If you have to deceive your participants you must at least get their consent that they want to take part and give them a debriefing on the true nature of your work at the end of your study.

You can also minimise demand characteristics in experimental work by using a **single-blind technique**. This is where the participant does not know to which condition of the independent variable (control or experimental) they have been allocated. There have been reports that cannabis helps alleviate symptoms of multiple sclerosis and Parkinson's disease. To test this in a scientific experiment using a group of MS or Parkinson disease participants, half of the experimental group would be given the cannabis pill, while the other half, the control group, a harmless sugar pill or **placebo**. No participant would know whether they had been given the cannabis or the placebo. All nonetheless record any effect. This is a good example of the single-blind technique where the participant doesn't know to which condition of the IV they have been allocated.

Experimental designs

An experimental design refers to the controlled structure, form or plan of the experimental procedure. Experimental designs help narrow down confounding variables, especially those concerning the participant. Designs also reflect an important principle of the experimental method, which is an ability to make sense of any data that is produced. This is because experimental designs allow us to compare one treatment of the independent variable with another. As we read earlier this produces data, the significance of which we test using statistics.

Experimental designs fall into two categories: related and unrelated. A related design generates data that are related; unrelated designs generate data that are unrelated.

Related experimental designs

There are two types of related designs used in experimental research – repeated measures, and matched pairs design.

Repeated measures

A repeated measures design (RMD) repeats the measure of performance, the dependent variable, under the differing conditions of the independent variable. A repeated measures design is particularly appropriate if you want to do a 'test–retest' comparison with two, and sometimes more, manipulations of the independent variable. A repeated measure is a **within-subjects design**, because each participant provides data for all manipulations of the independent variable.

To use an RMD in our alcohol experiment we would use one group of participants. They would first undergo condition A of the independent variable, no alcohol, and be asked to do the driving simulation test. They would then undergo condition B of the independent variable, alcohol, and repeat the simulation test. We are clearly repeating the measure with our group of participants – the measure being the number of errors made on the simulation test under the two conditions of the IV. This is a repeated measures design.

Mention must be made of another *participant variable* called **order effect**. Order effect refers to the influence on your results of practice, fatigue, or boredom. Order effect can pollute an RMD because you are asking participants to do something at least twice, in this instance a driver simulation test. What if, whether drunk or sober, they learned to do the simulation test better in condition B as a result of practice in condition A? In an RMD, practice can influence results, as can other order effects such as tiredness and boredom.

ABBA AND COUNTERBALANCING

If you use a repeated measures design and want to control for order effect, the trick is to use **counterbalancing**. Counterbalancing evenly distributes any order effect across the two conditions of the independent variable. In our example with ten participants, counterbalancing would see us randomly allocate participants 1–5 to undergo condition A first (no alcohol), then condition B (alcohol). Alternatively, participants 6–10 would be allocated to condition B first, and then condition A. Counterbalancing is an ABBA presentation to the two conditions of the IV. This means condition A then B for one half of our participants, and condition B followed by A for the other half. Counterbalancing using an ABBA exposure cuts down the likelihood of order effect in an repeated measures design.

ADVANTAGES AND DISADVANTAGES OF A REPEATED MEASURES DESIGN

The repeated measures design is very popular with psychology students in their experimental research. Its advantages include good control of participant variables and fewer participants are needed in comparison with a matched pairs design. Needing fewer participants probably helps its popularity with students! This is because with an repeated measures design you are of course asking the same group of participants to do something twice. Using an repeated measures design also distributes any individual differences the participants may have across the two conditions of the IV. Any individual differences will cancel each other out across condition A and condition B. In our example individual differences could be drinking experience, or lack of it, length of driving experience, sex of participant, body fat, and so on.

The main disadvantage of the repeated measures design is order effect – counterbalancing should be used to control for this. Another disadvantage is that of demand characteristics. The participants could guess the true purpose of our alcohol research and decide that it was not in their interests to behave as they might.

Matched pairs design

Another related design, termed a matched pairs design, is used when a test–retest procedure is difficult because of order effect. It is characterised by matching participants on the basis of the participant variables you think could give rise to an alternative explanation of any results you get. What are *relevant* confounding participant variables differs from experiment to experiment. In our alcohol study participants would be matched on the basis of sex, body fat, drinking experience, etc. Other participant variables like IQ (intelligence quotient), and socio-economic status (what you do, where you live, and how well off you are) are maybe not as relevant in this instance, but could be in others. Once matched, participants are randomly allocated to the control and experimental group conditions. Applying a matched pairs design to our example, we would match participants on the basis of relevant confounding variables, then randomly allocate each matched participant to either the control condition A, or the experimental condition B of the independent variable, and ensure that each group mirrors the other as far as possible. The control group would get no alcohol and do the driving simulation test. The experimental group would get alcohol and similarly do the simulation test. The scores obtained by each group under each condition of the IV would then be compared.

Advantages and disadvantages of a matched pairs design

The main advantage of the matched pairs design is that you avoid order effect. Participants, in whatever condition, are only asked to do one thing once. Here participants only undergo one manipulation of the IV (no alcohol, alcohol) and then do the driver simulation test. If you have matched participants properly on the basis of relevant confounding variables, it is a reasonably good procedure to control for participant variables. An MPD also gives you access to powerful inferential statistics such as the related *t* test.

The main disadvantage attached to an MPD is the question of whether you have matched on the basis of *relevant* confounding participant variables. You can never be entirely sure that you have accounted for all the important differences between people that may influence the results of your study. As a result it is difficult to control totally for all participant variables. Other disadvantages are the time and resources required to find out what individual differences are relevant to your study. These of course you have to match. You also need twice as many participants as in a repeated measures design.

INTERACTIVE

Why are repeated measures and matched pairs designs said to be related?

Unrelated experimental designs

The main unrelated experimental design is an independent group design (IGD). An independent group design is also referred to as an independent sample, or independent measures design. An unrelated design creates a situation where any data obtained is unrelated. This is because the participants undergoing each condition of the independent variable are unrelated to one another; they are 'independent' groups.

Independent groups design

An independent group design is a **between-groups design**. Each participant in each group experiences only one condition of the independent variable, and provides data for one manipulation of the independent variable.

To create an independent groups design as an example you could use two independent groups of participants, say the Kilmarnock History Club and Kilmarnock FC Supporters Club; you would toss a coin and randomly allocate one group to the control condition (no alcohol), and the other to the experimental condition (alcohol). Both groups would do the driving simulation test and you would compare their results.

An independent groups design is also appropriate where there is more than one condition of the independent variable. Take this example.

The participants of one group are each given a list of words and asked to repeat each word several times before going on to the next one. Participants in the second group are asked to form vivid mental images of each word, making links between that word and its successor. Both groups are then tested on memory recall.

There are two different conditions of the IV above: two different forms of remembering, rehearsal and imagery. The dependent variable in both instances is the number of words remembered under each of these conditions.

INTERACTIVE

1 What do you think is the aim of the above piece of research?

2 What do you think the outcome would be?

3 If one form of remembering were found to be better than the other, how confident would you be of your results (using an IGD)? Give reasons for your answer.

Advantages and disadvantages of an independent groups design

Order effects, such as practice, fatigue or boredom, do not arise because participants are allocated to only one condition of the independent variable.

As you may have worked out from the above Interactive, the main disadvantages of the IGD are participant variables, or individual differences. In our alcohol-driving ability investigation with the Kilmarnock History Club and the Kilmarnock FC Supporters Club you would definitely not be comparing like with like! The two groups differ entirely in the number of males and females involved, drinking experience, body fat and so on. Your results, comparisons and conclusions would be rather meaningless.

Another disadvantage of an IGD is that you need more participants in comparison to a repeated measures design. This is because you need two groups.

INTERACTIVE

Look at the data charts below. Identify the designs of these two experiments. Give reasons for your answer. Explain these designs, and give two advantages and two disadvantages for each.

Design 1

Participant number	Condition A results	Condition B results
1		
2		
3		
4		
5		
6		
7		
8		
9		
10		

Design 2

Condition A results	Condition B results
P1	P11
P2	P12
P3	P13
P4	P14
P5	P15
P6	P16
P7	P17
P8	P18
P9	P19
P10	P20

Types of experiments

There are three types of experimental procedure that adhere to the experimental method. These are laboratory, field and quasi-experiments. Each involves:

- the manipulation of an independent variable
- the observation of any effect this manipulation has on a dependent variable
- the control of extraneous variables.

The difference between the three types of experiment is their *location*. Location, or where the experiment takes place, affects the amount of *control* the researcher has over extraneous variables.

Laboratory experiments

The **laboratory experiment** involves the manipulation of an independent variable and the measurement/observation of the dependent variable. Laboratory experiments take place in the closed, heavily controlled setting of a psychology laboratory.

To ensure better control, a laboratory procedure standardises any instructions given to participants. Standardisation means that instructions to participants are agreed and checked for ambiguity before the experiment proper. Any ambiguities should have come to light in an earlier pilot study. **Standardised instructions** ensure all participants are told exactly the same thing. Standardised instructions are also important where participants are involved in non-experimental methods of research such as observation and the correlational technique. Now read the Study and Interactive on page 199 for an example of a laboratory experiment.

Field experiment

As we shall discover, the laboratory experiment is often accused of lacking in ecological validity. This means that they are 'unreal' and don't reflect a real-life situation. To avoid the question of ecological validity very often the experimental method is applied to a field experiment.

A **field experiment** also sees the manipulation of an IV and measurement/observation of a DV, but takes place away from the laboratory, indoors or out. A field experiment can occur in the natural environment of the participant, e.g. a school classroom, a playground, or the street, as Bickman's (1974) study illustrates on page 200.

Quasi-experiments

A **quasi-experiment** also occurs outside the laboratory but there is no manipulation of an independent variable, as the IV is already 'in place'. Measurement/observation of a DV does however follow. 'Quasi' means 'nearly' or 'almost'. A quasi-experiment is then *nearly* an experiment, but differs in one important respect. Participants are not randomly assigned to conditions of the IV by the experimenter. In a quasi-experiment the conditions of the independent variable are already in place.

Take the following example. You might be interested in the impact developmental changes have on intelligence. The development of intelligence is affected by biological, cognitive, social and emotional factors. Put another way, intelligence is affected by our nature (genetics), nurture (environment), and the outcome of the interaction of both. Nature and nurture, the changing factors

STUDY

Blakemore, C. & Cooper, G.F. (1970) 'Development of the brain depends on the visual environment.' *Nature*, 228, 477–78.

Aim: To investigate environmental influence on the development of perception.

Subjects: Kittens (non-human animals are called 'subjects' in psychological research).

Method: Laboratory experiment.

Independent variable: Independent variable: being raised in either a vertical or horizontal environment. Dependent variable: kittens' response to vertical and horizontal visual line stimuli.

Procedure: Blakemore and Cooper raised kittens from birth in complete darkness. For five hours each day the kittens were put into either a horizontal or vertical striped drum. Using an inverted cardboard funnel around their necks, the kittens were also sensorily deprived from seeing their own bodies. They could only look forward, so that stripes – horizontal or vertical – were the only stimuli they encountered.

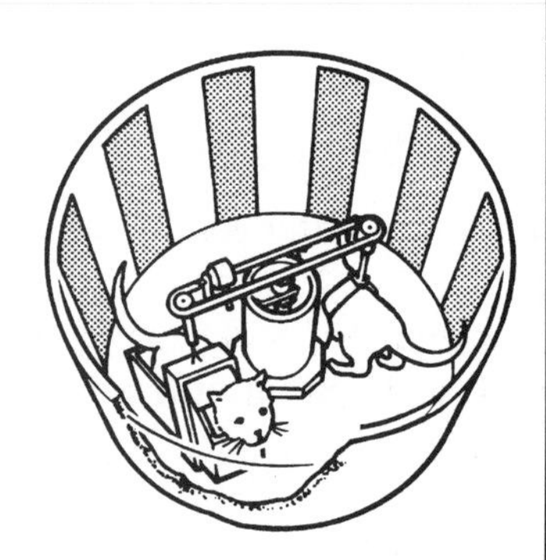

Figure 8.2 Blakemore and Cooper's cats

At five months old, the kittens were tested for line recognition by being presented with a moving pointer going in either a horizontal or vertical direction.

Results: The results showed that kittens raised in a vertical world only reacted to vertical line stimuli, while those kittens brought up in a horizontal world only responded to horizontal line stimuli.

The vertically raised kittens showed 'behavioural blindness' towards horizontal stimuli, and the horizontally raised kittens were 'behaviorally blind' towards vertical stimuli. Blakemore and Cooper discovered that this behavioural blindness corresponded with 'physiological blindness'. By placing electrodes in the kittens' visual cortex they found that the kittens raised in a vertical environment did not possess cells that 'fired' in response to horizontal line stimuli. On the other hand kittens raised in a horizontal stimuli did not have cells that fired off in response to vertical stimuli.

Conclusion: Environment affects the development of perception in some species at a physiological level. If an environment does not nurture aspects of perception, the species can suffer a deficit physiologically, which in this instance was behavioural/physiological blindness in either a horizontal/vertical environment.

INTERACTIVE

1. What was the aim of Blakemore & Cooper's (1970) study?
2. What was the IV and what was the DV?
3. Is this a repeated measures, matched pairs or independent groups/samples design? Give reasons for your answer.
4. What ethical issues does Blakemore & Cooper's (1970) study raise?

that influence intelligence, are here your independent variables; they are already in place and, as such, cannot be manipulated. This is the scenario of a quasi-experiment.

To conduct this quasi-experiment you would need to find a sample of participants and using a valid and reliable test, measure their intelligence at age 20, 30, 40, 50, 60 and 70. Any significant differences in participant intelligence scores would be put down to changing biological, cognitive, social and/or emotional factors in their life. These are in place and you have no control over these independent variables. You can measure their influence nonetheless.

Namikas & Wehmer (1978): A quasi-experiment

Namikas & Wehmer (1978) were interested in aggression shown by males and females in litters of mice. The independent variable was the number of male and female mice born to each litter. The IV (male/female ratio) was 'in place' and varied naturally from litter to litter. It is a quasi-experiment because they had no control over this. Namikas & Wehmer (1978) observed that a male mouse born in an overwhelmingly female litter was more aggressive than male and female mice born and raised together in a mixed litter.

STUDY

Bickman L. (1974) 'The social power of a uniform'. *Journal of Applied Social Psychology*, 1, 47–61.

Aim: To investigate obedience in a real-life setting.

Method/procedure: Experimental method. Field experiment.

Bickman wanted to investigate obedience in the streets of New York. He asked different confederates to wear a) a security guard's uniform b) a milkman's uniform and c) civilian dress. These were the different conditions of his independent variable. They were then observed on the streets of New York asking passers-by to pick up a paper bag, give a dime to a stranger, or move away from a bus stop.

Results: Bickman found that 80 per cent of passers-by obeyed the guard in comparison to 40 per cent who obeyed the confederate dressed as a civilian. The number who obeyed the milkman was the same as the number who obeyed the civilian.

Conclusion: We learn from our culture and social world to be more obedient to certain authority figures than others.

INTERACTIVE

Questions

1. In your everyday experience identify and describe a similar situation you have observed.
2. What were Bickman's conditions of the independent variable? What was the measure he used for the dependent variable?
3. Why is this a field experiment?

INTERACTIVE

Find another two laboratory experiments in this book. Write a short report on each identifying the name, date, aim, method (experimental: laboratory), procedure (what did the psychologist(s) do), results and conclusion(s).

Natural experiments

Confusingly, a natural experiment is often included under the heading of the 'experiment' in psychology. In a natural experiment the researcher usually observes an animal or human in their natural environment. There is no manipulation of an independent variable in a natural experiment. The researcher does not, and cannot, have one. As a result the 'natural experiment' is not a procedure that reflects the experimental method.

Using other non-experimental techniques such as survey, interview and case study, it would be possible to track individual genetic and environmental changes that might suggest a link with intelligence, were you to live long enough to conduct *this* **longitudinal study**. A longitudinal study in psychology lasts more than one year. This one stretches that a wee bit! Enough of all this talk about experiments – why not now try one?

STUDY

An investigation into taste perception or Scotland's Other National Drink

Aim: the aim of this investigation is to assess the influence of visual cues on taste perception.

Experimental hypothesis: H_1: *When visual cues are frustrated, taste perception will be adversely affected.*

This is a one-tailed hypothesis.

Null hypothesis: H_0: *The frustration of visual cues will have no adverse effect on taste perception at the 0.05 level of significance.*

Independent variable: *egg yellow food colouring in lemonade in Condition B.*

Dependent variable: *observation and measurement of participant response to the Condition B manipulation of lemonade/egg yellow.*

Method: Laboratory experiment. Repeated measures design.

Apparatus:
500ml of quality lemonade
500ml of quality orangeade
Disposable cups (4 per participant)
38ml of egg yellow food colouring
Data response sheet (see later)

Preamble: Earlier in the cognitive approach, we looked at a cognitive process called perception. We enjoy visual perception, auditory perception, taste perception, etc. Taste perception is a result of our sense of vision, taste and smell all working together. Previous past experience is also an issue. Questions in this experiment are, is taste perception frustrated when visual cues are absent?, and does previous past experience influence taste perception?

Procedure: Arrange to get participants from your school, college, workplace, etc. This is a random sample obtained by opportunity sampling because the participants are easily available! Ten would be a good number. If you have ten participants you will need forty disposable cups. Ask the participants beforehand if they mind taking part

co

in an experiment on taste perception. If they say yes, you have their consent to proceed. Also brief them as to the general nature of your research (an investigation into taste perception). At the end it would also be a good idea to debrief your participants telling them the precise purpose of your experiment, and what it was you found out.

Before they arrive do the following. Mix up some egg yellow with lemonade until it resembles the colour of Scotland's Other National Drink. Then get four cups per person and put a little lemonade into the first, orangeade into the second, orangeade into the third and lemonade with egg yellow into the fourth. For the second participant have the sequence orangeade, lemonade, lemonade/egg yellow, orangeade, and so on. What you are doing, as our chart illustrates, is **counterbalancing** in each condition of the IV to avoid **order effect**.

Table 8.2 Counterbalancing chart

Participant	Condition A		Condition B	
1	Lemonade	Orangeade	Orangeade	Lemonade/egg yellow
2	Orangeade	Lemonade	Lemonade/egg yellow	Orangeade
3	Lemonade	Orangeade	Orangeade	Lemonade/egg yellow
4	Orangeade	Lemonade	Lemonade/egg yellow	Orangeade
5	Lemonade	Orangeade	Orangeade	Lemonade/egg yellow
6 etc.	Orangeade	Lemonade	Lemonade/egg yellow	Orangeade

Invite your participants into your laboratory one at a time. A classroom will do. Get them to taste each cup in the sequence above and ask them what they think the liquid is that they are drinking. Note any comment they make. Any comment made by a participant is called introspection. These are useful in the writing up of psychology reports, over and above the discussion of empirical data. It is likely in the lemonade/egg yellow manipulation people say they can't taste anything much, or that it is a well-known Scottish soft drink. Which it is not of course!

Give one point for each drink correctly identified in each condition of the IV, i.e. 'lemonade' or 'orangeade'. If participant number one identifies both drinks in Condition A as lemonade and orangeade they get 2 points. If they identify only one as correct they get 1 point, if none, 0 points. Do the same for Condition B. Enter participants' responses in a Data Chart as below. Participant scores have been entered as an example.

Table 8.3 Data sheet: taste perception

Participant	Condition A Score	Condition B Score	B–A Sign of difference
1	2	1	–
2	2	1	–
3	1	2	+
4	2	1	–
5	2	1	–
6	2	1	–
7	2	1	–
8	2	1	–
9	2	1	–
10	2	1	–

continued

You are testing your experimental hypothesis using a statistic called the 'sign of difference' test, also called the Binomial Sign Test. Work out the sign of difference for each participant by subtracting the B score from the A score and entering the sign of difference (+ or –) in the last column of your data response chart. If there is no sign of difference, i.e. if you get 1 in condition A and 1 in condition B, or 2 and 2, or 0 and 0, leave the right-hand-side sign of difference column blank for these participants. You can ignore these.

Count up the number of times a sign of difference occurs (either + or –). Call this N. In our example above $N = 10$. This is because there is one (+) and nine (–) in our B–A column. 1+9=10.

Count up the sign that occurs least frequently and call this calculated s. In the above example, with 10 participants calculated $s = 1$, because there is only one +. Then consult the Binomial Sign Table.

Run your finger down the left hand column until you find your N. In our example $N = 10$. Go across to your level of significance, which in this example is 0.05 for a one-tailed hypothesis.

Here we find the critical value is 1. Calculated s must be equal to, or less than, this critical (tabled) value. Our results show that calculated $s = 1$, and with $N = 10$ the critical value at the 0.05 level is 1.

In this instance because calculated s is equal to its critical value we can therefore reject our null hypothesis and accept our experimental hypothesis, being: *When visual cues are frustrated taste perception will be adversely affected.*

An interesting aspect to this experiment being done in Scotland would be the influence of culture on taste perception, remembering that perception is understood as our senses, plus gestalten, plus meaningful past experience. Can you see why in this example?

Table 8.4 Binomial sign test table

N	**Level of significance for one-tailed test**				
	0.05	0.025	0.01	0.005	0.0005
	Level of significance for two-tailed test				
	0.10	0.05	0.02	0.01	0.001
5	0	—	—	—	—
6	0	0	—	—	—
7	0	0	0	—	—
8	1	0	0	0	—
9	1	1	0	0	—
10	1	1	0	0	—
11	2	1	1	0	0
12	2	2	1	1	0
13	3	2	1	1	0
14	3	2	2	1	0
15	3	3	2	2	1
16	4	3	2	2	1
17	4	4	3	2	1
18	5	4	3	3	1
19	5	4	4	3	2
20	5	5	4	3	2
25	7	7	6	5	4
30	10	9	8	7	5
35	12	11	10	9	7

Calculated S must be EQUAL TO or LESS THAN the table (critical) value for significance at the level shown.

Source: F. Clegg, *Simple Statistics*, Cambridge University Press, 1982. With the kind permission of the author and publishers.

INTERACTIVE

Having done the above, use http://www.uwsp.edu/psych/apa4b.htm to help you write up a report on the investigation. Use the recommended headings as much as possible.

Advantages of the experimental method

The advantages of the experimental method are fourfold: the ability to establish cause and effect, the control of variables, objectivity and replication.

Cause and effect and control

The experimental method is the only method of enquiry where a *cause–effect* relationship can be established between variables. This is because the experimental method emphasises the *control of variables*. When, using a particular experimental design, we control confounding variables and get data to support our experimental hypothesis, we can draw a cause and effect conclusion between our independent and dependent variables.

Objectivity, validity and measurement of the dependent variable

The validity of any conclusion we may reach on cause and effect is founded on objectivity. Precise measurement of the dependent variable helps produce objective and factual data, and this empirical data is the most scientific. We can thus be more confident of the results and conclusions of experiments in comparison to non-experimental research procedures, where data is more descriptive and subjective.

Standardisation, replication and generalisation

The standardisation of experimental procedure and instruction is another advantage attached to the experimental method. Standardisation of design and instructions to participants helps in the *replication* of your experiment. If others follow your standardised procedure, replicate your experiment and get the same results, all can be more confident of a probable cause and effect relationship regards the IV and the DV. With careful sampling of participants, the experimental method also allows you to generalise your results to the population from which your sample was drawn.

Disadvantages of the experimental method

Ecological validity

Lack of *ecological validity* is the main disadvantage of the experimental method. The situations for which psychological experiments try to establish a cause–effect relationship very often do not reflect real life. This was illustrated in our examination of the behaviourist approach in particular. Is there really no difference between the animal and human species? Do animals learn in the same way as we humans? By comparing animals with humans regarding how species learn, are behaviourist experiments lacking in their ecological validity?

Sampling bias

Sampling bias can also be a disadvantage in that a poor sample can prevent you from generalising your results to a larger population. A great number of psychological experiments involve student participants – indeed student participants who study psychology. Relying on participants from such a closed group shows *selection bias* (the exclusion of others).

Extraneous variables

Extraneous variables are also a major disadvantage of the experimental method. The situation, the experimenter, and the participant can all give rise to other explanations for the results. Absolute control of extraneous variables is an almost impossible task. One type, *random variables*, cannot be controlled, as they cannot be anticipated. They just happen. Other *confounding variables* such as the experimenter him-herself can influence results.

Confounding variables

Experimenter expectations, giving rise to experimenter bias, can be a problem. He or she can consciously or unconsciously create an experimenter effect (Rosenthal & Fode, 1963).

Participant variables are a particular confounding variable in experiments that can cause difficulty. Those concerning individual differences, even when controlled using a design, can never be entirely anticipated. *Participant expectancy*, or the Hawthorne Effect, can see participants behave in an unnatural way because they know they are the subjects of an experiment. How they know is because of the *demand characteristics* of the experimental situation. Cues are picked up that can reveal the true purpose of the experiment, and this can interfere with the thoughts, feelings, and behaviours of those taking part.

Table 8.5 Advantages and disadvantages of the experimental method

Advantages of the experimental method	Disadvantages of the experimental method
■ Cause and effect	■ Question of ecological validity
■ Control of variables	■ Control of extraneous variables
■ Objectivity	■ Confounding variables (participant)
■ Replication	■ Demand characteristics

Advantages and disadvantages of different types of experiment

Advantages of the laboratory experiment

The main advantage of the laboratory experiment is that it gives a clear *cause and effect* relationship between an independent and dependent variable. This is because it is easier to *control extraneous variables* in a laboratory than in other experimental situations.

The laboratory experiment also ensures greater accuracy in the measurement of our dependent variable. Devices to precisely measure behaviours are far easier to use in a laboratory than elsewhere. These objective measures of observed behaviour guarantee the *validity of our empirical data*. The laboratory experiment's standardised procedure also allows others to replicate what has been done. If after *replication,* this new empirical evidence is supportive, we can be even more confident that any cause and effect relationship is as a result of the manipulation of the IV on the DV, and not other extraneous chance factors.

Disadvantages of the laboratory experiment

The *control of all extraneous variables* is impossible. *Random variables,* for example, just happen, and cannot therefore be controlled. You can try to anticipate and control for *confounding variables* but can never be entirely certain that you have accounted for them all, until after the experiment, and then it is too late. The laboratory experiment is also often accused of lacking in ecological validity. This is because the results are often from an unreal situation, which is difficult to find in real life.

Who is to say that in our alcohol and driving ability example, our participants in real life would drink and then get behind the wheel of a car? Only an idiot would do this. *Generalisation* of results into a real world situation is therefore sometimes difficult because of a laboratory experiment's lack of real-life, ecological validity.

Advantages of the field experiment

A field experiment yields greater ecological validity than a laboratory experiment; and because it takes place in a real-life setting, any behaviour it observes is more likely to be natural. You avoid sampling bias because you access in the field a more representative sample of the population to whom you want to generalise your results. Demand characteristics can be minimised.

Disadvantages of the field experiment

It is more difficult to control for extraneous variables in a field environment than in a laboratory. Imagine designing a field experiment to investigate types of play behaviour in children from age four to eight years. The most appropriate field environment for this would be a primary school playground. You arrange everything, and on the day your field experiment is due to take place it rains! You have to call it off – yet the project us due in the next day! This is an example of a random variable in a field experiment. A student of psychology in Scotland would of course time manage their practical investigation better. Well at least in my classes!

Controlling for confounding variables in a field experiment is equally hazardous, there are just so many. An example of this is Feshbach & Singer's (1971) study.

Feshbach and Singer were interested in the influence violent/non-violent TV programmes had on male teenage behaviours. They predefined programmes such as 'Batman' as violent. Boys aged between nine and fifteen from seven residential schools were randomly assigned to either condition of the independent variable, which was to watch either violent or non-violent TV. Each group within each home was instructed to watch at least two hours of television per day for six weeks, watching in either condition of the IV.

For three of the seven schools tested, levels of aggression among those exposed to violent programmes were found to be *lower* than those of participants exposed to non-violent TV. According to Feshbach and Singer, this supports the *catharsis hypothesis*. The catharsis hypothesis says that watching violent TV provides a safe fantasy outlet for aggressive impulses and helps to reduce aggressive behaviours. This is in sharp contrast to Bandura *et al.*'s (1961) findings on naturally aggressive children. Bandura *et al.* found naturally aggressive children to be *more* aggressive as a consequence of observing and imitating aggressive adult models.

You might think Feshbach and Singer would appear to have made an important discovery. However Liebert & Sprafkin (1988) criticise Feshbach and Singer on two counts. Boys in the non-aggressive TV group in the three institutions where the catharsis effect appeared had rebelled against being told they could not watch 'Batman'. To keep the peace no doubt, Feshbach and Singer then proceeded to let them watch their 'banned' programme. This constitutes an important difference in comparison to the treatment of all the other groups. Further, Liebert & Sprafkin (1988) say:

> *'An important alternative explanation ... for the fact that some control subjects were more aggressive is that they resented being restricted to non-aggressive programmes, and this resentment was expressed in an increase in violence.'*

Resentment alone could have accounted for more violent behaviour in the non-aggressive control group.

INTERACTIVE

How many confounding variables can you find in the Feshbach and Singer field experiment that could provide an alternative account to their catharsis hypothesis?

Advantages of the quasi-experiment

The biggest advantage of the quasi-experiment is its high ecological validity. Quasi-experiments are more 'natural'; the IV is one that naturally occurs; the participants you access are in their natural environment. Their thoughts, feelings and behaviours are deemed to be more normal and natural as a result. In a quasi-experiment sampling bias disappears, as do demand characteristics. This is of course as long as participants *are* unaware they are part of a psychological experiment.

Disadvantages of the quasi-experiment

You have no control over the independent variable. In a quasi-experiment it is also extremely difficult to infer a cause–effect conclusion due to an inability to control extraneous variables. These could be other factors that give rise to your results (see earlier Feshbach & Singer, 1971).

Quasi-experiments are almost impossible to replicate. They take place at a particular time, a particular place and with a particular group of participants. A quasi-experiment has only spatio-temporal validity.

Quasi-experiments can also attract participant expectancy in that the demand characteristics of the situation might give participants a clue that they are taking part in an experiment. On the other hand, if participants do not know they are the subject of an investigation, the quasi-experiment can attract ethical criticism concerning privacy, disclosure, consent and debriefing.

Because of an inability to control the IV and extraneous variables, and an inability to replicate to confirm/deny the original results, the quasi-experiment is least like a procedure that adheres to the experimental method. Procedures that are recognised as 'true' experiments must see the manipulation of an independent variable, the observation and measurement of any effect of this manipulation on a dependent variable, and the control of extraneous variables.

Table 8.6 Advantages of types of experiments

Type of experiment	Advantages
Laboratory experiment	■ Cause and effect can be better established ■ Objectivity and precision measurement of DV ■ Control of confounding variables ■ Replication due to standardised procedures (design/instructions)
Field experiment	■ High ecological validity ■ Avoids sampling bias ■ Demand characteristics minimised
Quasi-experiment	■ Great ecological validity ■ Little, if any, sampling bias ■ Participants less influenced by demand characteristics

Table 8.7 Disadvantages of types of experiments

Type of experiment	Disadvantages
Laboratory experiment	■ Impossible to control for all extraneous variables ■ Lack of ecological validity due to artificial laboratory environment ■ Sampling bias, demand characteristics, experimenter expectancy can all influence behaviours, results and conclusions ■ Ethics (deception, etc.)
Field experiment	■ Difficult to control extraneous variables ■ Difficult to replicate ■ Precision measurement problematic ■ Ethics (consent, deception, privacy, etc.)
Quasi-experiment	■ Cause–effect difficult to establish between IV and DV ■ No control over IV ■ Little control over extraneous variables ■ Impossible to replicate ■ Only spatio-temporal validity ■ Ethics (consent, deception, privacy, etc.)

Summary

The experimental method of research is a controlled procedure that sees the manipulation of an independent variable (IV) to observe and measure any effect this has on a dependent variable (DV). The essential features of the experimental method are the control, observation and measurement of variables. Having the hallmarks of a science, the experimental method makes us more confident about the validity of any cause–effect relationship established between an independent and dependent variable. The experimental method also makes us more assured about the generalisation of its results to a wider population. The experimental method's emphasis on strict procedures helps others replicate the experiment to confirm, or otherwise, the original research findings. This is how scientific knowledge grows. The experimental method sets out to test a null hypothesis, which if rejected allows the researcher to accept the experimental, or research, hypothesis. Hypotheses will, more often than not, be tested at a level of significance. A level of significance is the wager, probability, or p value, a researcher places on themselves that their results happened by chance. Students of psychology generally set themselves a level of significance of 0.05, which means they are happy to accept that in the rejection of their null hypothesis, there is still a 1:20 chance that any cause–effect relationship established is due to chance or random factors.

These chance or random factors, which can be an alternative explanation for results in psychological research, are called extraneous variables and are of two kinds. Random variables just happen, making them impossible to control, and confounding variables, which *can* be anticipated and controlled. Examples of confounding variables would be any situational variable found in the experimental setting, experimenter variables, such as experimenter and expectancy effect, and participant variables, which are those participant peculiarities that can influence results. These include participant expectancy and demand characteristics.

To control for extraneous variables, the experimental method uses one of two kinds of design procedure, a related or within-subjects design (like repeated measures or matched pairs), or alternatively, an unrelated independent group/sample/measures design. Each category, and each type of design, has particular features. For example, the repeated measures design, where participants experience all conditions/manipulations of the independent variable, can attract order effect. Counterbalancing can control order effect. What design is adopted is often decided in anticipation of confounding variables that can arise in the different experimental situations, which are the laboratory, field and quasi-experiment. They differ in their location, and thus the degree of control a researcher has over confounding variables.

The laboratory experiment often attracts criticism on the grounds of ecological validity. The further away from the laboratory a researcher goes, however, the more likely it is that the (more ecologically valid) quasi- or field experiment will attract random and confounding variables. As a research method, the experimental method is assuredly the most rigorous of methodologies in psychology. To get an even better understanding as to why this can be said, let us now examine non-experimental designs.

INTERACTIVE

1. Go to http://www.essex.ac.uk/psychology/experiments/lexical.html and do the Lexical Decision Experiment. Make sure you take a copy of each page!
2. Please now write a short report of your experimental research under the following headings. Aim; Method; Procedure; Results; Conclusion.
3. Go to http://www.alleydog.com/quizzes/methodsquiz.asp and do the Research Methods Quiz. How did you do?
4. Read http://www.sytsma.com/phad530/expdesig.html. What questions do researchers have to consider when thinking about using an experimental design?

Structured questions with answer guidelines

1 *Describe and explain the experimental method of research.*

With reference to the preceding chapter, structure your answer as follows:

- Define the experimental method of research as being *a controlled procedure that sees the manipulation of an independent variable (IV) to observe and measure its effect on a dependent variable (DV)*. Then using examples to help you:
- Identify and explain the following features of the experimental method:
  - generalisation, replication and validity
  - the experimental hypothesis, one and two-tailed
  - the independent and dependent variable
  - the null hypothesis, probability and significance
  - extraneous and confounding variables
  - situational, experimenter and participant. Types, examples, control
  - experimental designs: RMD and IGD
  - types of experiment: laboratory, field and quasi
  - features of laboratory, field and quasi-experiments. Location and degree of control over IV and confounding variables.

2 *Evaluate the experimental method of research in terms of its advantages and disadvantages.*

Structure your answer as follows:

- Define the experimental method of research as being *a controlled procedure that sees the manipulation of an independent variable (IV) to observe and measure its effect on a dependent variable (DV)*. Then using examples to help you:
- Identify and explain advantages of the experimental method, i.e.
  - cause and effect
  - control of variables
  - objectivity
  - replication.
  - Then describe the specific advantages attached to specific types of experimental method.
- Identify and explain disadvantages of the experimental method
  - ecological validity
  - control of extraneous variables
  - participant variables
  - demand characteristics
  - Then describe specific disadvantages attached to specific types of experimental method.

Glossary

Between-subjects design: an unrelated design such as an independent groups design. Also called independent subjects/samples design

Counterbalancing: a technique used in an experiment to control for order effect, e.g. ABBA.

Demand characteristics: clues from the research situation that help the participant work out its purpose. Demand characteristics alter behaviour, and thus influence results

Dependent variable: in an experiment the DV is the variable that is measured or observed as a consequence of changing or manipulating the independent variable

Experimental design: the procedure adopted to control for participant variables in an experiment, e.g. repeated measures, independent groups

Experimental method: a research design only applicable to a laboratory, field or quasi-experiment. The experimental method is identified by the manipulation of an IV, the observation of any effect this has on a DV, and the control of extraneous variables

Experimenter effect: an aspect associated with the experimenter in research e.g. their behaviour, manner, age, sex, age etc. that influences the behaviour of the participant in some way

Field experiment: an experiment that takes place away from the laboratory in a more natural setting. The experimental method of control, observation and measurement of variables still occurs

Independent variable: in an experiment the IV is the variable that is changed or manipulated to measure/observe its effect on the dependent variable

Laboratory experiment: traditional setting of an experiment that adheres to the experimental method of control, observation, and measurement of variables

Longitudinal study: research of a year or more

Mean: a statistical average, e.g. the mean of 2 + 3 + 4 + 1 + 2 + 5 + 1 is 2.571 (18 divided by 7)

Order effect: the influence of tiredness, fatigue or boredom on participants in an experiment. Controlled by counterbalancing

Pilot study: a practice run of an experiment to identify any flaws, snags or ambiguity of instructions before conducting the experiment proper

Placebo: a placebo is the control condition of the IV that has no effect, e.g. a sugar pill

Quasi-experiment: a situation that is 'nearly' an experiment, which takes place in a real-world environment. The main difference between a quasi- and a field/laboratory experiment is that participants are already found in those conditions of the IV you are researching

Single-blind technique: used in experimental research where the participant does not know to what condition of the independent variable they have been allocated

Standardised instructions: agreed instructions to be given to participants in an experiment, usually formulated after a pilot study has been conducted

Treatment: the conditions or manipulations of an independent variable

Within-subjects design: related designs such as repeated measures and matched pairs

9

The observational method

BY THE END OF THIS CHAPTER YOU SHOULD BE ABLE TO:

- **identify by example the observational method of research**
- **define and explain the observational method of research with reference to its key features**
- **explain and evaluate the observational method of research in terms of its advantages and disadvantages.**

Overview of the observational method

Earlier in Chapter 7, when introduced to research methods, we discovered that the observational method is non-experimental in design – as are the interview, survey, and case study methods. When using the observational method there is no manipulation of an independent variable. As a consequence no cause–effect relationships can be made concerning your observations as to why the behaviour(s) may have occurred.

What all observational procedures share is the use of a standardised (planned and systematic) method in order to obtain accurate data on whatever behaviour is being observed. This gives the researcher accurate and detailed data from which to draw conclusions.

We find five types of observation used in psychological investigations:

- participant observation
- non-participant observation
- structured (controlled) observation
- unstructured (uncontrolled) observation
- naturalistic observation.

In all five, observation involves the planned gathering, analysis and interpretation of data on observed behaviour.

The observational method has both advantages and disadvantages as a research tool in psychology. Ethics and the issue of disclosure can be major headaches, but if the researcher adheres to the observational method – to plan, structure and conduct their observation in a disciplined way – the observational method may be seen as one of the purest forms of non-experimental research, as it taps directly into behaviour, rather than perceptions of it as might happen in a case study or interview.

What is the observational method?

The observational method of research concerns the planned watching, recording and analysis of observed behaviour as it occurs in a natural setting.

The study of naturally occurring behaviour

Given that psychology is the study of human behaviour and mental processes, it seems logical to suggest that in order to study the *behavioural* aspect of psychology we need to observe the behaviours of those around us. Indeed, much research that psychologists conduct involves observing behaviour at *some* stage in the research process.

Figure 9.1 Observing!

The observational method requires careful planning

The theme that runs through procedures using the observational method concerns the careful planning of *how* the behaviour under scrutiny is to be observed and recorded. We all observe each other on a daily basis. Indeed, your interest in psychology might encourage you to observe others much more closely than you did before! If you are in a supermarket you may glance at the purchases of other shoppers. While sitting in a café you may observe the interactions between people, their eating habits or their clothes. You cannot tell anything much from these casual observations of behaviours, although they may sow the seeds for later hypothesis testing, as the following exercise illustrates.

Key features of the observational method

Generating empirical data

The observational method requires us to pre-plan our approach to those behaviours we want to watch. A major part of this preparation involves us in deciding how our observations are to be recorded. This is because our records, and/or our recordings, can give us factual and objective measurements of our observed behaviour, i.e. empirical data. This empirical data is later analysed in order to draw factual conclusions on the behaviours observed.

INTERACTIVE

Go to a café, refectory or restaurant and *just observe* what is going on for a few minutes. You will find there is so much going on that you cannot properly observe everything, and what observations you do make will be influenced by your motivation, your mood, your concentration and your perspective (where you are sitting/standing). If you are hungry, the biological and cognitive approaches tell us you will be more motivated towards observing the food-orientated behaviours of those around us – such as people cooking, staff carrying food to tables, others eating, and so on. If you are tired the study of attention reminds us you will not be able to concentrate to observe anything much at all! You could test the influence of perspective on casual observation by also getting a friend to observe, but sit apart from you in the cafe. It is quite likely that the reports of your individual observations of the same scene will vary considerably. The need for careful planning and recording of any psychological observation should now be apparent. The observational method of research involves the *planned* watching, recording and analysis of behaviour as it occurs in a natural setting.

A good example of the generation of empirical data from an observation in everyday life is that of an athlete running 100 metres. All involved agree beforehand on the measurement of 100 metres. The athletes line up and start when they hear the gun. Electronic devices are used to identify false starts. The athletes' time to run 100 metres is objectively and factually recorded in seconds using stopwatches. The athlete who crosses the line first wins. By comparing times we are able to say how an athlete has performed in relation to the others in the race, and 100-metre athletes in the athletic world at large. We are able to draw many more conclusions about the athletes' running behaviour due to the generation of empirical data. This data tells us, for instance, who was fastest off the block, who was first to 50 metres, whether the athletes have achieved their personal best, and so on.

Data from observations can either be quantitative or qualitative. We have already met these terms.

Quantitative data

Quantitative data, in an observation, provides us with a *quantity* or *number* concerning the behaviours of people. We could observe, for example, the sex and film choice of people using a particular cinema complex during a particular period of time. You could decide to observe the first hundred people entering the cinema and record their sex and which film they go in to see. After this data has been collected, you would be able to quantify, or give a *measurement* to the sex of participants and their particular film choice.

Qualitative data

Qualitative data gives emotional details concerning behaviours. It is subjective, i.e. 'How was it for you?'

If you wanted to find out what those hundred people *thought* of the film you could also give them a short exit interview or survey that would allow you to collect *qualitative* data. Qualitative data is the rich, detailed, personal information provided by each individual on, here for example, the strengths and weaknesses of the acting, the story, the direction, the special effects and so on.

Data-gathering techniques

To get the most meaningful measurements of behaviour in observational studies some important questions should be considered. What is to be observed; why is it being observed; by whom; where and when is the observation to be conducted, and how is the recording of our observations to be carried out?

What?

The types of behaviours that can be observed in psychology are varied, and can be those of either human or non-human subjects, i.e. people or animals.

Why?

At the outset it is important to have an understanding of the topic under investigation and why you are conducting your research. You have to determine its purpose; you may begin by trying to answer a question out of simple curiosity, e.g. what is the sexual behaviour of people in a particular group? This would gradually become more specific as you refine your initial observations, such as, what are the specific behaviours of the male in this group; who attracts the most females, or what do men in this group do in social situations to attract a female. Or indeed *vice versa*.

By whom and where?

The observational method of research is particularly appropriate for social psychologists, developmental psychologists and animal behaviourists, primarily because of the participants/subjects used in their studies, i.e. social groups, children and animals. In each case, valid and reliable results would be more likely if behavioural observations occurred in the *natural environment* of the participants/subjects.

When?

When to observe can be problematic. To help us there are two methods of recording observed behaviours – continuous recording and time sampling. Continuous recording means recording all behaviours all the time. Time sampling records snapshots of behaviour.

- **Continuous recording** allows for an *exact* record of behaviours with the time they occurred (for events), or the time at which the behaviour started and finished (for states of behaviour, e.g. aggression).
- **Time sampling** involves the *periodic* recording of behaviour, e.g. recording a situation at five-minute intervals. Time sampling gives you less information, and an exact recording of the behaviour you are interested in is not *necessarily* obtained. You could be recording the wrong five minutes! However, time sampling is a way of condensing information in observational research, and with good prior planning a *sample* of the behaviour(s) you are interested in can be captured and recorded.

How?

How you get data from your observation is important to the generation of objective empirical data. Observations often use precise measures, such as audio/visual recordings and/or observation schedules.

Video recordings provide an exact audio and visual record of behaviour. They are particularly useful in situations where behaviours are being recorded over a lengthy period. Video recordings are also helpful when the behaviour under investigation is too fast, or too complex, to be analysed in real time. Tapes and recordings can then later be slowed down, stopped or freeze-framed to give a better idea as to why the behaviour may have happened.

Written records are also often used in observations, either on their own, or to complement audio and visual recordings. Called observation schedules or check sheets, they are carefully constructed in order to get an accurate picture of the behaviour under investigation. Codes and a **behaviour index** might also be used, as we can see in our example below.

Table 9.1 An observation schedule: check sheet using time sampling

Date/time xx/xx/xx 1 pm	Kitten A	Kitten B	Kitten C	Kitten D
Intervals				
0.30	F	S	Mw	S
1.00	F	S	S	S
1.30	F	S	S	T
2.00	F	S	Aw	T
2.30	S	S	Aw	F
3.00	F	S	Aw	F
3.30	F	F	P	F
4.00	S	F	P	F
4.30	F	F	F	F
5.00	F	F	F	F

Behaviour index:

S = kitten is sleeping

F = kitten is feeding from mother

P = kitten is playing or fighting with others in litter

Mw = the mother is washing the kitten

T = the mother is toileting the kitten by licking

Aw = the kitten is awake but still.

Figure 9.2 How would you categorise the behaviour on the right?!

Using time sampling, this observation schedule check sheet has been used to record behaviours of very young kittens. The date and time of recording would normally be inserted in the top left box. For recording purposes the four kittens in the litter were given a letter A–D. The time interval sampled was every 30 seconds over a 5-minute period. The behaviour index allowed the observer to quickly and accurately record what each kitten was doing at each particular time sampled. This is excellent quantitative empirical data essential for analysis and a considered conclusion.

INTERACTIVE

Why would the above observational check sheet give you quantitative data? Why would qualitative data be impossible in this situation?!

Obtrusive and unobtrusive measures

An **obtrusive measure** in an observation is where an observer uses a check sheet or observation schedule, 'scoring' the behaviours as they happen in front of them. A video camera or camcorder would also be deemed an obtrusive measure if in sight of those who are taking part.

An **unobtrusive measure** in an observation is a *hidden* measure of behaviour, such as the use of a one-way mirror, hidden camera/recorder, etc.

The use of obtrusive measures can be an extraneous variable in an observation, and give rise to an alternative explanation as to why the behaviour you observed has occurred.

Control of extraneous variables

Despite careful planning, extraneous variables or *variables from the outside* can give rise to alternative explanations in observations of behaviour. Extraneous variables are unavoidable and infinite. As researchers, we must try to make sure that extraneous variables are anticipated and controlled in our research procedures.

As we saw earlier in the chapter on the experimental method, extraneous variables are of two types. **Random variables** are extraneous variables that 'just happen'. You have no control over random variables. Examples would be the weather, or how a participant was feeling on the day.

The other type of extraneous variable that *can* be anticipated and controlled is called a **confounding variable**. An obtrusive measure in an observation could be a confounding variable because the presence of an observer with a check sheet or camcorder could influence the behaviour of those being observed.

One of the most effective types of observation used to avoid extraneous variables is, as we will see, a structured observation. Structured means controlled. Structured observations can give rise to a common type of confounding variable in observational research called observer bias (see Rosenthal & Fode (1963) on page 191).

Observer bias

Observer bias can occur if more than one observer is used, for instance, if different observers are recording data at the same time, or working on a shift basis over an extended time period.

Observer bias would be a confounding variable if one observer has a different understanding of what the codes used in a behaviour index mean, and fills in the schedule wrongly. Another example of observer bias would be where one observer has their own hypothesis and, consciously or unconsciously, selects *only* those observations for recording to substantiate this.

In order to control for observer bias there are two types of reliability check that can be used. These are called within-observer reliability, and between-observer reliability.

- **Within-observer reliability** measures the extent to which each individual observer obtains *consistency* when recording scores or ratings of the same behaviour on *different occasions*. Their video recordings and check sheet records of the 'same' behaviour on a number of occasions can verify this.
- **Between-observer reliability** measures the extent to which two or more observers obtain the *same* results when measuring the *same* behaviour on the *same* occasion. This can again be confirmed, or otherwise, using their video recordings and check sheets.

Within- and between-observer reliability can be further tested by correlating the records of different observers. The greater the statistical relationship of within- and between-observers' scores/ratings, the greater the level of **inter-rater reliability** an observational study is said to have. This strengthens the reliability of any conclusions that may be made.

You – the observer – can thus be a confounding variable in your own observational research. Guard against this by agreeing on what goes to make up the behaviour you want to observe. Agree a common coding system for this, construct a behaviour index and check sheet/observation schedule as in Table 9.1. You could increase the inter-rater reliability of your study by verifying your own, and others' coding of observed behaviour by using a correlation.

Types of observation

There are as indicated earlier five different types of observations that adhere to the observational method: participant observation; non-participant observation; structured observation; unstructured observation; naturalistic observation.

Participant observation

Participant observation sees the observer(s) set up and take part in the behaviour under investigation.

Participant observation can give an accurate record of what is actually happening in a situation. However, while the behavioural information may be accurate, it is also possible that the presence of an observer may alter the behaviour of those taking part. This is known as the **observer effect**, and is an example of another confounding variable in observational studies. You can avoid the observer effect by deciding not to disclose who you are. Called **covert observation**, this attracts obvious ethical criticisms, in that you are not being open and honest about your true purpose with fellow 'participants'. If your observation is known about, this is an **overt observation**. You are being open about what you are doing. Now please turn to the Study and Interactive on page 220.

Non-participant observation

Non-participant observation sees no participation *on the part of the observer.*

Non-participant observation is where the observer does not take part in the behaviour under investigation and observes and records what occurs from a distance. This eliminates the possibility of observer effect, and is usually a covert observation in that your measures would be hidden, or just too far away for anyone to be aware of them.

The behaviours being observed are thus prone to subjective interpretation on the part of the observer, and this could show itself in the form of observer bias which should be anticipated and controlled.

An example of non-participant observation is the study by Piliavin *et al.* (1969). It should be noted that here, observation was used in conjunction with the experimental method, since the researchers controlled a number of *independent* variables. Independent variables are, of course, a feature of any procedure that uses the *experimental* method. Now please turn to the Study and Interactive on page 221.

Structured observation

Structured observation is the planned watching and recording of behaviours as they occur within a controlled *environment.*

Structured observation sees the researcher first identify the behaviour(s) in which they are interested, and then observe its type or frequency over a set period of time using a pre-coded data-gathering instrument, such as a check sheet. Generally a structured observation would follow the procedure shown on page 222.

STUDY

Rosenhan, D.L. (1973). 'On being sane in insane places'. *Science*, 179, 250–58

Aim: To find out if those characteristics that lead doctors and other professionals to a diagnosis of mental illness are a result of the patient's actual condition, or because of the environment and context within which the patient is observed and diagnosed.

Method: Eight sane people presented themselves for admission to twelve different hospitals in the USA (**participant observers**). They complained of hearing voices such as 'dull' and 'thud'. Other than this symptom the eight **pseudo-patients** complained of no other ailments. After admission to the hospital they stopped complaining about hearing voices. They took part in the activities on the ward, and in their role as participant observers, wrote notes about staff and patients.

Results: Seven of the eight pseudo-patients received a diagnosis of schizophrenia. They were kept in hospital for between seven and fifty-two days (average nineteen). They were all released with a diagnosis of schizophrenia in remission. The only people who suspected that they were not genuine patients were some of the other patients in their ward.

Conclusion: Psychiatric professionals saw note-taking by the pseudo-patients as an aspect of their condition. Outside the context of a psychiatric ward this, and other behaviours, would not be seen as abnormal. David Rosenhan concluded that 'normal' behaviours were reinterpreted as 'abnormal', based on the context of the situation, psychiatric hospitals, and therefore the subsequent expectations of the staff. These expectations existed because of the labels they attached to the sane and insane.

From the perspective of participant observation it should also be noted that accounts given by the pseudo-patients of their experiences within a psychiatric ward are not necessarily representative of the experiences of 'real' patients, who do not have the comfort of knowing that they have been possibly misdiagnosed. It may be apparent that here it would have been difficult to use anything but participant observation.

INTERACTIVE

1. What evidence is there to indicate that Rosenhan's (1973) study is a participant observation?
2. Did Rosenhan (1973) generate empirical data? Give reasons for your answer.
3. Why is Rosenhan's study *not* a structured observation?

STUDY

Piliavin, I.M., Rodin, J. & Piliavin, J.A. (1969). 'Good Samaritanism: An underground phenomenon?' *Journal of Personality and Social Psychology,* 13, 289–299

Aim: In order to investigate passenger-response to an emergency in a *real-life* situation of a New York subway train and to ensure **ecological validity**, Piliavin *et al.* used non-participant observation within a field experiment. They were interested in the speed, frequency, and rate of passenger response to a manipulated 'emergency' involving stooges who were told to act in a particular way. Other aspects to helping behaviour (altruism) that were of interest were the number of passengers in the carriage where the emergency occurred, their race, and whether there was any difference in them offering help if the 'victim' was perceived as drunk or visually impaired.

Method: Incidents such as a black/white victim drunk or sober (with a cane) collapsing in a carriage of a New York subway train were staged at set times over a period of two months. Passengers on the trains were the participants. Each train carriage contained an average of forty-three passengers, with a racial mix of 45 per cent black and 55 per cent white. The researchers were four students (two male and two female). The females were the non-participant observers of the incidents enacted by their two male colleagues.

The observers recorded the race, age, sex and location of each passenger on pre-prepared sheets. They then recorded who and how many people helped the 'victim' and how long it took for them to respond.

Results: The cane victim received help on 62 of 65 trials. The drunk victim received help on 19 of 38 trials. On 60 per cent of all trials the victim received help from two or more helpers. On close analysis the sex of the 'first helper' was more likely to be male.

Conclusion: Passengers were more helpful than Piliavin had predicted and he attributed this to a delicate balance on the part of the helper between personal cost and personal reward. The cost of helping may be embarrassment; the cost of not helping, guilt. The rewards associated with helping may be praise and respect, while those associated with not helping may be 'no time wasted' in a busy day.

Piliavin *et al.* thought that what motivates someone to help is not altruism – a drive within us to help for helping's sake – but our need to remove/avoid a negative emotional state if we don't help. We feel bad about it.

INTERACTIVE

1. Why is Piliavin *et al.*'s (1969) study an example of non-participant observation?
2. What type of experimental design is also being used?
3. Can you identify any independent variables?
4. What do you understand by the term 'ecological validity'?
5. How was observer bias overcome?

In a structured observation you need to:

- define the behaviour or type(s) of behaviours to be studied
- identify the time frame during which the behaviour is to be observed
- develop a data-gathering instrument, e.g. observation schedule
- select an observer role – what is it you want the observers to do
- train observers if more than one is to be used
- conduct the observation(s) using your data-gathering instrument(s)
- verify data for reliability.

Structured observations: a controlled environment

If you were interested in toy preference among girls and boys in the under-five age group, a structured observation would be ideal. Having obtained the necessary permission to conduct your research you would find out prior to the observation those toys familiar to the participating children. You would then introduce an equal number of familiar and unfamiliar toys into the nursery situation, having also discovered from an independent source whether they were considered 'male toys' or 'female toys'. This could be done by contacting manufacturers, or by surveying members of the public and asking their opinion on which toy they thought more appropriate for which sex.

Once all this has been determined, you could enhance your structured observation of pre-five toy-preference by using a range of obtrusive measures such as a check sheet, plus utilise unobtrusive measures like a hidden video recorder or CCTV.

Structured observations and ethics

Structured observations are often used to protect the welfare of those being observed. An example of this is Ainsworth *et al.*'s (1978) study where a naturalistic observation of an infant's reaction to being separated from his/her mother would have been unsafe and unethical. The natural environment of a supermarket or park would have been too dangerous. The situation in Ainsworth *et al.*'s study is 'natural,' in so far as the child and mother could expect to find themselves in a similar situation at some time or another because it took place in an environment akin to a doctor's surgery. An important feature of this structured observation was the eight changing environments that occurred during the course of the observation.

NATURALISTIC OBSERVATION

Naturalistic observation is the planned watching and recording of behaviours as they occur within a natural environment

Naturalistic observation is often associated with **ethology**, a branch of psychology which studies the behaviour of animals in their natural environment. They do this in order to make species–species comparisons with humans in, for example, mother–infant attachment behaviours, aggression, etc. Naturalistic observation, or observations of real-life behaviours in a real-life natural setting, gives to what you discover ecological validity. This means behaviours are real because they have been naturally observed – but in a planned and systematic fashion.

STUDY

Ainsworth, M.D.S., Blehar, M.C., Waters, E. & Wall, S. (1978) '*Patterns of attachment: A psychological study of the strange situation*'. New Jersey: Lawrence Erlbaum Assoc. Inc.

Aim: To observe the emotional reactions of infants to brief separations from their caregivers in the presence of strangers, and of their behaviour when the caregiver returned.

Method: Using a structured observation procedure and a specially prepared observation room, interactions between infants and their caregivers, while in the presence/absence of a stranger/caregiver, were observed and recorded through a two-way mirror. There were eight stages (or strange situations) in the process. Each of the eight stages lasted approximately three minutes.

Stage	Situation
One	Mother and baby are shown into an observation room
Two	Mother does not get involved with her baby and baby is left to explore the room
Three	A stranger enters the room. For the first minute the stranger does not interact with either the baby or the mother. After one minute the stranger begins to speak to the mother. After another minute the stranger approaches the baby. At the end of another minute the mother leaves the room
Four	The stranger and baby are left together with the stranger playing/soothing as appropriate.
Five	The stranger leaves the room and the mother settles the baby into play once more.
Six	Baby is alone in room.
Seven	Stranger re-enters the room and begins to interact with the baby
Eight	Mother returns and greets the baby. The stranger leaves the room.

Observers recorded the reactions of the baby and the mother in each of the stages. They were interested in four types of behaviours evident during the strange situation, which they coded accordingly, i.e.

1 Separation anxiety – any distress the infant showed when mother left.
2 The infant's willingness to explore.
3 Stranger anxiety – anxiety shown by the infant when approached by the stranger.
4 Reunion behaviour – reaction of the infant after separation when mother returned.

Results: As a result of their observations, Ainsworth *et al.* concluded that there were three main types of attachment behaviours found between mothers and their infants: **Type A – Anxious–avoidant** (infant is ambivalent to mother's presence; they are more distressed by being left alone than by the mother's departure and find comfort with the stranger). **Type B – Secure attachment** (infant plays happily in the mother's presence, they are distressed at the

continued

mother's departure rather than because of their isolation. Although the stranger can offer some comfort, there is a clear difference between the comforts obtained from the caregiver and the stranger). **Type C – Anxious–resistant** (the infant is wary in mother's presence, they play and explore less than types A and B children. On the mother's return anxious–resistant infants both seek and reject her comfort at one and the same time. The stranger cannot comfort them).

Conclusion: Of the mother/infant pairings studied, 15 per cent showed type A anxious–avoidant behaviour; 70 per cent, type B secure attachment behaviour; and 15 per cent, type C anxious–resistant attachment behaviours. Sensitive mothers have infants who can tolerate short separations and explore strange environments independently, who seem safe in the knowledge that they can return to the mother for security (Type B). Insensitive mothers have infants who lack secure attachment to the mother, and demonstrate this by either ambivalence or anger at being separated from her (Types A and C).

INTERACTIVE

Read the Ainsworth *et al.* (1978) structured observation and consider the following questions.

1 What was the purpose of the study?

2 What procedures were undertaken to ensure this was a structured observation?

3 What ethical reasons might have prompted the use of structured observation in this instance?

4 Describe the coding system used by the researchers.

An example of a naturalistic observation would be if we wished to see the behavioural reaction of an animal to a new food source. We would obtain the most valid results if we observed food source changes in the animal's natural environment. Consider a troop of monkeys living in an area of the forest where their main food is banana. Researchers may wish to test if the monkeys can adapt to another food source, e.g. berries not native to the forest. They would provide quantities of the berries within easy reach of the monkeys and observe and record the monkeys' behaviour in relation to the new food source.

Figure 9.3 The feeding behaviour of monkeys could be studied by naturalistic observation

Naturalistic observation and children

Naturalistic observation is also often used with children. Children react to the slightest change in their environment – watch the reaction of a toddler when mum has to leave him/her with someone less familiar! In order to observe children's *natural* behaviours, psychologists would want to observe them in an environment familiar to them. Thus with infants and children, a *naturalistic* observation could take place in the home, school, playground, etc.

Naturalistic observation can be applied to our earlier example of toy choice among girls and boys in the pre-five age group. To be a naturalistic observation, you would arrange to go to the nursery, then using a pre-planned system, you would record the sex of each child, and length of time you observe each child play with the toys normally available to them. At the end of this you might be able to conclude that boys preferred particular toys, while girls preferred others.

Extraneous variables in naturalistic observations

There are problems with deducing too much from what you naturally observe in this situation. The boys' and girls' toy preference could have been influenced by a variety of confounding variables such as the toys available, their prior knowledge and experience of particular toys, and your presence as a stranger in the nursery. Random variables could also occur in that something may have happened to the child/children, which may have influenced their mood, and thus their behaviour, on the day of your observation.

Unstructured observation

Unstructured observation is the unplanned, informal, watching and recording of behaviours as they occur in a natural environment.

INTERACTIVE

How might **observer bias** influence an unstructured observation?

An unstructured observation is a form of observational study where the behaviour of interest, and/or the method of observation have not been clearly specified in advance. Unstructured observations are used when a specific behaviour being studied cannot be clearly identified, and when it is important to observe participants in their own environments rather than in, say, a laboratory setting. An example of an unstructured observation is that of a social psychologist going undercover to observe the behaviours of a gang of football casuals.

All that unstructured observations do is give the researcher a sense of *what is going on here?* The investigator does not have any measuring or recording instrument other than a notebook or memory. Particular attention must be paid to observer bias in unstructured observations. In the above example it would be foolhardy for the social psychologist to pull out a notebook and start taking the 'firm's' details! His later recall of events can however be influenced by personal opinion. Observations would not have been recorded in a planned, systematic and objective manner.

Examples of unstructured observations include Whyte in 1943 when he joined an Italian street gang in Chicago. He used a cover story that he was writing a book about the area. His true purpose was to observe the gang from a psychological point of view. He is remembered for his famous statement on his experiences: '*I began as a non-participating observer. As I became accepted into the community, I found myself becoming a non-observing participant.*'

Observation as a technique

Bandura *et al.* (1961)'s study is a classic piece of psychological research where a Canadian research team, led by Alfred Bandura, conducted an experiment and a non-participant observation into the transmission of aggressive behaviours from adults to children. As we can see from the study that follows they had three conditions of the independent variable.

They used observation as a technique, rather than a method in its own right. Observations occurred within a laboratory experiment. In their experiment they observed and recorded children's behaviours from behind a one-way mirror, later coding and analysing their recordings. On this evidence Bandura *et al.* (1961) concluded that children observe, then imitate and model themselves on the adult behaviours that they see.

Stanley Milgram's work into blind obedience is another example of structured observation being used as a technique to gather data within an experimental design. His 1963 laboratory experiment used film to observe and record his participants' emotional reactions to orders from an authority figure to inflict apparently lethal doses of electricity on another person.

STUDY

Bandura, A., Ross, D., & Ross, S.A. (1961). 'Transmission of aggression through imitation of aggressive models'. *Journal of Abnormal and Social Psychology*, 63, 575–582

Aim: To discover if aggression in children is influenced by observation, imitation and modelling of aggressive adult behaviour.

Method: Three groups of children were shown an adult being either rewarded, not rewarded or punished for aggressive behaviour towards a Bobo doll. Each child was then observed in an identical play environment with any resultant aggressive behaviour recorded onto film and later analysed, on a frame-by-frame, child-by-child basis.

Results: Children who had watched adult models engage in aggressive acts went on to exhibit more aggressive behaviours than those who had watched non-aggressive acts. Boys showed more aggression than girls. Male models induced more aggression in boys than female models. Male models induced more physical aggression, and female models, more verbal aggression in girls.

Conclusion: Children learn aggressive behaviours as a result of observing, imitating and modelling themselves on adults.

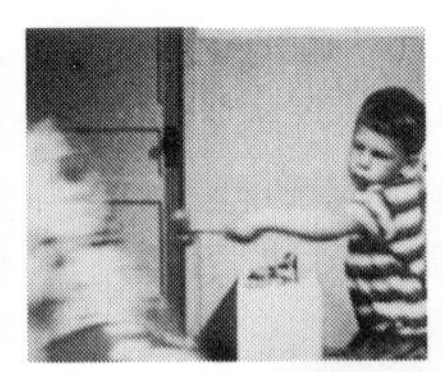

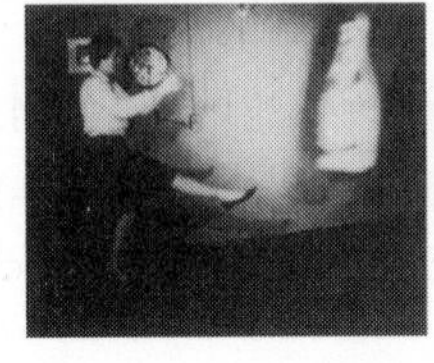

Figure 9.4 The aggressive behaviour of a female model, and the subsequent behaviour of a boy and girl who watched her (from A. Bandura *et al.*, 1961)

INTERACTIVE

1. Describe the features of this research that Bandura *et al.*'s (1961) study shares with the experimental method.
2. Identify the independent variables in this study.
3. What was the dependent variable in this study?
4. What did Bandura *et al.* discover?
5. Identify features of the observational method in this experimental situation.

Ethical issues and the observational method

Ethics in research

The following is based on the British Psychological Society (BPS) *Ethical Guidelines and Code of Conduct* (1985):

1. General consideration: always ensure that the research you do is carried out from the standpoint of the participants taking part. Research should never be offensive to anyone. This means that you should do nothing that threatens a person's health, well-being, or dignity. You should also be aware that we live in a multi-cultural country of diverse ethnic communities. Research should be considered from a socially inclusive, non-sexist, anti-racist and non-ageist perspective.
2. Consent: wherever possible consent should always be got from participants.
3. Deception: deception is not allowed if participants would be unlikely to co-operate without it. If in doubt the researcher should seek advice from a teacher, lecturer, etc.
4. Debriefing: any research must provide participants with an opportunity to discuss the outcomes of it. This is called debriefing, and allows discussion of the specific purpose of the research; interpretation of the participant's particular performance, scores, answers, etc., and give them an opportunity to ask questions.
5. Withdrawal from the investigation: all participants should give their permission to take part in your research. They should also be allowed to withdraw at any time if they so wish.
6. Confidentiality: unless subject to Scots law and UK statute, e.g. the Data Protection Act, confidentiality between participant and researcher should be observed at all times. If in doubt seek advice from your teacher, lecturer, etc.
7. Protection of participants: all participants taking part in research should be protected from any physical or mental harm.
8. Observational research: any observation should observe the privacy and psychological well-being of those studied. If consent to be observed is not possible, observations should only occur where it would be normal that those observed would/could be by others. If in doubt consult your teacher or lecturer.
9. Giving psychological advice: sometimes during research, the researcher will be asked their advice concerning a psychological matter that is of concern to a participant. The golden rule is not to give advice if not qualified to do so. If in any doubt you should seek advice from your teacher or lecturer.
10. Colleagues: everyone who studies psychology should abide by the above set of ethical principles. It is our duty to encourage others who carry out psychological research to observe these ethical guidelines at all times.

INTERACTIVE

Using the three studies detailed in this chapter, identify any ethical considerations you think are relevant to each. Give a reason, or reasons, for your answer. Please adhere to psychological conventions in your answer, i.e. 'Piliavin *et al.* (1969)', etc.

Advantages of the observational method

As a research tool the observational method can lead to a hypothesis for further study, and in so doing can save time and money being spent on a badly designed experiment, or other method of research.

The observational method provides 'real-life,' ecologically valid information, in that in an *ideal* situation, the researcher observes behaviour unobtrusively as it happens. Being in their natural environment, and *unaware* of the observer's presence (a covert observation), those being observed are more likely to behave naturally. The observational method can therefore avoid the problem of people behaving in a unnatural way if they know they are taking part in a piece of psychological research, if participants /subjects are unaware that they are being observed.

There are some subjects for whom the observational method is the only ethical method to use, e.g. young children and animals (outside captivity).

The standardisation of observational procedures gives sound evidence in the form of empirical data from which to draw conclusions about why participants/subjects behave as they do.

Table 9.2 Advantages of particular types of observation

Observational method	Advantages
Naturalistic observation	■ Particularly good for observing certain subjects ■ Provides ecologically valid recordings of naturally occurring behaviour ■ Spontaneous behaviours are more likely to occur
Structured observation	■ Allows control of extraneous variables ■ Reliability of results can be tested by repeating the study ■ Provides a safe environment to study contentious concepts such as infant attachment
Unstructured observation	■ Gives a broad overview of a situation ■ Useful where situation/subject matter to be studied is unclear
Participant observation	■ Gives an 'insiders' view ■ Behaviours are less prone to misinterpretation because researcher was a participant ■ Opportunity for researcher to become an 'accepted' part of the environment
Non-participant observation	■ Avoidance of observer effect

Disadvantages of the observational method

The main disadvantage of the observational method of research concerns replication. Replication of research allows for confirmation of results – or otherwise. Getting the same results the second, etc. time around allows you to be more confident of any conclusions you have previously drawn. Replication of observations is almost impossible. By their very nature future observations take place in a different time and space.

You cannot in any observation draw any cause–effect conclusions. There is no independent variable. These only occur in procedures that use the *experimental* method.

Another disadvantage is the lack of control of variables in most observational situations. You can never be *entirely* sure that you have identified, anticipated and controlled all confounding variables that could influence the behaviours you have observed.

Table 9.3 Disdvantages of particular types of observation

Observational method	Disadvantages
Naturalistic observation	■ Ethics: Where research is undisclosed, **consent** will not be obtained; where consent is not obtained, details may be used which infringe **confidentiality**
Structured observation	■ The implementation of controls may have an effect on behaviour ■ Lack of ecological validity ■ Observer effect ■ Observer bias
Unstructured observation	■ Only really appropriate as a 'first step' to give an overview of a situation/concept/idea
Participant observation	■ Observer effect ■ Possible lack of objectivity on the part of the observer
Non-participant observation	■ Detachment from situation so relies on perception which may be inaccurate

With all types of observation ethical considerations must be taken into account before, during, and after conducting your research

Summary

The observational method is non-experimental in design. The absence of an independent variable does not allow any cause–effect conclusions to be drawn from observational research. Sound evidence is however important to the observational method. Indeed, the observational method's key feature is a standardised, planned, and systematic approach to observe and record behaviour objectively. This is of course to generate all-important data upon which to base any conclusions. Observations, which can be overt or covert, are of five main types: participant observation, non-participant observation, structured observation, unstructured observation and naturalistic observation. Each involves the planned gathering, analysis and interpretation of mostly empirical data on observed behaviour. Each type of observation has its own features, advantages and disadvantages. Participant observation, for example, sees the researcher set up, and take part in the observation of behaviour under investigation. Non-participant observation sees no involvement on the part of the researcher, with recordings of observed behaviours being taken from afar. The observational method has both advantages and disadvantages as a research design in psychology. Covert observations can be problematic as to ethics and disclosure. Confounding variables also plague observations. These are infinite, and include observer bias and the observer effect. If the researcher plans, structures, and conducts their observations appropriately, the observational method can be seen as a most valid and reliable form of non-experimental research in psychology mainly due to its high ecological validity.

INTERACTIVE

1. Read the report of the working party chaired by Angela Costabile, Università degli Studi della Calabria at http://www.gold.ac.uk/tmr/reports/aim2_calabria1.html#CAT

   Make up a check sheet using time sampling to record incidents of aggressive behaviour in a school playground.

2. Read http://www.stream.fs.fed.us/streamnt/jul96/jul96a1.htm

   In what way is observer bias apparent in this piece of research? How was observer bias confirmed?

3. Go to http://www.wabash.edu/depart/psych/Courses/Psych220/LABNET%202001/ob4.html

   Based on this, design a simple observation to investigate types of play behaviour shown by pre-five-year-old boys and girls. Identify the purpose of your research, the aim of your observation, the method used (brief details of participants, materials and procedure), and how your results could be recorded and presented.

4. Go to http://ct.essortment.com/psychologybehav_rvjp.htm and read 'How do psychologists study behavior?'. In less than 250 words, compare and contrast the advantages and disadvantages of the experimental method, with those of the observational method.

Structured questions with answer guidelines

1 *Describe and explain the observational method of research.*

With reference to the preceding chapter, structure your answer as follows:

- Define the observational method of research as concerning *the planned gathering, analysis and interpretation of data on observed behaviour, as it occurs in a natural setting*
- Identify and explain the following features of the observational method:
  - non-experimental in design. Generally no IV, therefore no cause–effect
  - the need for empirical data. Types. Examples
  - detail of data-gathering techniques such as continuous recording, time sampling, audio-visual recorders, observation schedules, coding, behaviour index, and obtrusive and unobtrusive measures
  - control of extraneous variables, e.g. observer bias
  - types of observation, i.e. participant, non-participant, structured, unstructured, and naturalistic. Give definition of each
  - Describe some features of each type.
  - Refer to examples of research that use the particular type(s) of observational method you are writing about.

2 *Evaluate the observational method of research in terms of its advantages and disadvantages.*

Structure your answer as follows:

- Define the observational method of research *as the planned gathering, analysis and interpretation of data on observed behaviour, as it occurs in a natural setting*
- Identify and explain advantages of the observational method, i.e.
  - To help decide on behaviours for further study by *other* means, e.g. an experiment or a survey
  - It gives us accurate detail of natural behaviours. Ecological validity
  - Appropriate for the study of infants and animals (say why: refer to research)
  - Avoids unnatural behaviours (say why this is so)
  - Standardisation (of what?) – gives valid and reliable results (why?)
  - Then describe the specific advantages attached to specific types of observational method
- Identify and explain disadvantages of the observational method
  - Replication
  - No IV (implications: no cause–effect)
  - Control of extraneous variables, i.e. confounding – observer bias, observer effect; random – weather, mood state of participants
  - Ethics and covert observations
  - Then describe specific disadvantages attached to specific types of observational method.

Glossary

Behaviour index: an index used in observations to record the behaviour of subjects/participants

Continuous recording: the recording of *all* behaviour during the observation period

Covert observation: observations that take place without the subject's knowledge

Ethology: the study of animals in their natural environment

Observer bias: may occur in that the observer may be influenced by prior knowledge/experience or expectations of the subjects/situation under investigation

Observer effect: any changes in a participant's behaviour as a result of the observer's presence

Obtrusive measures: devices used to measure performance/behaviour that can be seen by the participants of observational studies, and can thereby affect behaviour, e.g. a video camera

Overt observation: open observation, where all who take part know they are participating

Pseudo-patient: as in Rosenhan's (1973) study, where researchers *pose* as patients in order to record observations

Time sampling: the recording of behaviour at particular set times

Unobtrusive measures: observational methods of measurement and recording that are hidden and as a result do not impact on the subject's behaviours, e.g. CCTV, video recordings

10

The survey method

BY THE END OF THIS CHAPTER YOU SHOULD BE ABLE TO:

- **identify by example the survey method of research**
- **define and explain the survey method of research with reference to its key features**
- **explain and evaluate the survey method of research in terms of its advantages and disadvantages**

Overview of the survey method

The **survey method** gathers quantitative data on thoughts, feelings and behaviours we have in common, or on which we differ. The survey method asks a representative sample of people the same questions about particular attitudes, opinions, values and beliefs. If the sample is truly representative, this allows generalisation of results to the population from which the sample came. Surveys can be used on their own or with other research methods such as the experiment, observation and the interview. The survey method shares an important feature with the more structured methods of interviews and observations. This is the gathering of data by self-report from a respondent or interviewee. Surveys can be conducted by post, face-to-face, by telephone, videophone and the Internet. A good survey will be designed well with **standardised** instructions and questions. A **pilot survey** is often conducted to allow this to occur. Survey questions can be either open or closed. **Open questions** give rise to candid, descriptive answers, while **closed questions** restrict respondents' choice of answer. Open questions can give you too much qualitative, descriptive information in answers, which makes defining our common or differing attitudes, opinions etc. difficult. Closed questions, which give quantitative or numerical answers, are useful, especially if a **Likert scale** of measurement is used. Advantages of the survey method of research are that it is cheap, easily administered, replicable, and a large amount of data can be got from a lot of people in a fairly short time. Most importantly, a well-designed survey, if given to a representative sample, allows the researcher to generalise results to the population from which this sample came. Disadvantages include poor design, **GIGO**, reliability and validity, **acquiescence response**, a tendency to give socially desirable answers, and response and sampling bias.

What is the survey method of research?

The survey method of research asks a representative sample of people oral or written questions to find out about their attitudes, behaviours, beliefs, opinions and values.

The survey method of research is non-experimental in design. In psychology the survey has two functions. It gathers quantifiable data on the behaviours of a target population, and it is also used to test hypotheses.

An example of the former is the 1999 Glasgow University Social and Public Health Unit survey. This was a two-year longitudinal survey into psychological development in early adolescence. In 1993–4 a survey was given to a large number of children in Primary 7 in West Central Scotland about their thoughts and feelings. Two years later in 1996–7, the children were again given a similar questionnaire. The children were now in their second year (S2) in forty-three secondary schools in and around the city of Glasgow. The number reporting feeling nervous, worried or anxious in P7 jumped from 40 per cent to over 50 per cent by S2. Those reporting feeling irritable and bad-tempered went from 40 per cent to 48 per cent over the same period. Those feeling sad and unhappy increased from 35 per cent to 40 per cent. Glasgow University concluded that respondent symptoms were indications of psychological ill health, which appears to increase during adolescence. The survey concluded that a substantial number of teenagers in Scotland suffer from low self-esteem during their early teenage years. Only time will tell if this low self-esteem is permanent and is related to mental ill health in the medium to long-term.

An example of the latter is Adorno *et al.*'s (1950) study, which aimed to find out about the authoritarian personality. This interest was strongly influenced by the rise of the Nazis, and the Second World War from 1939–45. The world was just waking up to the Holocaust. Psychology in general, and social psychology in particular, wanted to know whether we were all capable of such terrible atrocities, or was the horror the result of a particular and unique personality – an authoritarian one. Adorno *et al.* wanted to confirm whether there was an authoritarian personality, and, if so, to investigate how it came about.

INTERACTIVE

Read about Adorno *et al.* (1950) and answer the following questions.

1. What do you think the hypothesis was that Adorno *et al.* wanted to test?
2. What do you think Adorno saw as a contribution to the authoritarian personality? Give reasons for your answer.
3. Which two non-experimental methods of research did Adorno *et al.* use?
4. What results and conclusion did Adorno *et al.* (1950) reach?

Adorno and his colleagues designed a survey to reveal prejudice, which they thought was an important personality trait in the authoritarian personality. They posted it off and got two thousand replies from people from all sorts of backgrounds. The **volunteer sample** who returned the questionnaire included school and university students, nurses, prison inmates, psychiatric patients and workers. They were all white, native-born, lower middle, and middle-class Americans. Eighty were then invited to attend a clinical interview. On the basis of their completed surveys, these were the ones Adorno *et al.* had thought were the more prejudiced. At a clinical interview they were each asked a selection of more detailed, open questions about their background and upbringing. Initial survey and subsequent clinical interviews helped to then construct the famous Adorno F-Scale. The F-Scale is a measure of just how fascist and authoritarian an individual might be. This personality came about as a consequence of upbringing and environment.

The volunteer sample

A volunteer sample is problematic in all types of psychological research. A volunteer sample is one made up of those people who decide they want to participate in the research programme. Volunteers are not representative of the normal population. Rosenthal & Rosnow (1975), in *The Volunteer Subject*, New York: John Wiley, pp. 195–6, identify twenty-two characteristics of those who volunteer for research.

- Volunteers tend to be better educated than non-volunteers.
- Volunteers tend to have higher social-class status than non-volunteers
- Volunteers tend to be higher in need of social approval than non-volunteers.
- Volunteers tend to be more sociable than non-volunteers.
- Volunteers tend to be more intelligent than non-volunteers when volunteering is for research in general, but interestingly not when volunteering is for somewhat less typical types of research such as hypnosis, sensory isolation, sex research, small-group and personality research.

A volunteer sample can therefore give rise to **volunteer bias** in research.

SURVEY DESIGN

What makes a good survey is good design. This is easier said than done and demands some expertise. To begin to think about a survey as a method of research it is essential that you first clarify its purpose. Knowing exactly what it is you are trying to find out from any survey will shape the questions you want to ask. Having a clear purpose will help you in the design and standardisation of your survey.

Standardisation concerns the instructions and questions that you give to people to help them complete your survey. These should be worded so that your respondents know what is required of them. In essence, instructions and questions should be easily understood. Care should also be taken over the type of questions used. Open questions encourage respondents to give open or descriptive answers. Closed questions restrict respondents to give closed answers.

The type of question asked influences the usefulness of the data collected. If you ask open questions you get a lot of descriptive, opinionated answers, which are difficult to analyse. Closed or restrictive answers are easier to analyse but sometimes don't mean very much. Surveys are cheap and easy to administer, and can generate a lot of useful information, but have their disadvantages. We have seen that surveys can suffer from volunteer bias. They can also attract other extraneous variables like participant response set, acquiescence response set, social desirability, sampling, and interviewer bias. If constructed well, surveys are an excellent research tool, and it is to this that we now turn.

Key features of the survey method of research

The survey method includes any type of research that involves *asking people oral or written questions* about their thoughts, feelings and behaviours. It is thus important to realise that key features of the survey apply to questionnaires, structured/semi-structured/clinical interviews, and the more structured of observations.

Whatever their form, surveys aim to collect standardised data from a representative sample of people. As a method of enquiry the survey is passive, in that there is no manipulation of an independent variable. As a result *no* cause and effect conclusions can be made on the basis of a survey. As emphasised above the main feature of the survey method is that it is structured. As will be explained, a **structured survey** will feature the standardisation of instructions and questions, often after a pilot survey has been done. The types of questions asked, which can be either open or closed, can affect the type of data a survey can generate. This as we will see has implications for any conclusions made.

The unstructured survey

With all this emphasis on structure it seems odd to suggest that a survey can be unstructured. The unstructured survey is more commonly known as the clinical interview, which is examined in more detail in our next chapter. The reason the clinical interview is sometimes called an unstructured survey is it will always have a pre-prepared set of core questions that an interviewer will want to ask. These questions will have been developed beforehand, often after refinements have been made following a pilot study. The standardisation of oral questions in clinical interviews are as important as the standardisation of written questions in surveys.

The structured survey

The structured survey is used in all areas of life such as consumer research, psychological enquiry, politics, health, etc.

Surveys can be done by post, face-to-face, by telephone, videophone and the Internet. Their usefulness depends on how well the survey was designed, and the sample to which it was given.

What do I want to know?

In order to design a survey, you need to know what you want to do. Clarifying '*What is it exactly I am interested in, and what in particular am I trying to find out?*' helps you design relevant questions. You could design a survey to find out about attitudes to lowering the voting/driving age to sixteen, legalising cannabis, sex/violence on TV, what the silent majority of pupils think about bullying in school, etc. A survey could examine health-related behaviours such as underage drinking, investigate religious beliefs and church attendance, collect opinions on social and moral issues such as the ethics of genetic engineering, and so on.

Survey item design

Once you have decided on the purpose of your survey you must design the questions you want to ask. This is called item design. There are two types of item, or question, that the researcher can use in a survey – the open question and the closed question.

Open questions

An open question is a question that can have many different answers. An example of an open question in a survey is, 'What is the biggest problem facing Scotland today?' If this were given to a thousand different people you could get a thousand different answers. Concluding what these thousand people have in common would be impossible. Open questions like this are to be avoided. They give you too much descriptive or *qualitative* information with which you can do very little. To be of any value to the researcher data in a survey should be amenable to measurement. It should be quantifiable.

Closed questions

You can get measurable, quantitative answers to questions in a survey when you use what are called 'closed questions'. Closed questions are questions which offer *a restricted choice of answer or response* for the participant, probably the most simple example being 'yes' or 'no'. Closed questions, which have restricted answers, include questions on gender, age, where you live, occupation, etc. As can be seen below there is only one answer to these types of closed question. These answers are then counted or *quantified* by the researcher, against the relevant item.

Are you male or female?		What age are you?	
Are you employed/unemployed?		What is your postcode?	
What is your occupation?			

Figure 10.1 Examples of closed questions. Closed questions are restrictive but give quantifiable answers

Closed questions like this often appear at the beginning of a survey, and give valuable *quantitative* information. The answers to closed questions help the researcher work out how many men and women took part in the survey, their age, what district they live in, their occupation, etc. Postal code can reveal all sorts of things, the most important, certainly in consumer research, probably being your socio-economic status. Closed questions can generate very useful data that can have interesting results. In 2002 the Halifax plc bank was much embarrassed by the leak of a document based upon internal survey research advising their staff to be wary of doing business with taxi drivers, window cleaners and market traders. People reported being offended by what the Halifax's data analysis of customer occupations seemed to imply. What do you think that was?

Closed questions fall down when they try to get answers to complex questions. Consider the following closed question:

Please answer the question below. Please circle your response.

The biggest priority facing Scotland today is qualifying for the World Cup? Yes No

Figure 10.2

Here *you* are deciding that qualifying for the World Cup is Scotland's biggest priority, as opposed to say, the Health Service, education, housing, transport, etc.

The forced-choice nature of the response, *yes* or *no*, further does not allow people who genuinely *do not know* how to answer. You can add up and measure yes/no answers to questions, but if the question doesn't really apply to people's actual thoughts, feelings and behaviours then what you get is meaningless.

In summary, surveys hope to generate manageable quantitative data on complex issues. To do so, closed questions will be used, certainly at the beginning of the survey, to get numerical data on your sample. They are of less use in the body of a survey because of their forced-choice nature. Closed questions don't generate quality answers. Open questions only can do this, but these are notoriously difficult to analyse because of the many different responses you can get. This can be overcome by using a scale of measurement for your item/question responses.

Scaling items: the Likert scale

One way around the problem of generating meaningful quantitative answers to restrictive closed questions is to use a Likert scale. This is named after Renais Likert who designed it at the University of Michigan Institute for Social Research in the 1960s. It is often used in surveys today and is recognisable when you are asked to indicate your strength of feeling about a particular issue on a rating scale. Taking the above question 'The biggest priority facing Scotland today is qualifying for the World Cup?' by using a Likert scale you would indicate your strength of feeling on the matter by circling 1, 2, 3, 4, or 5 on a rating scale. Circling 1 would mean you strongly agree; circling 2, agree; circling 3, don't know; 4, disagree, and 5, strongly disagree.

Please indicate by circling 1, 2, 3, 4 or 5 your strength of feeling about the question below.

	Strongly agree	Agree	Don't know	Disagree	Strongly disagree
'The biggest priority facing Scotland today is qualifying for the World Cup?	1	2	3	4	5

Figure 10.3 Likert scale

This would allow other maybe more important questions on unemployment, homelessness, education or the National Health Service, to be asked elsewhere. At the end of the day *scaling* the answers to closed questions can generate statistical measurements of people's attitudes and opinions, such as those they feel are important in the Scotland of the twenty-first century. The use of a Likert and other scales of measurement in a survey yield both qualitative *and* quantitative data, and are nowadays relatively obvious and widespread. A survey's use of a Likert scale allows people to agree/disagree on the basis of their strength of feeling on an issue. It also allows people to say they have no opinion if the question isn't an issue for them. Likert scales help avoid forced-choice compliance.

Using a Likert scale, those numbers circled are used by the researcher as quantitative data. If 10,000 people circled 1 in the above example this would be analysed as a major priority in

Scotland. If 10,000 people circled 5, this would be analysed as a non-priority. Just how much of a non-priority would also depend on the Likert score obtained from other items in the survey hopefully covering unemployment, homelessness, education, and transport and the National Health Service.

Likert scale warning!

If you are ever asked to complete a questionnaire that uses an even number of Likert-type response choices, i.e. 1, 2, 3, 4 instead of 1, 2, 3, 4 or 5 – this is a fixed-choice compliance survey. Because it does not have an odd number of item response choices there is no room for a 'don't know' answer. Without this *DK filter* it forces respondents to say that '*Yes indeed this is an issue about which I have an opinion*' (when it may not be). Respondents then are forced to strongly agree/agree or disagree/strongly disagree. Take the following example.

Please indicate by circling 1, 2, 3 or 4 your strength of feeling about the question below.

	Strongly agree	Agree	Disagree	Strongly disagree
Changes should be made to the Higher psychology examination.	1	2	3	4

Why should you be wary of a fixed choice compliance survey, like the above?

THE PARENTAL AUTHORITY QUESTIONNAIRE

Opposite is an example of a Likert scale being used in a psychological test called the parental authority questionnaire (PAQ). The PAQ is a 30-item (question) questionnaire. The questionnaire is given separately to both the mother and the father. When all the items are complete, a score can be obtained. A permissive mother/father is measured by the likes of question 1, authoritarian mother/father by the likes of questions 2 and 3, and an authoritative mother/father by 4 and 5. If you are able to take the option in developmental psychology, you will find out more why parenting style influences the development of a child's personality.

INTERACTIVE

Consulting a dictionary of the English language or a dictionary of psychology find out what the words opposite mean:

- permissive
- authoritarian
- authoritative.

Recognise anyone?!

Questionnaire 1: The parental authority (PAQ)

Instructions: For each of the following statements, circle the number on the 5-point scale (1 = strongly disagree, 5 = strongly agree) that best describes how the statement applies to you and your mother. Try to read and think about each statement as it applies to you and your mother during your years growing up at home. There are no right or wrong answers, so don't spend a lot of time on any one item. We are looking for an overall impression regarding each statement. Be sure not to omit any items.

1 2 3 4 5 1 While I was growing up my mother felt that in a well-run home the children should have their way in the family as often as the parents do.

1 2 3 4 5 2 Even if her children didn't agree with her, my mother felt it was for our own good if we were forced to conform to what she thought was right.

1 2 3 4 5 3 Whenever my mother told me to do something as I was growing up, she expected me to do it immediately without asking any questions.

1 2 3 4 5 4 As I was growing up, once family policy had been established, my mother discussed the reasoning behind the policy with the children in the family.

1 2 3 4 5 5 My mother has always encouraged verbal give and take whenever I have felt that family rules and restrictions were unreasonable.

From Buri, J.R. (1991) ' Parental authority questionnaire'. *Journal of Personality Assessment*, 57 (1), 110–119, Lawrence Erlbaum Associates.

Standardisation

Standardisation concerns the careful construction of instructions and questions. The standardisation of instructions and questions asked of anyone in any type of research is vital. This is because respondents/participants at the very least need to know what is required of them. If the instructions are confusing, or the questions ambiguous and difficult to understand, then a survey is not particularly effective. Neither is any other procedure where the standardisation of instructions and questions is an issue. This would include the experiment; the structured, semi-structured and clinical interview; and structured observation.

Principles of survey design

On page 241 is a 12-step survey design. To achieve this, the following principles should be borne in mind.

- **Keep the language simple.** Ask yourself '*Who is the audience*?' and write your questions and instructions to this level. Parten (1950) suggests that language an eleven-year-old would understand is appropriate.
- **Keep questions short and on one issue.** Keep the number of questions to a minimum. The longer the questionnaire, the less likely a respondent will feel like filling it in. If what you need to find out is necessary, ask the question. If it isn't, then leave it out.

- ☐ **Avoid technical terms,** e.g. performance criteria, jargon or abbreviations such as SQA. This is unless you know for sure that your respondents understand these sorts of terms.
- ☐ **Avoid leading questions.** Leading questions are questions worded in a way that lead the respondent to a particular answer. An example of a leading question might be

  'Have you stopped smoking cannabis?' Yes/No

  Whichever way the respondent answers, he/she is 'admitting' to have have broken the law! Think about it.
- ☐ **Avoid emotive or moral questions.** The respondent may feel your survey is getting too personal. The 'best' and 'worst' example the author has ever seen of this was a survey given to female members of the public, by a non-psychology student, asking respondents for their names and addresses; and then Question 1 asked *'Have you ever had an abortion? Yes or No.'* This is definitely to be avoided. If you must use personal or emotional questions, place them at the end of the questionnaire. If in doubt always ask your teacher or lecturer.

12-step survey design

If you decide to use a survey as a research method you could adopt the following design model.

1. Select an area of psychological interest.
2. Research the topic area to get ideas about what questions to ask.
3. Write the questions down.
4. Use closed questions at the beginning of the survey to generate good quantitative data on your sample.
5. For better item analysis, use a Likert scale to get quantitative data on answers to your questions.
6. Decide on a sequence of questioning. What is to be Question 1, Question 2, etc.? It is always best to *randomise* your sequence in case the survey attracts **response acquiescence** set (see Disadvantages of the Survey Method).
7. Write down your *standardised instructions*. These should come at the beginning of your survey and make clear what is expected of the respondent. They should also make reference to the general purpose of the survey, confirming that the respondent agrees to take part, their right to withdraw etc. Please see http://www.bps.org.uk/about/rules5.cfm (or the previous chapter) for *The Psychologists' Code of Conduct*.
8. Conduct a pilot survey with a small group of people. It is best if they are from the group who will complete the final survey. Their job is to tell you if they understand the instructions, the questions, etc. Put simply, they highlight flaws.
9. Redraft the survey, and if necessary pilot it again.
10. Conduct your survey.
11. Debrief your respondents, and give them an opportunity to find out the results.
12. Analyse your results.

The should–would question

Should–would questions are interesting. Selltiz *et al.* (1963) suggest that survey respondents answer *should* questions from a social or moral point of view, and answer *would* questions in terms of their personal preference. Having *should* or *would* as part of questions on social, moral and personal issues can skew results and conclusions.

Taking our earlier issue:

Would you legalise cannabis? Yes Don't Know No

could produce a different answer to what at first appears an almost identical question:

Should cannabis be legalised? Yes Don't Know No.

INTERACTIVE

Try the above. Ask only one respondent one question! Get twenty responses for the first question, and 20 for the second. Make sure all respondents come from the same population, i.e. students in S5 and S6, students in a college etc.

Compare your results. Did you get a should–would effect?

Survey modes

Face to face

Survey mode refers to the way a survey is done. The most common survey mode used by psychology students is face to face with respondents. The face-to-face survey can attract extraneous variables such as interviewer bias and the interviewer effect. This is explored more fully in our next chapter on the interview method and concerns the subtle communication of 'expected' answers in face-to-face questioning situations. Face-to-face surveys can take place in the street, at your door, in your workplace, at your school or college, etc.

Figure 10.1 A face-to-face survey

Postal survey

INTERACTIVE

See postal surveys used by the Department of Health in the 1998 National Survey of NHS Patients at: http://www.doh.gov.uk/public/nhssurveyquestionnaires.htm

See results and analysis at http://qb.soc.surrey.ac.uk/surveys/nhsp/nhsmeth.htm#seven

The postal survey is also very common. Postal surveys are often used to find out about consumer behaviours, attitudes and opinions. They suffer from a very high non-return rate. A low return rate in a postal survey can throw doubt on its results. Unfortunately non-return rates in postal surveys are notorious. The very best of surveys, as in the government's NHS survey above, can get a 65 per cent return rate, but it is much more usual for a postal survey to have a return rate of between 15–25 per cent. This would be seen as a good result!

To increase the likelihood of return, it is a good idea to prepare people about the survey they are going to be asked to complete. The government's national census in 2002 saw a TV and billboard advertising campaign prior to the census taking place. A respondent would also expect their postal survey to include a stamped-addressed envelope, allowing them to return it at no expense. Consumer surveys may further entice completion by enclosing a pen, and/or some sort of return incentive, like a prize. Postcard and telephone follow-ups are also helpful in increasing return rates, as is collecting the survey directly from the respondent at their home. If households do not return their national census, they are visited by a series of census officials, and if they still don't hand it over, this can result in criminal prosecution. The national census prides itself on its very high return rate!

Postal surveys and volunteer bias

Because of their long-standing problem of low return rates, postal surveys suffer from volunteer bias, which we came across earlier when we looked at the problems of the volunteer sample. Because of the postal survey's very high non-return rate, volunteer bias and thus the unrepresentative nature of the respondents who actually *do* return them, the results of postal surveys are questionable.

Telephone, videophone, and online surveys

To try to avoid the problems of the volunteer sample it is becoming common nowadays to find surveys also being done by telephone, videophone, the Internet, and e-mail.

INTERACTIVE

Please go to http://www.psyresearchonline.com/trstudy/trindex.html and investigate the Reactions to the Terrorist Attacks of 11 September 2001 online survey being conducted by the University of Kentucky.

An example of an online survey

During November 2001–March 2002 the British Psychological Society was interested in finding out what school and FE college students in the UK thought of their psychology courses. Students were asked to complete the online survey at:
http://ess.ntu.ac.uk/sutton/formfiles/soc3banyape/bps.htm

Psychology student questionnaire

The British Psychological Society is interested in how students respond to their school and college courses in psychology. Please complete the following questions about the course in psychology that you are taking this year.

Please enter your age (in years)

[ ]

Please select your sex

- [ ] Male
- [ ] Female

What course are you on?

- [ ] AQA AS/A Level
- [ ] EDXCEL AS/A Level
- [ ] OCR AS/A Level
- [ ] SQA Higher Level
- [ ] Other

Why did you choose this course?

- [ ] want a career in psychology
- [ ] sounded interesting
- [ ] something different to study
- [ ] heard about the teacher
- [ ] my friends had chosen it
- [ ] I had read about it
- [ ] other

If 'other' please state the reason

[ ]

Psychology student questionnaire cont/d.1

Compared to other subjects I am studying or have studied, psychology is

- ☐ much more interesting
- ☐ slightly more interesting
- ☐ about the same
- ☐ slightly less interesting
- ☐ much less interesting

Compared to other subjects I am studying or have studied, psychology is

- ☐ much more relevant to my life
- ☐ slightly more relevant to my life
- ☐ about the same
- ☐ slightly less relevant to my life
- ☐ much less relevant to my life

Compared to other subjects I am studying or have studied, psychology is

- ☐ much more difficult
- ☐ slightly more difficult
- ☐ about the same
- ☐ slightly less difficult
- ☐ much less difficult

Compared to other subjects I am studying or have studied, psychology requires

- ☐ much more work
- ☐ slightly more work
- ☐ about the same
- ☐ slightly less work
- ☐ much less work

Psychology student questionnaire cont/d.2

My psychology course is

☐ very much as I expected

☐ fairly much as I expected

☐ different to what I expected

Do you want to study psychology further (after you have finished the course you are on)?

☐ yes

☐ maybe

☐ no

My favourite topic in my psychology course is ...

My least favourite topic in my psychology course is ...

What do you think would make the psychology course better?

What advice would you give to a friend who was thinking of studying psychology?

Psychology student questionnaire cont/d.3

Who do you think are the three most important or influential psychologists?

One

Two

Three

I am glad I chose to study psychology

Strongly agree 1 2 3 4 5 Strongly disagree

Thank you for completing this questionnaire. Please click the SUBMIT button.

submit clear

INTERACTIVE

1 Why is this a survey?
2 What is this survey's purpose?
3 Identify the standardised instruction in this survey.
4 Identify two closed and two open questions in this survey.
5 Why are these examples of 'closed' or 'open' questions?
6 Identify two survey questions that use a Likert scale.
7 How do these two questions avoid forced compliance answers?
8 What type of sample are the researchers trying to access? Give reasons for your answer.
9 Identify three uses of a qualitative question seeking a qualitative answer.
10 In your opinion is this a well-designed survey? Give reasons for your answer.

Sampling

In any psychological research sampling is crucial. In order to conduct research, psychology needs participants to study. It is usually impossible to study *everyone* of interest in your target population (group of interest), so psychologists sample from it instead. Poor sampling however will give you poor results and poor conclusions. Any sample used in any kind of research in psychology should therefore reflect the target population onto which the researcher wants to generalise their results and conclusions. Sampling issues are of critical importance to the survey method of research. This was vividly illustrated in the 1992 UK General Election. In the run-up to the 1992 election, national poll after national poll published by firms such as NOP, MORI and System 3 all pointed to a narrow Labour victory under Neil Kinnock. On polling day itself, four polls published that morning agreed that Labour were still one point ahead. In the election itself, the Conservatives were found to be eight points ahead. It was the biggest ever discrepancy in British polling history between what the polls had anticipated and what actually transpired (Butler & Kavanagh, 1992). One reason for the psephologists' mistake was poor sampling. They did not access those who went out and voted Conservative at the last minute. And just in case you ever appear on a quiz show, a psephologist is someone who studies political opinion polls.

Good sampling allows for the generalisation of your results onto the target population from which your sample is drawn. You can infer certain things, i.e. how the population of a country might vote. Because of the desire to generalise results and conclusions, a sample must be as representative of the target population as possible. Types of sampling method include the following.

Random sampling

Random sampling is where each member of a target population has an equal chance of being chosen to take part in your research. This could be achieved by drawing straws or pulling names from a hat. An example of random sampling would be if you wanted to get information from a college community about their potential use of a new college sports centre. You could use random sampling by previously deciding that every tenth person to come through the main entrance during a certain time is asked to participate in the survey. The people who complete the survey are your random sample. It is random because every person coming through the main entrance had an equal chance (1: 10 in this instance) of being chosen for the survey.

Stratified sampling

Stratified sampling occurs when you look at your target population and decide to make up a sample for your research reflecting the make-up of the target population. At a simple level, if your target population were 60 per cent male, and 40 per cent female, your stratified sample would reflect this gender balance. In a stratified sample of 100, 60 would have to be male and 40 female. You 'stratify' on the basis of the variables you think are important to your research.

Opportunity sampling

Opportunity sampling comprises exactly what it says. Your sample is made up from whoever is available and around at the time. If you need twenty participants, an opportunity sample will include the first 20 people you find willing to assist. Opportunity sampling is particularly popular in student research because it is convenient.

Quota sampling

Quota sampling is popular in consumer research. Quota sampling is having a sample from a particular stratum or subcategory in society, in equal proportion to their occurrence in the target population. If consumer researchers were interested in finding out the buying habits of 16- to 21-

year-old males who made up 10 per cent of a city's population of 100,000, a quota sample survey would survey only this age group and stop when the quota of 10,000 of the required age group were reached.

INTERACTIVE

1 What do you understand by the term 'sampling'?

2 Why is it important we use a representative sample of people in psychological research?

3 Explain four different types of sampling method and give an example of each.

Advantages of the survey method

The advantages of surveys are that large amounts of standardised information can be obtained from a large number of people in a short space of time. If designed well and completed by a representative number of people, survey results can be generalised onto the population from which the representative sample came.

Surveys are highly replicable, and can be used on a longitudinal basis to constantly update us on questions of interest. The BPS survey above should be permanently 'up' for this very reason. Such a longitudinal survey also allows for trends and changes in opinion to be gauged over time.

Surveys are also easy to score, unless of course open-ended questions are used. We get quantifiable data from a survey that can be useful to help develop and support hypotheses. A survey can also generate empirical data giving a measurement of behaviours, attitudes, opinions, beliefs and values of a target population.

One final advantage of the survey method is that it is cheap! If a survey is well designed it is a most useful tool of research in its own right, or as rich soil for future research using other methods of enquiry.

Disadvantages of the survey method

If a survey is poorly designed, as a credible research tool it can attract a wide variety of problems. Students of Higher psychology should be extremely cautious if considering designing their own survey for their practical investigation. Be warned!

Any research method that uses oral or written instructions/questions must first standardise them. This is to ensure that all participants/respondents get the same instructions/questions, and that these instructions/questions are clear and unambiguous. Unless this happens the issues of validity and reliability will arise. Validity concerns *whether the questions measure what they claim to measure?* A question of reliability would also arise if researchers didn't standardise instructions/questions beforehand. If left to their own devices to give instructions and ask questions, researchers would be inconsistent in what they said to different individuals. Any information got from such a non-standardised situation, and any claims made as a result, are questionable. It is not reliable as data to lend support to hypotheses, or as objective facts about behaviours, attitudes, opinions, beliefs or values. What you put into a survey by way of careful design, you get

Table 10.1 The advantages and disadvantages of sampling

Sampling method	Advantages	Disadvantages
Random sampling	If the random sample is large enough, random sampling gives the best opportunity for everyone in a target population to participate in your research. In a target population of 2000, a representative random sample of 1:20 would be more representative than one of 1:200. 1:20 as a representative random sample of 2000 would be an unbiased random sample. 1:200 would be a biased random sample.	The bigger the target population, the more difficult it is to randomly sample in it. You are unsure who the target population is. If it were a town of 60 000, for example, looking in the phone book and choosing every 1000th person would be a problematic random sample. Not everyone is in the phone book, people are ex-directory, thousands of people use only mobiles whose numbers are not listed.
Stratified sampling	When it is important that characteristics/subcategories/strata of a target population be investigated, stratified sampling is most useful. Stratified sampling gives you a truly representative sample of your target population on the basis of those identified characteristics you want to investigate.	Stratified sampling is time-consuming because characteristics in the target population have to be identified, and a calculation of their ratio of occurrence worked out. This is to ensure the correct ratios in your stratified sample.
Opportunity sampling	Opportunity sampling is extremely quick and economical. It is the most common method of sampling because it is convenient.	It is an unrepresentative method of sampling. There is a difficulty when using opportunity sampling to generalise your results to a meaningful target population. If your opportunity sample was 10 first-year pupils from a large secondary school, anything you might infer from a survey could only be applied to this small unrepresentative group.
Quota sampling	Quota sampling is a quick and efficient way to gather information on specific strata within a population. If you were a consumer intelligence firm and a client were a large fashion chain catering to females in the 16–25 age group, quota-sampling females in this age group above would be ideal from the point of view of efficient market research.	How the quota sample is chosen is often left up to the researcher. If 100 16–25-year-old females were to be the quota sample, an opportunity sample of 100 16–25-year-old female students might be used. This quota would not reflect all 16–25 year old females in the target population.

out of it in terms of valid and reliable data. Poorly designed instructions and questions see a survey suffer from the GIGO effect. Quite simply, 'Garbage in, garbage out'!

Earlier it was suggested that when a survey is designed the questions in the body of the survey should be scaled and randomly presented. This helps avoid acquiescence response, socially desirable answers, and response set. Acquiescence response is a tendency people have to agree, or say yes, especially to things that they think don't affect them that much. Consequently, surveys can be very prone to acquiescence response. Response set arises when respondents think they see a pattern of desired answers to survey questions, and answer accordingly. To avoid response set, scaling and the randomisation of questions are recommended. Scaling and randomisation also help prevent acquiescence response, and a tendency by people to give socially desirable answers.

As emphasised, features of the survey method also apply to other research methods where the asking of (oral or written) questions is important. What can jeopardise all these procedures, even when researchers adhere to good research design, is sampling bias. If your sample does not reflect a target population, you cannot make generalisations to this population because your sample is not representative of it. There are, as we know, different types of sampling techniques, such as random, stratified, opportunity and quota sampling. Each of these has particular advantages and disadvantages, which should be taken into consideration if thinking about using the survey method of research.

INTERACTIVE

Read over the advantages and disadvantages of the survey method of research and in no more than fifty words design a study aid to remember what they are.

INTERACTIVE

1. Read http://www.hr-survey.com/ItemConstruction.htm and discover how to design good survey questions.
2. Go to Phil's Homepage @ http://www2.ntu.ac.uk/soc/psych/Banyard and read, amongst other things, the Bl*ffer's Guide to writing psychology essays!
3. Go to http://trochim.human.cornell.edu/kb/scallik.htm. Why are Likert, Guttman and Thurstone scales of measurement said to be 'unidimensional'? Please use examples in your answer.
4. Go to http://www.consumerpsychology.com/brandlab/videos/videos.html and find out about consumer psychology.

Summary

The survey method of research is non-experimental in design. It is a method of enquiry that asks a representative sample of people oral or written questions. Surveys are often used in the likes of social and consumer psychology to support or develop hypotheses on our attitudes, opinions, beliefs, values and behaviours. A good survey is well designed, considering in its structure the use of open and closed questions, and scales of measurement such as a Likert Scale. To ensure a survey is worthwhile it is important to standardise the instructions to be followed beforehand and the questions you want to ask. Standardisation reduces ambiguity and respondents' acquiescence response. One way to achieve standardisation is to do a pilot survey, the purpose of which is to point out flaws. Surveys are nowadays conducted face to face, by post, telephone or online. These different survey modes can help reduce sampling bias, and increase your 'return' rate. Advantages of surveys are that they are cheap and generate a large amount of standardised information from a lot of people, which if quantifiable can be used as measurements upon which to base conclusions. Disadvantages of the survey method are that poor design gives poor results. If a survey is badly constructed, its results and conclusions can be accused of being invalid and unreliable.

Structured questions with answer guidelines

1 *Describe and explain the survey method of research.*

With reference to the preceding chapter, structure your answer as follows.

- Define the survey method of research as one that asks questions in oral or written form of a representative sample of people, to find out about their attitudes, behaviours, beliefs, opinions, and values.
- Identify and explain the following features of the survey method of research:
  - non-experimental in design. Gathers information on behaviours, etc. (give example), and to support/develop hypotheses (give example). Importance of good survey design.
  - open questions and closed questions. Pros and cons. Likert scale of measurement
  - standardisation of instructions and questions. Pilot studies. The should–would question
  - survey modes (how surveys are conducted nowadays).

2 *Evaluate the survey method of research in terms of its advantages and disadvantages.*

Structure your answer as follows.

- Define the survey method of research as one that asks questions in oral or written form of a representative sample of people, to find out about their attitudes, behaviours, beliefs, opinions, and values.
- Identify and explain advantages of the survey method, i.e.
  - great deal of standardised information, etc. in a short space of time. Give example
  - replicable. *What does this allow?*
  - easily scored quantifiable data. *What does this allow the researcher to do?*
  - cheap.
- Identify and explain disadvantages of the survey method, i.e.
  - poor design gives poor results
  - lack of standardisation of instructions/questions leads to questions of validity and reliability of the survey
  - GIGO effect
  - acquiescence response, socially desirable answers and response set. *Suggest how these can be avoided*
  - sampling bias. Volunteer samples/bias. Importance of a representative sample. *A good answer would indicate this could affect the results and conclusions using any research method.*

Glossary

Acquiescence response: a psychological tendency people have to agree with what is asked of them

Closed question: a question whose answer is restricted in some way, e.g. 'what age are you?' is a closed question. It only has one possible answer

GIGO: garbage in, garbage out. GIGO is the result of poor survey design

Likert scale: a scale of measurement often used in a survey that allows for a person's strength of feeling on a matter to be expressed. Likert scales also generate good quantitative (numerical) data on issues

Open question: a question that has a variety of possible answers

Pilot survey: a practice run of a survey to identify any flaws, snags or ambiguity of instructions/questions before conducting the survey proper

Structured survey: a survey whose instructions/questions will be standardised, usually after a pilot survey has been conducted

Survey method: the survey method of research asks a representative sample of people oral or written questions to find out about their attitudes, behaviours, beliefs, opinions, and values

Volunteer sample: a sample made up of people who volunteer to take part in your research. Can give rise to volunteer bias

11

The interview method

BY THE END OF THIS CHAPTER YOU SHOULD BE ABLE TO:

- **identify by example the interview method of research**
- **define and explain the interview method of research with reference to its key features**
- **explain and evaluate the interview method of research in terms of its advantages and disadvantages.**

Overview of the interview method

The interview method of research is used in psychology to get personal accounts of individual experiences. The purpose of the interview method is neatly captured in the phrase 'a conversation with a purpose'. Interviews are also often used in conjunction with other research methods as part of a larger investigation. As we will see, there are two categories of interview, structured and unstructured. The structured interview also includes the semi-structured interview and the clinical interview. The major difference between the categories is the ability to ask spontaneous questions of the client/participant/patient. This affects what kind of data that can be collected, whether the data can be generalised beyond those people being interviewed, and whether the data is valid and reliable. These advantages and disadvantages of the interview method will be explored, as shall advantages and disadvantages of particular types of interview.

WHAT IS THE INTERVIEW METHOD OF RESEARCH?

The interview method of research is a conversation with a purpose.

The interview method of research is non-experimental in design. It is a conversation with a purpose. The interview has the researcher collect detailed personal information from individuals in a one-to-one setting using oral questions. The interview is used widely in psychology, often alongside the survey, to supplement and extend our knowledge about a person(s)/psychological issue under investigation. Interview questions will be either 'open' or 'closed'. As we read earlier in the chapter on the survey method, an open question is one that can have a variety of answers. A closed question is one that restricts the answer given. Whatever types of questions are asked, interview data should be recorded using pre-prepared scales, notes, audio or videotape. Unless using a measure like a scale, interviews give us mostly qualitative, or descriptive, data about people's thoughts, feelings and behaviours. This is mainly due to the free-ranging nature of questioning in the less structured types of interview, which makes obtaining numerical or quantitative data difficult.

Open and closed questions

An example of an open question could be 'Why do you enjoy studying Higher psychology?' Ask this of a thousand students and you would get many different answers. Because answers would be very *descriptive*, this *qualitative data* would be very difficult to analyse. Open questions can give you too much data to analyse in a meaningful way.

A closed question could be 'Do you enjoy studying higher psychology, yes or no?' With closed questions you get *numerical*, or *quantitative data*. Here you might find 700 out of 1000 students enjoyed studying higher psychology. Closed questions can give you too little data to analyse in a meaningful way. You would probably want to know why 700 enjoyed Higher psychology. And more importantly *why* the other 300 didn't!

Key features of the interview method

Categories of interview

There are two categories of interview in psychological research, the structured interview and the unstructured interview.

The structured interview

The structured interview means you plan beforehand what questions are to be asked of those taking part. This standardisation, or your prior preparation, of interview questions, is a key feature of the structured interview. The questions asked will depend on the issue to be investigated.

Another recent feature, certainly of the structured interview, is its mode or setting. Interviews nowadays can be conducted face to face, by telephone, videophone and the Internet.

The unstructured interview

The other category of interview is the unstructured interview. The key feature of the unstructured interview is the free-ranging nature of the interview questions asked. You do not have to have, or stick rigidly to, any pre-set questions.

As we shall see when we look at advantages and disadvantages of the interview method, whether you pre-arrange your questions in a standardised format, or have a free-ranging discussion are both an advantage and disadvantage of the interview method. Standardisation in structured interviews *versus* free-ranging questioning in a less structured situation can influence the reliability and validity of your results and conclusions.

INTERACTIVE

Watch an interview on 'Parkinson' or Newsnight' and complete the following.

1 Identify the programme, interviewer and interviewee.

2 Was this a structured interview, unstructured interview or a bit of both? Give reasons for your answer.

Structured interviews: three types

There are three types of structured interview used in psychology, the structured interview itself, the semi-structured interview and the clinical interview. What they share is the *standardisation* of questions asked. Where they differ is the degree of freedom the interviewer has to deviate from these pre-set questions.

Structured interview

Structured interview: where the researcher plans and carefully constructs pre-set questions. These are the only ones asked.

A structured interview attempts to obtain a detailed understanding of a particular aspect of a person's mental processes and behaviours. To achieve this, the structured interview will have the researcher use pre-planned, carefully constructed and pre-set questions.

Structured interviews are often used to conduct research looking at a unique group of individuals who share a particular condition or problem. We also come across them in those structured interviews conducted by market research companies in our high streets. Very often they are collecting data on our attitudes and opinions on a wide range of subjects.

Standardisation of structured interview questions

The structured interview therefore consists of a pre-prepared set of specific questions.

Standardisation in a structured situation does not allow the interviewer to ask any questions other than those prepared beforehand. They could not inject anything 'extra' into the interview, and as a result the structured interview is mostly a 'question and answer' session. If the questions are pre-set, interviewers may well have a response sheet, or scale, which they score as the interview progresses. This numerical data is later used to give *quantitative* data upon which to base any results and conclusions. In a structured setting the interviewer attempts to be objective and tries not to influence the participant's replies.

Standardisation gives quantitative data

Di Nardo *et al.* (1994) point us to the Anxiety Disorder Interview Schedule (ADIS) used in the USA to help diagnose obsessive–compulsive disorder (OCD). In the United Kingdom OCD affects 1:50 people. In a good example of a structured interview that generates quantitative data, clients using ADIS are asked about their obsessions and compulsions. An obsession is a constant, often irrational, thought or feeling. A compulsion is a behaviour that you repeat over and over again, which is connected to your obsession. On an eight-point scale the client scores the frequency of their compulsive behaviours from 'never' through 'occasionally' to 'constantly'. This would see someone who is obsessed with hygiene probably 'constantly' wash his or her hands, or 'constantly' marking the same homework hour after hour, night after night.

The structured interview's ability to generate quantitative data is also found in personnel selection. Take someone who is applying for a job as a psychology lecturer in an FE college! To find out about their psychological knowledge, a structured interview *could* contain the following structured questions:

- ☐ What causes depression from the biological point of view in psychology?
- ☐ What stages are involved in Piaget's theory of cognitive development in young children?

We know from our look at the biological and cognitive approach that in each case there is a correct answer. Each candidate's answers to these pre-prepared pre-set questions could be scored on a scale of 1–10 to give the college a better understanding of someone's knowledge of psychology. This would be useful data upon which to base a decision.

Asking an individual a set of pre-arranged pre-set questions is thus called standardisation. The issue of standardisation in the *framing* of oral and written questions was explored when we looked at the survey method of research. As we discovered the construction of questions for structured interviews/surveys is not easy. These issues should also be taken into account when considering the interview as a research method.

Obsessive–compulsive disorder (OCD)

Obsessive–compulsive disorder is a psychological condition characterised by high anxiety. Symptoms include hand washing, constantly checking, i.e. that the gas is off /door is locked, ruminating – or thinking endlessly about things – being overly neat, tidy and ordered, hoarding and fearing harm. Body dysmorphic disorder also shares similarities with OCD. This is an obsession with how you look. OCD takes up a lot of a sufferer's time. It can also seriously affect their family relationships, work and social life. While the cause of obsessive–compulsive disorder is not known, it is thought by OCD support organisations to be possibly a result of a chemical imbalance in the brain. Symptoms seem to have nothing to do with the sufferer's basic personality. Nor is it likely OCD is caused by childhood experience. A Freudian analysis is inappropriate. People with OCD are usually aware that their compulsions and obsessions are irrational. Their perceptions of reality are usually not distorted in other ways. They 'function' normally in all other respects. It is other people's perception of their obsessive–compulsive behaviours that unfortunately adds to their problems. Others, put simply, write them off as 'mad'.

Dedicated to A.M.

Replication and generalisation

Standardisation of questions is also important because it allows the same questions about the same issue to be asked of different individuals. This *replication* of the same questions is another feature of the structured interview. When you give the same set of questions to a sample of individuals you are able to make *generalisations* about what you have found out to the population from which they came. We shall return to this when we look at advantages of the structured interview.

Structured interview modes

The mode or setting of the structured interview has, as indicated earlier, begun to be of interest to psychologists. Mode concerns whether the interviewer is present and face to face with the participant, or absent as when conducting the interview by telephone.

Donovan *et al.* (1997) compared information about personal health got face to face or by telephone interview from people in Perth, Western Australia. Two samples were put together; 1,000 in the face-to-face group, and 222 in the telephone group. From each group, a stratified sample was drawn (see Chapter 10). Each individual in each stratified sample took part in a number of interviews over a three-year period. All were asked the same structured questions, the only difference being the interview mode used – face to face, or telephone.

Telephone respondents reported significantly lower levels of smoking and higher levels of drinksing behaviours when compared to those interviewed face to face in their homes. Donovan *et al.* (1997) conclude we should be cautious about the results different structured interview modes can generate. Different modes can throw up different results even though the same questions are asked.

Semi-structured interview

Semi-structured interview: where the researcher prepares pre-set questions, but will occasionally ask some spontaneous questions.

Figure 11.1 A semi-structured student guidance interview

The semi-structured interview still has pre-arranged pre-set questions but the interviewer is a bit freer to explore the more interesting answers given by the client or participant.

Semi-structured interviews are used to diagnose affective, or mood disorders such as clinical depression. Clinical depression is a disorder that affects 20–30 men per thousand, and 40–90 women per thousand in the UK. In its diagnosis the clinician would use a semi-structured interview to confirm five of the symptoms shown in Table 11.1 on page 260.

The semi-structured interview is also used in the personnel selection in the workplace. In order to get the best person for the job, a personnel department would put together structured interview questions matched to the job specification. All candidates would be asked these questions, but if someone says something particularly interesting, the interviewer(s) might ask them to expand on this. Very often, in this now *semi-structured* situation, a candidate discloses interesting personal detail that gets them the job. Or doesn't. Remember and watch the *Trainspotting* video!!

Table 11.1 Symptoms of clinical depression (based on Spitzer *et al.*, 1978)

In order to be said to be suffering from clinical depression, a person should have experienced a number of the following symptoms together over a period of time.	
A	Persistent low mood (for at least two weeks)
plus	
B	At least five of the following symptoms: **1** Poor appetite or weight loss, or increased appetite or weight gain (change of 1 lb [450 g] a week over several weeks or 10 lb [4.5 kg] in a year when not dieting). **2** Sleep difficulty, or sleeping too much. **3** Loss of energy, fatiguability or tiredness. **4** Body slowed down or agitated (not mere subjective feeling of restlessness or being slowed down, but observable by others). **5** Loss of interest or pleasure in usual activities, including social contact or sex. **6** Feelings of self-reproach, excessive or inappropriate guilt. **7** Complaints or evidence of diminished ability to think or concentrate such as slowed thinking or indecisiveness. **8** Recurrent thoughts of death or suicide, or any suicidal behaviour.

Clinical interview

Clinical interview: where the researcher has some pre-set questions, but will ask spontaneous questions. What spontaneous questions are asked depend on the previous answer given by the participant.

A clinical interview is similar to a structured and semi-structured interview. It has some pre-arranged pre-set questions and also an option to ask free-ranging questions. However it would go further and get respondents to expand even more on their interesting answers.

Piaget used the clinical interview to discover whether four-year-old children had acquired the ability to conserve volume. Indeed it was he who coined the phrase 'clinical interview'.

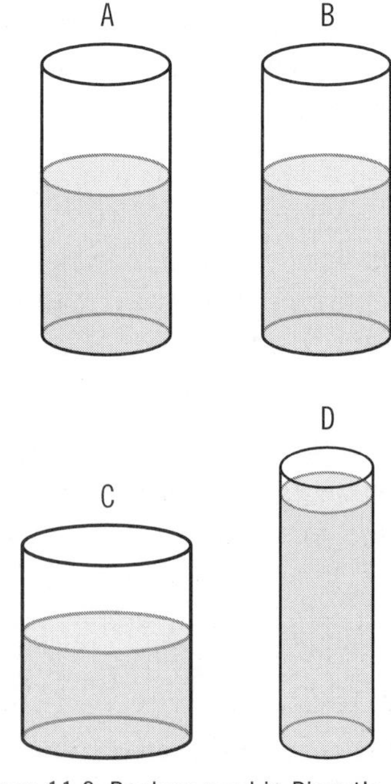

Figure 11.2 Beakers used in Piaget's experiment

Piaget had a one-to-one clinical interview with four-year-olds. He put equal amounts of liquid into two identical beakers, A and B (Figure 11.2). He then poured the contents of A into a same-shaped glass C, and the contents of B into a different-shaped glass D. Each child was then asked which one they wanted (C or D) and why. They invariably chose the tall thin glass D over the short fat one C.

Piaget (1952) believed this was because at four, children have not yet acquired the ability to conserve volume. This means that they are mentally unable to consider two aspects of an object simultaneously. They can only take on board that the tall thin glass *looks bigger* than the small fat one. They are unable to use **transformation**, to move the liquid back and forth from glass to glass, to work out that both contain the same amount of liquid. With different children Piaget slightly varied the questions asked in response to their last answer given. This is what makes this a clinical interview.

Sigmund Freud also used the clinical interview method. The detail he got went on to form many of his case studies. Believing that most of our psychological problems lie in our unconscious Freud used connected, free-ranging but focused oral questioning with many of his patients to get to their specific fears and worries. He believed these fears and worries were to blame for their hysterias or phobias. Once exposed, and these connections made, Freud hoped his patients would have a greater understanding of why they were thinking or behaving in a dysfunctional way. As a consequence they could overcome their problem better. Freud's use of what would be recognised today as a clinical interview laid the basis for such important works as *The Interpretation of Dreams*.

THE UNSTRUCTURED INTERVIEW

Unstructured interview: where the researcher has no pre-set questions. He or she asks free-ranging questions.

The 'unstructured' interview does not have pre-arranged pre-set questions and as such is freer ranging. The unstructured interview is used to explore an issue or area of enquiry *generally*. It may throw up some interesting ideas to be researched later using more structured research methods.

In an unstructured interview the researcher *can* ask the same sort of questions, as with a structured interview, but their style is free-flowing rather than rigid. It is much more conversational. Questions can be adjusted according to how the interviewee is responding. The interviewer may even inject their own opinions, humour or ideas to stimulate the interviewee's responses. The unstructured interview requires much more skill and is much more complex in process and analysis than a structured interview.

The humanistic approach with its use of the client-centred interview is a good example of an unstructured interview. In the past in humanistic psychotherapy the client-centred interview was entirely non-directive. It was an unstructured interview in extreme form where the client led the pace. It was they who decided what was to be talked about. The counsellor helped the client to explore self, using genuineness, empathy and unconditional positive regard only. Nowadays humanistic psychotherapy is more directive. This is because the non-directive interview method was found to be rather wasteful of time. It was just too loose and free-ranging. Nobody got anywhere particularly fast. The unstructured interview will probably nowadays have *some* direction to it, as is illustrated below.

Examples of unstructured interview questions

'Could you tell me more about ...'

'I'm not sure I understood what you meant by ...., could you explain that in a bit more detail?'

'I find that fascinating! Tell me more.'

'What was happening in your life when this problem started?'

'How did you feel then?'

'How did this all start?'

Unstructured interviews are useful for general information gathering.

Training

Whatever type of interview used – structured or unstructured – the interviewer, researcher or psychologist will have undergone lengthy training. A clinical psychologist will have studied for over six years completing undergraduate and post-graduate study in psychology. They will also have undergone supervision as a probationer clinical psychologist. Many careers officers in Scotland will also have studied and trained in interview techniques at postgraduate level. This is in order to give considered careers advice when interviewing young people and adults who require their assistance. Training is essential to conduct interviews. As a method of research for a Higher psychology practical it is not really recommended!

Advantages of the interview method

Generally interviews allow for the production of a large amount of data about individuals, which can be very detailed. Depending on the interview method used, i.e. structured or unstructured, this data can be quantifiable (numerical), or qualitative (descriptive). This very much depends on the type of question asked. That is, whether it is an open or closed question, and whether it was planned, or asked on the spur of the moment. Closed questions can be quantified. Open questions cannot. Planning to ask a question gives you an opportunity to prepare a measure to quantify an answer. Spontaneous questions lead to open answers, which are notoriously difficult to quantify and analyse.

Further, the more structured the interview the more able the researcher is to generalise their results to whatever population their interview sample came.

Disadvantages of the interview method

The interview method is unreliable as it is based on self-report from patients/clients/participants. They could be lying or economical with the truth. At a job interview, are you likely to inform the panel of your past misdeeds?!

Another disadvantage associated with the interview method is that no cause–effect relationship can be made. There is no manipulation of any independent variable upon which a cause–effect relationship can be based.

Interviewer inexperience or lack of training is often seen as an extraneous variable with the interview method of research. The **interviewer effect**, produced by their manner, style of questioning, type of questioning, and so on, may not encourage a natural response from participants. As a consequence, replies got may be the interviewee responding to the interviewer's behaviours. This could influence any results and conclusions that might be drawn.

Table 11.2 Advantages and disadvantages of the interview method of research

Advantages of the interview method	Disadvantages of the interview method
■ Large amount of quantitative/qualitative data obtained	■ Self-report by the interviewee is an unscientific method of gathering data
■ Gives detailed understanding of issue under investigation	■ Cannot make any cause and effect relationship
■ Generates further research	■ Inexperience and lack of training of interviewer can be an extraneous variable

Advantages and disadvantages of different types of interview

Advantages of the structured interview

As it asks the same questions of different individuals, a structured interview can give you quantifiable data. In using a structured interview market researchers ultimately get a count of the types of cars people own, the shops they frequent, their buying habits, and so on. Standardisation of questions allows researchers to be confident that any data they generate is reliable. Reliability means that you are asking successive individuals the same questions assured that the issue is being investigated *consistently*.

Reliability: Investigating the issue by way of an interview in a consistent manner.

Another advantage of the structured interview is that because you are asking the same questions of a group of individuals, you can generalise your results out to the population from which the interview sample was drawn.

Disadvantages of the structured interview

The structured interview restricts those being interviewed to answer only the questions asked. It is an insensitive way to conduct research in that people don't enjoy answering questions in an automatic fashion.

Further, the rat-a-tat-tat manner of structured interview questions does not allow for the rich qualitative data people often prefer to give you about their life. It may be in this descriptive data that a better clue to the issue under investigation is lurking. Because of the stilted nature of the questions asked, structured interviewing needs substantial training. This is to try and avoid it becoming too awkward or too uncomfortable for those taking part.

Validity: Are your interview questions investigating the issue?

In a structured interview, indeed any interview, the researcher gets to make up the questions. A structured interview could then be accused of lacking *validity* if the researcher asks the 'wrong' questions in their search for the 'right' answer. See also the survey method.

ADVANTAGES OF THE SEMI-STRUCTURED INTERVIEW

The freer ranging nature of the semi-structured interview overcomes the insensitivity of the structured interview. You may, at least occasionally, allow participants to express themselves.

The semi-structured interview gives *reasonably* reliable results, in that the majority of questions are pre-set and asked consistently of everyone. This makes *these* answers easier to quantify and analyse.

DISADVANTAGES OF THE SEMI-STRUCTURED INTERVIEW

Its free-ranging nature encourages qualitative answers. Descriptive answers are difficult to quantify and analyse. In a job interview, the occasional spontaneous question asked of some candidates may be seen as unfair to others.

ADVANTAGES OF THE CLINICAL INTERVIEW

The clinical interview is flexible and responsive to where the client/patient/participant is coming from. It is sensitive to what they are saying and what they would like to say. Information got from a clinical interview is reasonably valid in that the core questions concerning the issue will be prepared beforehand. Answers/responses to these can then be analysed relatively easily.

DISADVANTAGES OF THE CLINICAL INTERVIEW

Spontaneous questions in clinical interviews can give rise to problems of replication and generalisation. Being too sensitive, flexible and wide-ranging in your spontaneous questioning makes replicating the same clinical interview with others difficult. If you had to give a clinical interview to twelve people and came up with useful spontaneous questions with interviewee number 8, what do you do about those already interviewed and those still to be interviewed? Indeed, does your spontaneous question have relevance to what you are investigating? Is it valid? Further, if you can't replicate the same procedure you cannot generalise your findings out to the population from where your sample came.

The occasional nature of spontaneous questions could be seen as bias on the part of the researcher, and is a further disadvantage of the clinical interview. The client may say something that fits the researchers' 'pet' theory, and the researcher encourages this with a spontaneous question or two! This is known as interviewer bias.

INTERVIEWER BIAS AND THE INTERVIEWER EFFECT

Interviewer bias and the interviewer effect thus describe situations where the interviewer affects the kind of responses given in an interview. The interviewer may subtly communicate expectations in the same way as an experimenter might with experimenter bias. This we came across earlier in the Rosenhan study and the self-fulfilling prophecy.

Psychology has discovered that participants search for clues about how to behave in a research study and are prone to being influenced by a researcher's expectations. This is especially so of child participants. Interviewer bias is also a problem in unstructured interviews, where the interviewer thinks of questions as he/she is going along.

LEADING QUESTIONS

Interviewer bias can be explained in terms of leading questions. Psychological research has demonstrated how the language used in a question can affect the answer given. Two classic examples come from Loftus. In Loftus & Palmer's (1974) study participants were asked to estimate the speed of a car that was involved in an accident. When participants were asked 'How fast were the cars travelling when they *hit* each other?' they reported a lower speed estimate than when asked 'How fast were the cars travelling when they *smashed* into each other?' In this instance they reported a higher speed. The use of the words 'hit' and 'smashed' appeared to influence the participants' perception of the speed of the car.

In another study, Loftus & Zanni (1975) showed how the use of the words 'a' or 'the' in a question can change the way people answer a question. Loftus and Zanni asked participants two slightly different questions about a car accident. The first question was 'Did you see the broken headlight?' which assumes that there was a broken headlight in the situation. The second question was 'Did you see a broken headlight?' which is more open. Participants had been shown a film of a car accident. There was no broken headlight in the film, but 17 per cent of those asked about '*the* broken headlight' said there was one, while only 7 per cent of those asked about '*a* broken headlight' reported they had seen one.

ADVANTAGES OF THE UNSTRUCTURED INTERVIEW

An unstructured interview can give you highly detailed data on an individual. Its more relaxed atmosphere can capture their particular point of view, as we saw earlier with humanistic psychotherapy. It is an extremely flexible non-experimental method that has high ecological validity because it is more natural for those taking part.

DISADVANTAGES OF THE UNSTRUCTURED INTERVIEW

The free-ranging nature of the unstructured interview gives rise to problems of reliability, replication and generalisation. Because questions are 'unstandardised', an unstructured interview if given to a series of individuals could be accused of inconsistency or unreliability. This is because different individuals would be asked different questions. For this reason, unstructured interviews cannot be replicated.

An inability to replicate the unstructured interview means you cannot generalise out, or apply your findings, to a wider population from those interviewed. Unstructured interviews, given the free-ranging and spontaneous nature of questioning, also makes what is revealed by participants difficult to quantify and analyse. Another disadvantage to the unstructured interview is the validity of the unplanned question asked. Does it investigate what you want it to investigate?

Wiesner & Cronshaw (1988) analysed 151 employment studies conducted by government bodies in the UK, USA, Canada, Europe and Australia. They wanted to compare the effectiveness of the

Figure 11.3 Advantages and disadvantages of different types of interview

Type of interview	Advantages	Disadvantages
Structured interview	■ Standardisation of all questions can give quantifiable data ■ Replication ■ Data is more reliable as the issue is being investigated in a consistent way ■ Allows generalisation of results/ conclusions to the population from which the sample was drawn	■ Restrictive questioning leads to restrictive answers ■ Insensitive to participants' need to express themselves ■ Validity of questions asked. Are they the right ones?
Semi-structured interview	■ Standardisation of most questions gives quantifiable data ■ Replication ■ Data is therefore reasonably reliable ■ Ability to ask some spontaneous questions is sensitive to participants' need to express themselves	■ Its use of an occasional spontaneous question makes these answers difficult to quantify and analyse ■ Spontaneous questions asked of some and not of others can be seen as unfair, especially in personnel selection
Clinical interview	■ Flexible, responsive and sensitive to participants ■ Preparation of core questions should ensure validity ■ Core questions and responses should be reliable and analysed easily	■ Difficult to replicate ■ As a result, an inability to generalise your findings to a wider population ■ Possible interviewer bias in their use of leading spontaneous questions
Unstructured interview	■ Flexible, responsive and sensitive to participants ■ Relaxed and natural for those taking part ■ Highly detailed and ecologically valid qualitative data	■ Difficult to replicate ■ As a result, an inability to generalise your findings to a wider population ■ Possible interviewer bias in 'selective' use of leading, and spontaneous questions

unstructured and structured interview techniques as a predictor of later job performance. Applying a correlation of category of interview against later job performance, Weisner *et al.* found the validity of structured interviews to be higher ($\rho = 0.34$ in 10,080 cases) when compared to unstructured interviews, where $\rho = 0.17$ in 5,518 cases. Wright *et al.* (1989) further report the validity of category of interview against job performance at 0.14 for unstructured interviews and 0.39 for structured interviews.

What both these studies highlight is the thorny issue of the validity of spontaneous questions asked in the less structured kind of interview (see Figure 11.3). A question that is particularly problematic for the unstructured interview is '*Are these spontaneous and free-ranging questions actually investigating the issue?*' In Wiesner & Cronshaw's (1988) and Wright *et al.*'s (1989) studies, the issue was what category of interview gave you a better chance of getting the right employee. The unstructured interview was not particularly helpful in the prediction of actual job performance when later compared to the structured interview.

Given that a perfect positive correlation is when $\rho = +1.00$, both the structured and unstructured interview would here appear to fall short of the mark, if their purpose was to predict conclusively future ability to do the job.

Figure 11.3

Summary

The interview method of research is a conversation with a purpose. It is non-experimental in design. The interviewer on a one-to-one basis collects detailed personal information from individuals, using oral questions. The interview is used widely to supplement and extend our knowledge about individual(s). Interviews can give us both quantitative and qualitative data about participants' thoughts, feelings and behaviours. This is due to the standardisation and/or free-ranging nature of questions asked. The more structured or standardised interview questions are, the more able you are to get quantitative data. Quantitative data is reliable and easy to analyse. The less structured and freer ranging the interview questions, the more qualitative your data becomes. Qualitative data is difficult to analyse and is not as reliable.

There are two categories of interview, the structured interview and unstructured interview. The key feature of the structured interview is the pre-planning of all the questions asked. Structured interviews also allow for replication of the interview with others, which further enables generalisation of what you find out to the population from which your interview sample came. Structured interviews are conducted in various modes: face to face, by telephone, videophone and the Internet. There are three types of structured interview. The structured interview itself, the semi-structured interview and the clinical interview. A major feature, and difference, is the degree to which each uses standardised and unplanned questions. Standardisation helps the reliability of your results and conclusions. The greater the use of unplanned questions, the less structured the interview becomes. Unplanned spontaneous questions are a key feature of the unstructured interview. Spontaneous questioning is more responsive to the participant. However spontaneous questioning does not allow for generalisation. Spontaneous questions can also be accused of generating invalid results and conclusions. Thus standardisation *versus* the free-ranging nature of questions is both the main advantage and disadvantage of the interview method of research, in general and in particular.

INTERACTIVE

1. Go to http://facultyweb.cortland.edu/~ANDERSMD/PIAGET/a1.HTML

   Write a short report on how Piaget tested a child's ability to conserve area. You may use graphics to help you.

2. Go to http://www.beta.nl/regado2000_book/projects/07_Knibbe_0457_0457_AA.htm

   Why is it important that this project standardises its alcohol questions?

3. Read http://ericae.net/pare/getvn.asp?v=5&n=12

   In your opinion what five steps are involved in designing a structured interview?

4. Print off and read the Certification of Psychological Disability Form produced by the University of California at Berkeley at http://dsp.berkeley.edu/PYcert.html

   In its completion what type of interview would the clinician most likely use? Give reasons for your answer. What advantages and disadvantages does this method attract?

Structured questions with answer guidelines

1 *Describe and explain the interview method of research.*

With reference to the preceding chapter, structure your answer as follows:

- Define the interview method of research *as a conversation with a purpose*. Explain its purpose in terms of *getting personal accounts of individual experiences.* Then go on to identify and explain the following features of the interview method:
  - categories of interview. Structured and unstructured
  - three types of structured interview. Structured, semi and clinical
  - explain structured interviews. Definition, purpose, standardisation, quantitative data (with examples), generalisation, modes
  - explain semi-structured interviews. Definition, similarity and difference to structured interviews, examples of its use
  - explain clinical interviews. Definition, similarity and difference to structured/semi-structured interviews, examples of its use
  - explain unstructured interviews. Definition, purpose, features (free flowing spontaneous questions), examples of its use
  - need for interviewer training in whatever interview situation.

2 *Evaluate the interview method of research in terms of its advantages and disadvantages.*

Structure your answer as follows:

- Define the interview method of research *as a conversation with a purpose*. Explain its purpose in terms of getting *personal accounts of individual experiences*. Then go on to identify and explain the following:
- Identify and explain advantages of the interview method, i.e.
  - generates large amounts of detailed information on the person(s) or psychological issue under investigation
  - often prompts more structured research by other means, e.g. an experiment or a survey
  - depending on interview method used, obtains quantitative and/or qualitative data
  - standardisation (of what?) – may give valid and reliable results (why?)
  - the specific advantages attached to specific types of interview method.
- Identify and explain disadvantages of the interview method, i.e.
  - self-report unscientific. Why?
  - no IV (implications: no cause–effect).
  - interviewer as an extraneous variable. Why?
  - the specific disadvantages attached to specific types of interview method.

Glossary

Interviewer effect: the influence an interviewer may have on the person being interviewed, because of their manner, style of questioning and so on

Transformation: this is the cognitive ability we develop to move and manipulate objects, etc. in our minds. Piaget said that children as young as four had not yet developed transformation, which was necessary to solve his conservation of liquid problem. The children had to move the liquid back and forth from glass to glass to work out that both glasses contained the same amount of liquid, and were unable to do so. For Piaget, a four-year-old is at the pre-operational stage of cognitive development, and cannot yet think or problem-solve like the older eight-year-old. This is because a child's brain is still developing. Children think differently from adults because of biological maturation. Study developmental and cognitive psychology to find out more

12

The case study method

BY THE END OF THIS CHAPTER YOU SHOULD BE ABLE TO:

- **identify by example the case study method of research**
- **define and explain the case study method of research with reference to its key features**
- **explain and evaluate the case study method of research in terms of its advantages and disadvantages.**

Overview of the case study method

The case study method of research is a detailed in-depth investigation into a single-case happening. **Idiographic** in nature, a case study can be about a person, a family, an organisation or an event. The case study is often used by the psychoanalytic approach, developmental psychology, and in the study of individual differences such as personality, intelligence and atypical behaviour. The case study is a method of enquiry that generates rich, mostly qualitative, descriptive detail about a unique individual, episode or situation. As a method of research, the case study is said to be ecologically valid, in that it is true to life. A case study can be **retrospective** or **longitudinal**, and can involve the use of case histories, interviews, questionnaires, **psychometric tests**, diaries, observation and experimental research. These features will be addressed in this chapter, as will the advantages and disadvantages of the case study method.

WHAT IS THE CASE STUDY METHOD OF RESEARCH?

The case study method of research is a detailed in-depth investigation of a single case happening concerning a person, a family, an organisation, or an event.

Because it investigates the 'single case', as a research method the case study is idiographic in nature. It is centred on the individual or unique situation or event. Sigmund Freud, the founding father of the psychoanalytic approach, made the case study famous. He used the **retrospective case study** method in the development of his theories about the unconscious and personality. His two most renowned case studies were Little Hans (1909) and Anna O. (1910). These case studies were *retrospective*, which means that Freud collected rich, qualitative, descriptive detail about his participants' *pasts*. These case studies required his participants to *self-report* from their point of view. Also known as **introspection**, self-report is an individual's personal subjective account of an experience. Subjective self-report is however one of the main criticisms of the case study, as we will see.

Case studies can also be **longitudinal**. This type of case study follows a unique occurrence, episode, or situation for at least a year into the future. An example of a longitudinal case study could be one investigating the psychological impact on an individual, family, or organisation following the 11 September 2001 attack on the World Trade Centre. Another is the BBC's longitudinal study into the biological, cognitive, social and emotional development of a group of Millennium babies (i.e babies born on 1 January 2001). Presented by Lord Robert Winston, one of Britain's leading scientists, it is a study to be televised annually until 2020 and is of much interest to developmental psychology. Developmental psychology is all about biological, cognitive, social, and emotional development in and across the human life span. This series looks at such developments in infancy, childhood, adolescence and early adulthood, and is a must for anyone with an interest in psychology.

INTERACTIVE

Gregory & Wallace (1963) discovered that a 52-year-old patient, SB, blind almost from birth, was to have an operation to restore his sight. They were particularly interested in his newfound visual abilities, but also became intrigued by the influence the restoration his sight had on his emotions. They studied his past hospital records, and examined his developing visual sense in controlled experimental conditions. They found that SB perceived more and more detail about a stimulus as a result of greater experience and exposure to it. Perception is more than merely 'seeing' or visually sensing. What we perceive involves the biology of the eyes, gestalten and past experience, plus cognitions such as attention, language, memory and thinking. Gregory and Wallace also interviewed SB. A great deal of qualitative data was recorded about SB's cognitive and emotional change after his operation. SB told them that he was initially delighted with his new ability but had became depressed. Vision was not all that it was cracked up to be. He had thought the sighted community could see a lot better than they did. He thought sight meant a better ability to see in the dark, and that what the sighted saw equated with beauty. He could not understand acceptance of impure visual surfaces like chalk marks on a board, flaky paint, and so on. Gregory & Wallace (1963) say SB's case lends support to the development of visual perception being an interaction of nature, our biology, and nurture, our experiences in our environment.

Questions

1 What features indicate that Gregory & Wallace's (1963) study is a case study?

2 What was the purpose of this case study?

3 Was this a longitudinal or retrospective case study? Give reasons for your answer.

4 What did Gregory and Wallace discover about SB's visual, perceptual and emotional development?

5 According to Gregory & Wallace (1963), how does perception develop?

Key features of the case study method

We have identified the case study method as a detailed in-depth investigation of a single case happening concerning a person, a family, an organisation or an event. The subject of a case study is anything or anyone who is found to be unique in some way. What psychologists use to construct a case study will differ from participant to participant, subject to subject, issue to issue. Before we turn to these elements, let us look at first feature of the case study method, its subject matter.

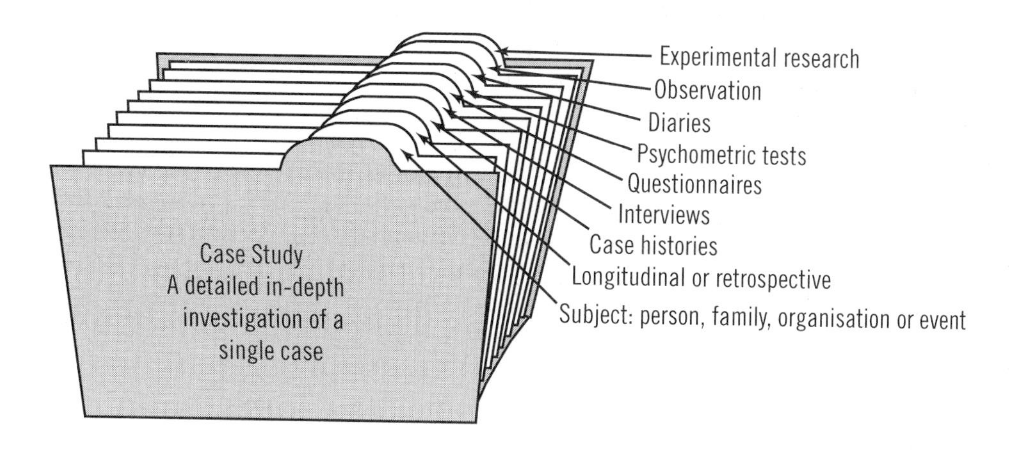

Figure 12.1 The case study method

The case study: a single case happening

The case study is usually about a single case concerning an individual. It can also be applied to organisations and even animals, as the following should illustrate.

Case study: the individual

Koluchová (1972, 1976, 1991) is a classic longitudinal case study of identical twin Czechoslovak boys, PM and JM, born in 1960. Their mother died when they were born and the babies were fostered for the first eighteen months of their lives. They were then returned to their father and stepmother, who subjected them to an extremely cruel regime. They were isolated from everyone, kept malnourished, given no exercise or intellectual stimulation and beaten severely. When found at age seven they were physically, cognitively, socially, and emotionally retarded. Medical records indicated that they were small for their age, had rickets and had little speech. Their new social surroundings terrified them. They were put into a home, assessed by interview and natural observation, and sent to a school for children with severe learning

Figure 12.2 A case study concerns an individual who is unique in some way. Eat your heart out David Beckham!

difficulties. Due to being unable to read, write or speak very well, their intelligence had to be estimated. They were assessed as having the intelligence of a three-year-old. The twins were in fact seven years of age.

PM and JM were then adopted by two sisters, who immediately started to nurture, love and cherish them. Over the next seven years, they gradually began to catch up with physical, cognitive, social, and emotional developments of children of their own age. When Koluchová revisited the boys at age 14, and using intelligence tests and questionnaires, interviews with the boys, interviews with the sisters and school, she concluded they showed no sign of atypical behaviour or physical abnormality. They attended a normal secondary school and were average pupils. When they left school they did a technical apprenticeship, later going to an FE college to study electronics. Both served in the army, got married and had children. Another visit by Koluchová in 1989, when the twins were twenty-nine, saw her report them as entirely normal, stable, and in a permanent, loving relationship with their respective wives and children.

Case study: the organisation

Hayes & Lemon (1990) used the case study method to examine the successful management of change within an organisation. Their clients were a small computing firm in the UK who had got into a rut. The biz and the buzz associated with a computer company were missing. This is fatal to any business, but more so for one at the cutting edge of new technology. They needed some help. After observing the day-to-day running of the business, they conducted interviews with the management and workers, the conclusions of which went into a report. The report recommended that management work more as a team to promote an internal and external company identity. It also recommended that shop floor issues be addressed concerning the future of the business. The management agreed to implement all the recommendations. The researchers revisited the firm six months later. They again observed the day-to-day running of the business, but this time to gauge the degree and effect of change. They also conducted more interviews to see how happy the workers and management were with what had been implemented. Hayes and Lemon reported that most of the earlier suggestions had been successfully implemented. Management were more cohesive. Everyone worked more as a team. Management, the workers and the company had found their common identity, and this was paying dividends on the business front. Management spoke to the workers more and took more of their concerns on board. They were more aware of the importance of good management–employee relations in the successful running of a business.

Figure 12.3 A case study can also investigate an organisation

INTERACTIVE

1. Is Hayes & Lemon's (1990) study a retrospective or longitudinal case study? Give reasons for your answer.
2. How did Hayes and Lemon generate their reports for this case study?
3. Do Hayes and Lemon adopt a case study approach? Give one reason for your answer.

CASE STUDY: THE ANIMAL

Gardner & Gardner's (1998) study, which looked at teaching sign language to chimpanzees, is a good example of a case study of a non-human animal. The use of the case study to investigate animals is by no means exceptional in psychology. The method has been used with non-human animals such as Gua the chimpanzee (Kellogg & Kellogg, 1933), the peppered moth (Kettlewell, 1955) and Koko the gorilla (Patterson, 1978).

ELEMENTS OF THE CASE STUDY

A retrospective case study gathers in information about the past.

A longitudinal case study gathers in information for at least a year into the future.

Case studies which can be retrospective or longitudinal are made up from a variety of sources. These include case histories, interviews, questionnaires and psychometric tests, diaries, observation and experiments. As we will see, almost all research methods looked at in the previous chapters can be used in the construction of a case study. It is, then, appropriate that this book end with such an all-embracing research method.

CASE HISTORIES

Case histories are records of case notes from the past that have a bearing on the present issue under investigation. Examples of sources for a case history could be school and college records, medical records held by a GP, records held by other professionals such as social workers, the police and the criminal justice service. A researcher sifts through these for relevant information concerning the matter under scrutiny. An example of this could be with a person thought to be schizophrenic. The researcher, or mental health professional, would read relevant records to look for previously reported symptoms such as signs of withdrawal, loss of friendships, voice hearing, reporting messages from strange sources telling him/her to do things, or paranoia.

INTERVIEWS

An individual is often interviewed to find out how things from their past, or present, have influenced their thoughts, feelings, and behaviours. This information can contribute, in whole or in part, to a case study. An example of interviews being used to form a retrospective case study was illustrated earlier with Freud's Little Hans and Anna O.

Investigations into the the impact of tragic events on individuals, communities or organisations often use interviews as a major part of any programme, report, or piece of research on those

STUDY

Sign Language Studies of Human-Fostered Chimpanzees, Gardner & Gardner (1998)

Figure 12.4 Moja – and human friends

Aim: Gardner and Gardner raised an infant chimpanzee named Washoe in a home as close as possible to the home of an infant human being to see how the chimpanzee would develop like a human child. Washoe lived in a human house, slept in a human bed, and played with human toys. She ate human food at a human table with forks and spoons, and she had to help set the table and clear up after. She learned to use a human toilet, undressing herself, wiping herself, flushing the toilet, and even asking to go the toilet during lessons and chores. A human member of her foster family was with her all her waking hours every day of the year.

Procedure: Earlier Hayes & Hayes (1951) raised chimpanzee Viki like a child, but they only spoke English to Viki and a chimpanzee vocal tract cannot make the sounds of English. The modern human vocal tract evolved over millions of years. True human fostering requires a common human language. Instead of speech, Gardner and Gardner spoke to Washoe in American Sign Language, ASL, the visual-gestural language of the deaf in North America, because chimpanzee hands are so much like human hands. Using a human language permitted Gardner and Gardner to compare Washoe with human infants acquiring ASL. Gardner and Gardner replicated Project Washoe with four more infant chimpanzees, Moja, Pili, Tatu and Dar, who were human-fostered from birth.

Gardner and Gardner taught ASL the way human parents teach human infants. They modelled ASL for the infants, named interesting objects and events, and asked and answered questions. Skinner's operant conditioning was obviously inappropriate for human-fostering. Later, a student of Skinner attempted to teach a caged chimpanzee by strict operant conditioning with very little success (O'Sullivan & Yeager, 1989).

Results: Extensive daily records showed that Washoe, Moja, Pili, Tatu and Dar signed to friends and to strangers. They signed to each other and to themselves, to dogs and to cats, toys, tools, even to trees. Along with their skill with cups and spoons, pencils and crayons, their signing developed stage for stage much like the speaking and signing of human children (Gardner & Gardner, 1998). They also inflected their signs in the elementary ways that deaf children inflect their signs. They performed far above chance on tests in which observers could see the chimpanzees but could not see what the chimpanzees were naming.

Later in a communal laboratory setting, Fouts and Fouts introduced 10-month-old Loulis to the human-fostered chimpanzees. Humans ceased signing when Loulis could see them, which was nearly all the time. Under these conditions, Loulis learned over 50 signs of ASL that he could have learned only from other chimpanzees (Fouts *et al.*, 1989).

Conclusion: Treated like human children, chimpanzees develop like human children in all ways, including conversation in American Sign Language. Conversational skill develops in stages that are parallel to the stages of human development, only slower.

affected. These interviews could contribute to a longitudinal case study, with the programme makers, reporters or researchers revisiting and re-interviewing the individual, community or organisation at a later date.

It should also be noted that interviews could also take place with relatives, friends, doctors, social workers or teachers, concerning the individual subject, or **target**, of the case study.

Interviews that contribute to a case study are fairly loose and unstructured. A clinical interview may be given to an individual or group of individuals. As we read earlier, a clinical interview would feature some pre-set core questions asked of all being interviewed. The clinical interview gives a researcher flexibility to explore issues that arise from the interviewees' more interesting answers. An unstructured interview would have some idea about what questions could be asked by a researcher, but is even more flexible in style when compared with the clinical interview. The questions asked in the unstructured interview really depend on the previous answer given by the participant. Or any answer at all.

As we saw when we looked at the interview method of research, interviews give us mostly qualitative, or descriptive data about peoples' thoughts, feelings and behaviours. This is mainly due to the free-ranging nature of questioning in the less structured types of interview, which makes obtaining numerical, quantitative data difficult.

Questionnaires and psychometric tests

Questionnaires and psychometric tests, on the other hand, do give a researcher quantitative, numerical data. These *facts* are useful in any case study.

A case study concerning an organisation would almost certainly use a survey to assess the organisation and those individuals in it. A survey is a pre-prepared standardised written questionnaire. Surveys give a researcher quantitative data on the issue being investigated. The survey could be used to find out why an organisation is at it is, and how this might be changed. The results of the survey would generate empirical data. This would be used as empirical evidence to identify problem areas and suggest remedies.

Case studies of individuals often use psychological questionnaires and psychometric tests to assess attitudes, intelligence, personality, and so on. A **psychometric test** gives you a *measurement of a human characteristic* such as personality and intelligence.

Take, for example, the psychometric measurement of intelligence. Intelligence is normally distributed in a population. What this means is that relatively few people are extremely intelligent, the vast majority are of average intelligence, and the relatively few are unintelligent. The vast majority have an IQ, or intelligence quotient, of around 100 (the average) as measured by psychometric tests. Giving someone a psychometric test of intelligence allows their score to be compared with others in and outside their age group. In Koluchová's case the twins were initially assessed as having an IQ of 40. In comparison with other seven-year-olds, the twins had a comparable intelligence more like that of a three-year-old. This is valuable in a case study in that it can be used as a baseline to measure any improvement in intelligence as a consequence of change in environment or dedicated learning programme. In Koluchová's case, the love, care and affection given to the twins by the sisters was the key variable to their improvement from 'abnormal' to 'normal' in less than seven years. These dramatic changes were measured by psychometric tests of intelligence, amongst other things.

DIARIES

The case study can also involve a participant being asked to keep a diary. This would be used to record how they thought, felt and behaved over the course of the study. A pharmaceutical company may ask volunteers in a new drug trial to keep a diary and a doctor might do the same with a patient being put on new medication. A family might be asked to keep a diary if piloting a new product for a company. New technology has seen the advent of palm-held electronic diaries where participants in a study enter data on whatever the case study concerns. Electronic diaries have begun to be used by native trackers in the South African bush to help in animal conservation work. The trackers are trained to record the many different species of animal they come across by pressing a particular picture icon on their hand-held palm tops. Video diaries are the basis of the success of a lot of fly-on-the-wall TV programmes. Individuals often use video diaries to vent their frustrations and reveal how they *really* feel during the course of the programme. This everyday realism is most attractive to us, the TV audience!

OBSERVATION

Observation can be another element to a case study. The observational method of research concerns the planned watching, recording and analysis of observed behaviour as it occurs in a natural setting. Observation, as a method of research can be structured or unstructured, participant or non-participant. More usually, however, any observation that is used in a case study is naturalistic. Something happens that the observer sees as an important element to their research. The importance of Freud's natural observation of Anna O.'s hysterical attacks laid the foundation to his theories and the psychoanalytic approach. Gardner and Gardner's observation in the wild that chimpanzees communicated by gesture laid the basis of an important contribution to the psychology of language, research that continues to this day.

EXPERIMENTS

An experiment, or series of experiments, can also contribute to a case study. These experiments would be laboratory-based in the main. An excellent example is that of an experiment contributing to a case study of a unique condition like anterograde amnesia. In anterograde amnesia a victim is unable to remember anything after a particular point in time. This can be caused by brain infection, as in the case of Clive Wearing, the former chorus master with the London Sinfonietta, or a surgical operation, as with H.M., a case study conducted by Milner *et al.* (1968).

H.M.'s medical records indicated that he had suffered massive and frequent epileptic fits from age sixteen. When he was twenty-seven he accepted radical surgery. This involved the removal of his hippocampus on the left and right-hand side of his brain. His life-threatening epilepsy was cured, but he suffered anterograde amnesia as a result of the operation, where he can remember mostly everything about life before his operation, but nothing thereafter. To discover the extent of his memory deficit, and gain an insight into the role of the hippocampus and memory, Milner *et al.* set H.M. various laboratory-based memory tasks. They report that his short-term memory (STM) is normal and has a duration of around fifteen seconds. He is unable to transfer much information from STM into his long-term memory (LTM). The very limited information he can transfer into LTM he cannot retrieve and use later on. From observations they also suggest that H.M. cannot learn anything from the present. Any news item he reads or sees cannot be recalled. He has no concept of time unless he looks at a clock and cannot remember family details, such as the death of his father, since his operation. The present is meaningless. He greets everyone he has come across since the removal of his hippocampus as complete strangers, even though they may meet him many times a day. As Blakemore writes:

> *'... new events, faces, phone numbers, places, now settle in his mind for just a few seconds or minutes before they slip, like water through a sieve, and are lost from his consciousness'*
> *(Blakemore, 1988).*

INTERACTIVE

1. Why, in your opinion, is this study of H.M. a case study?
2. What causes anterograde amnesia? What are the effects on memory?
3. What radical surgery did H.M. undergo?
4. What were the consequences for him?
5. Identify three different research elements that contributed to the case study on H.M. by Milner *et al.* (1968).

Advantages of the case study

The main advantage of the case study is that it can give excellent in-depth, mainly qualitative information about a single case happening concerning an individual, organisation or animal. It is a very useful research tool that is used to investigate one-off phenomena in a rich and detailed way. It treats those whom it investigates with respect, and has the welfare of the individual at heart. This is one of the reasons why a case study is a more appropriate research method to use when investigating controversial topics such as child abuse.

Case studies usually give researchers information high in **ecological validity**. What this means is that the information a case study generates is real. It is an investigation into a happening that has an individual self-report on an actual experience as it has affected them. In recent years case studies of similar rare occurrences have begun to be pooled on a global basis. The pooling of information helps contribute to our overall knowledge of something of unique interest. The study of the paranormal is maybe an obvious example.

Throughout the course of history, some individuals have been reported to possess paranormal powers, such as telepathy, clairvoyance, extra-sensory perception (ESP) and psychokinesis. The study of ESP includes *precognition*, or the ability to foresee the future. Psychokinesis, or PK, is a paranormal ability to move and manipulate objects without touching them. Individuals with paranormal powers are rare in any one country. One way of investigating the paranormal is to use a meta-analysis of pooled case studies of individuals from all over the world. A meta-analysis examines a number of reported cases of these exceptional individuals. Meta-analysis is then a 'study of all the studies'. It aggregates and averages the results of a large number of similar, but independent studies of a particular phenomenon.

Disadvantages of the case study

The main disadvantage of the case study method is that it is idiographic in orientation. This means that because the case study is geared towards the individual and the single case, its findings cannot consequently be applied to everyone. As a case study is about a unique happening concerning an individual or organisation, any generalisation of results and conclusions to the population from which the individual or organisation comes is impossible.

Further, because the case study is about a single case happening it cannot be replicated. Replication helps confirm earlier results and conclusions. The ability to replicate a case study, to find support or otherwise for *its* earlier results and conclusions is impossible. The difficulty in the replication and confirmation of results is related to another disadvantage to the case study method, its subjectivity.

A case study gathers in mainly qualitative, descriptive information about an individual. This information is obtained from case histories, interviews, diaries, etc. and is subjective because it is based on an *individual's personal feelings and opinions*. Another flaw with subjective self-report data is that its worth depends on the individual being truthful. We should be circumspect about self-reported information for all sorts of reasons, the main reason being that we are never entirely truthful! We forget things, we miss out things that we think are irrelevant, we lie (even to ourselves), we are 'economical with the truth', we exaggerate, we disclose some things about ourselves and keep other things hidden. The reliability of information got by self-report is therefore suspect.

The case study can also attract ethical concerns about the *privacy* of individuals whose life histories may be publicised after their death. If a case study is to be carried out, it is advised that the individual/organisation's real names are not revealed. *Confidentiality* should also be observed, with aliases for participants being used wherever possible.

Each component used by the case study also attracts its own disadvantages, a number of which we came across in earlier chapters. The unstructured interview forms the main element to a number of case studies. Unstructured interviews are prone to interviewer bias. Interviewer bias occurs where the interviewer subtly communicates his or her expectations to the interviewee, which are then reflected in the responses given to the questions asked. Leading questions can also be a problem in the more unstructured of interviews, particularly when the interviewer asks spontaneous questions. Could these questions be leading the interviewee to give an answer that fits the researcher's theory or idea? Fisher & Greenberg (1977) think that Freud had a tendency to select or emphasise information that fitted psychoanalytic interpretation. Also, a lot of psychoanalytic ideas came to Freud as he naturally observed his patients. He took no notes during his psychoanalytic sessions, thinking this would distract his patients in therapy. Instead, he wrote up the case notes for his case studies several hours after his patients had left. His case studies were his memories of what had happened in therapy some time after the event. Nothing exists to substantiate what Freud says he observed. Such subjective or opinionated observation as the foundation to theory is not good science. The case study then lacks scientific validity. It is not an objective, controlled method of research and is prone to bias. One final disadvantage is that because it is a non-experimental method of research, *no cause–effect conclusions* can be drawn from any data generated in a case study.

Figure 12.5 Advantages and disadvantages of the case study method

Advantages of the case study method	Disadvantages of the case study method
■ Detailed in-depth information obtained of a single case concerning a person, a family, an organisation or an event ■ High ecological validity ■ Sensitive to the individual, and sensitive issues concerning the individual	■ Cannot generalise results ■ Replication impossible, to confirm earlier results ■ Reliability of information got by self-report ■ Interviewer/observer bias ■ Lack of scientific validity: no cause–effect conclusions can be drawn

Summary

The case study method of research is a detailed in-depth investigation into a single-case happening concerning an individual, organisation or animal. Because of its interest in the single case the case study is said to be idiographic in nature. It is a method of enquiry that generates rich, mostly qualitative, descriptive detail about a unique individual, episode, situation, etc. The case study has been used in the psychoanalytic approach, examples being Freud's Anna O. and Little Hans. Developmental psychology has also used the case study as with Koluchová (1972, 1976, 1991), while the study of individual differences sees its use in single cases of interest concerning intelligence, personality, and atypical behaviour. A case study can be retrospective or longitudinal, and can involve the use of case histories, interviews, questionnaires, psychometric tests, diaries, observation and experimental research. As a method of research the case study's main advantage is its ecological validity. It is true to life. It gets detailed in-depth information about a single case happening concerning an individual, organisation or animal in a humane manner. Its disadvantages include an inability to generalise results, difficulties of replication and confirmation of earlier results, and the subjectivity and reliability of information got by self-report. Interviewer and observer bias further reduces its usefulness as a scientifically credible method of research.

Thank you for taking the time to read this book.

INTERACTIVE

1. Using the Internet please write short case notes on the following targets of case studies:
   - **a** Genie by Curtiss (1977) and
   - **b** Kitty Genovese by Darley & Latané (1968).
2. Read http://www.fairfax.bham.sch.uk/psychology/gardnergardner.html

   What are the strengths and weaknesses of the Gardner & Gardner (1969) study?
3. Do the Implicit Association Test at http://buster.cs.yale.edu/implicit/index.html
4. Go to the University of Cardiff Careers Service site at http://www.cf.ac.uk/caas/student/psychometric.html to investigate a variety of psychometric tests.

Structured questions with answer guidelines

1 *Describe and explain the case study method of research.*

With reference to the preceding chapter, structure your answer as follows:

- Define the case study method of research as a detailed in-depth investigation of a single case happening concerning a person, a family, an organisation, or an event.
- Identify and explain the following features of the case study method:
  - non-experimental in design. Idiographic. Give examples of its use
  - retrospective and longitudinal. Explain
  - elements: case history, interviews, questionnaires, psychometric tests, diaries, observation and experiments. Give some detail.

2 *Evaluate the case study method of research in terms of its advantages and disadvantages.*

With reference to the preceding chapter, structure your answer as follows:

- Define the case study method as a detailed in-depth investigation of a single case happening concerning a person, a family, an organisation, or an event
- Identify and explain advantages of the case study method, i.e. detailed in-depth information of a single case happening concerning a person, a family, an organisation, or an event. Illustrate with examples
  - high ecological validity. Why?
  - sensitive to the individual and sensitive in its investigation of issues concerning the individual.
- Identify and explain disadvantages of the case study method:
  - inability to generalise results. Why?
  - impossible to replicate. Why?
  - information got by self-report of doubtful reliability. Why?
  - extraneous variables: interviewer and observer bias. Explain.
  - lack of scientific validity. No IV (implications: no cause–effect)
  - ethics and confidentiality.

Glossary

Idiographic: an investigative approach centered on a unique or single case happening concerning a person, an organisation, a family or an animal

Double-blind technique: a technique in which neither the researcher–observer nor the participant knows to which condition of the independent variable they have been allocated. This helps avoid confounding variables

Ecological validity: research that reflects real life. Laboratory experiments are often accused of lacking in ecological validity

Introspection: self-reporting of experience by participants in research. Used by Sigmund Freud and Wilhelm Wundt

Longitudinal case study: a case study following the future of a participant/subject/organisation

Psychometric test: a psychological test that measures psychological factors, e.g. personality, intelligence, aptitude and so on

Retrospective case study: a case study investigating the past of a participant/subject/organisation

Target: the subject (person, organisation, family, animal) of a case study

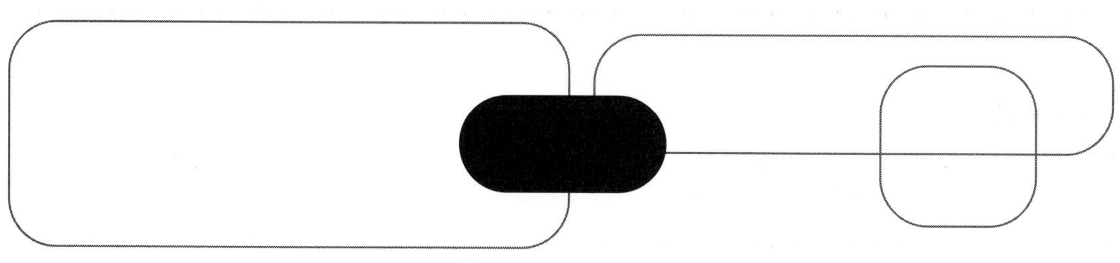

References

Adler, A. (1927) *The Practice and Theory of Individual Psychology*. New York: Harcourt Brace Jovanovich.

Adorno, T.W., Frenkel-Brunswick, E., Levinson, J.D. & Sanford, R.N.(1950) *The Authoritarian Personality*. New York: Harper & Row.

Ainsworth, M.D.S. & Wittig, B.A. (1969) 'Attachment and exploratory behaviour of one-year-olds in a strange situation.' In B.M. Foss (Ed.) *Determinants of Infant Behaviour*, Volume 4. London: Methuen.

Ainsworth, M.D.S., Blehar, M.C., Walters, E. & Wall, S. (1978) *Patterns of Attachment: A Psychological Study of the Strange Situation*. Hillsdale, New Jersey: Lawrence Erlbaum Associates Inc.

Argyle, Michael (1983) *The Psychology of Interpersonal Behaviour* (4th edition). Harmondsworth: Penguin.

Asch, S.E. (1955) 'Opinions and social pressure.' *Scientific American*, 193(5), 31–35.

Atkinson, R.C. & Shiffrin, R.M. (1968) 'Human memory: A proposed system and its control processes.' In K.W. Spence & J.T. Spence (Eds.) *The Psychology of Learning and Motivation*, Volume 2. London: Academic Press.

Atkinson, R.C. & Shiffrin, R.M. (1971) 'The control of short-term memory.' *Scientific American*, 224, 82–90.

Axline, V.M. (1964) *Dibs: In Search of Self*. New York: Ballantine.

Ayllon, T. & Azrin, N.H. (1965) 'The measurement and reinforcement of behaviour of psychotics.' *Journal of the Experimental Analysis of Behaviour*, 8, 357–83.

Ayllon, T. & Azrin, N.H. (1968) *The Token Economy: A Motivational System for Therapy and Rehabilitation*. New York: Appleton-Century-Crofts.

Baddeley, A.D. (1976) *The Psychology of Memory*. New York: Basic Books.

Baddeley, A.D. (1990) *Human Memory*. Hove: Lawrence Erlbaum Associates.

Bandura, A., Ross, D. & Ross, S.A. (1961) 'Transmission of aggression through imitation of aggressive models.' *Journal of Abnormal and Social Psychology*, 63, 575–82.

Barlow, D.H. & Durand, V.M. (2000) *Abnormal Psychology: An Introduction* (2nd edition). Media Edition, Pacific Grove, CA: Wadsworth Publishing Co.

Bateson, P. (1986) 'When to experiment on animals.' *New Scientist*, 109 (14960), 30–2.

BBC TV 'Tomorrow's World', 13 March 2002.

Beck, A.T. (1967) *Depression: Causes and Treatment*. Philadelphia: University of Philadelphia Press.

Beck, A.T. (1974) 'The development of depression: A cognitive model.' In R.J. Friedman and M.M. Katz (Eds.) *The Psychology of Depression: Contemporary Theory and Research*. New York: Wiley.

Berkowitz, L. (1989) 'The frustration–aggression hypothesis: Examination and reformulation.' *Psychological Bulletin*, 106, 59–73.

Bickman, L. (1974) 'The social power of a uniform.' *Journal of Applied Social Psychology*, 1, 47–61.

Blakemore, C. (1988) *The Mind Machine*. London: BBC Publications.

Blakemore, C. & Cooper, G.F. (1970) 'Development of the brain depends on the visual environment.' *Nature*, 228, 477–8.

Bleuler, E. (1911) *Dementia Praecox or the Group of Schizophrenias,* J. Avikin (Trans.). New York: International University Press.

Bouchard, T.J., Lykken, D.T., McGue, M.M., Segal, N. & Tellegen, A. (1990) 'The sources of human psychological differences: The Minnesota study of twins reared apart.' *Science*, 250, 223–8.

Breuer, J. & Freud, S. (1895) 'Studies on hysteria.' In J. Strachey (Ed. and trans.) *Standard Edition of the Complete Psychological Works of Sigmund Freud* Volume 2, London: Hogarth.
British Psychological Society (1993) 'Ethical principles for conducting research with human participants' (revised). *The Psychologist*, 6 (1), 33–5.
British Psychological Society & The Committee of the Experimental Psychological Society (1985) *Guidelines for the Use of Animals in Research*. Leicester: BPS.
Brown, R. (Ed) *New Directions in Psychology*. New York: Holt, Rinehart & Winston.
Brown, T.A., Di Nardo, P.A. & Barlow, D.H. (1994) *Anxiety Disorders Interview Schedule for DSM-IV (ADIS-IV)*. San Antonio, TX: The Psychological Corporation.
Bruner, J.S., Goodnow, J.J. & Austin G.A. (1956) *A Study of Thinking*. New York: Wiley.
Buri, J.R. (1991) 'Parental Authority Questionnaire', *Journal of Personality Assessment*, 57 (1), 110–9, Lawrence Erlbaum Associates.
Buss, A.H. & Plomin, R. (1984) *Temperament: Early Developing Personality Traits*. Hillsdale, New Jersey: Erlbaum.
Butler D. & Kavanagh D. (Eds.) *The British General Election of 1997*. Macmillan.
Butterworth, G. & Harris, M. (1994) *Principles of Developmental Psychology*. Lawrence Erlbaum Assoc.: UK.
Cardwell, M. (2000) *The Complete A–Z Psychology Handbook* (2nd edition). London: Hodder & Stoughton.
Carlsmith, J.M., and Anderson, C.A. 'Ambient temperature and the occurrence of collective violence: New analysis.' *Journal of Personality and Social Psychology* 37 (1979): 337–44.
Chomsky, N. (1959) 'Review of Skinner's verbal behaviour.' *Language*, 35, 26–58.
Chomsky, N. (1968) *Language and Mind*. New York: Harcourt Brace Jovanovich.
Christensen, L. (1988) 'Deception in psychological research: When is its use justified?' *Personality and Social Psychology*, 14, 665–75.
Clamp, A.G. (2001) *Evolutionary Psychology*. London: Hodder & Stoughton.
Coolican, H. (1999) *Research Methods and Statistics in Psychology* (3rd edition). London: Hodder & Stoughton.
Cohen, D. (1979) *J.B. Watson: The Founder of Behaviourism*. Boston: Routledge & Kegan Paul.
Coopersmith, S. *The Antecedents of Self-Esteem*. San Francisco: Freeman.
Cottingham, J. (1992) *The Cambridge Companion to Descartes*. Cambridge University Press.
Craik, F.I.M. & Lockhart, R. (1972) 'Levels of processing.' *Journal of Verbal Learning and Verbal Behaviour*, 11, 671–84.
Craik, F.I.M. & Tulving, E. (1975) 'Depth of processing and retention of words in episodic memory.' *Journal of Experimental Psychology*: General, 104, 268–94.
Curtiss, S. (1997) *Genie: A Psycholinguistic Study of a Modern Day 'Wild Child.'* London: Academic Press.
Darwin, C. (1859) *The Origin of Species by Means of Natural Selection*. London: John Murray.
Darwin, C. (1871) *The Descent of Man and Selection in Relation to Sex*. London: John Murray.
Darwin, C. (1871) *The Expression of Emotion in Man and Animals*. London: John Murray.
Davison, G. & Neale, J. (2000) *Abnormal Psychology* (8th edition). Chichester: Wiley.
Delfabbro, P.H. & Winefield, A.H. (1999) 'Poker-machine gambling: An analysis of within session characteristics.' *British Journal of Psychology*, 90, 425–39.
Delgado, J.M.R. (1969) *Physical Control of the Mind*. New York: Harper & Row.
Dollard J., Doob L.W., Miller N.E., Mowrer O.H. & Sears R.R. (1939) *Frustration and Aggression*. New Haven, CT: Yale University Press.
Dostoyevsky, F. (1880) *The Brothers Karamazov*. Oxford University Press.
Dunckner, K. (1939) 'The influence of past experience upon perceptual properties.' *American Journal of Psychology*, 52, 255–265.
Eagly, A.H. & Carli, L.L. (1981) 'Sex of researchers and sex-typed communications as determinants of sex differences in influenceability: A meta-analysis of social influence studies.' *Psychological Bulletin*, 90, 1–20.

Ebbinghaus, H. (1885) *On Memory*. Leipzig: Duncker.
Effective Health Care (1999) 'Drug treatments of schizophrenia.' *Effective Health Care*, 5, 6.
Ellis, A. (1973) *Humanistic Psychotherapy.* New York: Julian Press.
Ellis, W.D. (1938) *A Source Book of Gestalt Psychology*. New York: Harcourt, Brace & World.
Elkind, D. (1980) Erik Erikson's eight ages of man. *New York Times Magazine*, 5 April.
Erikson, E.H. (1963) *Childhood and Society* (2nd edition). New York: Norton.
Erikson, E.H. (1968) *Identity: Youth and Crisis*. New York: Norton.
Erikson, E.H. (1980) *Identity and the Life Cycle*. New York: Norton.
Eysenck, H.J. (1947) *Dimensions of Personality*. London: RKP.
Eysenck, H.J. (1952) 'The effects of psychotherapy: An evaluation.' *Journal of Consulting Psychology*, 16, 319–324.
Eysenck, H.J. (1985) *Decline and Fall of the Freudian Empire*. Harmondsworth: Penguin.
Fechner, G.T. (1860) *Elemente der Psychophysik*. Leipzig: Bretkopf and Hartnel.
Feshbach, S. & Singer, R.D. (1972) 'Television and aggression: A reply to Liebert, Sobol and Davidson, and Sobol review and response.' *Television and Social Behaviour*, Vol. V.
Fisher, R.P. & Geiselman, R.E. (1988) 'Enhancing eyewitness memory with the cognitive interview.' In M.M. Gruneberg, P.E. Morris & R.N. Sykes (Eds) *Practical Aspects of Memory: Current Research and Issues*. Vol 1. Memory in Everyday Life. Chichester: Wiley.
Fisher, R.P., Geiselman, R.E. & Amador, M. (1989) 'Field test of the cognitive interview: enhancing the recollection of actual victims and witnesses of crime.' *Journal of Applied Psychology*, 74, 722–727.
Fisher S. & Greenberg R. (1977) *The Scientific Credibility of Freud's Theories and Therapy*. Harvester.
Flanagan, C. (1999) *Early Socialisation: Sociability and Attachment.* Routledge Modular Psychology Series, London: Routledge.
Fouts, R.S., Fouts, D.H. & Van Cantfort, T.E. (1989) 'The infant Loulis learns signs from cross-fostered chimpanzees.' In R.A. Gardner, B.T. Gardner & T.E. Van Cantfort (Eds.), *Teaching Sign Language to Chimpanzees*. Albany, NY: SUNY Press.
Freud, A. (1936) *The Ego and Mechanisms of Defence*. London: Chatto and Windus.
Freud, Sigmund. Standard Edition of the Complete Psychological Works of Sigmund Freud. (Trans.) Strachey, J. Vol. IV, *The Interpretation of Dreams* (I) (1900).
Freud, Sigmund. Standard Edition of the Complete Psychological Works of Sigmund Freud. (Trans.) Strachey, J. Vol. V, *The Interpretation of Dreams* (II) and *On Dreams* (1900–1901).
Freud, Sigmund. Standard Edition of the Complete Psychological Works of Sigmund Freud. (Trans.) Strachey, J. Vol. VI, *The Psychopathology of Everyday Life* (1901).
Freud, Sigmund. Standard Edition of the Complete Psychological Works of Sigmund Freud. (Trans.) Strachey, J. Vol. VII, *A Case of Hysteria, Three Essays on Sexuality and Other Works* (1901–1905).
Freud, Sigmund. Standard Edition of the Complete Psychological Works of Sigmund Freud. (Trans.) Strachey, J. Vol. X, *The Cases of 'Little Hans' and 'The Rat Man'* (1909).
Freud, Sigmund. Standard Edition of the Complete Psychological Works of Sigmund Freud. (Trans.) Strachey, J. Vol. XV, *Introductory Lectures on Psychoanalysis* (Parts I and II) (1915–1916).
Freud, Sigmund. Standard Edition of the Complete Psychological Works of Sigmund Freud. (Trans.) Strachey, J. Vol. XVI, *Introductory Lectures on Psychoanalysis* (Part III) (1916–1917).
Freud, Sigmund. Standard Edition of the Complete Psychological Works of Sigmund Freud. (Trans.) Strachey, J. Vol. XVIII, *Beyond the Pleasure Principle, Group Psychology and Other Works* (1920–1922).
Freud, Sigmund. Standard Edition of the Complete Psychological Works of Sigmund Freud. (Trans.) Strachey, J. Vol. XIX, *The Ego and the Id and Other Works* (1923–1925).
Freud, S. (1924) 'The passing of the Oedipus complex.' In E. Jones (Ed.) *Collected Papers of Sigmund Freud*, Volume 5, New York: Basic Books.
Freud, S. (1933) *New Introductory Lectures on Psychoanalysis*. New York: Norton.
Freud, S. (1949) *An Outline of Psychoanalysis*. London: Hogarth Press.

Galton, F. (1869) *Hereditary Genius: An Inquiry onto its Laws and Consequences*. London: Macmillan.
Garcia, J. & Koelling, R.A. (1966) 'Relation of the cue to consequence in avoidance learning.' *Psychonomic Science*, 4, 123–124.
Gardner, B.T. & Gardner, R.A. (1969) 'Teaching sign language to a chimpanzee.' *Science*, 165 (3894), 664–672.
Gardner, B.T. & Gardner, R.A. (1998) 'Development of phrases in the early utterances of children and cross-fostered chimpanzees.' *Human Evolution*, 13, 161–188.
Gardner, R.A. & Gardner, B.T. (1998) 'Ethological study of early language.' *Human Evolution*, 13, 189–207.
Geiselman, R.E., Fisher, R., Mackinnon, D. & Holland, H. (1986) 'Enhancement of eyewitness memory with the cognitive interview.' *American Journal of Psychology*, 99, 385–401.
Gershon, E.S. & Rieder R.O. (1992) 'Major disorders of mind and brain.' *Scientific American*; September 88.
Glasgow University Social and Public Health Unit 1999 survey.
Glassman, W.E. (1995) *Approaches to Psychology* (2nd edition). Buckingham: Open University.
Goffman, E. (1971) *The Presentation of Self in Everyday Life*. Harmondsworth: Penguin.
Gottesman, I.I. (1991) *Schizophrenia Genesis*. New York: W.H. Freeman.
Gottesman, I.I. & Shields, J. (1976) 'A critical review of recent adoption, twin and family studies of schizophrenia: Behavioural genetics perspectives.' *Schizophrenia Bulletin*, 2, 360–398.
Gregory, R.L. (1972) 'Visual illusions.' In B.M. Foss (Ed) *New Horizons in Psychology*, 1. Harmondsworth: Penguin.
Gregory, R.L. (1973) *Eye and Brain* (2nd edition). New York: World Universities Library.
Gregory, R.L. (1980) 'Perceptions as hypotheses.' *Philosophical Transactions of the Royal Society of London*, Series B, 290, 181–197.
Gregory, R.L. & Wallace, J. (1963) *Recovery from Early Blindness*. Cambridge: Heffer.
Gregory, R.L. & Coleman, A. (Eds) *Sensation and Perception*. London: Longman.
Griffiths, M. (1990) 'The cognitive psychology of gambling.' *Journal of Gambling Studies*, 6, 401–407.
Griffiths, M. (1997b) 'Selling hope: the psychology of the National Lottery.' *Psychology Review*, 4 (1), 26–30.
Gross, R. (1995) *Themes, Issues, and Debates in Psychology*. London: Hodder & Stoughton.
Gross, R. (1996) *Psychology: The Science of Mind and Behaviour* (3rd edition). London: Hodder & Stoughton.
Gross, R. (1999) *Key Studies in Psychology*. London: Hodder & Stoughton.
Gross, R. (2001) *Psychology: The Science of Mind and Behaviour* (4th edition). London: Hodder & Stoughton.
Gross, R., McIlveen, R., Coolican, H., Clamp, A. & Russell, J. (2000) *Psychology: A New Introduction*. London: Hodder & Stoughton.
Hayes, N. (1998) *Foundations of Psychology* (2nd edition). Surrey: Nelson.
Hayes, N. & Lemon, N. (1990) 'Stimulating positive cultures in growing companies.' *Leadership & Organisational Change Management*, 11(7), 17–21.
Heather, N. (1976) *Radical Perspectives in Psychology*. London: Methuen.
Heim, A. (1970) *Intelligence and Personality – Their Assessment and Relationship*. Harmondsworth: Penguin.
Higher Still Development Unit (2000) *Higher Still Support Materials HSDU*: Edinburgh, Scotland.
Higley, J.D., Suomi, S.J. & Linnoila M. (1992) 'A longitudinal assessment of CSF monoamine metabolite and plasma cortisol concentrations in young rhesus monkeys.' *Biological Psychiatry*. 32:127–145.
Hilgard, E.R., Atkinson, R.L. & Atkinson, R.C. (1979) *Introduction to Psychology* (7th edition). New York: Harcourt Brace Jovanovich.
Hobbes, T. (1651) *Leviathan*. London: Dent, 1914.
Homicide in Scotland 2000, Scottish Executive 2001.

Honzik, M.P., MacFarlane, H.W. & Allen, L. (1948) 'The stability of mental test performance between two and eighteen years.' *Journal of Experimental Education*, 17, 309–324.
Howie, D. (1952) 'Perceptual defence.' *Psychological Review*, 59, 308–315.
Hull, C.L. *Principles of Behaviour*. New York: Appleton-Century-Crofts.
Hume, D. (1757) *Four Dissertations, IV, Of The Standard of Taste*. London: Millar.
Iversen, L.L. (1979) 'The chemistry of the brain.' *Scientific American*, 241, 134–149.
Izard, C. (1977) *Human Emotions*. New York: Plenum Press.
Jacobs, M. (1992) *Freud*. London: Sage Publications.
Johnstone E.C., Owens D.G.C., Crow, T.J. *et al.* (1989) 'Temporal lobe structure as determined by nuclear magnetic resonance in schizophrenics and bipolar affective disorder.' *Journal of Neurological and Neurosurgical Psychiatry*; 52:736–741.
James, W. (1884) 'What is an emotion?.' *Mind*, 9, 188–205.
James, W. (1890) *The Principles of Psychology*. New York: Henry Holt & Company.
Jung, C.G. (1963) *Memories, Dreams, Reflections*. London: Collins/RKP.
Jung, C.G. (1964) (Ed) *Man and His Symbols*. London: Aldus–Jupiter Books.
Kagitçibasi. Ç. (1996) *Family and Human Development across Cultures: A View from the Other Side*. Mahwah: Lawrence Erlbaum.
Kamin, L.J. (1974) *The Science and Politics of IQ*. Potomac, N.J.: Lawrence Erlbaum Associates.
Keegan, G. (2002) 'Delirium on helium.' *Psychology Review*, Vol 9 Phillip Allen Updates.
Keegan, G. (2002) *Developmental Psychology Staff Resource Pack Advanced Higher*. Dundee: Learning and Teaching Scotland.
Keegan, G. (2003) *Cognitive Psychology Staff Resource Pack Advanced Higher*. Dundee: Learning and Teaching Scotland. In press.
Kellogg, W.N. & Kellogg, L.A. (1933) *The Ape and the Child*. New York: McGraw Hill.
Kempermann, G. & Gage, F.H. (1999) 'New nerve cells for the adult brain.' *Scientific American*, 280 (5), 38–43.
Kettlewell, H.B.D. (1955) 'Selection experiments on industrial melanism in the Lepidoptera.' *Heredity*, 9:323–42.
Koffka, K. (1935) *Principles of Gestalt Psychology*. London: Lund Humphries.
Kohler, W. (1947) *Gestalt Psychology*. New York: Liveright.
Koluchová, J. (1972) 'Severe deprivation in twins: A case study.' *Journal of Child Psychology and Psychiatry*, 13, 107–114.
Koluchová, J. (1991) Severely deprives twins after 22 years observation. *Studia Psychologica*, 33, 23–28.
Kreuz, L. & Rose, R. (1972) 'Assessment of aggressive behaviour and plasma testosterone in a young criminal population.' *Psychosomatic Medicine*, 34, 321–2.
Kuhn, T.S. (1970) *The Structure of Scientific Revolutions* (2nd edition). Chicago: Chicago University Press.
Laing, R.D. (1959) *The Divided Self: An Existential Study of Sanity and Madness*. London: Tavistock.
Laing, R.D. (1961) *Self and Others*. London: Tavistock.
Laing, R.D. (1967) *The Politics of Experience and the Bird of Paradise*. Harmondsworth: Penguin.
Laing, R.D. & Esterton, A. (1964) *Sanity, Madness and the Family*. London: Tavistock.
Laird, J.D. 'Self-attribution of emotion. The effects of facial expression on the quality of emotional experience.' *Journal of Personality and Social Psychology*, 29, 475–486.
Lange, C. (1885) 'Om Sindsbevaegelser. Et psychko. Fisiolog. Studie.' English translation in K. Dunlap (Ed) *The Emotions*. London: Haffner, 1967.
Latané, B. & Rodin, J. (1969) 'A lady in distress. Inhibiting effects of friends and strangers on bystander intervention.' *Journal of Experimental Social Psychology*, 5, 189–202.
Lennenberg, E.H. (1967) *Biological Foundations of Language*. New York: Wiley.
Levinger, G. & Clark, J. (1961) 'Emotional factors in the forgetting of word associations.' *Journal of Abnormal and Social Psychology*, 62, 99–105.

Likert, R. (1932) 'A technique for the measurement of attitudes.' *Archives of Psychology*, 22, 140.

Liebert R.M. & Sprafkin J. (1988) *The Early Window: Effects of Television on Children and Youth*. New York: Pergamon Press.

Locke, J. (1690) *An Essay Concerning Human Understanding*. New York: Mendon (reprinted, 1964).

Loftus, E.S. & Palmer, J.C. (1974) 'Reconstruction of automobile destruction. An example of the interaction between language and memory.' *Journal of Verbal Learning and Verbal Behaviour*, 13, 585–589.

Loftus, E.S. & Zanni, G. (1975) 'Eyewitness testimony. The influence of wording on a question.' *Bulletin of the Psychonomic Society*, 5, 86–88.

Lowe, G. (1995) 'Alcohol and drug addiction.' In A.A. Lazarus & A.M. Coleman (Eds.) *Abnormal Psychology*. London: Longman.

Maddi, S.R. (1996) *Personality Theories: A Comparative Analysis* (6th edition). Pacific Grove, CA: Brooks/Cole.

Malinowski, B. (1929) *The Sexual Life of Savages*. New York: Harcourt Brace Jovanovich.

Manic Street Preachers, 'I'm Not Working.' Lyrics, Nick Jones.

Markle, S. (1969) *Good Frames and Bad* (2nd edition). New York: Wiley.

Marr, D. (1982) *Vision: A Computational Investigation into the Human Representation and Processing of Visual Information*. San Francisco, CA: W.H. Freeman.

Martin, P. & Bateson, P. (1996) *Measuring Behaviour* (2nd edition). Cambridge, UK: Cambridge University Press.

Martin S.M., Manning J.T. & Dowrick C.F. (1999) 'Fluctuating asymmetry, relative digit length and depression in men.' *Evolution and Human Behaviour,* 20: 203–14.

Maslow, A. (1954) *Motivation and Personality*. New York: Harper & Row.

Maslow, A. (1968) *Towards a Psychology of Being* (2nd edition). New York: Van Nostrand Reinhold.

Maslow, A. (1970) *Motivation and Personality*. (2nd edition). New York: Van Nostrand Reinhold.

McDougall, W. (1908) *An Introduction to Social Psychology*. London: Methuen.

Milgram, S. (1963) 'Behavioural study of obedience.' *Journal of Abnormal and Social Psychology,* 67, 371–8.

Milgram, S. (1974) *Obedience to Authority*. New York: Harper & Row.

Miller, G.A. (1956) 'The magical number seven, plus or minus two. Some limits on our capacity for information processing.' *Psychological Review*, 63, 81–97.

Miller, G.A. (1978) 'The acquisition of word meaning.' *Child Development*, 49, 999–1004.

Miller, N.E. (1941) 'The frustration–aggression hypothesis.' *Psychological Review*, 48, 155–78.

Milner, B. (1971) 'Interhemispheric differences in the localization of psychological processes in man.' *British Medical Bulletin*, 27, 272–7.

Mowrer, O.H. (1960) *Learning Theory and Behaviour*. New York: John Wiley.

Neisser, U. (1976) *Cognition and Reality*. San Francisco CA: W.H. Freeman.

Olds, J. (1956) 'Pleasure centres in the brain.' *Scientific American*. October. 105–6.

Olds, J. (1958) 'Self-stimulation of the brain.' *Science*. 127, 315–23.

Olds, J. & Milner, P. (1954) 'Positive reinforcement produced by electrical stimulation of the septal area and other regions of a rat brain.' *Journal of Comparative and Physiological Psychology*, 47, 419–427.

Orne, M.T. (1962) 'On the social psychology of the psychological experiment with particular reference to demand characteristics and their implications.' *American Psychologist*, 17, 776–83.

Orne, M.T. & Holland, C.C. (1968) 'On the ecological validity of laboratory deceptions.' *International Journal of Psychiatry*, 6, 282–93.

Ornstein, R. (1986) *The Psychology of Consciousness* (2nd edition). Harmondsworth: Penguin.

O'Sullivan, C. & Yeager, C.P. (1989) 'Communicative context and linguistic competence.' In R.A. Gardner, B.T. Gardner & T.E. Van Cantfort (Eds.), *Teaching Sign Language to Chimpanzees*. Albany, NY: SUNY Press.Parten M.B. (1950) *Surveys, Polls and Samples*. New York: Harper.

Paul G. & Lentz R. (1977) *Psychosocial Treatment of Chronic Mental Patients*. Cambridge, Mass.: Harvard University Press.

Pavlov, I.P. (1927) *Conditioned Reflexes*. Oxford: OUP.

Penfield, W. & Roberts, L. (1959) *Speech and Brain Mechanisms*. Princeton: Princeton University Press.

Pennington, D.C., Gillen, K., Hill, P. (1999) *Social Psychology.* London, UK: Arnold.

Peterson, L.R. & Seligman, M.E.P. (1984) 'Causal explanations as a risk factor for depression: Theory and evidence.' *Psychological Review*, 91, 347–74.

Piaget, J. (1950) *The Psychology of Intelligence*. London: Routledge & Kegan Paul.

Piaget, J. (1952) *The Child's Conception of Number*. London: Routledge & Kegan Paul.

Piaget, J. (1963) *The Origin's of Intelligence in Children*. New York: Norton.

Piaget, J. (1973) *The Child's Conception of the World.* London: Paladin.

Piaget, J. & Inhelder, B. (1956) *The Child's Conception of Space*. London: RKP.

Piaget, J. & Inhelder, B. (1969) *The Psychology of the Child*. London: RKP.

Piliavin, I.M., Rodin, J. & Piliavin, J.A. (1969) 'Good Samaritanism: An underground phenomenon?' *Journal of Personality and Social Psychology*, 13, 289–99.

Pinel, J.P.J. (1993) *Biopsychology* (2nd edition). Boston: Allyn & Bacon.

Pinker, S. (1997) *How The Mind Works*. New York: Norton.

Plomin, Robert & DeFries, John, C. (1998, May). 'The genetics of cognitive abilities and disabilities.' *Scientific American, 278* (5), 62–9.

Plutchik, R. (1994) *The Psychology and Biology of Emotion*. Harper Collins

Popper, K. (1968) *Conjecture and Refutations: The Growth of Scientific Knowledge*. New York: Harper & Row.

Postman, L., Bruner, J.S. & McGinnies, E. (1948) 'Personal values as selective factors in perception.' *Journal of Abnormal and Social Psychology*, 43, 142–54.

Psychiatric Morbidity Among Prisoners (1997) ONS (Office of National Statistics) survey.

Roethlisberger F.J. & Dickson, W.J. (1939) *Management and the Worker*, Cambridge, Mass.: Harvard University Press.

Rogers, C.R. (1942) *Counselling and Psychotherapy: Newer Concepts in Practice*. Boston: Houghton Mifflin.

Rogers, C.R. (1951) *Client-centered Therapy – Its Current Practices, Implications and Theory*. Boston: Houghton Mifflin.

Rogers, C.R. (1961) *On Becoming A Person*. Boston: Houghton Mifflin.

Rogers, C.R. & Dymond R. (1954) *Psychotherapy and Personality Change*. University of Chicago Press.

Rosenhan, D.L. (1973) 'On being sane in insane places.' *Science*, 179, 250 –8.

Rosenthal, R. (1966) *Experimenter Effects in Behavioural Research*. New York: Appleton-Century-Crofts.

Rosenthal, R. & Fode, K.L. (1963) 'The effects of experimenter bias on the performance of the albino rat.' *Behavioural Science*, 8, 183–89.

Rosenthal R. & Rosnow, R.L. (1975) *The Volunteer Subject*. New York: John Wiley.

Rubin, E. (1915) *Synsoplevede Figurer*. Kobenhaun: Gyldendalske.

Rubin, Z. & McNeil E.B. (1983) *The Psychology of Being Human* (3rd edition). London: Harper & Row.

Ryckman, R.M. (2000) *Theories of Personality* (7th edition). Pacific Grove, CA: Brooks/Cole Publishing Co.

Schacter, S. & Singer, J.E. (1962) 'Cognitive, social, and physiological determinants of emotional states.' *Psychological Review*, 69, 379–99.

The Scottish Executive Central Research Unit 2002. *Scottish Crime Survey 2000.*

Scottish Qualifications Agency (1997) *Arrangements for Psychology* (1st edition). Glasgow, Scotland.

Scottish Qualifications Agency (2000) *Arrangements for Psychology* (4th edition). Glasgow, Scotland.

Scottish Qualifications Authority (2001) *Arrangements for Psychology* (5th edition). Glasgow, Scotland.

Segall, M.H., Dasen, P.R., Berry, J.W. & Poortinga, Y.H. (1999) *Human Behaviour in Global Perspective* (2nd edition). Boston: Allyn & Bacon.

Seligman, M.E.P. & Hager, J. (Eds) (1972) *Biological Boundaries of Learning*. New York: Appleton-Century-Crofts.

Selltiz, C. *et al.* (1976) *Research Methods in Social Relations.* (3rd edition). New York: Holt, Rinehart & Winston.

Skinner, B.F. (1948) 'Superstition' in the pigeon.' *Journal of Experimental Psychology*, 38, 168–72.

Skinner, B.F. (1950) 'Are theories of learning necessary?' *Psychological Review*, 57(4), 193–216.

Skinner, B.F. (1953) *Science and Human Behaviour.* New York: Macmillan.

Skinner, B.F. (1954) 'The science of learning and the art of teaching.' *Harvard Educational Review*, 24(2), 86–97.

Skinner, B.F. (1957) *Verbal Learning.* New York: Appleton-Century-Crofts.

Skinner, B.F. (1968) *The Technology of Teaching.* New York: Appleton-Century-Crofts.

Skinner, B.F. (1971) *Beyond Freedom and Dignity.* New York: Knopf.

Stephenson W. (1953) *The Study of Behaviour: Q-technique and its Methodology.* University of Chicago Press, Chicago.

Thorndike, E.L. (1898) 'Animal intelligence: An experimental study of the associative processes in animals.' *Psychological Review*, Monograph Supplements, No. 8). New York: Macmillan.

Thorndike, E.L. (1911) *Animal Intelligence.* New York: Macmillan (Reprinted Bristol: Thoemmes, 1999).

Tolman E.C. & Honzik C.H. (1930) Introduction and removal of reward and maze-learning in rats, *University of California Publications in Psychology*, 4, 257–75.

Watson, J.B. (1913) 'Psychology as the behaviourist views it.' *Psychological Review*, 20, 158–77.

Watson, J.B. (1919) *Psychology from the Standpoint of a Behaviourist* (1st edition). Philadelphia, PA: Lippincott.

Watson, J.B. & Rayner, R. (1920) 'Conditioned emotional reactions.' *Journal of Experimental Psychology*, 3(1), 1–14.

Weins, A.N. & Menustik, C.E. (1983) 'Treatment outcome and patient characteristics in an aversion therapy program for alcoholism.' *American Psychologist*, 38, 1089–96.

Wolpe, J. 'Psychotherapy by reciprocal inhabitation.' In C.H. Patterson (Ed.), *Theories of Counselling and Psychotherapy.* New York: Harper & Row, 1973.

Wundt, W. (1897) *Outlines of Psychology.* Wilhelm Engelmann.

Whyte, W.F. (1943) *Street Corner Society. The Social Structure of an Italian Slum.* Chicago: University of Chicago.

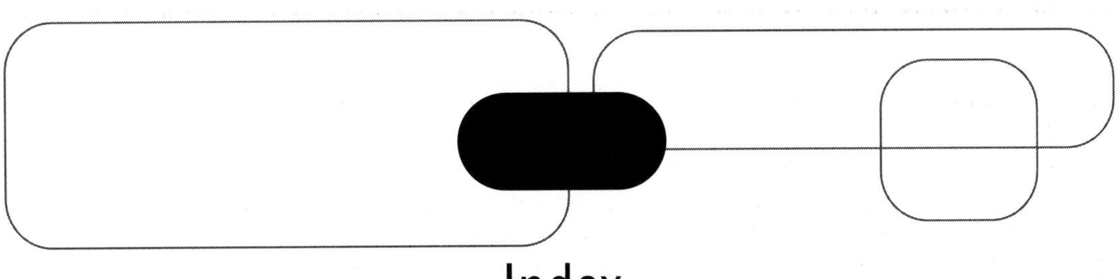

Index